Child Abuse and Moral Reform in England, 1870-1908

Child Abuse and Moral Reform in England, 1870-1908

GEORGE K. BEHLMER

STANFORD UNIVERSITY PRESS 1982

STANFORD, CALIFORNIA

Published with the assistance of the
National Endowment for the Humanities

Stanford University Press, Stanford, California
© 1982 by the Board of Trustees of the
Leland Stanford Junior University
Printed in the United States of America
ISBN 0-8047-1127-5
LC 81-51331

FOR MY PARENTS

Preface

THE IDEA that children possess a "right" to reasonable treatment from their parents came of age in the late nineteenth century. This assertion may strike some living in the late twentieth century as puzzling. The staunchly present-minded will point out that not until 1962 did American pediatricians coin the emotive phrase "battered child syndrome." Prior to the classification of battering as a pathological problem—that is, as behavior stemming from compulsion rather than from random fits of temper—could the *need* for a children's rights campaign be widely appreciated? The English and American philanthropists who founded the first societies for the prevention of cruelty to children during the 1870's and 1880's were, admittedly, far less sophisticated than latter-day experts in attempting to explain why parents brutalized their offspring. Yet the early reformers did understand that this behavior was often habitual, apt to be repeated if intervention was not forthcoming. Moreover, with greater experience these reformers grew as concerned about the impact of long-term neglect as about direct physical assaults on children. Convinced that strict law, conscientiously applied, would promote better care of the young in their own homes, the child-savers sought to create a public demand for such law. Why this agitation did not start sooner is an intriguing problem.

The earliest experiments in family policing were conducted in the northeastern United States, but it was in England that the prevention of cruelty to children became a truly national preoccupation. Above all, the London (later, National) Society for the Prevention of Cruelty to Children preached the gospel of children's rights in both town and country, a mission for which the society was cursed as well as thanked. An analysis of its work forms the core of this book.

Professor Peter Stansky of Stanford University guided the present study through its dissertation stage with a rare blend of contagious enthusiasm and critical rigor. I prize him as a mentor and a friend. Paul Seaver's creative shredding of an early draft brought to light numerous conceptual flaws, and Paul Robinson fought to save me from my prose. Alasdair Macphail gave much useful advice. Parts of the expanded manuscript have profited from the insights of Leslie Parker Hume, Norris Pope, Kirk Willis, Tom Laqueur, Geoffrey Tyack, Howard Malchow, Catherine Ross, and Michael MacDonald. Naturally, the errors and inadequacies remain my own.

I should also like to acknowledge a long-standing debt of gratitude to Professors Robert Kelley and Alfred Gollin of the University of California, Santa Barbara, who did not directly contribute to this book, but who introduced me while an undergraduate to the pleasures of history.

The staffs of many institutions have been most generous with their time and assistance. The Reverend Arthur Morton, formerly the Director of the NSPCC, was particularly kind to an impatient graduate student. He and Miss Marion Bones introduced me to the society's sometimes sensitive records, without in any way trying to shape my conclusions. David Rozkuszka, of the Stanford Library's Government Documents Department, placed a fine collection of British parliamentary papers at my disposal.

My research was carried out with the financial support of a Stanford University Fellowship, a Whiting Fellowship in the Humanities, a summer grant from the American Council of Learned Societies, and an award from the Boys Town Center for the Study of Youth Development at Stanford University. The Boys Town Center and the University of Washington helped defray the costs of manuscript preparation.

G.K.B.

Contents

Eight pages of illustrations follow p. 110

Child Abuse and Moral Reform in England, 1870-1908

The Last Refuge of Cruelty

O N APRIL 5, 1860, a couple calling themselves Frederick and Maria Staines stood in the dock of London's Lambeth Police Court, charged with mistreating their three-year-old daughter. Mrs. Maria Tanner explained that the prisoners occupied an apartment in her house, and that for the past few weeks she had often heard the father thrash his little girl with what sounded like a piece of cane. About eleven on the previous morning the couple had gone out, leaving the child locked up in the room. Mrs. Tanner used this opportunity to visit the girl. She found her lying naked on a bed, so horribly marked that Mrs. Tanner nearly fainted. The child's torso, legs, and arms were covered with grotesquely colored welts, and the contusions on her back still oozed blood. Mrs. Tanner sent for a constable who in turn carried the child to a workhouse and placed her under a surgeon's care. The parents were taken into custody when they returned at seven that evening.[1]

A week later the prisoners appeared before the Hon. G. C. Norton for final examination. By this time the court had gleaned a good deal more information about the couple, most of it coming from people who had chanced to read newspaper accounts of the case. "Mrs. Staines" was in reality Mary Elliott, a widow; the battered girl was the youngest of her four children. Frederick Staines, it seemed, had a reputation for rough conduct in the neighborhood. Whether he had really once broken the arm of his own mother remained uncertain, but no doubt surrounded the prison term he had served for assaulting a former paramour. After weighing all the evidence Norton recommended that Elliott seriously consider placing her child with one of the benevolent persons who had written to the court to offer Mary Ann a home. Such an arrangement the widow flatly refused. Thus there remained only the sentence to set: six months' hard labor at Wandsworth House of Correction for each prisoner.[2]

The trial of Staines and Elliott is noteworthy not because their crime was rare but because the court meted out a comparatively stiff penalty. Had Mrs. Tanner not been a meddlesome landlady, of course, the child's condition probably would have gone undiscovered. And had the accused been man and wife, they would likely have heard a longer lecture on parental responsibility and suffered shorter jail terms. For in mid-Victorian England, then the most prosperous and self-consciously civilized society in the world, parents still enjoyed virtually unfettered power over all offspring who remained at home. Complained John Stuart Mill in *On Liberty* (published the year before Staines and Elliott went to Wandsworth): "It is in the case of children, that misapplied notions of liberty are a real obstacle to the fulfillment by the State of its duties. One would almost think that a man's children were supposed to be literally, and not metaphorically, a part of himself, so jealous is [public] opinion of the smallest interference of law with his absolute and exclusive control over them; more jealous than of almost any interference with his own freedom of action."[3]

According to most theories of family government the subordination of child to parent made for a well-ordered "little society" wherein the lessons of self-discipline could be learned by the young. Within the patriarchal home, restraint was imposed on children and accepted as guidance. Here too, explained an advocate, "the will finds its highest freedom in obedience, because it chooses to obey."[4] How harsh in exacting such obedience fathers and mothers might be was a thornier issue, however, since to specify the limits of parental power was by definition to violate the privacy of family life.

This does not mean that English society in the middle of the nineteenth century was blind to the problem of cruelty or indifferent to the plight of suffering children. On the contrary, most educated men and women would have agreed with Macaulay that human nature reached its lowest state when the sight of pain became an agreeable amusement. Unlike Hobbes, who two centuries before had defined cruelty as the drive "to hurt without reason," Macaulay was referring to a more sinister deformation of character that feeds upon itself, compelling the warped personality to find—sometimes to create—new sources of pain.[5] Such behavior was both embarrassing and threatening to middle-class culture; sadism not only grated against the bourgeois self-image of toleration and humanity but also posed the danger of contagious moral degeneration. The campaign against cruelty to animals had taken firm root in England by mid-century, and a major premise of animal lovers was that brutality to beasts encouraged savagery among men.[6] Admittedly, some of the early humane leaders were lampooned for their convictions. In his "Ode to Richard Martin," Tom Hood noted that the architect of England's first animal welfare law was short of admirers, at least among his own kind:

> Drovers may curse thee,
> Knackers asperse thee,
> And sly M.P.s bestow their cruel wipes;
> But the old horse neighs thee,
> And zebras praise thee,
> Asses, I mean—they have as many stripes![7]

But the impressive growth of animal protection societies demonstrated that Martin's cause had been adopted by influential sections of the middle and upper classes.

Even more clearly the mid-Victorian generation gave unprecedented attention to children and the problems facing them. Both the bulk and the sentimentality of child-centered literature from this period are striking. Dickens's novels reflected and reinforced the image of children as reservoirs of sensitivity in an increasingly materialistic world.[8] Specially sensitive as well as physically weak, the young were therefore wholly unsuited to the drudge labor of factories and coal pits. So argued Elizabeth Barrett Browning in what must qualify as the most maudlin example of this genre, "The Cry of the Children" (1843). Her weary toilers weep, sob, or shed tears sixteen times before they ask: "'How Long, . . . O cruel nation, Will you stand, to move the world, on a child's heart?'"[9] Nor was this sentimental view of the young restricted to literature. Lord Shaftesbury, the pious defender of the rights of working children, was superbly adept at the politics of pathos.[10] Although Shaftesbury never allowed himself to bask in his parliamentary triumphs, many of his contemporaries took pride in an "enlightened" public policy toward the young. *Notes & Queries* remarked in 1862 that as recently as 1839 a boy nine years old was hanged at Chelmsford for arson; the nation, it seemed, had grown appreciably more tolerant of childish error within living memory. That 1,990 boys and girls under the age of twelve still occupied English jails in 1856 failed to dampen this enthusiasm over rapid social progress.[11]

Despite such glaring exceptions to the rule of humanity, children raised in England during the 1850's and 1860's were on the whole treated more gently than in the past. Nevertheless, caution must be exercised when generalizing about the nature of parent-child relations over time. "There can be no doubt," Lawrence Stone has argued, "that more children were being beaten in the sixteenth and early seventeenth century, over a longer age span, than ever before."[12] Many young people in the Tudor-Stuart period endured ferocious discipline when parents, obsessed with the innate sinfulness of children, sought to crush all signs of self-assertion in their offspring. Not all Englishmen embraced Puritan child-rearing advice, however. Sir Thomas Elyot wrote about the education of young gentlemen: "I wolde not have them inforced by violence to lerne, but . . . to be swetely allured thereto with praises and suche praty gyftes as children delite in."[13] A staunch humanist who had no children of his own, Elyot was hardly a typical Tudor parent. Yet it seems improbable that Puritan patterns of discipline entirely replaced older, less stringent parent-child relations. Moreover, even in a Puritan-dominated society such as the Massachusetts Bay Colony, parental prerogative had its bounds. "If any parents . . . shall exercise any unnaturall severitie towards them," declared a provision of 1641, "such children shall have free libertie to complaine to Authoritie for redresse."[14]

Granted that harsh corporal punishment of the young was common in England throughout much of the Tudor-Stuart era, there is substantial evidence to suggest that the eighteenth century witnessed a lessening of parental severity among the upper social strata. The reasons for this shift in child-rearing behavior are still somewhat obscure. Older accounts state simply that "gentler relations" began to prevail between young and old, and that a new spirit of humanity was "creeping" into domestic life under whose influence parents "were almost beginning to consider their children as the same flesh and blood as themselves."[15] Equally weak in explanatory power is the recent assertion that an "intrusive mode" of child care emerged during the eighteenth century as western European culture reached the "psychogenic" stage, characterized by parental assumption of full responsibility for molding the young.[16]

Parents in the privileged classes still demanded obedience from their children, but, particularly after mid-century, they were more apt to shame or frighten than to whip them into submission.[17] It is harder to demonstrate that the eighteenth century ushered in a "new world" for children of the lower-middle and laboring classes. Though Locke's view of the infant mind as a tabula rasa and Rousseau's notion that the child is born naturally good gained wide acceptance in this period, these ideas probably did not hold sway in families of modest means. Poor parents could ill afford to treat their offspring as superior pets when family survival demanded that toddlers be steered into mill work, chimney sweeping, and professional begging.[18]

If the eighteenth century was not an era of permissiveness for all English children, neither did the early years of the nineteenth century bring a dramatic reversion to the older, harshly patriarchal family pattern. The disciplinary rigor of the evangelicals and Methodists cannot be denied, but it can be exaggerated. Although John Wesley preached the need to break the will of the child, he also hoped that parents could avoid punishing their young. Where punishment proved essential, "You should take the utmost care to avoid the very appearance of passion. Whatever is done should be done with mildness; nay, indeed, with kindness too."[19] Joseph Barker, born in Yorkshire in 1806 to Methodist parents, recalled being chastened as a very young child. "The next thing I remember was being put into a dark cellar, and told that the *boggard* [goblin] should have me. This was the most terrible affair of all. I was dreadfully frightened. I really believed that there was a boggard in the cellar, and for any thing I knew to the contrary, I saw it plainly, at the bottom of the cellar steps." Significantly, however, Barker added, "Little did my mother imagine the horrible effect that fright had on my mind."[20] The London tailor and Radical Francis Place suffered greater hardship at the hands of his father. "Beating and that too in excess was with him the all in all in the way of teaching." But Place senior was not so much a religiously inspired man as one whose "passions were strong, and too little under control to permit him to produce effects by examples."[21] Both Wesley, the guiding light of Methodism, and Lord Shaftesbury, after the death of Wilberforce England's most prominent evangelical, would have rebuked Place senior for his brutal ways.

To the extent that memoirs can be trusted, it appears that early

Victorian fathers in comfortable homes were often remote and imperious, but not necessarily harsh. Rich men, of course, could afford to delegate disciplinary chores to nannies, governesses, and schoolmasters, reserving for themselves the presentation of gifts and the delivery of sage advice.[22] The paterfamilias in an evangelical household commonly took direct responsibility for correcting his young. Still, even these solemn fathers in their black frock coats tended to be admonitory rather than tyrannical.[23]

By mid-Victorian times, therefore, parental discipline was growing less retributive among some social classes. Yet at law children remained defenseless, since charges of mistreatment were seldom brought against natural parents. Limits to parental power, of course, did exist. A century before, Blackstone had held that a parent "may lawfully correct his child, being under age, *in a reasonable manner*; for this is for the benefit of his education."[24] Similarly, English common law assumed that parents were obligated to provide for the basic physical needs of their legitimate issue. But what constituted "reasonable" correction and adequate support were far from clear, and the state had no wish to clarify these issues. Indeed, Parliament's reluctance to step between parent and child is underscored by the legislation passed to aid the young outside their homes.

Apprentices were the first major youth group to win statutory protection. The conditions of parish apprenticeship, a system introduced by the Elizabethan Poor Law of 1601, were especially hard during the late seventeenth and early eighteenth centuries. After the 1662 Act of Settlement, local authorities could and did rid themselves of pauper children by "dumping" them on masters in distant parishes, thereby abandoning all supervision of the unfortunate youths.[25] But if these children frequently suffered severe ill-treatment, their masters, at least from the mid-eighteenth century, ran an increasingly high risk of punishment. In 1740, for example, Mrs. Elizabeth Branch, "a gentlewoman of great substance," was executed for beating to death her servant girl. Despite an annual income of £300—with which she retained no fewer than eight attorneys—and regardless of her reputation for parish charity, Mrs. Branch received scant sympathy from her peers at the Taunton Assizes. The 1767 case of Elizabeth Brownrigg stirred still greater indignation. A prosperous midwife and apparently tender mother of nineteen children, Mrs. Brownrigg terrorized the pauper girls she used as housekeepers. For one of the two apprentices found imprisoned in the family pig cellar, rescue came too late; with her body "covered with gashes from head to foot," her head "swelled to an enormous size, and her speech gone," the girl soon died. After her arrest Brownrigg narrowly escaped dismemberment by a "vast" crowd surrounding the Mansion House, only to hang later at Tyburn.[26] Translating popular outrage into reasoned argument, Jonas Hanway fought to ease the lot of apprentice chimney sweeps. "In a well-regulated free community, every child is as much an object of the protection of the state as the adult," he held; "but what adult *submits*, much less *contracts* for such treatment as is shewn to these poor children?"[27]

Continued public concern found expression in the 1802 Act that required overseers and guardians of the poor to keep a register of the children they bound out.[28] Subsequent legislation passed in 1844 and 1851 empowered the Poor Law Commissioners to prescribe terms and conditions by which children were indentured, and provided for the periodic visitation of pauper apprentices by guardians. Additionally, the 1851 Act specified a maximum jail term of three years for willful neglect of or malicious assault on an indentured child.[29] Interest in safeguarding young apprentices and servants persisted throughout the mid-Victorian period, with unsuccessful amending measures brought before Parliament in 1863 and again in 1868.[30] In 1877, Caroline Carter, a servant struck with a shovel by her Buckinghamshire master, received ample legal assistance against him. Farmer Morris and his wife thought it more prudent to abscond, forfeiting £400 in bail, than to face prosecution.[31]

The factory reform movement likewise proved that a troubled public conscience could move Parliament to shield the working child. With the realization that both Peel's 1819 Factory Act and Hobhouse's 1826 amending legislation had failed to ensure adequate protection of young people employed in textile mills, reformers in the north unleashed a new campaign of unprecedented moral fervor. In September 1830, Richard Oastler, a forty-year-old estate agent, wrote his celebrated letter on "Yorkshire Slavery," comparing local conditions with those in the Caribbean plantations:

Thousands of our fellow-creatures . . . are this very moment existing in a state of slavery *more horrid* than are the victims of that hellish system, "*colonial slavery*." . . . The very streets which receive the droppings of an "Anti-Slavery Society" are every morning wet by the tears of innocent victims at the accursed shrine of avarice, who are *compelled*, not by the cart-whip of the negro slave-driver, but by the dread of the equally appalling thong or strap of the [factory] over-looker, to hasten, half-dressed, *but not half-fed*, to those magazines of British infantile slavery—the *worsted mills in the town and neighbourhood of Bradford*!!![32]

Soon Oastler, Michael Sadler (a Leeds banker who assumed early parliamentary leadership of the factory agitation), and their allies began to promote the Ten Hours Bill as the "Cause of God." By the mid-1830's mill owners who opposed further reduction of working time for children or who attempted to circumvent existing regulations found themselves branded "Lawbreakers, Tyrants and Murderers."[33]

Central to the factory-child debate was the question of physical and moral suffering. Reformers harped on the abuse dealt out by adult operatives. Particularly where the young worked for spinners who were paid on a piece-work basis, beating served as a spur to greater productivity or as a reprisal for costly absence.[34] Sadler's exhibition in the House of Commons of heavy leather thongs used to discipline young workers was good theater, conjuring up the real-life saga of Robert Blincoe, a former pauper apprentice whose body had reputedly never been free from wounds during his ten years at a Derbyshire mill. So common was physical cruelty to mill children, argued one reformist organ, that factories should have "protectors" to guard the young.[35]

The "wearisome uniformity," "close confinement," and "constrained positions" characteristic of mill labor were another source of suffering. Attempting to add precision to the reformers' cause, John Fielden, MP for Oldham, ascertained from experiments conducted in his Lancashire factory that child employees commonly walked twenty miles during their twelve-hour shifts.[36] Under these conditions irreparable harm was bound to occur, the reformers maintained. Further, the child's natural sense of joy was sure to be crushed along with his health. The "young heart is a living laboratory of love," wrote Peter Gaskell; but "everything which goes on before the eyes of the unfortunate factory children, is . . . calculated to nip in the bud . . . the flower which was springing up from within them."[37]

Those opposed to child-labor legislation systematically denied these claims. When Sir George Head made his tour of northern factories in the early 1830's, he saw "on every side, a crowd of appar-

ently happy [little] beings, working in lofty well-ventilated buildings."[38] Rosier still were the scenes sketched by Andrew Ure. At no
time during his surprise visits to the factories in and around Manchester did Ure see children looking careworn. Rather, they always
seemed cheerful and alert, "taking pleasure in the light play of their
muscles,—enjoying the mobility natural to their age." And at the
end of the day these elfin creatures went skipping from the mills
into the streets.[39]

Despite their polemicists, the foes of factory legislation ultimately yielded to the combined weight of evangelical conscience,
fear of social unrest, and the sentimental view of childhood.[40] After
Sadler lost his seat at the general election of 1832, it was Lord Ashley (later the seventh Earl of Shaftesbury) who became the parliamentary spokesman for reform. Lord Ashley's key role in amending
and extending the Factory Acts is well known, as are his battles to
aid child mine workers and the "climbing boys." Since "the State
has an interest and a right to watch over and provide for the moral
and physical well-being of her people," he reasoned, legislation to
guard defenseless children made compelling sense.[41] Yet neither
Lord Ashley nor any of his mid-Victorian allies pushed this argument to its logical end—that is, justifying statutory limits on parental power by virtue of state "interest." To patrol industry on behalf
of the young was England's Christian duty. To patrol the home was
a sacrilege.

This is not to say that the idea of legal interference with family
life was utterly foreign to the mid-Victorian generation. Some of
those who took up the problem of criminal youth surely wished for
greater legal authority with which to save children from the degrading influence of their parents. The first thorough study of juvenile
delinquency—indeed, the first use of that phrase—appeared in an
1816 report compiled by London philanthropists. Even at this early
date the role of parental neglect in fostering criminal behavior
among children received close attention. Three decades later, growing worry over juvenile crime and the resulting debate over the relative merits of imprisonment, transportation, and reformatory
detention as punishments for youthful offenders brought this relationship into still sharper focus. Testifying before an 1847 select
committee of the House of Lords, John Adams, recent Chairman of
the Middlesex Sessions, revealed that a high proportion of the children who appeared before him had either "profligate" parents or

else stepfathers or stepmothers who abused them.[42] Studies of juvenile delinquency pointed to the nexus between the availability of intoxicating drink, cruelty by drunken parents, and the readiness of some children to forsake their homes in favor of the streets.[43] In a slightly different scenario offered by Sidney Turner, the first government inspector of reformatories, drink and greed combined to send the child on his road to ruin:

The blow and the curse were his first catechism. . . . At an age when the children of the wealthy would be carefully tended, and on no account allowed to leave the precincts of the nursery, he was sent out to beg or pilfer, beaten if unskilled or unlucky, rewarded and praised if clever and successful. He had . . . brutal and unnatural parents, who traded in their children's depravity, and locked them in the cellar or garret after they had despoiled them of the fruits of their dishonesty and begging, careless whether they lived or died, while they themselves revelled in the gluttony and drunkenness which their children's crimes had purchased.[44]

Although unanimous in condemning the influence of parental abuse, mid-century students of juvenile delinquency did not agree on the purpose of reformatory action. Gathered in one camp were the "realists," those whose primary goal was the prevention of crime. These reformers were convinced that some children had made a conscious decision to break the law. Thus they wanted all juvenile offenders punished as a warning to others contemplating similar deeds.

Opposed to the realists were the "humanitarians," whose first aim was rescue.[45] The humanitarians believed that most criminal children had acted without discernment. They emphasized rehabilitation over retribution and insisted that young offenders be sent directly to reformatory institutions without suffering the hardening experience of a preliminary prison term. Foremost among proponents of this school was Mary Carpenter, the daughter of a Unitarian minister and prime mover behind charitable work for the destitute and criminal youth of Bristol. All humans possess a "weary longing" for kindness from their fellowman, Carpenter wrote in 1851. "But to children it is an absolute necessity of their nature, and when it is denied them, they become no longer children." Love, particularly when dealing with the young, "draws with . . . cords far stronger than chains of iron."[46] Such thinking informed all Mary Carpenter's work for wayward youth—work that did much to win parliamentary recognition of reformatories and industrial schools in 1854 (17 & 18 Vic., c. 86) and 1857 (20 & 21 Vic., c. 48), respectively.

Although very imperfectly enforced, these acts marked both a major change in English penal policy and an advance of the state into family life.[47] The Industrial Schools Acts passed between 1857 and 1880 specified three conditions under which children might be removed from the custody of their parents: first, when parents could not "control" their offspring; second, when it appeared from evidence given in court that parents were teaching children to be "depraved and disorderly"; and third, when parents were incarcerated. Few children in the mid-Victorian period were rescued from mistreatment through the Industrial Schools Acts, and those who were generally earned judicial notice because they seemed ripe for a life of crime. Nonetheless, the laws that Mary Carpenter and her associates helped secure gave latter-day child-savers a base upon which to build more radical arguments.[48]

The ragged school movement also confronted its patrons with the wreckage wrought by unfeeling mothers and fathers. Originally designed to provide religious instruction for London's wastrel children, the ragged schools soon expanded their range of activity to include reading lessons, the "industrial training" of slum youths in honest trades, the provision of food, clothing, and shelter for faithful pupils, and juvenile emigration to America and the colonies.[49] Lord Ashley and Charles Dickens became interested in ragged schools during the 1840's, though Dickens saw the movement less as a godly mission than as a practical step toward rehabilitating emotionally and physically damaged children. The author of *Nicholas Nickleby* and *Oliver Twist* had already demonstrated a familiarity with boys whose "every young and healthy feeling [had been] flogged and starved down" by their parents. Even so, Dickens was deeply moved by his first glimpse of ragged school pupils. "I have very seldom seen," he wrote to Angela Burdett-Coutts, "anything so shocking as the dire neglect of soul and body exhibited by these children. . . . The children in the Jails are almost as common sights to me as my own; but these are worse, for they have not arrived there yet, but are as plainly and certainly travelling there, as they are to their Graves."[50] Precisely because the young could be maimed so early by vicious parents, Dickens eventually decided that ragged schools could accomplish very little in isolation. Above all, neglectful and brutal parents must face severe punishment for their deeds.

Without such power the state could no more hope to halt juvenile crime "than we could hope to extinguish Mount Vesuvius, in eruption, with a watering pot."[51]

Dickens and Mary Carpenter understood the need for a legal redefinition of parental power. But not until the 1880's would a child's right to reasonable treatment within the family emerge as an issue of pressing public interest. There was, therefore, a major discontinuity between the late-Victorian anticruelty campaign and earlier reform efforts on behalf of apprentices, working children, and youthful offenders. This discontinuity resulted in large part from the persistence of the idea that the domestic relations of parent and child were immune to government regulation. It is an irony of the English past that animals received broad legal protection half a century before children. Less often noted but perhaps more important, widespread concern for the physical safety of women also predated that for the young. Of the two sacred family ties, the relationship between husband and wife drew legislative interference before that between parent and child.

Though reformers talked about shielding women and children in the same breath, they clearly were preoccupied with the former. In 1853, proposing England's first statutory prohibition of violence against women and children, Henry Fitzroy announced the government's intention to prevent the "dastardly and cowardly assaults . . . constantly perpetrated upon defenceless women by brutes who . . . [call] themselves men." Fitzroy predicted accurately that this evil, which was "so universally acknowledged, so rapidly growing, and constituted such a blot upon our national character," would spur the Commons to quick action. Significantly, the subject of child abuse did not merit a single remark in this or subsequent debates on the bill.* A parliamentary return ordered the following year shows that local authorities administered the new Act with women exclusively in mind. J. Hammill reported for the magistrates at London's Worship Street Police Court: "With regard to women of the town, I have continually laid it down to them, that as long as

---

*Hansard, 3d ser., 124 (March 10, 1853), cols. 1414–19. In the Lords, Earl Granville recited with disapproval the "old jocular proverb": "A woman, a dog, and a walnut tree, / The more they are beaten the better they'll be." Hansard, 3d ser., 127 (May 26, 1853), col. 551. The Act for the Better Prevention of Aggravated Assaults upon Women and Children (16 Vic., c. 30) provided a maximum prison term of six months or a fine of up to £20 for attacks on all females and on males under fourteen that resulted in actual bodily harm.

TABLE I
Metropolitan Police Statistics: Relationship Between Male
Party Charged with Assault and Complainant,
June 1, 1850–June 1, 1853

Relationship	Number of cases
Lambeth	
Husband and wife	176
Male person and concubine	12
Son and parent	8
Father and child	5
Brother and sister	3
No known relation	350
TOTAL	554
Westminster	
Husband and wife	72
Male person and concubine	11
Son and parent	4
Father and child	2
Brother and sister	2
Master and servant	2
Stepfather and child	1
Brother and sister-in-law	1
Uncle and niece	1
Cousins	1
No known relation	458
TOTAL	555

SOURCE: Return Relating to Charges Preferred Against Male Persons for Assaults on Women and Children, P.P., 1854, LIII.

they conduct themselves quietly in the streets they are as much entitled to protection as any other class of Her Majesty's subjects, which seems to cause astonishment to the people who hear it, so accustomed have the brutal population of this region been to knock down these poor creatures as if they were so many ninepins, and without feeling." [52]

Although returns from most police districts failed to differentiate between women and children as victims of assault, two exceptions, those from Lambeth and Westminster, are suggestive (see Table I). [53] The high proportion of assaults committed by males neither related to nor living with their victims (63 percent in Lambeth; 83 percent in Westminster) implies that many of the incidents recorded were public brawls. [54] That few children appear to have been assaulted is natural; the young either could not or dared not prefer charges against adult males. But how many contemporaries noted this statistical bias? It is likely that figures such as these perpetuated the "invisibility" of child abuse relative to the mistreatment of women.

More than two decades later, renewed government concern about violence to women prompted another poll of judges and police officers. The Metropolitan Commissioner of Police and a number of County Chief Constables declared in their reports to the Home Secretary that brutality to women and children was on the rise. Officials attributed this trend to higher wages and shorter working hours, which contributed respectively to "increased drunkenness and increased time and opportunity for domestic and out-door brawling." The wretched dwellings of the poor and the want of "any provision for their comfort and amusement" also merited mention. Violence against the weak plainly angered those polled. Many respondents, like P. H. Edlin, Chairman of the Middlesex Quarter Sessions, normally regarded the use of the cat as "retrograde and barbarous" but condoned flogging in cases of assault upon women and children.[55] Viewing the problem from a feminist perspective, Frances Power Cobbe, the prominent antivivisectionist, believed that if flogging were added to existing penalties for wife-beating, women would be even less apt to testify against their husbands. Instead, she endorsed legislation whereby wives of men convicted of aggravated assault could obtain a protection order from the court, equivalent to a judicial separation.[56] Cobbe assumed that all cruelty, whether directed against animals or humans, stemmed from the same personality defect: "heteropathy," or "anger excited by signs of pain." So it was that "the joyless little faces and timid crouching demeanour" of beaten children sometimes provoked "fresh outrage" rather than pity. Still, like the great majority of her contemporaries, Cobbe assumed that the problem of child abuse paled by comparison with that of brutality to women.[57]

A close examination of the judicial statistics for England and Wales belies to some extent contemporary fears about increasing violence to females. Between 1861 and 1891 the number of persons summarily convicted for aggravated assaults against women and children steadily declined both relative to population and in absolute terms. Interestingly, the sharpest decrease in convictions over a five-year period occurred between 1876 and 1881, just when Cobbe was denouncing "wife torture" (see Appendix C, Fig. 1). Though the conviction rate for common assault also fell (after reaching a peak in 1871 of 304.5 per 100,000 of the population aged fifteen and over), the rate for aggravated assault declined proportionally faster.[58] A waning public interest in the protection of women cannot explain the decline in convictions; continued expressions of concern rule out this possibility. In 1882, for example, four MPs introduced a bizarre scheme designed to discourage violence against women. Any male over fifteen convicted of "grievously assaulting" a female could, at the court's discretion, be exposed for as long as four hours in a pillory; further, there would be "exhibited near above his head a board or placard setting out, in legible letters at least two inches in length, the name of the offender, and the words . . . 'wife-beater.'" Though "child-beaters" would have received equal treatment under this short-lived bill, the defense of the young was a secondary consideration.[59]

A more plausible explanation for the long-term decrease in convictions for aggravated assault is that brutality to women, especially that meted out by husbands, actually declined. This hypothesis is consistent with the finding that all crimes of violence against the person dropped sharply in late Victorian England.[60] It has been suggested that a rising standard of living lessened stress on laboring men as providers, thereby rendering them less sensitive to female assertiveness.[61] The same logic would imply a lower level of violence against working-class children, though in the absence of reliable statistics this assumption cannot be tested.

Community justice as well as parliamentary debate gave precedence to the defense of women. For generations common people had taken it upon themselves to chastise the transgressors of social norms by resorting to a variety of rituals known collectively as "rough music." In an effort to humiliate, for example, a widower who had chosen a scandalously young second mate, or a woman who had committed adultery, local citizens might gather to serenade the offender with a cacophony of cleavers banging on kettles, blasts on rams' horns, and shouts of derisive laughter.[62] Husbands thought to have been excessive in disciplining their wives—one convention held that a man should never strike his spouse with an instrument thicker than his thumb—could receive similar treatment. Yet communities very rarely applied "rough music" sanctions against abusive parents. The child *belonged* to its father and mother, and neighbors were loath to meddle with a proprietary interest.[63]

During the last quarter of the nineteenth century, however, this view of parental right would change dramatically. What caused its decline was more than the slow spread of humane sentiment. If the late Victorian campaign against child abuse was to win wide public support, its leaders needed a new moral vision in which justice for the young took precedence over the claims of parenthood. Interestingly, the men and women who created this vision would do so by arguing that the security of the home demanded it. The Englishman's castle was to be breached for the good of the castle, and, ultimately, for the good of the Englishman as well. Thus, child-savers labored also to save parents.

The reformers would bristle at the word "charity." Anticruelty work meant not benevolence but upholding children's rights and enforcing parental duty. Although the reformers never acknowledged the point, they disowned charitable motives partly because they wished for strategic reasons to avoid the appearance of social condescension or class bias. Overwhelmingly genteel, the leaders of the child protection movement naturally brought their domestic prejudices to bear on their work, but, as we will see, they were ready to chastise the comfortable as well as the dispossessed.

The erosion of parental power and the problem of class interest in moral reform are major themes of this book. A third theme is the play between private and state initiatives in social welfare. The growth of central government during Victoria's reign has attracted a great deal of scholarly attention, if not much agreement about its causes. Whatever the preferred agent of change, however, historians now seem to accept that the identification of intolerable social ills led the state to take responsibility for their cure. Parental abuse of the young emerged as an issue of pressing national concern in the 1880's, yet the state refused to supervise the treatment of children at home. Here, then, is a case study of how voluntary effort created its own central government to cope with an obvious evil.

CHAPTER 2

Doctors and Baby-Farmers

To SAVE INFANTS from systematic destruction, reformers took a halting first step into the home. Beginning in the mid-1860's a small group of English doctors assumed responsibility for exposing the plight of "nurse children," infants who were placed with professional foster parents. The case for protection had two strengths. First, medical men could trade on their reputations for public service and scientific expertise; narrow self-interest was rarely one of the charges hurled against them. Second, the defenders of the rights of nurse children could stress the commercial nature of adoption, thereby lessening fear that the monitoring of foster parents might create a precedent for interfering with "normal" family relations. * Opposing the physicians was a coalition of interests whose common cry became "the liberty of the individual." The strength of this opposition ultimately kept reformers from winning the radical legal changes that they sought.

Many physicians and their lay allies grew concerned about the fate of unwanted babies through their study of infanticide. During the early 1860's England was witnessing a true "slaughter of the innocents," social critics warned. London newspapers told of infants found stuffed down privies, tossed into the ornamental ponds of Regent's Park, or simply left in gutters, their necks either slashed or discolored from strangulation. Some provincial towns offered large rewards for information leading to the arrest of child-killers in their midst. The *Saturday Review* spoke for a large audience when it lamented this "foul current of life, running like a pestilential sewer beneath the smooth surface of society." [1]

---

* Technically, adoption in the sense of the transfer of parental rights and liabilities was unknown under English common law until 1926.

TABLE 2

Some Causes of Death for Infants under One Year, 1864

Contemporary classification	Number of deaths		Percent of deaths from all causes	
"Zymotic [infectious] diseases"	25,322		22.4%	
Diarrhea		9,818		8.7%
Whooping cough		3,483		3.1
Smallpox		1,882		1.7
"Constitutional diseases"	7,517		6.7	
Hydrocephalus		2,836		2.5
Tabes mesenterica		2,659		2.4
"Local diseases"	42,671		37.8	
Convulsions		20,821		18.4
Pneumonia		8,382		7.4
Bronchitis		7,400		6.6
"Developmental diseases"	32,596		28.9	
Premature birth		8,339		7.4
Teething		2,142		1.9
"Violent deaths"	1,730		1.5	
Suffocation (accidental and negligent)		906		0.8
Homicide		192		0.2
Burns and scalds		133		0.1
"Sudden deaths" (causes unascertained)	794		0.7	
"Causes not specified"	2,305		2.0	
Deaths from all causes	112,935		100.0%	

SOURCE: Twenty-Seventh Annual Report of the Registrar-General.

It is difficult to judge how far such alarm reflected reality. Even at the height of the infanticide scare violent death played a small part in overall infant mortality. During 1864, for example, violence accounted for just 1.5 percent of infant deaths. Thus diarrhea was nearly eight times as lethal as the combined threat of suffocation, burns, and murder (see Table 2). Yet a close study of homicide statistics shows that children under the age of one formed a far higher proportion of all murder victims than they do today. From the 5,314 cases of homicide listed by the Registrar General for the period 1863–87, a grim 3,355 cases—or 63 percent—involved infants. By contrast, in 1977 only 6.1 percent of all English murder victims were children under one year of age.[2] If not "slaughtered" en masse, mid-Victorian infants clearly were more apt to be killed than people of all other age groups combined.

The Stirring of Reform

In late 1862 a group calling itself the Association for the Preservation of Infant Life petitioned Parliament to repeal the Poor Law Amendment Act of 1844, insisting that the social stigma of bastardy, if distributed more equitably between mother and putative father, would not then so often lead to crime.[3] This was the first of many attempts by ad hoc associations to attack the "root causes" of child-murder. Unfortunately, few philanthropists could agree on priorities for reform. Uncoordinated and even contradictory, their calls to action produced little in the way of concrete results. The ambitiously titled National Society and Asylum for the Prevention of Infanticide, inaugurated on September 3, 1863, sought reform without the help of Parliament. Its founders proposed "to stimulate a healthy national sentiment" on the subject "not by exciting a maudlin sympathy with guilt, even under the garb of desertion and suffering in the hour of travail, but by boldly confronting the dark crime of child-murder, and making a resolute effort to absterge from the national escutcheon the foul blot that in Christian England in this nineteenth century many a mother does 'forget her suckling child,' and mercilessly destroy the 'fruit of her womb.'"[4] To this end the new organization proposed to establish a "Maternal and Affiliation Institution," which would combine the benefits of a retreat and a moral reformatory for the shame-stricken mother and her offspring. In its capacity as guardian of these illegitimate children, the institution would compel contributions from the mother and, where possible, from the putative father.[5] Whether this scheme ever went into effect is uncertain because mention of the National Society soon vanished from the London press. Vague references to groups of gentlemen calling for a revitalized foundling hospital or for an inquiry into the operation of the bastardy laws suggest a continuing, if ineffectual, interest in the protection of infant lives. More visible but also lacking political force were the resolutions of the Health Department of the Social Science Association, which recommended the compulsory registration of all births and deaths.[6]

When Parliament finally decided to address the subject of infanticide, it did so within a narrow judicial context. Between November 1864 and March 1865, the Commission on Capital Punishment solicited opinion from England's best legal minds on the sanctions against homicide. In the course of these hearings the commissioners learned not only that child-murder had ceased de facto to be punished as a capital offense, but also that in many instances judges had actively conspired with laymen to circumvent the law. The former Home Secretary Spencer Walpole gave two explanations for such courtroom farces.

First of all, the public do not consider that a child just born can be regarded in the same light as a person who, we will say, has grown up and is deprived of all those rights and enjoyments which then belong to him; and secondly, looking at what is the foundation of all your law with reference to murder, namely the presupposed malice and malignity, you cannot say that this is the case at least in the public estimation with regard to most of the instances in which a woman kills her child.

But, as Walpole also confessed, where to draw the line between infanticide and the more heinous act of murder posed a knotty problem. Although he himself favored a grace period of three months after birth, his fellow witnesses were less lenient, inclining toward the three-day exemption allowed in France. Ultimately, the commissioners decided that "an Act should be passed making it an offense, punishable with penal servitude or imprisonment at the discretion of the court, unlawfully and maliciously to inflict grievous bodily harm or serious injury upon a child during its birth, or within seven days afterwards, in case such child has subsequently died. No proof that the child was completely born alive should be required."[7] The theory behind this formulation was sound; if presented with the option of a verdict somewhere between the poles of concealment of birth and outright murder, juries would be more apt to convict, thus reinfusing the law with a deterrent value. Capital punishment amendment bills incorporating the commissioners' recommendations came before Parliament in 1866 and again the following year, only to die before gaining a second reading in the Commons.[8] Despite the urgings of Walpole and his allies, most MPs were reluctant to make statutory distinctions between different types of murder.

Simultaneously, however, the government began to feel a new wave of pressure for reform. This reawakening of moral outrage stemmed mainly from the sensational trial of Charlotte Winsor. On February 15, 1865, a parcel lying by the roadside near Torquay in Devonshire was found to contain the body of a dead infant wrapped in newspaper. The child belonged to Mary Harris, aged 23, a servant. Both she and Charlotte Winsor, aged 45, with whom the baby had been placed, were arrested and tried for murder. After a first trial in which the jury failed to reach a verdict, the Devon Spring Assizes resumed the case, this time with Harris giving Queen's evidence. The facts as they now surfaced proved that infanticide was not always the act of misguided mothers, but sometimes rather the product of "a system," as one outraged correspondent wrote to *The Times*, "with regular practitioners and fixed fees."[9]

Born in the sleepy Devonshire parish of Halberton, the second of eleven children, Charlotte Winsor had been raised by a father who labored in the fields and a mother who read fortunes. Although she too began as an illiterate field worker, Winsor discovered a more lucrative calling by the time she married her third husband. When Mary Harris obtained a situation, she entrusted her illegitimate child to Winsor for the sum of three shillings a week. The latter mentioned that she also "put away" bastards in exchange for premiums of £3 to £5. Although Harris at first declined this special service, she returned to Winsor's home a few weeks later and stood by while the older woman smothered the child under a bed.[10] Apprised of these details, the jury returned a swift verdict of guilty. By summer's end the "Torquay Murder" had become the focus of national and even international attention. London's *Illustrated Police News* dispatched an artist to sketch Winsor's now infamous cottage, while readers across the Atlantic learned that infanticide in England was a "recognized eventuality."[11]

One journalist remarked that public furor over the Torquay case evaporated soon after Winsor went to prison.

It was only while our tender feelings were suffering excruciation from the harrowing story of baby torture that we shook in wrath against the torturer. Considering what our sufferings were (and from the manner of our crying out they must have been truly awful) we recovered with a speed little short of miraculous. Barely was the trial of the murderess concluded and the court cleared, than our fierce indignation subsided from its bubbling and boiling, and quickly settled down to calm and ordinary temperature.[12]

The English public, it is true, had often heard of "wise men" and "herbalists" whose potions were meant to induce miscarriage, and of midwives whose services ranged from mid-term abortion to delivery by means of a meat hook thrust through the child's head.[13] Thus, for many people the crime of Charlotte Winsor was gross enough to excite momentary horror, but not so uncommon as to sustain a long-lived reform campaign. Yet this revelation of professional infanticide did make a lasting impression on certain London doctors.

On May 17, 1866, John Brendon Curgenven, Honorary Secretary of London's prominent Harveian Society, proposed to his medical associates that they address themselves to the issue of child-murder "in its social aspect, rather than to the pathological evidences to be found in the various modes of death." Curgenven reveled in action. As a medical student he had been the second person in the west of England to test ether. Later he spent two months as a volunteer surgeon in the Crimea, where his patients included Florence Nightingale.[14] Curgenven's fellow members were enthusiastic about the idea of a full-scale inquiry. Dr. Charles Drysdale, an expert on syphilis and future President of the Malthusian League, stressed that "the stigma of society should not, as now, be so severe against the maiden-mother who had *one* child, whilst it was so lenient to the other woman who entailed, even in the married state, suffering and ignorance upon a numerous and guiltless progeny." The President of the Harveian Society, W. Tyler Smith, agreed that the underlying causes of child-murder needed exposure. The committee appointed to conduct this investigation consisted of Smith, Drysdale, Curgenven, Ernest Hart, soon to be editor of the *British Medical Journal*, William Hardwicke, a Middlesex Deputy Coroner, J. S. Burdon-Sanderson, Medical Officer of Health for Paddington and later Regius Professor of Medicine at Oxford, Benson Baker, M.O.H. for Christ Church district in St. Marylebone, and a Mr. Sedgwick.[15]

The membership of this committee bears closer analysis. With the exception of Sedgwick, for whom no biographical information has been found, all these men were devoted to improving public health. Both Tyler Smith, an obstetrician, and Charles Drysdale, a venereologist, had witnessed the human cost of conceiving children in poverty and disease. For Drysdale, at least, infanticide and prostitution were symptomatic of the same disorder: the social and economic oppression of women in England.[16] Drysdale's feminism would soon lead him to take an outspoken and highly unpopular stand in favor of birth control, a stand that very few mid-Victorian doctors were willing to share.[17] Nonetheless, his Harveian Society peers did agree that since infanticide was usually the act of single women abandoned by their lovers, men must be held accountable for the bastards they sired.

William Hardwicke, J. S. Burdon-Sanderson, and Benson Baker, all public employees, naturally saw child-murder as a threat to the communities they served. Moreover, in 1866 London coroners and medical officers of health would have been particularly sensitive to rumors of mass infanticide, for it was one of their own, Edwin Lankester, who had done so much to fuel these rumors. Coroner for the Central District of Middlesex since 1862, Lankester estimated that London alone harbored 16,000 women who had destroyed their babies.[18]

Neither J. B. Curgenven, a general surgeon, nor Ernest Hart, an ophthalmic surgeon, was drawn to the infant protection issue by reason of his medical specialty. Rather, their activism here, as on many other reform fronts, seems linked to a strong need for social recognition. No doubt Curgenven and Hart were temperamentally suited to be humanitarians. But it is also significant that both young men entered the London medical world as in some sense outsiders. Curgenven, then 35, was from Cornwall; although he studied at St. Bartholomew's Hospital, he never held a hospital or medical school post, the possession of which distinguished elite consultants from ordinary practitioners.[19] Hart, by contrast, became Dean of the St. Mary's Hospital Medical School in 1863. Still just 31 in 1866, he could look forward to a prestigious and well-paying career. Yet this wunderkind was a Jew, and his faith kept him from going to Queen's College, Cambridge, on the scholarship he had won at the City of London School.[20] To suggest that Hart and Curgenven became reformers partly out of a quest for social esteem makes sense in terms of their backgrounds and the general anxiety about status felt by members of the mid-Victorian medical profession. As Jeanne Peterson has argued, "medicine's all too recent associations with the occupations of artisan and shopkeeper tied the profession to the world of competition and profit, both of which were antithetical to status as a gentleman." The drive for gentility and the desire to serve mankind were complementary motivations for many doctors.[21]

The infanticide committee of the Harveian Society met once a month during the latter half of 1866. Gathering information occupied most of its time; correspondence from doctors and charitable institutions together with reports obtained from the Foreign Office on the care of illegitimate children on the Continent formed the bulk of its evidence. After digesting this material, the committee drew up a list of twenty recommendations for presentation at the society's annual meeting on January 3, 1867. The recommendations ranged widely, from calling for the compulsory registration of all births and the endorsement of the Royal Commission's stand on the punishment of infanticide, to insisting on the supervision of all persons hired as day-nurses of illegitimate children and the revision of the Poor Law to increase the sum recoverable from putative fathers. On a motion by Curgenven, the meeting agreed to press Walpole, once again Home Secretary in Derby's third cabinet, for an interview, at which the need for government action along these lines would be urged.[22] As an attempt to place infanticide in its larger social context, the committee's report was impressive. Ironically, however, its very comprehensiveness rendered it less effective as a lever for reform. On January 28, 45 Harveian Society members heard Walpole explain that such domestic legislation entailed much doubt and difficulty. The deputation's timing was poor. A government preoccupied with the franchise question and a Home Secretary wary of competition for his own Homicide Law Amendment Bill did not make eager allies.[23] Moreover, the report's facile assumption that illegitimacy was rising—deduced from a comparison of bastardy statistics in 1830 and 1860, without taking into account the shift from parish to civil registration—marred its credibility on other points.[24] The doctors seemed to have reached a dead end.

J. B. Curgenven, however, was prepared to campaign alone. On March 18, he read a paper entitled "The Waste of Infant Life" to the Health Department of the Social Science Association. Curgenven's paper is noteworthy both because of its forceful argument that the state should assume responsibility for infant welfare and because it presaged the next issue in the child protection debate. The central government, he held, had neglected its duty to the child. The state's willingness to provide for the feeble-minded but not for the young was indefensible: "Why should the helpless infant receive less consideration than the lunatic? The former has a life that may be of value; but the life of the latter, though valueless, is preserved, in the case of paupers, at the cost of the country, at great expense, and under the care of a special department which the legislature has provided for the purpose."[25] Curgenven's case carried conviction, at least among the sanguine reformers of the Social Science Association. On May 13, the association's Health Department gave unanimous support to two of his resolutions: first, that a maternity fund be established in connection with every factory, out of which the woman lying-in would receive a sum equal to her weekly wages for a period of two months after the birth of her child, if it lived; second, that every encouragement be given to the establishment of infant day-nurseries for the children of working women. But only after "considerable discussion" did Curgenven's third resolution pass:

It having been proved that very great mortality exists among illegitimate children in the care of hired nurses, a fact which shows the existence of much ignorance, carelessness, and culpable neglect on the part of these nurses, the Health Department of this Association is of opinion that protection should be accorded by the State to illegitimate children, by requiring that all persons taking charge of them should be registered, or licensed, and placed under the supervision of the Poor Law Medical Officer of the district in which they reside.[26]

References to the term "baby-farming," that is, the practice of receiving infants to nurse or rear by hand in exchange for payment, multiplied in early 1867.[27] By September the *Pall Mall Gazette* was denouncing "suspicious" newspaper advertisements for child adoption. These advertisements often appeared in papers that catered to women seeking work. Servants looking for situations, or females interested in openings for "feather-hands," "artificial flower-hands," or plaiters of ribbon and net would have read such notices.[28] The *British Medical Journal* first alluded to baby-farming on October 19, in connection with a coroner's inquest revealing that all four children belonging to a hairdresser's wife had been put out to nurse and had subsequently died. Before the end of the year *The Times* noted that professional adoption of infants by "respectable" married couples, sometimes for as much as £30, seemed to be a "regular institution" in Edinburgh.[29]

So far the allegations of criminality associated with baby-farming were vague and unsubstantiated. More than anyone else the person responsible for making tangible these hazy suspicions of foul play was Ernest Hart, then editor of the *British Medical Journal*. Like Curgenven, Hart had already distinguished himself as a medical activist. While on *The Lancet*'s editorial board, Hart persuaded the journal to initiate a special study of nursing in London's Poor Law infirmaries. The findings of *The Lancet*'s commission, together with Hart's own *Fortnightly Review* article "Hospitals of the State," proved instrumental in persuading Home Secretary Gathorne Hardy to secure the Metropolitan Poor Law Amendment Act of 1867, legislation that greatly improved medical treatment of paupers in London.[30] Hart, therefore, had reason to trust in the efficacy of public exposure as a tactic for prompting parliamentary action. And he was now determined to use his own *Journal* to lay bare the evils of baby-farming.

In early January 1868, Hart took the first step in his new campaign, obtaining permission from the Registrar General to inspect local registers in the hope of tracing houses where large numbers of children had died. When he found that loopholes in the registration law prevented this, he tried another tack. Working with Dr. Alfred Wiltshire, Hart drew up newspaper advertisements requesting a nurse to assume responsibility for a child. Within a week they had received 333 replies to their offer of a £5 premium. Although only a few of the respondents gave their home addresses, it was possible to locate a majority of the letter writers, for those who left post office addresses generally consented to a rendezvous. Under the guise of a distressed father burdened by an illegitimate child, Wiltshire paid visits to the homes of as many respondents as possible. The outcome of these inquiries, as Hart saw it, "was to establish beyond doubt . . . that many of these women carried on the business [of adoption] with a deliberate knowledge that the children would die very quickly and evidently with a deliberate intention that they should die."[31]

Between January 25 and March 28, 1868, the *British Medical Journal* carried five leading articles based on Hart's research. The editor prefaced these reports with a stinging critique of official inaction.

But for the surprising apathy which our governmental powers display, and the attitude of indifference or, at the best, of expectancy with which, from constitutional scruples, or upon grounds of mysterious policy, they are apt to regard all the developments of social misdoing and misery, not flagrantly forced upon their attention, we should have hesitated to undertake single-handed the task of inquiring into and exposing the details of the system of baby-farming and baby-murder—terms frequently convertible—which, no one will be surprised to hear, is now carried on in the metropolis and in the provinces, after a fashion destructive to life, utterly immoral, and not uncommonly felonious.[32]

Hart succeeded in capturing public attention. A week after the publication of his first exposé, the *Pall Mall Gazette* ascertained that a boy with three and sixpence could easily insert an offer for concealed delivery or professional adoption in the *Daily Telegraph*, so lax were that newspaper's advertising standards.[33] By early April Lady Petre had raised a large sum of money with which to establish a crèche in the impoverished district adjacent to Manchester Square. Much had been said about female frailty, but little had been done to ease the lot of working mothers. Lady Petre hoped that her crèche would lighten the burden of maternity for a few women in this predicament.[34] The subject of diabolical adoption also intruded upon literature, when Lady Wood wrote about an evil Essex nurse in *Sorrow on the Sea* (1868). Somewhat later Arthur Sullivan's very unsinister Buttercup would confess

> A many years ago,
>   When I was young and charming,
> As some of you may know
>   I practiced baby-farming.[35]

The government remained impassive, however. Acting on behalf of Hart, Lord Shaftesbury asked the Duke of Marlborough, then Lord President of the Council, if official notice had been taken of the baby-farming revelations, and whether, as a result, remedial action was contemplated. Marlborough diplomatically conceded the existence of a traffic in nurse-children, "under which the grossest crimes might be committed." And though the matter seemed "rather one of police than of sanitary investigation," he predicted that the government would turn their attention to it during the parliamentary recess.[36]

Had Hart been able to exert political pressure earlier in the session, Gathorne Hardy might have responded with a serious departmental study. Unfortunately, though possessed of a potent propaganda tool in the *Journal*, Hart did not at this time control the British Medical Association's legislative nerve center, its Parliamentary Bills Committee. Organized in 1863, the P.B.C. set reform priorities and planned lobbying strategy for a membership of four thousand. In its *Fifth Annual Report* the committee indicated that the protection of infant life rated as but one of the association's legislative aims. During the previous year, for example, the P.B.C. had devoted special effort to amending both the Irish vaccination scheme and the government's Artizans' Dwellings Bill. Dr. Septimus Gibbon, Honorary Secretary of the committee, suffered "protracted attendances" at the Houses of Parliament and arranged repeated interviews with legislators in order to promote the association's view on these subjects.[37] Without a concrete plan to regulate baby-farming, Gibbon had little for which to agitate. Moreover, Hart may have been at odds with other members of the B.M.A. hierarchy, for between July 1869 and June 1870 he stepped down as editor of the *Journal*—the only hiatus in a regime that spanned 31 years.

Hart would later recall that the baby-farming question "went to sleep" from the autumn of 1868 to the summer of 1870.[38] A change of ministries following the general election of November 1868, together with subsequent parliamentary absorption in Irish affairs and elementary education, deterred reformers from mounting a new assault on the Home Office. Yet individual voices continued to decry the hazards of professional adoption. In March 1869 Curgenven presented another paper, "On Baby-Farming and the Registration of Nurses," to the Social Science Association, in which he calculated that fully two-thirds of the illegitimate children born annually in England and Wales were placed with caretakers. A majority of these bastards, he insisted, fell into the hands of "ignorant and unscrupulous women." If Curgenven intended these arbitrary estimates to spark a legislative response, he failed.[39] The one hint of parliamentary action came in the form of the Marquess of Townshend's own Infant Life Protection Bill. This hastily conceived plan to require a magistrate's license for every person taking charge of an infant under five years collapsed when critics pointed out that it would encumber poor parents as well as baby-farmers.[40]

The dormant period ended suddenly in mid-June 1870. On the morning of June 12, two infant bodies were discovered in Brixton. The first, found among some lumber, had been wrapped in a piece of blue cloth and fastened up with paper. Discernible on the outer wrapping was the name "Mrs. Waters." The second body, also bundled up, had been found by a lamplighter underneath a railway arch. Since both corpses were badly decomposed, the coroner's jury returned verdicts of "found dead" on each. But Acting Inspector Hammond of the Metropolitan Police knew that sixteen more bodies of infants had been picked from neighboring streets within recent weeks. Under these circumstances the advertisement in

Lloyd's Weekly Newspaper seemed highly suspicious: "Adoption—
a good home, with a mother's love and care is offered to any respectable person wishing her child to be entirely adopted. Premium
£5, which sum includes everything. Apply, by letter only, to Mrs.
Oliver, Post Office, Grove-Place, Brixton." Hammond, therefore,
had one of his officers, Sergeant Relf, investigate. Relf arranged a
meeting at a railway station and then shadowed Mrs. Oliver to her
home. It was not, however, until he traced a seventeen-year-old
mother of an illegitimate child to the same house that the sergeant
felt ready to act. Then, accompanied by the girl's father, who demanded to see his grandchild, Relf gained admission to the house.
Inside he found not only the baby in question, "dreadfully emaciated and apparently dying," but also ten other infants, all of them
neglected except for Oliver's own child.[41]

Slowly, in the course of seven hearings held during the following
month, details emerged about what *The Times* called "one of the
most horrible . . . stories ever brought to light in a Court of Justice." "Mrs. Oliver," it transpired, was only one of several aliases
used by Margaret Waters, aged 31. The widow Waters, in partnership with her 29-year-old sister Sarah Ellis, ran a deadly trade. A
servant girl testified that the standard infant formula at Waters's establishment consisted of common lime mixed with water. Sergeant
Relf had confiscated three bottles from the house, one containing
laudanum and the other two poison. Not unexpectedly, the bastard
child of Jeanette Cowan soon died of starvation exacerbated by the
ingestion of narcotics. Four more infants eventually perished. Tickets discovered in the house showed that in May and June alone the
women had pawned over one hundred items of children's clothing,
including two shirts bearing labels that suggested aristocratic clien-
tele. When Waters and Ellis went on trial at the Central Criminal
Court, they faced prosecution for murder, manslaughter, conspiracy, and obtaining money under false pretenses. Sarah Ellis escaped
with a conviction on the last charge alone, but her sister did not
fare as well: Margaret Waters was hanged on October 11.[42]

Some observers doubted that her fate would deter other women
similarly employed. This demonstration of professional risk, critics
reasoned, would only prompt baby-farmers to raise their prices,
thus encouraging unwed mothers to perform their own killings.[43]
Clearly, however, the "Brixton horrors" did stimulate a new and
more effectual attempt to secure remedial legislation. The idea of an

Infant Life Protection Society open to laymen as well as doctors originated with Curgenven and W. T. Charley, the Conservative MP for Salford. Although plans for such an alliance seem to have been formulated soon after the unmasking of Mrs. Waters, it was not until October 14 that the I.L.P.S. convened its inaugural meeting in Charley's Temple chambers. Aiming for a more diverse membership than that of the Harveian Society, the founders of this new body nevertheless agreed that social reform was the province of "gentlemen"; membership in the I.L.P.S. required a minimum annual subscription of half a guinea, or a donation of five guineas. The composition of the central committee also reflected this same bias. Serving with Curgenven as Honorary Secretary was the Reverend Oscar Thorpe, Vicar of Christ Church, Camberwell; and W. T. Charley, by profession a barrister specializing in conveyancing, became Treasurer. Other prominent figures included George Hastings, Secretary of the Social Science Association, W. T. Manning, Coroner of the Queen's Household, Francis Peek, a prominent philanthropist and the contributor of £100 towards the committee's expenses, and Ernest Hart. Once again ensconced as editor of the *Journal*, Hart welcomed the I.L.P.S., arguing that "State inspection of the helpless buntings" was an issue "eminently medical." [44]

The society hastened to publicize its aims and to act upon them. Curgenven's *Prospectus*, published in December, outlined four "principal objects":

I. To prevent the destruction of Infant Life, and the moral and physical injury to young children, caused by the present system of Baby-farming; and with this in view, to promote a Bill in Parliament requiring that any person taking charge of an infant or young child for gain should be certified as of good character and be registered; and that every child so placed out shall be subject to proper supervision.

II. In the event of the proposed Bill being passed by Parliament, to promote the formation of District Committees, with a view to the selection and supervision of nurses of good character resident in suitable locations.

III. To promote the boarding out of destitute orphans and deserted children in healthy places, and with trustworthy persons, instead of their being left under the injurious moral and physical influences of Workhouse Nurseries and Schools.

IV. To promote the amendment of the Laws relating to Bastardy, and to Registration of Births and Deaths; and of the Law of Evidence in cases of Infanticide. [45]

Significantly, the I.L.P.S. not only proposed legal reform on a wide range of subjects affecting the physical safety of infants, but also sought to protect older children placed with foster parents by Poor Law authorities. In November, G. J. Goschen, President of the Poor Law Board, had issued an order permitting unions to settle workhouse children with persons living outside their districts, provided that local committees be responsible for the selection of suitable homes and that inspectors answerable to those committees carry out inspection of children so placed. With 51,939 persons under ten years of age living in English workhouses as of July 1, 1868—roughly 14,000 of whom were orphans—the boarding-out system promised to expand rapidly. I.L.P.S. leaders wanted to insure that this new form of outdoor relief did not degenerate into state-sanctioned neglect. Implicit in this concern was the notion, as yet embryonic, that all children deserved the special protection of the state.[46]

On November 9, the Home Secretary, H. A. Bruce, greeted an I.L.P.S. delegation bearing a draft bill that incorporated these objects. Bruce appeared more receptive than his Tory predecessors. In addition to offering general approval of the proposals on infanticide and baby-farming, he urged the society to introduce a clause for the suppression of secret accouchements.[47] Bruce's request stemmed from the failure of law enforcement officials to break up clandestine lying-in homes. Throughout 1869, for example, the Metropolitan Police kept under surveillance a Mrs. L. Martin, self-styled "certified accoucheur," who ran an establishment located at 33 Dean Street, Soho. According to an anonymous informant, Mrs. Martin supplied abortions for sums varying from £10 to £50, depending on the financial resources of her patients. Women who came to her at full term were delivered over a vessel filled with water, thereby drowning the newborn child. Altogether she boasted of having eliminated no fewer than 555 infants and fetuses during one ten-month period. Further investigation confirmed that Martin's house received "numbers of well-dressed females." Yet Martin's care in preventing incriminating evidence from leaving her house, combined with the refusal of patients to testify against her, left the authorities powerless to prosecute. When the former washerwoman and hospital nurse died suddenly in November 1869, her son and her paramour assumed control of this profitable business. The

Home Secretary was thus understandably well disposed toward legislation that might rid London of such dens.[48]

Nine weeks later Hart and Charley met with the President of the Poor Law Board. Though he too sympathized with the aims of the bill, he expressed concern that its provisions for inspecting boarded-out children might conflict with regulations set out in his recent order. Therefore, the measure that Charley and co-sponsors William Brewer (Liberal, Colchester) and Lyon Playfair (Liberal, Edinburgh and St. Andrews universities) introduced in the Commons on February 21 exempted Poor Law children.*

Even so, their bill called for some sweeping changes. The second clause made it illegal for any person "to receive or retain for hire or reward" an infant under the age of six without having first obtained a license from a justice of the peace. The JP, in turn, could grant such a license only after seeing a certificate from another magistrate, clergyman, or registered medical practitioner, vouching for the applicant's good character and ability to provide adequate food and lodging for the child. The license would remain in force one year. These regulations, the bill stipulated, should not extend to the relatives or legal guardians of a child, to persons having the care of children whose parents were resident abroad, or to boarding schools and public orphanages. But nurses who contravened the law by accepting a child under the age of six would be guilty of a misdemeanor and, therefore, liable to a maximum prison term of six months. Children retained for less than 24 hours did not come under the provisions of the bill.

Other clauses delineated a complex inspection system. Licensees were required to enter in a register the name of any child taken for hire, and, in the case of one kept longer than a week, to give its name and birth certificate to the local Poor Law medical officer. The latter would personally inspect every child at least once a month and send a written report on its condition to the Poor Law Board every three months. Further, the board had to appoint and finance a Registrar of Children together with a "sufficient number

---

* Select Committee on Infant Life Protection, P.P., 1871, VII, Q. 73. Both of Charley's co-sponsors were public health activists. William Brewer was a doctor and at the time Chairman of the Metropolitan Asylums' Board. Lyon Playfair had enrolled at Edinburgh University intending to pursue a medical degree, but subsequently switched to chemistry, earning a Ph.D. in that field. He had participated in several parliamentary studies, including the 1844–45 Commission on the Health of Towns.

of Inspectors and Sub-Inspectors to carry out the provisions of the Act." And finally, the bill obligated licensees to notify the district coroner within a day of the death of a nurse-child. Coroners would automatically hold inquests on the bodies of such children unless presented with a doctor's certificate stating that the death arose from natural causes. No nursling could be buried without a coroner's authorization.[49]

That Charley's bill provoked instant controversy was not surprising. Any scheme for social reform that entailed intrusion of the central government risked antagonizing champions of "individual liberty." But what did startle I.L.P.S. members was the criticism of their plan, in meticulous detail, by the fledgling women's suffrage movement. In the lengthy pamphlet *Infant Mortality: Its Causes and Remedies*, the Committee for Amending the Law in Points Wherein It Is Injurious to Women branded the bill superficial and meddlesome. The moving force behind this attack seems to have been Lydia Becker and her Manchester branch of the National Society for Women's Suffrage. With the founding in March 1870 of the *Women's Suffrage Journal*, edited by Becker, and the introduction in May of the first parliamentary legislation devoted exclusively to the female franchise, advocates of votes for women were just beginning to find their political feet. To pioneers in this crusade, Charley's bill offered a target far more vulnerable than Gladstone's Government.[50]

Becker's arguments were persuasive. According to her, the Infant Life Protection Bill aimed at removing the "apparent and proximate causes of the fearful mortality prevailing among nurse-children," leaving "the real and ultimate causes untouched." Infanticide and baby-farming sprang from the inequitable bastardy laws, from social prejudice against employing unwed mothers, and from basic maternal ignorance. None of these problems found a remedy in the I.L.P.S. measure. Furthermore, the bill failed to discriminate between women who assumed total responsibility for children and those who only shared that responsibility with one or both parents. Becker and her companions denounced the kind of blanket registration envisioned by the I.L.P.S., which would prevent single mothers from leaving their children with friends and neighbors for short periods.[51]

The note resonating throughout the pamphlet was laissez-faire. By increasing "officialism, police interference, and espionage," the proposal would add to "the already oppressive burden which the ratepayers have to fear . . . [and] weaken in the community that sense of responsibility to conscience and to God in which virtue, national as well as personal, has its root." Rounding out this catalog of abuses was the charge of male presumption. The bill, though

dealing with women in the performance of that domestic office which is, by common consent, regarded as peculiarly their own—namely the nursing of infants—. . . places the entire supervision, regulation, and authority in these matters in the hands of men. *Men only* are to grant the licenses—*men only* are competent to certify to the qualifications of the licensee—and *men only* are to visit the babies in their own nurses' charge. This minute and galling supervision by men of the domestic and nursery arrangements of women, would be felt as grievously vexatious by the women of this nation, especially by the poorer classes.[52]

Although the Manchester feminists did not say so, they must also have seen Charley's bill as a threat to work opportunities for widows, spinsters, and other self-supporting women.

Curgenven and other members of the I.L.P.S. felt unfairly treated. In its *Reply*, the society contended that most of Becker's criticisms arose from misunderstanding. It was wrong, Curgenven argued, to characterize the bill as a male incursion into the female sphere, for he and his associates intended that "ladies" should, as sub-inspectors, play a vital part in the inspection of nurse-children. Similarly, the charge of ignoring the underlying causes of infanticide and baby-farming was inappropriate because amendment of the bastardy laws required separate legislation, as did any scheme for the training of women in mothercraft.[53] Yet one irreducible difference of opinion remained: whereas the I.L.P.S. viewed state regulation of adoption as a safeguard whose benefits to potentially endangered infants outweighed possible inconveniences to their mothers and caretakers, women of the N.S.W.S. considered the plan repugnant precisely because it infringed upon the freedom of the individual female.

Parallels between this debate and the controversy surrounding the Contagious Diseases Acts are striking. The idea of controlling venereal disease in garrison and dockyard towns through licensing and inspecting brothels, incorporated in the 1864 Act, derived from the Parisian system of *maisons tolérées* and their regulation by a special *Police des Moeurs*. The I.L.P.S., in turn, looked to the

French hospice plan as a model for effective supervision of nurslings. Mothers unable to provide for their illegitimate offspring could, after an interview with the authorities, leave them at regional centers or hospices, where the young would be placed in the care of resident wet nurses. Returning to their own homes, the nurses reared these children in exchange for a standard annual fee that decreased as their charges grew older. "Assisted" children stayed under state guardianship until they reached the age of 21. In 1869 the Paris hospice alone employed two chief inspectors, 25 sub-inspectors, and 278 paid medical officers to supervise the care of some 25,486 minors. But most important, the mortality rate of Parisian hospice infants stood at 12 percent, compared to an estimated death rate of 75 percent among unsupervised adoptees.[54]

Medical men were prominent in campaigning for both the extension of the Contagious Diseases Acts and the regulation of babyfarms. Early on, the Harveian Society urged mandatory inspection of suspected prostitutes in all large towns. Its recommendation was based on a report, written by Curgenven and Charles Drysdale, that pointed to a serious shortage of hospitals with venereal wards.[55] And just as this society had spawned the ad hoc infanticide committee, so it also gave birth, in July 1867, to the Association for Promoting the Extension of the Contagious Diseases Act of 1866. Predictably, J. B. Curgenven became an Honorary Secretary of the latter. Although the *British Medical Journal* had in 1864 assailed the newly introduced Contagious Diseases Bill as the most "iniquitous interference with the liberty of the subject . . . since the days of Charles I," the *Journal,* under Hart's editorship, became markedly less antagonistic.[56] Plainly, some doctors were gravitating to the view that coercion in the interest of medical safety was defensible. Thus, the energy with which physicians urged the inspection of prostitutes and baby-farmers alike may be seen as stemming from disillusionment with the voluntary principle as it applied to problems of public health. Contemporary medical campaigns for compulsory vaccination and for mandatory training and registration of midwives were motivated by similar sentiments.

Finally, opposition to the Contagious Diseases Acts and to W. T. Charley's bill sprang from related sources. Women spearheaded both attacks—Josephine Butler the former, and Lydia Becker the latter. Though it would be misleading to categorize Butler's Ladies National Association for the Repeal of the Contagious Diseases

Acts as a suffragist group, the followers of both Butler and Becker espoused women's rights. And it was James Stansfeld, later Butler's leading parliamentary ally, who convinced Charley to abandon his bill. Soon after replacing Goschen as President of the Poor Law Board in March 1871, Stansfeld impressed upon an I.L.P.S. delegation his displeasure with the bill's rigid licensing provisions. He would go no further than pledge his support for a parliamentary investigation of baby-farming. Faced now with sure government opposition, the society really had no choice but to accept Stansfeld's offer.[57]

Ultimately, this concession benefited the I.L.P.S., since the resulting Select Committee on the Protection of Infant Life gave the cause a national forum. Advocates of regulation figured prominently in the inquiry. The seventeen-member committee included Charley, Playfair, and Brewer, and among the 21 witnesses were Curgenven, Hart, Lankester, Benson Baker, the Reverend Oscar Thorpe, and Alfred Wiltshire. Hart and Curgenven argued their case effectively. The inspection of baby-farms, Hart insisted, was not a pet plan of sentimental philanthropists but rather the logical responsibility of the state for its "infant citizens." Moreover, as a commercial venture analogous to the operation of lodging houses, this trade demanded regulation. If, during 1870, 1,134 Liverpool lodging houses been registered, necessitating 34,823 day and 5,706 night visits by municipal inspectors, comparable supervision of baby-farms should not prove unmanageable.[58]

From the evidence presented, the committee drew various conclusions about the regional distribution and mechanics of professional adoption. Baby-farming appeared most prevalent in London and its environs and in the Scottish cities of Edinburgh, Glasgow, and Greenock. The densely populated manufacturing districts of Lancashire and Yorkshire, by contrast, seemed virtually immune to this social blight. E. Herford, Coroner of Manchester since 1849, had heard of only one case of fraudulent child adoption taking place in his county. At the same time, Dr. E. J. Syson, M.O.H. for nearby Salford, estimated that between 80 and 90 percent of the children sent out for the day by working mothers perished during infancy.[59] Baby-farming in this region may have been rare, therefore, not because northern mothers placed a greater value on infant life than London mothers, but because a reliable method for disposing of children was already at hand. The select committee also concluded that, in London at least, infants frequently came to negligent nurses via secret lying-in establishments. Typically, owners of these houses would receive a lump sum of money for undertaking to care for newborn children—with the explicit understanding that the mother would never again see her offspring. The enterprising owner then arranged with individual baby-farmers to accept the infant along with generally inadequate weekly payments. This business apparently blossomed when newspapers began to refuse to insert adoption advertisements. Mary Hall, whose establishment in Cold Harbour Lane, Camberwell, supplied Waters and Ellis with several infants, had £800 in her possession when arrested.[60]

Thanks again to Sergeant Relf's detective work, the select committee learned a great deal about the child disposal system run by Mrs. Hall. Originally a cook, this "stout and repulsive" woman had done very well for herself. She and her husband, formerly a ship's carpenter, owned their own seven-room home in south London, where as many as six ladies could be accommodated at once. Neighbors remarked that although a stream of pregnant women entered this home, none ever left carrying a baby. Still more sinister, Mr. Hall used to do the washing after confinements, and had been seen to throw "lumps" out of the bloody bedclothes to his cats. Stories such as these drove Relf to track down and question some of the servant girls who had worked in the house. They, in turn, told the police about a few of the women who had been confined there. It seemed that directly across the street lived a chemist who sold Mrs. Hall laudanum syrup, no questions asked; small wonder that the neighbors never heard a child crying at No. 6, Chapel Place. Drugged infants were removed from the house, often at night, and farmed out to a variety of women, some of whom lived within walking distance and some as far away as Gloucestershire. Not all the children delivered by Mrs. Hall left her house, however. After the police found several holes in the garden "full of cinders, ashes, lime, and a quantity of earth, wet and slimy, containing maggots in abundance," the presumption of cold-blooded murder became irresistible.[61]

Assured by no less than the Superintendent of Metropolitan Police that baby-farming was "a matter so wrapt up and so delicate" as to defeat conventional law enforcement, the committee issued a

Report favorable to regulation on July 10. Its recommendations were fourfold:

1. That there should be a compulsory registration of all births and deaths within a limited period after the occurrence of those events.
2. That there should be a compulsory registration of all private houses habitually used as lying-in establishments.
3. That there should be a registration of persons who take for hire two or more infants under one year of age to nurse for a longer period than a day; but so guarded as not to interfere with temporary arrangements of an unobjectionable character.
4. That voluntary registration should be encouraged in the case of nurses who are not required to register compulsorily.[62]

Adopting these guidelines, the I.L.P.S. prepared to present a revised bill in the new parliamentary session. At meetings held in W. T. Manning's Westminster offices on January 7 and 23, 1872, the society completed its work, and then sent the measure to Home Secretary Bruce.[63] Introduced in the Commons on February 7, the bill came up for its second reading one month later. A normally combative Charley now found himself in the unusual position of having to defend his scheme against charges of timidity. Its failure to provide for stringent inspection of private homes, its decision to ignore day-nurseries, its exemption from registration of those who accepted only one child at a time—all these concessions had been granted, he explained, in order to secure unanimity. Coupled with separate reforms of the bastardy and registration laws, however, this legislation would ideally give local authorities a weapon with which to wage war on the destroyers of infant life.[64] In its watered down form the plan won quick parliamentary approval.

Fruits of the Campaign

Objectively assessed, the 1872 Infant Life Protection Act was a resounding failure. The "local authorities," with whom persons receiving babies for reward had to register their homes, varied widely. Responsibility for administering the Act in London fell to the Metropolitan Board of Works; elsewhere borough councils and, in the counties, magistrates in Petty Sessions found themselves saddled with this duty. Most zealous in attempting to fulfill its obligations was the Metropolitan Board of Works. A body governed by 45 delegates from London vestries, the board had become far more than a sanitary authority since its establishment in 1856. From the oversight of drains and sewers, it had moved on to large-scale slum clearance, street widening, and park acquisition schemes, all in the cause of "better management" for Europe's largest city.[65] Parliamentary statute was now stretching the board's regulatory net wider still. From November 1, 1872, when the Act took effect, this body used "every means in its power" to publicize the requirements of the law. Notices were inserted in newspapers and circulars posted at police stations and workhouses throughout London. At the board's urging, vestrymen, Poor Law Guardians, and the Commissioner of Police instructed their officers to report to the board their discovery of all illegal nursing establishments.[66] Yet despite its exertions, the board registered only five houses and authorized the reception of a mere ten infants during the last two months of 1872. The following year saw a proportionally more meager harvest of ten registered homes taking in 23 nurse-children. And this total proved the largest for another four years.

These extraordinarily low registration figures sparked premature optimism in some circles. In March 1876 the *British Medical Journal* announced triumphantly that "the Act has operated in the most beneficial way in which penal Acts can operate, by prevention rather than by punishment. Nearly all the baby-farmers have broken up."[67] The Metropolitan Board of Works had arrived at a far different conclusion, however. As early as May 1873 it informed Bruce that evasion of the Act was rife and suggested as a partial remedy that "infant" be redefined to include all persons under seven years old. Not unexpectedly, Bruce rejected any amendment of the 1872 statute, as did his Conservative successor, R. A. Cross, when presented with a similar suggestion four years later. Resigned to improvising on its own, the board in February 1878 appointed Samuel Babey as its inspector of nurse-children. This officer's findings proved that baby-farming in London was far from defunct. During his first year on the job, Babey discovered twenty persons infringing the 1872 statute. More significantly, he also found 284 children, the majority of them illegitimate, at unregistered houses. But none of these children could be touched by the board because only a single infant under one was in residence. In 1879 and 1880 Babey unearthed 324 and 339 such cases respectively.[68]

The late 1870's brought sharp disappointment to those who had labored long on behalf of the unwanted infant. A "searching inquiry" conducted by the sanitary officer of St. Luke's parish, London, in mid-1877 revealed that though not one house in his district had been registered under the 1872 Act, widows and spinsters living in cramped, single-room flats ran "numerous" unlicensed nurseries. Worse, a correspondent in *The Times* described a notice that had been deposited in the letter box of a West End home. Addressed to "The Master of the House. Private," this notice offered bluntly: "Gentlemen's children removed and provided for. Medical certificates [of death] provided if required." Nor did London monopolize the bad news. The conviction in 1879 of John Barnes and his wife for murdering three nurslings underscored the fact that the Birkenhead Town Council, like most municipal governments, had ignored the 1872 statute. By the end of the decade doctors were clamoring for the inclusion of lone nurslings in a new baby-farming bill.[69] Very little seemed to have been accomplished.

Yet viewed more broadly, the mid-Victorian movement to protect infant lives did achieve important results. The I.L.P.S., true to its stated aims, pressed for legislative reform on several fronts. At the same time that it drafted the revised baby-farming measure in January 1872, the society mapped strategy for the introduction of its Bastardy Laws Amendment Bill. This proposed three major changes: first, to allow courts more latitude in assessing putative fathers for child-support; second, to enable boards of guardians to assist mothers in recovering maintenance costs; third, to extend the father's liability for support until his offspring reached the age of sixteen. Introduced by W. T. Charley on April 9, the bill encountered little opposition when it came up for its second reading two months later. Blessed with James Stansfeld's enthusiastic support, it rapidly passed into law (35 & 36 Vic., c. 65) and remained the basis for dealing with the financial maintenance of illegitimate children until 1957.*

Another victory attributable in part to the I.L.P.S.'s persistence was the tightening of registration procedures. Acting on the 1871

---

* *The Times*, January 30, 1872, p. 4; Hansard, 3d ser., 211 (June 19, 1872), cols. 1972–76. The mother could now make a claim against the putative father before her child was born or at any time within a year of its birth. Her maximum weekly support rose from two shillings and sixpence to five shillings.

select committee's recommendation, Dr. Lyon Playfair brought to the Commons late that same session a plan for the compulsory registration of births and deaths. Government assurance that it intended to pursue this subject, however, persuaded Playfair to withdraw his bill. Impatient peers introduced two similar measures during 1872 and 1873, both of which flew through the Lords only to stall in the Commons because of government obstruction. Official foot dragging won few friends and forced the Home Office to temporize with single-minded representatives of the British Medical Association, the Obstetrical Society of London, and the I.L.P.S.[70] Thus, when Disraeli's new administration decided to move (the Liberals had only talked), Conservatives gained favor with public health reformers of both parties. The Registration Act of 1874 set a maximum 40-shilling fine for failure to report births within 42 days and deaths within eight days. Persons neglecting to inform registrars within a week of finding an abandoned child alive faced the same penalty. Graveyard officials were prohibited from burying stillborn infants without a medical certificate or written declaration stating that the child had been born dead. Similarly, no more than one body could, without written justification, be deposited in a single coffin. Noncompliance with the latter two provisions brought a possible ten-pound penalty. For willfully giving false statements or certificates, offenders might spend up to two years in prison. The 1874 statute failed to satisfy reformers on only one score: stillbirths continued to go unregistered.[71]

Reformers also tried repeatedly to strike infanticide from the list of capital crimes. Once again, W. T. Charley assumed the leadership in this ultimately unsuccessful effort. In each parliamentary session from 1873 to 1876, Charley brought in I.L.P.S.-backed schemes for reclassifying the fatal infliction of "grievous bodily harm" on children during or immediately after birth as a felony, punishable by penal servitude for up to ten years. Charley's 1874 version actually passed the Commons and received a second reading in the House of Lords before progovernment peers engineered its death by postponement. Although public opinion was now receptive to such legislation, sufficient opposition still existed to sustain government leaders in their maneuvering to forestall amendment of the common law.[72]

Given the wide reform net cast by I.L.P.S. members and their allies within the medical profession, it is tempting to view subsequent child protection activity as deriving from the mid-Victorian crusade against baby-farming and infanticide. Although such a picture would be neatly linear, emphasizing the continuity in reform effort, it actually obscures as much as it explains. In March 1873 A. J. Mundella, the Liberal Member for Sheffield, joined three other MPs in proposing a bill for the better defense of children. Hansard barely mentions the bill, for Mundella's measure never reached the debate stage. Indeed, the powers it outlined must have seemed preposterous to the vast majority in Parliament: when a parent was convicted for doing "bodily harm" to a child under twelve, courts could appoint a guardian for the victim. In some instances this guardian might remove the child to his custody, and in other instances, armed with a court order, he might invade the parents' home to inspect their offspring.[73] Little noticed by contemporaries and forgotten by historians, this scheme nevertheless represented the first glimmer of a new legislative attitude toward English children. According to Mundella's plan, once the physical safety of the young had been jeopardized, even that most hallowed of Victorian ideals, the inviolability of family life, could and should be set aside.

Through their exposure of baby-farming, J. B. Curgenven and Ernest Hart had demonstrated that the abuse of infants was sometimes both premeditated and systematic. They had shown further that the traffic in unwanted children fed upon the privacy surrounding domestic relations. Even so, it was one thing to advocate burdening a comparatively small segment of the female population with periodic inspection of their home-based trade and quite another to propose sweeping restraints on the freedom of all parents to rear their children as they saw fit. Significantly, neither Mundella nor his co-sponsors had been active in the I.L.P.S. cause. A staunch supporter of compulsory education, Mundella approached the issue of child welfare from the perspective of Dickens and Mary Carpenter. As he informed Parliament in 1870:

I have recently explored some of the crowded parts of London, and the sights which I have seen were of the most horrible character. I saw courts in which children, poor, miserable, squalid, and neglected, were as thick as flies in a sugar cask. . . . Within a few yards of this House there are thousands of children who never come in contact with human love, who never hear a virtuous sentiment, who never have any teaching but that of the streets, whose parents are to be found in the gin-palaces and the public-houses; and yet the state neglects these children because, forsooth, it respects the "liberty of the parents."[74]

Mundella and his backers had decided that the state's refusal to interfere with tyrannical parents made bad sense. This was a radical conclusion for its time—and one that would remain radical until like-minded philanthropists mounted a new campaign against cruelty to children.

CHAPTER 3

Organizing in Defense of the Young

In the early 1880's English philanthropists began to denounce child abuse as a gross social ill. As previously suggested,
this new reform effort was more complex than the fight to protect
infant lives. Whereas those vilified as baby-farmers had been, with
very few exceptions, women, neither sex monopolized cruelty to
the young. Further, the great majority of nurslings were fatherless,
so their inspection posed no challenge to paternal power. And finally, whereas the protection of infant life had been most actively
promoted by doctors, those who led the war against cruelty to children were laymen from many callings. The medical profession
never ceased to defend misused children. After 1880 as before, *The
Lancet* and the *British Medical Journal* were instrumental in focus-
ing public attention on dangers threatening the young. But the anticruelty campaign grew so fast that one professional group could
neither manage nor finance it.

The Problem of Timing

Why did philanthropists take up the child-protection cause when
they did? In Germany the 1880's saw the rise of scientific child-
study, a discipline pioneered by physiologists such as T. W. Preyer.
The same period in France found lawmakers building a standard-
ized public school system and debating plans to curb *puissance pa-
ternelle*, the authority of the father, by amending parts of the Civil
Code.[1] It may be true—the connection is hard to prove—that English reformers were encouraged by such Continental developments
to press their case against parental sin. Unfortunately, this thesis is

not particularly helpful in explaining the birth of anticruelty groups in 1883 and 1884.*

The founding of these groups did coincide with a protest over the mistreatment of schoolchildren. By 1880 the flogging of scholars in both public and school board schools had diminished appreciably, though some masters would continue to wield the birch rod with brutal abandon. Increasingly, even "mild" scholastic punishment evoked public anger. Thus, *The Lancet* could decry the "evils and injuries likely to result from the boxing of ears and the smacking of faces" and wish that "some hard lesson . . . [be] taught the pedagogues who resort to this stupid mode of stimulating the dull intellect."[2] But what most disturbed Englishmen in the early 1880's was the alleged "overpressure" of schoolchildren. Since a teacher's salary depended on the percentage of children he could "push through the ordeal of examination," there was an incentive to load down boys and girls with home lessons. Occasionally the fear of failing an exam drove children to mental collapse and even suicide. More often their home lessons left them with "flushed and throbbing brow," prime candidates, some experts felt, for epilepsy and chorea.[3] In 1883 Lord Stanley of Alderley asked in the Upper House whether there might be a link between the country's rising lunacy rate and scholastic overpressure.[4] It is striking that 1883 also saw the founding of England's first anticruelty group. Having noted this coincidence, however, we are still left without a link between the two phenomena, for the teacher, though he stood in loco parentis, was not a parent, and the criticism of home lessons was not a criticism of home life.

It does not seem, moreover, that intervention against cruel parents became possible because belief in the sanctity of the home was weakening. Ruskin's "Of Queens' Gardens," published in 1865, epitomized the ideal of a self-contained domestic life: "So far as the anxieties of the outer life penetrate into it, and the inconsistently-minded, unknown, unloved, or hostile society of the outer world is allowed by either husband or wife to cross the threshold, it ceases

---

* Still less enlightening is the assertion that "concern over parental mistreatment of children has been directly related to the decline of sanctioned violence toward children themselves . . . in the form of child labor, indenture, slavery and other means of enlisting children as a source of cheap labor." Jeanne M. Giovannoni, "Parental Mistreatment: Perpetrators and Victims," *Journal of Marriage and the Family*, 33 (November 1971), 651.

to be home; it is then only a part of the outer world which you have roofed over, and lighted fire in."[5] Legislation enacted during the next twenty years put state servants on the Englishman's doorstep. The 1880 Education Act made elementary instruction truly compulsory by requiring school boards to appoint attendance officers. Henceforth, poor parents would find it difficult to avoid yielding up their children for at least part of the day.[6] More intrusive still were the medical officers of health and the canal boat inspectors who, during the 1870's, began to check sanitary conditions in homes and aboard residential craft.[7] Yet school attendance officers could meddle with domestic relations only insofar as truancy was at issue, and sanitary inspectors, though capable of drastic interference with family life, attacked health hazards that threatened whole communities. The late Victorian literature of moral improvement continued to place the home at the center of God's social order. In the words of one writer: "Estimate the healing, comforting, purifying, elevating influence which is ever flowing from this fountain, and you will understand the sacred ministry of the home to the higher culture of mankind. It is a mighty restraint of the selfish passions. It is the centrifugal force which continually widens the orbit of life, and bears us into the light of distant suns."[8]

If advocacy of child protection cannot be tied to a waning regard for domestic privacy, neither can we argue that the young merited special attention because of their key industrial role. Between 1851 and 1881 children under fifteen years of age constituted the fastest growing age-group in the nation. According to a study by Charles Booth, this category accounted for 35.4 percent of the total population in 1851, 35.6 percent in 1861, 36.1 percent in 1871, and 36.5 percent in 1881.[9] Comparatively abundant, children were at the same time of diminishing economic importance. In 1851 young people under fifteen made up 6.9 percent of the work force. Thereafter, this proportion fell to 6.7 percent in 1861, 6.2 percent in 1871, and 4.5 percent in 1881. Extended factory legislation had rendered young workers less profitable to some employers, and elsewhere they were displaced by technological advances such as the introduction of steam power in the lace and pottery trades. As Musgrove remarks, "compulsory education was a necessity by the 1870's not because children were at work, but because increasingly they were not."[10] Correspondingly, the need to shield the young from parental misuse became palpable because late Victorian children spent more time at home, in closer contact with their mothers and fathers, than did working children two generations earlier. That the campaign against child abuse first took root in large cities suggests something further. One result of England's rapid industrialization was the spawning of virulent slums in most of her urban centers. Citizens who could afford to do so began to flee these blighted central districts for healthier neighborhoods. Gradually, therefore, the social gulf between the urban rich and poor expressed itself in an ever sharper geographical segregation of classes.[11] "Left to grow up like forest trees, taking their chance of storm and sunshine," the urban masses came to be regarded by their now distant social superiors as a race apart. In 1846 Lord Ashley sketched this exotic picture of London's slum-born:

Every one who walks the streets of the metropolis must daily observe several members of the tribe—bold, and pert, and dirty as London sparrows, but pale, feeble, and sadly inferior to them in plumpness of outline. Their business, or pretended business, seems to vary with the locality. At the West End they deal in lucifer-matches, audaciously beg, or tell a touching tale of woe. Pass on to the central parts of the town—to Holborn or the Strand . . . and you will find that there the numbers very greatly increased: a few are pursuing the avocations above mentioned of their more Corinthian fellows; many are spanning the gutters with their legs, and dabbling with earnestness in the latest accumulation of nastiness; while others, in squalid and half naked groups, squat at the entrances of the narrow, foetid courts and alleys that lie concealed behind the deceptive frontages of our larger thoroughfares. . . . But it is in Lambeth and Westminster that we find the most flagrant traces of their swarming activity. There the foul and dismal passages are thronged with children of both sexes, and of every age from three to thirteen. . . . Their appearance is wild; the matted hair, the disgusting filth that renders necessary a second inspection, before the flesh can be discerned between the rags which hang about it; and the barbarian freedom from all superintendence and restraint fill the mind of a novice in these things with perplexity and dismay.[12]

No novice himself, Lord Ashley feared that if left to their "barbarian freedom" these swarming slum children would grow up even wilder than their parents.

Those at the top of the social scale tended to believe the worst about inner-city life. Mid-century descriptions of the large manufacturing towns, for example, agreed that industrialization had wrecked the nuclear family, alienating husband from wife, brother from sister, and parent from child.[13] In reality, as Michael Anderson has shown in his study of Preston, urban working-class families and kin groups could be remarkably cohesive.[14] But impressions carried the weight of conviction, and when considered in the context of real social and economic crises, they drove the privileged to take defensive action. Thus, in London during the 1840's and early 1850's, worry about cholera, Chartism, and the influx of Irish immigrants produced a corresponding peak of philanthropic zeal.[15] "We cannot replant seignorial influence in England, or reinstate aristocracy on its olden throne," cautioned one observer in 1849. Yet the "higher orders" still had it in their grasp, through "chastening and Christianizing," to render the urban masses "discreet and temperate."[16]

The early 1880's ushered in another period of heightened concern about the conduct of inner-city denizens. Since 1875 an economic slump had cut profits and contributed to high unemployment. Confronted with the prospect that material progress might be finite, middle- and upper-class Victorians began to see the function of charity less as assistance to the "deserving" poor than as a vital stimulant to the reintegration of the poor into productive society. Also contributing to a sense of philanthropic urgency was the revelation that slum clearance schemes had not eased and in some cases had actually exacerbated overcrowding. In London, the demolition of rookeries, street-widening projects, and the building of railways succeeded in displacing those least able to afford better housing. Tied to the central districts by their work, both casual and skilled laborers competed for scarce living space. By 1883, eight years after passage of the Artizans' Dwellings Act, the number of London families occupying single rooms was seen as still "enormous."[17] Social protest pamphlets such as George R. Sims's *How the Poor Live* and Andrew Mearns's *The Bitter Cry of Outcast London*, both published in 1883, underscored the need for new strategies to combat urban blight. *The Bitter Cry*, magnified by a sensationalist press, "touched the hearts of tens of thousands, and awoke deep feelings of indignation, pain and sympathy in every direction."[18]

Disquieting as living conditions may have been in central London, they were probably worse in Liverpool. With 552,508 inhabitants in 1881, Liverpool ranked as the nation's second-largest city. More significantly, it had by far the highest population density of any large town in England, approximately 109 persons per acre. According to Hugh Farrie, assistant editor of the *Liverpool Daily Post*, this figure rose to a choking 1,210 persons per acre in some of the most squalid areas—all of them located on a strip of land about four miles long, bordered on the west by the River Mersey and extending at its widest point about a mile eastward.[19] Severe overcrowding provided an ideal medium for the transmission of infectious disease. At mid-century, Liverpool had been the nation's unhealthiest town; thirty years later it still produced a higher mortality rate than any other English city.[20] By 1882, the Corporation had eliminated many of Liverpool's infamous cellar dwellings and had built new working-class housing on its northern perimeter. But such action barely scratched the surface of Liverpool's misery and did little to lessen the port's reputation as a haven for crime, drunkenness, and social disaffection.[21]

Perhaps more clearly in Liverpool than in any other English city, slum dwellers seemed to live beyond the reach of law and order. The poorest neighborhoods were heavily Irish. In 1851 nearly 25 percent of Liverpool's population was Irish-born, and though this percentage had dropped substantially by 1881, immigrants were still abundant enough to feed stereotypes of the Celt as a subhuman species, addicted to drink and bloodshed.[22] It was shameful that Irish fathers went on regular "sprees," when, primed by liquor, they battered their wives and children and smashed their few sticks of furniture. But even worse from the perspective of Liverpool's middle classes, these men also made certain streets "wholly impassable."[23] This was no trivial matter. In 1879, according to Silas Hocking, policemen and rent collectors who ventured alone into the maze of streets between Scotland Road and the docks were risking mayhem.[24] Further, unskilled dockhands, upon whose cheap and docile labor depended much of the city's commercial wealth, also inhabited these mean streets, and the threat of slum-bred disorder infecting the casual labor force could not be ignored.[25] Whether Irish or Anglo-Saxon, then, the poor of central Liverpool had become a social and economic menace. And here, where respectable citizens would have felt most compelled to exercise some influence over the behavior of the urban poor, Englishmen began to organize in defense of the young.

This is not to say that Liverpool philanthropists were inspired primarily by fear. Indeed, the earliest child-protection literature never mentions class conflict or crime as stimuli for reform. But the failure of conventional charity to cleanse slum life had grown so obvious by the early 1880's that benevolent men and women were now more receptive to new schemes for civilizing their city.

From Liverpool to London

The first call for an agency to shield children from domestic harm came in the spring of 1881. On April 15 of that year, the *Liverpool Mercury* published a letter from George Staite, Vicar of Ashton-Hayes, Cheshire, which argued that cruelty to children required specialized philanthropic attention. Staite could not say that Liverpool had ignored its children. The disadvantaged young were in fact objects of particular concern to local humanitarians—a preoccupation evidenced by the plethora of children's charities ranging from shoeblack brigades for destitute juveniles to the provision of wooden clogs for barefooted "waifs." And by 1884 the Central Relief Society was collecting and distributing £22,000 annually to some 77 charities, twenty of them devoted exclusively to children.[26] But, as the Reverend Staite observed, none of these sufficed:

Amongst benevolent institutions there does not appear to be one for getting at unrevealed cases of cruelty to children. Most neighbourhoods furnish such instances, which are freely talked about by neighbours, but receive no further attention. There seems to be wanted an organisation for looking into doubtful cases of real or supposed cruelty and neglect, and not waiting for them to come to light of themselves, which many never do. . . . Existing agencies are inadequate for reaching such cases. For instance, the district visitor looks upon her avocation as being more spiritual than temporal, and more to the adults than to the children. She leaves her tract, with a kindly inquiry for the general spiritual welfare of the family, and is in most instances young and inexperienced in the matter of children. The school attendance officer gives an occasional perfunctory call, but his sole business is to get children to school. If the family want parish relief the relieving officer calls, and if satisfied with their indigence (the squalid condition of the family being rather a recommendation than otherwise), he relieves them to the extent of two or three shillings a week, and there his duty ends. Nor can much reliance be placed on neighbours as regards taking the initiative. . . . The sad effects of cruelty and privation during childhood are but too clearly shown in the mental stupidity and ill-developed frame, and brutality of the matured life. And can nothing be done to mitigate and reduce these evils to a minimum?

Answering his own question, Staite proposed the formation in Liverpool of a society with a threefold function: to appoint voluntary correspondents in different districts to investigate any rumored cases of cruelty; to show parents and guardians of children their proper responsibilities "by preaching, lecturing, and distributing good, wholesome, sanitary literature"; and "to aim generally at doing works for children in their homes, and to influence public opinion on the subject." Such a society, he believed, would be relatively inexpensive and, more importantly, could enjoy interdenominational support.*

Shocked by a subsequent wave of inquests on infants overlain by their mothers,[27] Staite sent off a second letter on the subject. Overlying was only one of the many dangers faced by children, wrote Staite; the extent of undetected child abuse, considered in all its forms, must be vast. Cases of "cruelty" were divisible into three categories:

(1) Intentional, or those which come under the law; (2) Unintentional, which do not come under the law; (3) Accidental or careless, which may or may not be amenable to the law. The first group would include those cases in which it clearly appeared cruelty was intended, such, for example, as positive ill-treatment, by beating, starving, and systematic persecution. The second group would embrace the many cases arising chiefly from ignorance and where negative rather than positive cruelty was manifested—allowing young children to suffer from want of bodily attention, from sour and improper food, often given in dirty bottles, and ending not infrequently in convulsions and deaths. . . . The third group would include by far the greatest number of instances—those resulting principally from drunkenness, gossiping and neglect—the overlying of babies, falls, burns, scalds, runovers and all that class.[28]

Conceived in these broad terms, cruelty to children was a social evil that demanded immediate redress. Others agreed with Staite. One correspondent, a month later, suggested that a child-protection agency might act as a parliamentary pressure group, lobbying for the defense of "poor little victims of parental wickedness."[29]

* *Liverpool Mercury*, April 15, 1881, p. 7. Since the division between Protestants and Catholics was an important fact of Liverpool life, Staite understood that to succeed on a broad scale a Liverpool society for the prevention of cruelty to children would have to remain strictly nondenominational. See R. B. Walker, "Religious Changes in Liverpool in the Nineteenth Century," *Journal of Ecclesiastical History*, 19 (October 1968), 195.

Staite himself felt that charitable effort would have to be supplemented by statutory reform. Hoping to find a legislative spokesman, he wrote to Lord Shaftesbury in the summer of 1881. In reply, Shaftesbury agreed that the evils of child abuse were "enormous and indisputable," but that they consisted "of so private, internal, and domestic a character as to be beyond the reach of legislation." The subject, indeed, "would not . . . be entertained in either House of Parliament."[30] Shaftesbury's message was clear: a campaign against cruelty to children would have to be fought on the local level, without parliamentary assistance.

As philanthropic opinion in Liverpool warmed to the idea of a child-protection agency, the organizational blueprint for such a scheme waited in America. Credit for transmitting news of the American experiment to England belongs to Thomas F. A. Agnew, a Liverpool merchant and banker.[31] While touring New York City in 1881, Agnew noticed signs advertising a Society for the Prevention of Cruelty to Children. Hearing that the recently established society had gained the confidence of both the public and the New York state legislature, he called upon its President, Elbridge T. Gerry, at the society's shelter.[32] In reality New York had given the SPCC a cool reception. At least one newspaper had accused the society of prejudice against the poor, and among the poor themselves rumors persisted that the SPCC stole children from their parents.[33] Nonetheless, Gerry's description of his society so impressed Agnew that he went on to visit similar groups in Boston, Chicago, and Philadelphia. When Agnew returned to Liverpool in 1882, he brought with him the annual reports of those institutions.

The model of the New York SPCC heavily influenced the work later undertaken by Agnew and his Liverpool associates. From the beginning the New York society had taken care not to alienate public goodwill. Discretion was exercised in the prosecution of offenders. Unless aggravated assault was involved, the society's action consisted of a warning to the parent or guardian, followed by occasional visits from an inspector. Similarly, in dealing with the problem of child begging, officials attempted to distinguish between "those driven to it by actual want and suffering, and those sent out merely to support parents in a life of vice and drunkenness."[34] To avoid charges of religious partisanship, the society urged that children removed from parental custody by courts be committed to institutions governed by persons of the parents' faith. In large measure the New York SPCC owed its success to Elbridge Gerry, the distinguished lawyer who became its President in 1879.[35] Convinced of the deterrent value of selectively applied sanctions, Gerry exuded confidence that child abuse could be controlled, if not eradicated. Moreover, he emphasized the social utility of child protection. Gerry maintained:

In a social and moral point of view, the well-being of society imperatively demands that the atmosphere in which they [children] live and the treatment which they receive from those having their custody or intrusted with their care, shall be such as to insure habits of industry, temperance, honesty, and chastity. Cruelty to children produces mental and physical disease, and the prevention of such cruelty is a matter, therefore, of grave public importance.[36]

The New York SPCC's approach to child protection clearly impressed Liverpool philanthropists. After arousing the interest of the Central Relief Society, Agnew turned to Samuel Smith, Liberal MP for the city. In Smith the idea of an organization to combat child abuse found a potent ally. Since the early 1870's he had been active in the "maelstrom" of Liverpool philanthropy, immersed in work for the Y.M.C.A., the Council of Education, and various groups pressing for the emigration of destitute children to Canada. In connection with emigration projects, Smith had frequently witnessed cases of "abominable neglect" of children, "caused by dissolute parents forcing them to trade on the streets in all weathers."[37] Now, conscious of the New York precedent, Smith attended a local meeting of the Royal Society for the Prevention of Cruelty to Animals in early 1883, where he converted a proposal for the formation of a Dog's Home into an appeal for the defense of misused children. The Mayor of Liverpool, heeding Smith's request, offered to call a town meeting to discuss the subject, providing that Agnew submit a public petition in favor of the project. This was accomplished, and on the evening of April 19, 1883, the Liverpool Society for the Prevention of Cruelty to Children came into being.[38]

From the speeches delivered at this inaugural meeting it seems that public opinion favored a conservative campaign against child abuse. Christopher Bushell, Deputy-Chairman of the Central Relief Society and President of the Council of Education, thought that whereas prosecution of parents or guardians might be desirable "in extreme cases," the new organization should emulate the RSPCA in giving priority to humane education. The tough-minded Liverpool Coroner and magistrate Clarke Aspinall suggested that the society concentrate on enforcing the existing law as it pertained to the treatment of children. T. F. A. Agnew stressed that the society was not a radical departure from traditional philanthropy, but rather the product of consultation with established institutions such as the school board, the magistracy, police, medical officers of health, and Poor Law officials. Even Samuel Smith sounded a cautionary note: "He thought that the work of this Society should at first be tentative. The School Board had had in its earlier days to take soundings in the great sea of human ignorance and lay down the course on which it was to proceed. So the Society will have to take soundings in the great sea of human cruelty and neglect; and it will have gradually to develop a scheme of action suited to the exigencies of the case."[39] Those most active in advocating child protection clearly recognized the potential for controversy inherent in their new commitment.

The procedural conservatism preferred by the founders of the Liverpool society was matched by the respectability of its membership. The majority of the organization's 42 officers and committee members were professionally successful and philanthropically prominent. All were male.* Christopher Bushell and Samuel Rathbone, the latter Chairman of the Liverpool School Board, acted as Vice-Presidents, along with Samuel Smith and two other Liverpool MPs, Edward Whitley and Lord Claud Hamilton, both Conservatives. One-third of the 36-member general committee served as justices of the peace. Responsibility for the society's routine work fell to an executive committee of twelve men, chaired by Agnew. With four wealthy merchants, three lawyers, two bankers, and an eminent surgeon serving on it, this inner ring was a microcosm of the city's socioeconomic establishment. As a group, the executive committee members were middle-aged—they averaged 49 years old— and tended to be associated with some educational enterprise. Half of them either had served on the Liverpool School Board or had been involved in the establishment of University College. There does not seem to have been a marked political or religious align-

---

* Although Samuel Smith described the society's work as "one in which ladies might well cooperate," few posts were open to women. Initially, women appear to have helped care for children brought to the society's shelter and to have collected funds. *Report for 1883*, pp. 4, 9.

ment on either the executive or the general committee. At least two of the twelve men on the executive committee were Catholic: the organization would never wield wide influence if it struck the Irish poor as a tool of Protestantism.[40]

Thoroughly respectable in composition and committed to moral suasion as a reform tactic, the Liverpool SPCC nevertheless appeared innovative to contemporaries. The society drew a firm distinction between its work and that of traditional children's charity. Although empowered by its *Rules* to use shelters for the "temporary reception and disposal of children," the society was "not formed with a view to permanently housing, clothing, feeding, or otherwise providing for children, but rather for the purpose of increasing, and, if need be, enforcing such duties upon parents, guardians, or others entrusted with the care of children."[41] Moreover, the society's definition of cruelty presupposed a broad conception of parental responsibility and a major extension of children's rights. As seen by the Liverpool SPCC, cruelty to children included:

(a) All treatment or conduct by which physical pain is wrongfully, needlessly, or excessively inflicted, or

(b) By which life or limb or health is wrongfully endangered or sacrificed, or

(c) By which morals are imperilled or depraved;

(d) All neglect to provide such reasonable food, clothing, shelter, protection, and care, as the life and well-being of a child require;

(e) The exposure of children during unreasonable hours or inclement weather, as pedlers or hawkers, or otherwise;

(f) Their employment in unwholesome, degrading, unlawful, or immoral callings;

(g) Or any employment by which the powers of children are overtaxed, or the hours of labour unreasonably prolonged; and

(h) The employment of children as mendicants, or the failure to restrain them from vagrancy or begging.[42]

To some degree the society's early work belied its broadly defined scope. Certainly the Liverpool SPCC was scrupulous about projecting an image of moderation. The executive committee, for example, sifted through 151 applications in its search for a discreet first inspector.[43] And the society endeavored "to deal directly with the parents, and to reform the home rather than to punish the culprits."[44] But the rare cases that went to court usually involved gross neglect of or serious assault upon a child—eminently newsworthy items. Paradoxically, therefore, the society gained notoriety precisely because it prosecuted with reluctance.

The Liverpool SPCC's mission soon drew national notice. Shortly after the founding of the society, Samuel Smith announced in the *Nineteenth Century* that a new era of social reform had arrived, a period in which "new principles of legislation will be introduced, and fresh powers will be asked and obtained to stem the tide of misery." The direction in which these powers must be sought, he held, lay "in the more strict enforcement of parental obligations." Airing the society's view, Smith continued: "We have forgotten that the State, which bears the consequences, should have a voice in the matter. We accepted this principle in part when compulsory education was adopted, which was vehemently opposed by the then advocates of the 'liberty of the subject.' We require now a further extension of this principle; we wish to make it obligatory on a parent to feed, clothe, and bring up his child in a decent manner."[45]

Smith's plea for legislative redress of wrongs to children received important backing from Angela Burdett-Coutts, next to Lord Shaftesbury England's premier philanthropist.[46] Baroness Burdett-Coutts had long championed a variety of animal welfare causes, from the care of horses used on tramways and the guarding of songbirds against inhumane trapping, to the promotion of bee-culture— not, perhaps, unusual interests for one who doted on her dogs, llamas, and preternaturally glib parrot. Through her association with Charles Dickens she had also been an early supporter of ragged schools.[47] Now she threw her considerable influence behind the Liverpool SPCC. Writing to the Home Secretary on its behalf, she pointed out a grave defect in English law with respect to the young, "namely that after conviction and punishment of offenders against the person in the cases of children, there is no subsequent protection whatever to those children; they remain again in the custody and absolute power of those who have already injured them." Besides, it was in England's self-interest to defend its young: "While unnatural parents pass on . . . lightly to death the children they as lightly brought into life, these children . . . are lost to the country."[48]

The Baroness's public letter did not stand alone. Throughout late 1883 *The Times* paid unusually close attention to incidents of child abuse. Beginning in November it published three separate accounts of the West case, which involved a boy so savaged by his parents that he was unable to speak.[49] Shocked by these revelations, Florence Davenport-Hill, a proponent of the boarding-out of pauper children and the author of the widely read *Children of the State*, proposed that "parents legally convicted of cruelty should thereby be deprived of authority over their children until they can produce a satisfactory guarantee of good conduct towards them in the future." Child abuse was endemic among the poorer classes, she remarked.[50] Hesba Stretton, a well-known author of children's stories, and, like Baroness Burdett-Coutts, a former friend of Dickens, agreed that few people had "any idea of the extent of active cruelty, and still more of cruel neglect, towards children among our depraved and criminal classes." Observing that the Liverpool society had recently handled 86 cases in one month, Stretton concluded that a national child protection agency was required. Moreover, "the need for a national society of this kind . . . will become greater; for the growing love of liberty developing in the girls of the lower classes, which gives them a distaste for domestic service with its restraining and refining influences, tends also to an increasing roughness and coarseness of manner, which will unfit them for becoming kind, patient, and gentle mothers in the future."[51] The *Pall Mall Gazette* reasoned that since the reported incidents of cruelty to children "bear only a small proportion to those which never come into public notice at all," a national organization made excellent sense.[52] "Either greater publicity is given to these pitiable cases, owing, perhaps, to a healthy growth of opinion amongst the poorer classes, or they are greatly on the increase," ventured the *British Medical Journal*. Both interpretations argued for remedial action on an expanded scale.[53]

Eventually, any campaign to establish a national child-protection agency would have to take root in the Metropolis. London, like Liverpool, abounded in charities devoted to children. Philanthropists there were beginning to echo Mary Carpenter's argument that in addition to decent food, clothing, and shelter, the young also possessed a "natural right" to affection.[54] At least a few middle-class humanitarians felt that children's rights should include the opportunity to enjoy childhood—one of the assumptions behind the practice of taking London slum children for "fresh air" holidays in the country.[55] Indeed, a bewildering array of charitable institutions were created to make life less harsh for the young. *The Charities Register and Digest* for 1884 distinguished between those offering the child "relief in affliction," "relief in sickness," "relief in distress (permanent)"—this category alone fills 72 pages—"relief in distress (temporary)," "reformatory relief," and miscellaneous services such as emigration. The most elaborate mechanism for promoting juvenile welfare was the child-rescue agency. By the mid-1880's three organizations dominated this work, Dr. Stephenson's Children's Home, the Church of England Waifs and Strays Society (the CEWSS), and the Barnardo group.*

Of these, the last was the largest and best known. Born and raised a Protestant in Dublin, Thomas John Barnardo approached the reclamation of abandoned children with a strongly evangelical bias. Beginning in London's East End in 1866, Barnardo established a series of refuges for the outcast young, proceeding on the assumption that such children could be molded into useful citizens if removed from their degrading environment, exposed to the proper religious influences, and given vocational training. By 1885 his organization comprised nine separate institutions, with an annual budget exceeding £46,000.[56] Barnardo believed that only voluntary enterprise could cope with the estimated 20,000 homeless children living in London. Massive social problems demanded large-scale remedies, and so Barnardo had little use for the "cut-and-dry theorists and high-falutin reformers of the Charity Organisation school," who sought to encourage self-reliance among the poor by restricting the availability of charitable relief.[57]

He recruited candidates for his homes in two ways. Obviously most satisfying to Barnardo—and a method also employed by Dr. Stephenson and the CEWSS—was the philanthropic hunt.

For the better extension of my work among street boys, I adopted the plan of patrolling the streets nightly, during the most inclement season, on the look-out for homeless and destitute children amongst what may be well termed the purlieus of the Metropolis. After the hour of midnight, and guided by rescued lads whom I had at different times admitted to the Home, I have gone forth with bull's eye lantern to search low lodging-houses, noisome courts, unpleasant-looking streets and alleys, deserted markets, wharves and other places down by the waterside, and even on board barges.[58]

---

*Thomas Bowman Stephenson, a Wesleyan minister, opened his first home for destitute children in 1869. See William Bradfield, *The Life of the Reverend Thomas Bowman Stephenson* (1913). The Church of England Waifs and Strays Society was a more recent development, founded in 1881 by Edward de Montjoie Rudolf, a young civil servant. It concerned itself exclusively with the provision of homes for needy Anglican children. See *The First Forty Years* (1922).

If ferreting out individual children was one method of reaching needy youths, the mass selection of "street arabs" was another. During the winter of 1882, for example, some 1,400 boys and girls gathered in an East End coffee palace, where Barnardo's agents (having previously issued "tickets" to urchins found in various unsavory locations) chose the most pitiable for aid.[59] But whatever the means by which they were located, Barnardo's children usually showed the marks of long-term parental neglect.

The very size of such rescue operations seemed to prove London's need for an agency specializing in the prevention of child abuse. The Liverpool SPCC's first *Report*, published in April 1884, further convinced reformers that the work begun in Lancashire was of "great social importance" and should be attempted elsewhere.[60] Fortunately, the Liverpool group encouraged imitation. Shortly after the founding of the society, T. F. A. Agnew began to alert other cities to the possibility of organizing in the defense of children. His efforts met with success in both Bristol and Birmingham, where autonomous committees were formed. Attention next turned to London. Here, the misnamed Society for the Protection of Women and Children obviously could not "take cognizance of every species of cruelty" perpetrated upon the young; it dealt primarily with assaults by husbands against wives, and very selectively at that.* Therefore, in May 1884 Samuel Smith persuaded the Lord Mayor of London to lend the Mansion House for a public meeting. The next month, Agnew arrived in London to consult with Smith, Baroness Burdett-Coutts, and Hesba Stretton about creating a society modeled on the Liverpool SPCC. Finally, Stretton introduced Agnew to her friend Benjamin Waugh, a Congregationalist minister and editor of the *Sunday Magazine*. Short, bearded, with piercing blue eyes and an excess of nervous energy, Waugh would soon emerge as the driving personality behind child-welfare reform.

The Pioneers and Their Work

Benjamin Waugh was born in 1839, at Settle, in the West Riding of Yorkshire, the son of a saddler of Scottish descent. The senior

---

* *Charities Register and Digest* (1884), pp. 638–39. Although in operation since 1857, the Society for the Protection of Women and Children was perennially hampered by lack of funds. In 1882 its total income amounted to only £446. This society attempted unsuccessfully to profit from publicity given to the Liverpool SPCC. See *The Times*, January 11, 1884, p. 7.

Waugh was a staunch nonconformist whose belief in the liberty of conscience made him a supporter of Catholic Emancipation. Broadmindedness also characterized Benjamin's mother, Mary Harrison, who came from an old, and thoroughly Congregationalist, Yorkshire yeoman family. Although she died when he was only eight, Benjamin's mother seems to have instilled in her eldest son a strong humanitarian sentiment.[61] At the age of nine, the boy was sent to a small school kept by an uncle in Warwickshire, where he spent six happy years. His father had intended to article him to a firm of solicitors, but, when Benjamin reached fourteen, his health forced a reconsideration. Instead he went to Southport, a small town on the Lancashire coast, where he became apprenticed to Mr. Samuel Boothroyd, a well-established linen and woolen draper.[62]

Waugh's Southport years (1853–62) proved important for both the formulation of his religious views and the cultivation of his leadership abilities. Boothroyd and his sister-in-law, with whom Waugh lived, were ardent Congregationalists, and between them supervised the boy's orthodox religious training. Southport itself, then in the first stages of ebullient commercial growth, must have furnished an ideal climate for the nurture of a confident nonconformity. Predictably Benjamin developed into an honest, industrious, and somewhat self-righteous young man. His religious rectitude, coupled with a flair for administration, made him an effective temperance worker; while still very young he was appointed Honorary Secretary of the local branch of the United Kingdom Alliance.[63]

Gravitating toward the ministry, Waugh at 23 entered Airedale College, a theological school in Bradford. Service in the name of the Lord came naturally to one whose God appeared very personal and compassionate. As Waugh reflected at this time:

In reviewing my life, during the period that I can recollect, I am deeply impressed by God's goodness to me. Since the time of my being left without a mother, to the present time, I have been guided in a way that has been beset with many kind friends, and other mercies; and though it has been (and still is) a trial for me to leave Southport, yet I have come amongst strangers who are made friends of a most useful kind. Man deviseth his way, but God directeth his steps.[64]

Waugh was a diligent, if not brilliant, theological student. He prepared his sermons with almost painful carefulness. His delivery, however, always seemed fresh and unforced, a quality that endeared him to his first congregation in Newbury. It was with reluctance that Waugh left Newbury when his wife (the eldest daughter of his Southport master) became ill. In 1866, therefore, he accepted the pastorate of the Independent Chapel, Maze Hill, Greenwich.

One of London's many impoverished areas, Greenwich supplied a laboratory for the testing of Waugh's social conscience. Among the young minister's first projects was the visitation of families living near his church, an effort that involved the organization of temporary relief for the sick and destitute. Gradually Waugh grew interested in social work for the children of East Greenwich. With the aid of his congregation, he established a children's day-care center in Maze Hill. Waugh's growing concern about the problem of juvenile delinquency led him to join John MacGregor, a popular author and champion of the ragged school movement, in forming the Waste Paper and Blacking Brigade—a day institution designed to discourage juvenile crime by eliminating idleness. As an alternative to prison for young delinquents, Waugh and MacGregor arranged with local magistrates to place first offenders on deep-sea fishing smacks.[65] In appreciation for his efforts, four borough trades unions nominated Waugh to a position on the first London School Board. Explaining that he had consented to stand for election because he was "deeply interested in the welfare of neglected children whom it is the object of the Board to benefit," Waugh advocated a free school in every district, compulsory attendance, and most controversial of all, the exclusion of "every form of sectarianism" from the classroom.[66] With twelve candidates for four seats, including MacGregor and Emily Davies, a pioneering advocate of university education for women, the Greenwich campaign was fiercely contested. Assisted by his congregation, Waugh managed to place fourth in the poll.

Waugh's participation on the London School Board strengthened his conviction that new powers were wanted for curbing parental negligence. As a member of the visiting committee for the districts of Woolwich, Plumstead, and Sydenham, he listened to the excuses of parents for the non-attendance of their children at school. His investigation of the root causes of absenteeism persuaded him that the laws relating to the care of children at home were "absolutely inadequate and insufficient."[67] More generally, Waugh's school board experience impressed upon him the superiority of fact to emotion in debate. Particularly influential was the example set by

T. H. Huxley, the biologist and agnostic, through whom Waugh discovered that sharply focused propaganda best elicited "emotions of charity and sentiments of justice" and best imparted "simplicity and grandeur to appeals."[68] Waugh continued to press for "efficient and undenominational" education until, in 1876, poor health forced him to resign from the board.

Three years prior to his retirement from public life, Waugh had written *The Gaol Cradle, Who Rocks It?* (1873), a book noteworthy for its anticipation of future reform and its analysis of the origins of crime and poverty. Far from discouraging juvenile crime, the book argued, the imprisonment of young offenders actually reinforced criminality. The judicial treatment of these children was "altogether too severe," making few allowances for "small faults" and "foolish deeds."[69] But the author resisted the temptation to attack outrageous judgments by individual magistrates. Instead, he concentrated his assault on the parliamentary statutes that permitted imprisonment of the young. It was at the national level that Waugh's remedy applied: the provision of a special system of juvenile courts. Ordinary court proceedings traumatized children to the point where they could not give a proper account of their actions. But under a system of separate tribunals for children, Waugh believed, the magistrate would be

released from enforcing all juvenile criminal laws, instructed broadly to consider all circumstances—youth, natural propensities, temptations, and the lot; [permitted] to allow all reasonable excuses; to declare not simply guilty of the action charged, but also the reasonableness or unreasonableness of the person who makes it; whether the blame, if any, rests with the child or with the parents; . . . and in the evident interests of the child, the accuser and the community, immediate and remote, to pronounce on the expediency or inexpediency of punishment, and of what sort it should be, providing always that use shall not be made of either lock-up or gaol.[70]

Waugh prophesied that "the time will come when Englishmen will be ashamed that they ever dealt with the naughtiness of a child by police-courts and prisons, as they now are ashamed that they had ever traded in slaves."[71]

Equally perceptive was Waugh's critique of the Poor Law philosophy of public relief. The Poor Law, he observed, failed to differentiate between the needy and the ne'er-do-well, but rather assumed that the poor were "bad in the lump." In stipulating that public relief be accompanied by the humiliation of the workhouse, the Poor Law destroyed self-respect and transformed poverty into pauperism. Discussing the ideal of relief without penalty, Waugh outlined a system of social security far in advance of contemporary opinion.

Let the principle of the mutual benefit be taken up by the community; let there be established a national "club"; let it . . . provide for the exigencies of labour, of sickness, of accident, of age, and of death; . . . let its benefits rank as a sick club allowance, a fire insurance payment, a disabled soldier's pension, or an ex-minister's annuity; and let it by no means be a department of "Poor Law" administration. The demoralizing association would be fatal. . . . Let it rank among new institutions of the State, and be worked under new auspices—let its benefits be available as a right, a purchased, proprietary right.[72]

Waugh's visionary plan for national insurance as well as his proposal for children's courts presupposed state action on a massive scale. But despite Waugh's advanced views, *The Gaol Cradle* earned considerable praise from those concerned about the treatment of the young. The book so impressed Francis Peek, a member of the second London School Board, that he bought three hundred copies and, assisted by the Howard Association, distributed them to magistrates throughout England.[73]

Waugh's withdrawal from public life in 1876 had been a medical necessity, but retirement at the age of 37 did not suit his activist temperament. The resumption of work for the *Sunday Magazine* in 1880 partially satisfied Waugh's urge to be "useful."[74] Here, in addition to his editorial duties, he wrote a series of didactic tales called "Sunday Evenings with the Children." These stories often dealt with the theme of compassion for the young. Thus, the French soldier who paused in his flight from Moscow to carry a half-frozen drummer boy illustrated the truth that there is "loveliness" hidden in the hearts of the most unlikely people.[75] Waugh, however, had been used to more direct forms of public service and so welcomed the opportunity in 1884 to help form a London Society for the Prevention of Cruelty to Children.

Using the Ludgate Hill offices of the *Sunday Magazine* as headquarters, Waugh, Agnew, and Hesba Stretton began to publicize the society's inaugural meeting, scheduled for early July. The success or failure of this gathering would in large part determine the future of the organization. Samuel Smith had optimistically obtained the Mansion House's Egyptian Room, which could seat around six hundred, so a poor attendance would be disastrous. Moreover, a large and distinguished audience would facilitate the recruitment of prestigious supporters.[76] In preparation for the event an enormous petition, eighteen feet in length, was assembled. Hesba Stretton, in a letter to *The Times*, stressed both the plight of mistreated children and the determination of the society to "enlist the sympathy and cooperation of the honest and benevolent poor themselves" in its work.[77] Finally, Agnew appeared before the RSPCA's annual meeting to plead for last-minute support.

Careful planning brought its reward. On July 8 a capacity crowd filled the Egyptian Room and the elite of English philanthropy graced the speakers' platform. Alderman Cotton (Conservative MP from London), representing the Lord Mayor, occupied the chair, flanked on his right by the Earl of Shaftesbury and on his left by the Baroness Burdett-Coutts. In addition to Cotton and Shaftesbury, the speakers included Agnew, Samuel Smith, J. Allanson Picton (Liberal MP from Leicester), the Earl of Aberdeen, Dr. Barnardo, William Fowler (Liberal MP from Cambridge), Cardinal Manning (the Catholic primate of England), C. Kegan Paul (the publisher), and Waugh. T. F. A. Agnew, ever the voice of moderation, reminded those present that zeal for child welfare should be tempered by deference to established institutions: "Never, if you can help it, put yourself in opposition to those in authority; recognize their difficulties and respect their opinion, even when it differs from your own. By courtesy and patient consideration you will win the confidence and respect of the departments with which you have to deal and will get much more of your own way than by a less conciliatory tone."[78]

Some disagreement about the role of the new society surfaced during the meeting. Lord Shaftesbury felt that the present law was "quite sufficient to punish the perpetrators of acts of cruelty upon children," whereas Cardinal Manning insisted that legal loopholes would have to be eliminated by the London SPCC before it could operate efficiently.[79] Given the good will of the occasion, however, this rather fundamental difference of opinion did not prove disruptive. On the contrary, the Mansion House meeting yielded an impressive group of supporters, through whom the London society would attempt to attract a still larger following.

What kind of person backed the London SPCC in its infancy? The society's *First Annual Report* lists a total of 119 officers, in-

cluding committee members. By comparing this list with those for
other contemporary organizations, one can test, roughly, the correlation between interest in child protection and interest in other
selected social reforms.[80] Most striking is the relatively high proportion of London SPCC officers who advocated animal welfare:
twenty (17 percent) belonged to either the RSPCA or the Victoria
Street Society for the Protection of Animals from Vivisection.[81] Not
surprisingly, the London SPCC also attracted a number of officers—sixteen (13 percent)—who were currently associated with
large-scale rescue work for children.[82] Prior experience in education
was another common factor: fifteen (13 percent) had sat on the
London School Board for at least one three-year term.[83] The link
between child protection and the temperance movement was somewhat weaker, with thirteen (11 percent) of the London SPCC's officers belonging to at least one of four major anti-drink associations.[84] The campaign for sexual purity, which gained momentum
during the 1880's, claimed only seven (6 percent) of the society's
early officers.[85] These correlations held even more strongly within
the executive committee. Here, eight of 23 members (35 percent)
were connected with child-rescue work, five (22 percent) with animal welfare, and three (13 percent) with the London School Board.
Links with the temperance and sexual purity movements remained
more tenuous, each with only two supporters (7 percent) on the executive committee. It seems, therefore, that the first members of the
London SPCC were humanitarians, some of whom had gained
through prior charitable work direct knowledge about the misuse
of the young. Further, their attention tended to focus on the condition of the child itself, not on issues such as drink and chastity that
obscured the question of children's rights.

The London SPCC's officers almost all shared one other characteristic: they tended to be from the middle or upper classes.
The Honorary Secretaries—Benjamin Waugh, a saddler's son, and
E. de M. Rudolf, once an office boy—held unusually modest social
credentials. Founding officers were far more often successful busi-
nessmen, already prominent philanthropists, university-educated
clerics, parliamentary politicians concerned with the "social question," and titled aristocrats. In other respects, however, the membership was less homogeneous. Unlike the Liverpool SPCC, the
London society did not bar women from decision-making positions; the vital parts played in the founding of the society by the

Baroness Burdett-Coutts and Hesba Stretton precluded sexual segregation. Thirty-nine officers (33 percent) were in fact women.[86] In terms of political orientation, the society was avowedly nonpartisan; of the MPs who officially supported the society, ten were Liberals, six Conservatives. The London SPCC also appealed to a wide religious spectrum. Prominent Catholics, such as Cardinal Manning and Lady Holland, and prominent Jews, such as F. D. Mocatta and Jacob Montefiore, closed ranks with Anglicans and nonconformists.

With respect to religious disposition (as distinct from denominational preference), many of the society's early backers did not fit an evangelical mold. Evangelical Protestantism, with its emphasis on sin, conversion, and service, is estimated to have distinguished "as many as three-quarters of the total number of voluntary charitable organizations in the second half of the nineteenth century" and is credited with inspiring much of the child-welfare work in this period.[87] The London society itself has been described as an outgrowth of the evangelically inspired ragged school movement.[88] Insofar as ragged schools familiarized philanthropists with the consequences of parental neglect, they may be regarded as one important precursor of the campaign against cruelty to children. That an evangelical spirit also suffused the latter movement does not necessarily follow, however. Voluntary groups accepted the challenge of combating parental brutality because the state had proved manifestly unwilling to do so. Further, the need for a philanthropic mechanism to fight child abuse became associated, in many advocates' minds, with the necessity for legal change leading to the weakening of parental authority. Evangelicals were not inclined to smile upon such far-reaching reform.[89] Admittedly, the London SPCC did elect as its first President the incarnation of evangelical philanthropy, Lord Shaftesbury. Yet this choice reflected tactical rather than theological considerations. Now in his 84th year, Shaftesbury virtually personified Christian sympathy for the weak and defenseless classes in society, particularly children. The inclusion of Shaftesbury's name among the leaders of any voluntary enterprise dealing with children was thus nearly indispensable.[90]

The London SPCC, like its Liverpool counterpart, drafted a formidable charter:

The object of the Society is the prevention of cruel treatment, wrongful neglect, or improper employment of children; also all conduct by which life, limb or health, is wrongfully endangered or sacrificed, or by which morals are imperilled or depraved. Such objects are pursued by (a) remonstrance and moral suasion; (b) enforcement of the existing laws; (c) promotion of any amendment of the law that may prove to be necessary or desirable.[91]

Fulfilling these goals would be far more difficult. After the triumphant inaugural meeting, the society found itself blessed with warm wishes and little else. One unanticipated problem was lack of capital. As Hesba Stretton explained in an appeal to London's benevolently inclined: "We imagined we had only to make our object known through the medium of the press, which very kindly and very generously lent us its influence, and by the means of a large and influential meeting at the Mansion House, in order to secure an immediate and enthusiastic response. I . . . feared we should have too much money showered upon us when such a purpose was made known. . . . It is not so. We have not even enough money for our first winter's work." [92] Insufficient funds prevented the society from renting an office. During the late summer of 1884, therefore, the executive committee met in the board room of the RSPCA's Jermyn Street headquarters.

The ties between the London SPCC and the RSPCA went beyond the sharing of facilities. Founded in 1824, the RSPCA had emerged as a principal voice for humane sentiment in England; it subsumed 105 branches and auxiliary committees throughout England and employed 51 inspectors.[93] As already noted, a significant overlap existed between RSPCA and London SPCC officials. Another measure of affinity was financial: 32 RSPCA subscribers contributed £178 to the London SPCC's coffers (20 percent of its total income) between July and December 1884. Both organizations, moreover, relied on the same guarantor, Messrs. Coutts & Company.[94] John Colam, Secretary of the RSPCA since 1860, sat on the London SPCC's executive committee, and his son Robert served as the SPCC's chief legal counsel. A humane zealot—on one occasion he was injured while attempting to stop a bullfight—John Colam emphasized the interrelation between animal and child welfare. The motto of the RSPCA's newspaper, *Animal World*, was, he pointed out, "Man and bird and beast"; and its "argument . . . invariably [had] been that cruelty to animals breeds cruelty to human beings, which must be stopped directly or indirectly." [95] Yet Colam's support of the London SPCC may have been as much pragmatic as principled. The RSPCA, to safeguard its status as a moderate extra-parliamentary pressure group, had to resist the demands for uncompromising reform made by extremists. One way to circumvent these demands was to encourage enthusiasts to form distinct agencies for narrower ends—hence the proliferation of homes for dogs and horses, groups urging the prohibition of fox hunting and rabbit coursing, and societies for the suppression of vivisection. Similarly, the advocacy of a separate organization for child protection would have been politically expedient for Colam and the RSPCA.[96] As early as 1870 letters appeared in *Animal World* calling for the inclusion of children in an enlarged "Society for the Prevention of Cruelty to Children and Dumb Animals," but, probably for the reasons noted above, these suggestions failed to educe an official response.[97]

In any event, the London SPCC did not secure its own headquarters until the autumn of 1884. On October 27, Sheriff Faudel Phillips, representing the Lord Mayor of London, formally opened the society's office and shelter at 71 Harpur Street. Theoretically, the London society regarded the provision of temporary accommodation for children as subordinate to the task of preventing systematic mistreatment. It had nevertheless become clear that some facility more commodious than the Reverend Waugh's home would be required. Above all, a shelter served as an unofficial place of safety for brutalized boys and girls. The Waifs and Strays Society noted that the Liverpool SPCC's facility had been used to this vital end:

A warehouse worker hit and kicked his little daughter, who ran to a policeman for help. The policeman couldn't interfere with the matter, so he directed her to the Shelter of the Liverpool Society. There, the Society decided to issue a summons against the man, rather than to remonstrate with him as was the general policy.

As the Society harboured the girl in its shelter until the day of the trial, the father wasn't able to intimidate his daughter. Thus, the father was found guilty and fined £2 or, alternatively, two months in jail. . . . The little girl was returned to her mother.[98]

Though effective, this strategy hardly merited legal applause; a parent could—but, apparently, rarely tried to—regain custody of his child with a writ of habeas corpus. During the year ending in March 1884, the Liverpool society kept children in its shelter for an average of thirteen days. The following year, 329 children stayed for an average of eleven days.[99] A new facility donated by William Cliff in the summer of 1884 (at a cost of £2,315) may have tempted the Liverpool SPCC to expand its child-rescue operations. At first the London society also put its shelter to heavy use; between October 1884 and June 1885 Harpur Street dispensed 779 nights' lodging and 2,294 meals.[100]

The exigencies of child protection promoted another development: the professionalization of the two societies. In the late summer of 1884 T. F. A. Agnew moved to Hull, leaving the Liverpool SPCC temporarily adrift. As his replacement, the executive committee made Major George Leslie Secretary of the society at an annual salary of £200. Though this amount paled by comparison with, for example, the £500 granted annually to C. S. Loch, Secretary of London's Charity Organisation Society, it accounted for nearly one-quarter of the Liverpool SPCC's total expenditure in 1884.[101] In London, Benjamin Waugh, obviously now the administrative power in his organization, remained unpaid, no doubt because his pastoral and editorial duties already provided an income. During the last six months of 1884, the London SPCC did spend £107 10s. 6d. on salaries—12 percent of its funds.[102]

As the societies grew more professional, they began to issue propaganda. Believing that knowledge of the penalties for child abuse would deter parents from cruel behavior, the Liverpool executive committee decided to circulate placards "in the low quarters of the City" informing citizens that a Mrs. Graham had received fifteen months' imprisonment for the manslaughter of her child. At the same meeting, the committee approved payment of three guineas to a *Liverpool Mercury* reporter for preparing a summary of the speeches at the society's annual meeting.[103] The London SPCC likewise trusted in publicity "to discompose the reckless, inducing them to think and check cruel impulses." Thus, thousands of announcements were scattered in localities where "work seemed likely most to lie," and special permission was obtained to post notices of the society's operations in all police stations and Poor Law Union relieving offices.[104]

The London SPCC claimed to be no respecter of persons. "Whenever cruel practices have been [noted]," the *First Annual Report* pointed out, the society "acted with exactly the same promptitude and firmness." Its intervention in the King's College case received special notice:

C.F.B.—Boy, aged 12, killed by school fellows. On his return from school complained of sickness, became exceedingly ill, medical aid was called in, death shortly followed. Under examination of doctors, reluctantly told that as he was leaving school, 12 of the big boys had arranged themselves along the corridor and, as he passed, they each gave him a blow on the back with the fist. Other little boys were treated the same. He had suffered the same sort of thing on two previous occasions. The cause of death was concussion of the spine. After inquest, the boy's father was at once asked to give his sanction and help to a public inquiry and prosecution of the guilty boys for the sake of thousands of little fellows whose lives were made miserable by bullies in their schools. The father declined to assist the Society. . . . The Society also addressed the College authorities asking if they would aid the Society in discovering the culprits and bringing them to punishment, stating its determination to put down cruel actions irrespective of the place where they occurred.

All legal proceedings by the society ceased when the Home Secretary, Sir William Harcourt, announced in Commons that the matter had been referred to the Public Prosecutor.[105] But the London SPCC had clarified its policy in two respects. First, child-savers had shown themselves willing to meddle with the prosperous as well as with the poor. Although rare in these early days, prosecutions of middle-class offenders did take place. Second, the anticruelty campaign, though directed at the domestic sphere, was not to be confined to it. That the society envisioned a wide-ranging crusade against child abuse received further confirmation in the Frampton Cotterell case. The fining in January 1885 of a Sister of Mercy for beating two orphan girls provoked an argument in *The Times* between Hesba Stretton and "Common Sense." Backing his fellow executive committee member, E. de M. Rudolf promised that the society would investigate the question of corporal punishment in voluntary homes for the young.[106]

During its first year the society dealt with 95 cases involving 175 "domestic victims" and a "much larger number in public institutions." Of the former, 53 cases involved aggravated assault, 30 pertained to deliberate starvation, and twelve concerned "an evil which is altogether unmentionable" (sexual assault or incest).[107] Beyond shocking London's reading public with illustrations of parental inhumanity, however, the society contributed little to an understanding of the causes of child abuse. With one inspector to patrol a population approaching four million, conclusions about the mistreatment of the young were perforce crude. Individual cases fell into categories of "severe" or "mild." "Mild" cruelty denoted action that did not result in gross physical injury. As a result the society could regard as mild the behavior of the "orange woman," who, to keep her child out of school, "put her little boy of seven into an empty orange box, corded it up, thrust it under the bed and left it there till she turned her key in her room again at night, day after day, week after week, [until] . . . the quiet little fellow was almost insane." [108] Initially, London SPCC propaganda stressed the causal connection between intemperance and brutality—by implication locating cruelty's epicenter among the besotted poor. The *First Annual Report* suggested facilely:

In the past, drink shops had not had time to accomplish those second generation effects which are now coming to light. The process of natural selection is having its way, and drink everywhere within reach is in the long run producing among both men and women a totally incredible character, into whose hands a world of little folks is consistently coming, to live lives of unnatural suffering and unmentionable shame, and to die early deaths. [109]

The Liverpool society's analysis of the problem was somewhat less superficial. During the year ending March 1885 it assisted 844 children, of whom 61 had been the victims of "violence," 407 of "cruel neglect," 307 of "begging, vagrancy, and exposure," and 69 of "immorality." Significantly, violence accounted for only 7 percent of the Liverpool cases as compared to 56 percent of the London total. This discrepancy could be explained by a higher incidence of assaults on London children or, alternatively, by the Liverpool society's ability to detect less blatant forms of mistreatment. The latter explanation is more likely in view of the Liverpool SPCC's broad information network (see Table 3). The society, it would appear, was well known and generally trusted by the public.

Reviewing its work, the Liverpool SPCC found child abuse to be a complex problem. Though intemperance again ranked as the foremost contributor to mistreatment by parents, a variety of other conditions left their mark on "suffering childhood" (see Table 4). The single-factor listing of causes of mistreatment in Table 4 tends to conceal the interrelation of circumstances that encouraged adult misconduct. To take the most obvious example, poverty doubtless drove some parents to drink, desertion, or prostitution. What does emerge from this hierarchy of "causes," however, is the notion that

TABLE 3
Sources of Information for Liverpool SPCC Cases, 1884–85

Source	Cases	
	Number	Percent
Officers of the society	122	14.4%
Relations of children	102	12.0
General public	90	10.6
Neighbors of children	87	10.3
School board officials	74	8.7
Police officers	68	8.1
Schoolteachers	58	6.8
Newspaper paragraphs	57	6.7
Missionaries, Biblewomen, etc.	51	6.0
Charitable institutions	30	3.6
Children who came to the shelter	24	2.8
Liverpool SPCC executive committee	23	2.7
Anonymous letters	15	1.8
Relieving officers	13	1.5
Sanitary officers	13	1.5
Doctors	10	1.2
Clergymen	6	0.7
Employers	5	0.6
TOTAL	848	100.0%

SOURCE: Liverpool SPCC, *Report for 1884.*

TABLE 4
"Apparent Cause of Trouble" in Liverpool SPCC Cases, 1884–85

Cause designated by the society	Cases	
	Number	Percent
Drink and its consequences	300	35.5%
Father dead	90	10.7
Poverty	66	7.8
Mother neglectful	61	7.2
Deserted by parents	55	6.5
Mother dead	45	5.3
Parents living apart	35	4.1
Parental immorality	31	3.7
Both parents dead	29	3.4
Illegitimate	28	3.3
Unkind stepparents	24	2.9
Want of proper care	24	2.9
Wilfulness of children	24	2.9
Parents in prison	15	1.8
Hasty temper	10	1.2
Parents blind	7	0.8
TOTAL	844	100.0%

SOURCE: Liverpool SPCC, *Report for 1884.*

mistreatment of the young rarely stemmed from personal characteristics of adults ("hasty temper") or children ("wilfulness"). Rather, the society's statistics suggest that child abuse was, at base, an environmental problem, and as such its elimination would require drastic improvement in the social and economic conditions of inner-city life. Not surprisingly, therefore, the Liverpool SPCC declined to elaborate on findings that could be interpreted as showing the futility of its own work.

Sensationalism and Self-Restraint

Perhaps the London SPCC might have devoted more attention to the dynamics of cruelty to children if the society had not become immersed in the question of sexual abuse of young girls. On July 6, 1885, the *Pall Mall Gazette* printed the first installment in its well-known series about child prostitution. "The Maiden Tribute of Modern Babylon" scandalized the English public because it chronicled the purchase of a thirteen-year-old girl. By exposing the traffic in white slavery, W. T. Stead, editor of the newspaper, hoped to revitalize the long-neglected Criminal Law Amendment Bill. Stead's revelations came as no surprise to the London SPCC. In the course of its work the society had discovered that sexual assaults upon children were "strangely widespread," and although "odious . . . to the conscience of the country, . . . almost unpunishable." [110] The virtual immunity of this crime from prosecution resulted in part from legal restrictions placed upon the testimony of the young. Finding confirmation of Stead's claims in the *First Annual Report*, Lord Shaftesbury, speaking at the anniversary meeting of the society, challenged the government to take action.

After the exposures in the *Pall Mall Gazette* of the most awful, and some say criminal, character—whether proper or improper, expedient or inexpedient, he would not stop to consider—there was but one course for the Government to pursue. Now that the statements had been made and corroborated by such a Report as that now presented to them, the Government must take the matter in hand and make a searching inquiry. If the facts were overstated, the public would be consoled by the knowledge; if confirmed, the Government must act boldly, and surrendering almost every other object they had in view devote their whole attention to the eradication of the evils which St. Paul says should hardly be named, and compared with which the affairs of India and Ireland were comparatively unimportant. [111]

Shaftesbury had long maintained that incest was a hideous product of overcrowding.[112] But no environmental ill, he felt, could excuse this trade in young flesh.

The society's policymakers placed less faith in the efficacy of moral outrage. With its firsthand knowledge of the problem, the London SPCC, like Stead, might have launched a frontal attack on the sexual abuse of children.[113] Instead, it chose to wage a narrow campaign for legal reform. The society's executive committee drew up a "Memorial" to the government, which asserted:

That when a girl under 12 years of age has been carnally known, the necessity of understanding the nature of an oath in order to [allow] the reception of her evidence operates greatly against the enforcement of the existing law in cases of very tender years and tends greatly to the aggravation of the evil wrought upon little children.

That the necessary delays, commitments and adjournments are unfavourable to the ascertaining of the truth of a charge, and that little children are not able to remember five or eight weeks what actually took place, and especially to undergo cross-questioning upon the testimony. Your Memorialists urgently plead on these two grounds, 1st that where there is evident truthfulness in a little child, her statements may be received without oath, in support of the charges and in corroboration of other evidence: 2nd, that the committing Justices may take down in writing her statement to be used at the trial.

Further, the "Memorial" requested that "parents, guardians or any other person having *bona fide* interest" in a young girl be granted summary powers "to immediately enter any premises where they have reasonable ground for suspecting that she is detained for unlawful purposes." And lastly, it advocated raising the age of consent to eighteen. On July 22 the "Memorial" was presented to Home Secretary R. A. Cross. Although two MPs (Samuel Smith and J. A. Picton) joined the society's deputation, Cross rejected the proposals.[114]

Rebuffed by the government, the society turned to backbench support in the Commons. On July 9, the Criminal Law Amendment Bill had at last won a second reading in the Lower House. Three weeks later Cross announced that the English people could no longer tolerate violation of the "purity of their households and the honour of their daughters." Some MPs questioned this assessment. Charles Hopwood (Liberal, Stockport) opposed the bill on the grounds that the House was simply "riding on a storm created by

sensational statements of a filthy character in a public journal."
Besides, if the measure passed, young men would fall prey to "de-
signing creatures" whose aim was blackmail. Hopwood was not a
foe of social purity, but he opposed raising the age of consent for
the same reason that he had opposed the Contagious Diseases Acts:
all violated the individual's right of free choice.[115] Other MPs
shared Hopwood's doubts. Reiterating the extortion argument,
Cavendish Bentinck (Conservative, Whitehaven) added that the
white slavery issue had been manipulated—presumably by a dema-
gogic Stead—"as a means of irritating the humbler classes against
those above them in circumstances."[116]

But efforts to halt deliberation on the bill failed. The following
evening, July 31, Samuel Smith brought up the first of the London
society's legal amendments, the abolition of the oath for girl victims
of sexual assault. J. A. Picton reminded his fellow MPs "that unless
this Amendment or something like it was passed, they might as well
pass no Act at all . . . so far as little children were concerned." Although others agreed with him, opposition quickly developed. Perhaps most damaging, Cross criticized the proposal because it required a "total change" in the existing law. Hopwood, in turn,
warned that "the danger of a child's evidence was that it too readily
persuaded judge and jury"; remove the oath and childish imagination would play havoc with justice. Ultimately, legal conservatism
prevailed and Smith's amendment lost by a narrow margin.[117]

The next morning the *Pall Mall Gazette* assailed the vote as
"utterly preposterous," commenting angrily on the success of "Mr.
Hopwood, Mr. John Morley, and other well-known opponents of
imposing the oath on Members of Parliament . . . in making [a
child's] inability to understand the nature of an oath . . . an offence
punishable by liability to be violated with impunity."[118] Still, the society's amendment had nearly passed, which gave rise to the hope
that with vigorous lobbying the vote could be reversed during the
report stage. Waugh began to haunt the Commons, buttonholing
MPs at every opportunity, and outside the House, he arranged a
meeting for MPs in the Westminster Palace Hotel.[119] At some point
during these negotiations, Sir Henry James, the former Attorney
General, agreed to reintroduce Smith's amendment. On August 7,
Sir Henry kept his word. The Home Secretary now declared a
change of heart about the clause. Encouraged, Smith tried to secure
the society's second objective. In a rider, he proposed that state-

ments made by a girl victim before a magistrate and taken down in writing be acceptable later as evidence in court. As it happened, this was asking for too much. Sir William Harcourt called Smith's new idea "most dangerous," since it would place men at the mercy of children who had been "coached up" to give false evidence. Sir Henry James even threatened to withdraw his sponsorship of the original amendment. Thus, Smith's rider failed. But to the delight of the London society's supporters, the oath clause carried without a division.[120]

The oath provision was obviously not the centerpiece of the Criminal Law Amendment Bill that gained final approval from the House of Commons on August 14. By this legislation the age of consent rose to sixteen, white slavery met with new penalties, and brothels where females appeared to be unlawfully detained could be searched and their captives taken to a place of safety—changes that struck contemporaries as constituting an "extensive and radical alteration in the law."[121] To the London SPCC, the passage of Samuel Smith's amendment represented a substantial victory. Waugh and his associates regarded this concession as the thin edge of the wedge in their effort to give legislative form to the concept of children's rights. Yet the society's reforming style may have been as important as its actual accomplishments. Waugh explained to the crowd gathered in Hyde Park on August 22 "to express their shame and indignation at the prevalence of criminal vice in their midst" that the society viewed indecent assaults on the young "not as a question of morality, but [as a question] of protecting weak and little children." Disassociating itself from the furor over sexual corruption, the society emerged from the white slavery agitation with a reputation as an eminently practical advocate of child welfare.[122]

At the same time, the London SPCC benefited from Waugh's loyalty to W. T. Stead. Unlike the rest of his society, Waugh became personally involved in Stead's trial for the well-intentioned but illegal abduction of Eliza Armstrong. The journalist appeared to Waugh as a "knight" who had "dealt . . . manhood's blow at the whole herd of fornicators, adulterers, and whoremongers." Stead had, in the words of one contemporary, taken a "dynamic view of evil," and Waugh admired him for the frankness with which he had smashed the "conspiracy of silence" surrounding child prostitution.[123] Even after the pronouncement of the inevitable guilty verdict, Waugh continued to assist his friend. His letter to the *Pall Mall*

Gazette describing the editor's sickly condition was largely responsible for Stead's subsequent transfer to Holloway Prison and his treatment as a first-class misdemeanant.[124] Grateful, Stead turned his newspaper into a powerful voice for the young society.

Voluntary organization for the defense of abused children had developed rapidly throughout Britain since the Reverend George Staite first broached the subject in 1881. Soon after the London SPCC's birth, anticruelty groups also formed in Glasgow and Edinburgh, again partly due to the labors of T. F. A. Agnew.[125] Educated Scots and Englishmen were growing increasingly sensitive to the problem of parental cruelty and were now prepared to countenance a cautious child-protection effort. But effective prevention of child abuse, particularly that which occurred in the privacy of the home, would require fundamental changes in both parliamentary statute and public attitude. As late as 1885 Dr. Barnardo was still resorting to philanthropic kidnapping to rescue endangered children.[126] The gulf between "moral law" and "judicial law" remained wide.

CHAPTER 4

Toward the Children's Charter

THE ANTICRUELTY groups that emerged in the early 1880's reflected a growing public concern for child welfare and, in turn, reinforced that concern by dramatizing the defenselessness of the young. Officials of the London and Liverpool societies had attempted with some success to adapt their work to a legal system that was, in Benjamin Waugh's words, "little more than the survival of utterly pagan traditions practically modified, though but slightly, by modern Christian sentiment."[1] But voluntary effort, regardless of its sophistication, could not effectively shield children from harm without the aid of explicit limits on parental power. What were the prospects for such reform? The "Modern Babylon" scandal had finally forced Parliament in 1885 to crack down on the white slave trade, and in so doing, Parliament grudgingly conceded to the London SPCC a modification in the law of evidence for child victims of sexual assault. Now the storm of public outrage was subsiding. New protective legislation would therefore require a fresh moral mandate.

Remarkably, within four years Parliament passed Europe's most comprehensive law against parental misconduct. As we shall see, this landmark measure was won only after protracted debate in both Houses of Parliament. But Parliament would not have tackled so controversial a matter had the reality of starved and battered children not been thrust squarely in its face. Much of the credit for transforming child abuse into a national issue belongs to the London SPCC, whose three-pronged campaign of legislative analysis, wrenching propaganda, and organizational growth in the end proved to be decisive.

Law and Public Opinion

SPCC leaders early recognized the need for statutory reform. The London society's *First Annual Report* gave considerable attention to the legal conditions that militated against the prevention of cruelty to children. Most serious among these were the reluctance of Poor Law guardians to punish parents for willful neglect; the inability of women, "who are the last to yield to their surroundings, and are protectors of their offspring until drink and constant example have done their work," to give evidence against cruel husbands; and the father's "absolute right" to the custody of his children.* Mindful of the need for precision in its work, the society's law committee asked its Honorary Counsel, Robert Colam, to assemble a handbook on legislation pertaining to child protection. The resulting *Manual*, a carefully annotated 68-page abstract, made accessible in "plain and popular form" hitherto scattered statutes and parts of statutes, and it also set out the legal rationale for much of the society's subsequent reform argument. As the author observed, circumventing the father's hold over his offspring provided the key to child protection:

To do this will probably be the most difficult and yet most important work of the Society; for where the child is regarded as an adult for the purpose of the criminal law, as he is where the offender is neither father nor standing *in loco parentis*, adventitious help is not required so much as when the offender is one who mistreats and yet has a legal and almost indefeasible right to retain possession and control of his victim. In such cases, to remove the child beyond the range of the father's influence, may be the only means of saving it from a life of misery or destruction. Yet to do this without incurring the consequences of such interference . . . will require knowledge

---

* London SPCC, *First Annual Report* (1885), pp. 9–12. Strictly speaking the father's right to custody was not absolute. By the 1873 Custody of Infants Act (36 & 37 Vic., c. 12), Chancery could grant mothers access to or custody of children under sixteen; separation deeds, wherein the father surrendered control of his offspring to the mother, became valid. Still, the Act specified that the court need not enforce a maternal claim that appeared to operate against the infant's "benefit." The significance of this qualification was perhaps best illustrated by the 1879 dispute between Annie Besant and her husband, an Anglican clergyman, over the custody of their daughter. Although Mrs. Besant possessed full legal control of the child, the mother's atheistical views together with her part in publishing the supposedly indecent marriage manual, *Fruits of Philosophy*, persuaded the court to return the girl to her father.

of the Law, great care, and in some cases a considerable expenditure of time and money.[2]

Challenges to paternal power were most successful in the context of Chancery proceedings. Here the jurisdiction for the court to interfere with the custody of the child did not depend on estate but rather on Chancery's representative capacity derived from the Crown as *parens patriae*—that is, as "parent of the nation." Taken to its logical conclusion, the concept of *parens patriae* sanctioned the defense of all children as subjects of the Crown. Or so the London SPCC would contend.

Members of the Liverpool SPCC also expressed keen interest in legal reform. As early as April 1884, the society's counsel, W. J. Stewart, compiled a *Report as to Existing Laws* that focused on the problem of punishing parental neglect. Stewart held that although section 37 of the 1868 Poor Law Amendment Act empowered boards of guardians to prosecute neglectful parents, other agencies were competent to institute proceedings by treating these offenses as misdemeanors under common law.[3] The latter opinion posed serious difficulties, however. First, the prosecution had to convince a jury that the accused did in fact possess the means to supply adequate food, clothing, medical aid, and shelter for his child. Then, to sustain a conviction, it was necessary to show that the health of the victim had been seriously injured; proof that the child had suffered would not suffice. Finally, as an indictable offense, child neglect required a trial at the Quarter Sessions instead of the Police Court, entailing a substantial delay between detection and correction of the crime. In view of these obstacles, Stewart outlined a parliamentary amendment whereby upon summary conviction, parents whose negligence caused injury to their child's health could receive a prison term of up to six months.[4] Citing Stewart's plan, T. F. A. Agnew wrote the Home Secretary, Sir William Harcourt, in July 1884, to request appropriate amendment of the 1868 Act. Officials greeted Agnew's petition with benign indifference. Although the Local Government Board expressed "no objection" to such an amendment, Home Office bureaucrats generally ignored the issue until December, when the Assistant Under-Secretary, Godfrey Lushington, concluded that it was not a "matter of urgency."[5]

To expect Home Office support thus appeared illusory. But could substantive legal reform succeed without governmental sponsor-

ship? Leaders of the London and Liverpool societies felt compelled
to find out. A common assumption motivating these activists was
that guidelines for proper treatment of the young would, if given
statutory force, create large-scale changes in patterns of child care.
As Waugh and Cardinal Manning put it: "That the national will
can effect immense revolutions in the conditions of child existence
is beyond doubt—not alone because it can impose direct annoy-
ances and miseries on its savage abusers, but because it can set up a
standard of right and wrong, and community obligation, which is a
still more powerful influence."[6] The idea of a "straightforward
Draconian code" derived primarily from the New York State Penal
Amendment Act of 1884. This broad measure, which prohibited
not only child neglect but also a variety of employments deemed
harmful to the health and morals of the young—including acroba-
tic performances, begging, and theatrical exhibitions—had been
forwarded by the New York SPCC to its English counterparts.[7] Envious of the Act, Colam, Waugh, and other members of the London
SPCC's law committee pieced together their own "Bill for the Better
Prevention of Cruelty to Children" during the winter of 1885–86.
By early March, when Waugh invited the Liverpool, Edinburgh,
and Glasgow societies to discuss possible parliamentary action, the
London society had already drafted a concrete proposal.[8] At the ensuing meeting provincial delegates discovered that legislative confirmation, not consultation, was the order of the day. Representatives
from Liverpool felt betrayed, having arrived eager to share their
own reform ideas only to find a fait accompli.[9]

This dictatorial display by the London SPCC reflected an impatience for reform that, if impolitic, was nevertheless understand-
able. With the exception of the abortive 1873 Children's Protection
Bill,[10] no attempt had yet been made in England to deal comprehensively with the problem of child abuse. Those who managed the
young society were convinced that such legislation could pass only
if promoted by a single voice; a loose federation of anticruelty
groups, with each member beholden to different local interests, was
not apt to act cohesively. Furthermore, London SPCC leaders had
reason to believe that they were best positioned to shape public interest in the plight of ill-used children.

Competition between "cause" groups for public support typified
an era that expected so much of voluntary effort. Canon Barnett,
Vicar of St. Jude's in Whitechapel and founder of Toynbee Hall,

perceived an impatience for social reform underlying the "growing disposition among all classes to trust in 'societies,' whose rules become the authority for the workers and whose extension becomes the aim of their work. Men give all their energies to get recruits for their army, recognition of their clubs, and more room for their operations. 'Societies' seem thus to be very fountains of strength, and the only method of action. . . . A 'society' has indeed taken over in many minds the place of a priest." This trend toward charity stimulated by self-interest rather than by a religious sense of mission Barnett attributed in part to the growth of philanthropic "advertising."[11] Within the London SPCC, recognition of the power of propaganda inspired the founding in January 1887 of a monthly magazine, the *Child's Guardian*. Modeled on the RSPCA's *Animal World*, the new journal aimed "to inform such persons as are already interested in the condition of little victims of cruel treatment, wrongful neglect, and improper employment what they can and cannot do to stop these evils." At the same time, by publicizing the "substantial facts" of cases (both those that had been tried and those "which at present it would be useless to carry into court"), the society hoped to arouse "worthier and nobler sentiments" about children.[12]

The creation of an official voice served yet another function, self-defense. As operations expanded from a total of 95 cases in 1884–85 to 258 in 1886–87, so also did the risk of public censure. In the first issue of the paper, Waugh, as editor, hastened to defuse the rumor that a Protestant zealot from Manchester, charged with stealing a child from its Catholic parents, had acted under London SPCC orders.[13] Imputations of religious partisanship could damage public confidence in and generosity to the supposedly nonsectarian society. Equally serious, allegations of hostility to the poor threatened to discredit the organization in working-class neighborhoods. Accused in July 1887 of committing a "gross libel on the poorer classes," Waugh issued a soothing denial. The normally combative Secretary observed that the poor, far from being criminally disposed, as a whole "are marked by a marvellous energy and personal sacrifice for their children, which is at once the strength and the credit of this country."[14] More often, however, the *Child's Guardian* countered criticism with defiant self-righteousness. If its grisly tales of suffering sometimes surpassed the limits of good taste, the fault had a noble sanction: "We are resolved to inflict cruelty on the public fancy till the public cease to be so indifferent to the cruelties inflicted in the minds and hearts of English children who have no organ to portray the atrocities from which they have all too long and all too silently suffered."[15]

In its efforts to impress contemporaries with the urgency of child protection, the young society received invaluable support from London newspapers. The *Pall Mall Gazette* was unrivaled in propagating the views of Benjamin Waugh. As a valued member of Stead's "team," Waugh, and by extension his organization, reaped the benefits of the "new journalism."[16] In January 1886, before the society could safely indulge in attacks on public officials, the *Gazette* lambasted a magistrate for his misdirected leniency. " 'Beating the baby' will doubtless become a popular pastime in St. Giles's," it noted caustically, "after the encouragement afforded to amateurs of the act by Mr. Mansfield at Marlborough-street yesterday." Later in the same year Stead's paper gloated ("a hypocrite well punished") over the society's successful prosecution of Edward Steele, a Westminster preacher who regularly savaged his son for sloth in hawking religious tracts.[17] Other Metropolitan newspapers expressed their support by providing a forum for the London SPCC. Access to the pages of *The Times*, for example, proved immensely useful in disseminating propaganda. When a correspondent wrote to protest Dr. Henry Williams's horsewhipping of his little girl, *The Times* immediately notified Waugh, permitting the Secretary to publish an explanatory note beside the original letter. Waugh observed solemnly that his organization, which had undertaken the prosecution at the surgeon's Shrewsbury trial, routinely dealt with such horrors. Apparently expecting others to share his retributive zeal, Waugh added: "It may be comforting to the outraged feelings of English parents to know that the whole cost of the sad affair to the culprits can not be less than £2,000. Medical practice and house have had to be given up; the family have left the country." This pronouncement understandably angered the defendant's solicitor, who replied that by spending some seventy guineas to retain a "legal luminary" as its counselor, the society had deliberately persecuted a parent for what amounted to an honest mistake. He concluded that citizens ought to "consider whether such societies are desirable, and whether they are not, in fact, a danger to the public welfare." Yet Waugh had the last word in this exchange. A minute description of the six-year-old's lacerated body effectively stifled allegations of malicious meddling; and to charges of legal harassment Waugh responded, somewhat disingenuously, that the society had only placed at the service of the child an advocate as able as her father would employ.[18] Also supportive of the London SPCC's work were the *Daily News*, *Truth*, the *City Press*, the *Christian*, the *Guardian*, and Waugh's own *Sunday Magazine*.[19]

No doubt some members of the London press were intrigued by the society's reforming style—a blend of philanthropic aggression and legal acumen. The *Child's Guardian* took special pleasure in chronicling the downfall of cruel but socially prominent parents, thereby casting the society as an even-handed dispenser of social justice. The organization's own statistics seemed to vindicate its methods, for the London SPCC obtained convictions in the great majority of the cases it brought to trial. That these statistics were suspect contemporaries either failed to note or else chose to ignore. Of the 1,521 cases investigated by the society during its first five years, only 246, or 16 percent, resulted in prosecution; and these appear to have been selected as much on the basis of probable success as on the gravity of the offense. The law committee excelled at picking winners. In April 1887 the *Child's Guardian* proudly reported the chastising of Mrs. Leonard Charles, "a powerful lady of property," for beating her daughter with rubber tubing. Significantly, however, the society initiated its prosecution only after the High Court of Justice had ruled that Mrs. Charles could not regain custody of her child from a sheltering neighbor.[20]

The London SPCC was also adroit in capitalizing on notorious provincial cases. According to the *Pall Mall Gazette*, the society deserved "the gratitude of all human beings" for prosecuting Alice Clay, wife of a veterinary surgeon, at the Derbyshire Quarter Sessions in late 1887. It is noteworthy that the offense for which Mrs. Clay served six months with hard labor—applying a hot poker to her daughter's groin—occurred in August 1884. A lapse of over three years did not deter the society from bringing charges, once a servant formerly employed in the Clay household volunteered the facts.[21] Using different tactics, the London SPCC forced national attention on another Derbyshire case, this one involving the flogging of a boy for stealing a watch. On three occasions during the summer of 1887, Sir Walter Foster, Liberal MP for the district and Council President of the British Medical Association, questioned Home Secretary Matthews about the brutal punishment of seven-year-old James Buckberry. Acting for the society, Foster pointed out that the child, already frail in health, had been arrested in the middle of the night and subsequently subjected to four strokes of an illegally shortened birch rod, resulting in severe damage to his back. Eventually Matthews acknowledged that the arrest was "unnecessary and injudicious" and the punishment "far too severe." Further, he advised local law enforcement officials henceforth to consult doctors about the propriety of corporal punishment for child offenders.[22]

By 1887 the London SPCC had become a clearinghouse for national and even international cases. The executive committee cast a wide net during its third year, petitioning the Home Office to prohibit the imprisonment of young imbeciles, requesting the aid of the India Office in tracing immigrant children, and negotiating with the New York SPCC for the return of child stowaways in ships bound for America.[23] As experts in child welfare, leaders of the society felt entitled to special dispensations from the government. Waugh must have been irked, therefore, when the Home Office denied him access to Liverpool Police Court records, and frustrated when he was barred from entering workhouses and boarding-out homes. "We long to get our . . . inspectors in among these places to help to expose them," admitted the *Child's Guardian*.[24]

Counterbalancing the society's sometimes truculent tone and legitimizing its claims in the eyes of "respectable" opinion was the allegiance of rich and powerful patrons. With the death of Shaftesbury in October 1885, the office of President passed to the second Duke of Abercorn, a Donegal landlord best known for his hostility to Irish home rule. But the dominant aristocratic voice still belonged to Angela Burdett-Coutts. The Baroness and her coterie of noblewomen formed a distinct faction within the society. An ad hoc Children's Safety Committee, which included Countess Spencer, the Countess of Iddesleigh, the Countess of Aberdeen, Lady George Hamilton, Viscountess Midleton, Lady Tavistock, and Lady Nottage, periodically met at the Baroness's Stratton Street home to discuss rescue work. Although primarily concerned with the operation of the society's shelter, these women did not hesitate to advise the executive committee on policy matters.[25] Shocked by the contrast between their own domestic security and the nightmarish home lives of the shelter's inmates, they heartily endorsed the separation of children from abusive parents. Unquestionably, without their involvement the London SPCC would have been considerably less solvent. Society functions such as the benefit concert held at Grosvenor House in June 1885 attracted glamorous guests—Princess Mary of Cambridge, the Duke and Duchess of Westminster, the Duchess of Mecklenburg-Strelitz, the Duchess of Marlborough —and added hundreds of pounds to the coffers.[26] Waugh unabashedly courted aristocratic women, confident that their sponsorship of fashionable bazaars, garden parties, and amateur theatricals would attract both money and members from the title-conscious middle class. At the same time, these ladies lent credence to the society's propaganda. If someone as consummately genteel as Baroness Burdett-Coutts described cruelty as a "lust," who could complain of sensationalism?

Cardinal Manning's support of the London SPCC paid a different dividend, the goodwill of Catholic England. According to one biographer, Manning's Christian activism led him "to identify . . . with practically all major philanthropic schemes and social reforms of the second half of the nineteenth century."[27] This tells us little about his reform priorities. Manning in fact favored frontal assaults on social ills and preferred tightly organized campaigns. Hence his advocacy of teetotalism and his admiration for the United Kingdom Alliance—"a great Nasmyth's hammer which has struck a dent into the conscience of England." Speaking to an Exeter Hall audience in 1878, Manning extolled the alliance's tactics: "I do not believe that any man, or any number of men without organization, without local establishment and centres, without a perpetual agency in word and in writing, could by any manner of means have caused the conscience of the country to know and to acknowledge the real curse [a growing number of public houses] which is upon us."[28] Empathy with the oppressed and persecuted formed another component of Manning's Christian ethic. His humane instincts led him to support the antivivisection movement. Here his chosen vehicle for protest was Frances Power Cobbe's militant Victoria Street Society, of which he served as a Vice President from 1876 to his death in 1892. Manning hoped to entice his coreligionists into humane activity. Such causes were not only noble but also useful as a means of drawing the insular Catholic community into English public life. As he noted ruefully in old age, "It is not that our Catholics deliberately refuse [to participate in humanitarian movements], but partly they do not take the pains to know, partly they are . . . unconscious that Lazarus lies at their gate full of sores."[29] Thus the aggressive, proselytizing style of the London SPCC naturally appealed to him. From his first meeting with Benjamin Waugh in July 1884, Manning became a zealot in the defense of mistreated children, rivaling even the Secretary in his rhetoric.[30]

Together, in 1886, Waugh and Manning wrote the society's first and arguably most influential tract, "The Child of the English Savage."[31] Published initially in the *Contemporary Review*, it argued that "the Christianity and the civilization of a people may be measured by the treatment of childhood." The specific claims of child-life originated in the love of the Eternal Father for His Eternal Son. Since "a divine consanguinity bound man to God and man to man," it followed that parents should naturally cherish their offspring. Moreover, the child stands unique in the eyes of the Lord, for "of all His creatures it is the most like Himself in its early purity, beauty, brightness, and innocence." By injuring a child, the Christian brands himself an apostate as well as a coward. The protection of the young is thus a religious duty, and the protective agency's power of prosecution a Godly instrument. But probably most arresting to Victorian minds was the article's depiction of suffering childhood:

To paint a picture of the "Triumph of the Innocents" one has no need to go to Egypt for the groundwork, nor to Herod's pitiable victims for the figures. Its air might be filled with angel-children, once bruised with blows, crippled with kicks, and faint with hunger, looking down watching the little company of playing children in some grimy London court, where, since they had been abused out of this world, the Society for the Prevention of Cruelty to Children has prosecuted a man. Their little eyes, which used to weep, should be made glad with the sight of their old comrades rejoicing in the new and happier times.[32]

Fifteen thousand copies of the article were distributed throughout the country during the latter half of 1886. One of these accompanied Waugh's January 1887 letter to the Home Office requesting government support for the society's bill.[33] At this point Waugh was grasping at straws. Shortly after attending the London SPCC's 1886 Mansion House meeting, Lord Iddesleigh had agreed to introduce the bill in the Upper House. Prospects for parliamentary approval seemed bright. Lord Herschell, the former Liberal Lord Chancellor, had given his blessing to the objects of the measure—albeit after repeated interviews with the indefatigable Waugh.[34] Unfortunately, Iddesleigh's sudden death on January 12 dashed these hopes.

The Home Office, as expected, remained unwilling to sponsor substantial protective legislation. But this time the society's bill at least received serious study. A seventeen-page memo by unnamed civil servants sympathized with the bill's proposed penalties for juvenile street trading and willful neglect of the young, though the memo criticized provisions relating to the sale of alcohol to children and the deprivation of parental custody in cases of cruelty.[35] With respect to the regulation of children working in city streets, favorable Home Office opinion mirrored the feeling of municipal officials throughout England. Too often, it seemed, young people hawked newspapers, matches, and flowers to support their indolent parents. Although the use of children, particularly the deformed and sickly, to excite casual charity had long flourished in urban centers, sustained reform sentiment arose only after the institution of compulsory education. Beginning in 1877 the Charity Organisation Society launched a campaign against the exhibition of Italian begging children, victims of the so-called padroni system. Typically an entrepreneur, the padrone, would offer minimal compensation to poor Neapolitan parents for the use of their children, subsequently marching his charges to foreign cities. There, posing as street musicians, the often ill-clad and undernourished children would support their master with the alms they solicited.[36] By the late 1870's these troupes were common sights in London, Liverpool, and Bradford, as well as in various French, Swiss, and American cities. Communication between padroni enabled them to avoid localities where authorities were troublesome.[37] Angered perhaps more by promiscuous charity than by children shivering through English winters, C.O.S. leaders joined Italian consular authorities in persuading the Home Secretary, Sir Richard Cross, to take action. Between July and December 1877 33 padroni were convicted and sentenced to prison terms ranging from fourteen to 60 days. Government officials shipped the children back to their homeland.[38]

The padroni problem proved important because it focused public attention on the lot of the child street vendor. Some observers saw "casual employment" as a danger to juvenile morality. The Reverend James Nugent, Chaplain of the Liverpool Borough Gaol, insisted that England should follow the lead of certain American cities in prohibiting girls from plying wares in public. As Nugent explained to an 1882 Lords select committee, Liverpool women carried baskets filled with everything from fruit and fish to newspapers and rags.

Now these basket girls begin at a very early age, and they can earn from, we will say 6d., up to as much as 10s. a day; they are carrying heavy loads; they are comparatively innocent at first, but by degrees they get into the habit of drinking, and when a girl begins to drink, and gets into prison two or three times, though she may carry a basket, there is very little difference between her and a prostitute, and sometimes these girls are more lawless, obscene, defiant in their language, than even the common prostitute on the streets.[39]

Generally, however, municipal leaders regarded juvenile street trading less as a threat to sexual purity than as an embarrassing civic nuisance. English town authorities envied the Scottish Education Act of 1878, which stipulated that absolutely no child under ten, and only those between ten and fourteen who had obtained certification of their ability to read and write, could engage in casual employment after 7 P.M. during the winter months and after 9 P.M. during the summer.[40] Noting that these provisions had worked well in Glasgow, the 1882 Select Committee on Police and Sanitary Regulations approved a modified form of the Scottish law for inclusion in a Manchester Corporation Bill. Shortly thereafter local bylaws embodying similar regulations came into force in Birmingham, Bradford, Bristol, Hull, Leicester, Lincoln, Liverpool, Newcastle, and Nottingham.[41]

An absence of comparable bylaws for London severely hampered the society's efforts to protect children forced to beg by their parents. Public opinion was not entirely favorable to remedial legislation for the Metropolis. The *St. James's Gazette*, for example, described proposals to restrict juvenile street trading as "signs of the ever-narrowing liberties of man." This attitude received short shrift from a frustrated London SPCC: "That the parasitic lives which feed on weary dying children should be called 'men,' and their base habits be called 'liberties' of men, is most unfortunate."[42] Legally able to act only when child begging occurred without the pretense of selling, the society sometimes went beyond the law by spiriting away young hawkers to its shelter. This drastic procedure was better, it insisted, than the heartless efforts of the C.O.S. to eradicate mendicancy by withholding alms. "What of the . . . wretched drudge?" wondered the *Child's Guardian*. "While fewer people give and buy, it [the child] must only stand longer hours before it dares to go home, or else risk a beating within an inch of its life."[43] London SPCC leaders had found that the exigencies of child protection often could not be squared with the rules of scientific charity, and Waugh's willingness to advertise this conflict would make his organization suspect in the eyes of the C.O.S.

Despite all efforts at suppression, however, juvenile hawking continued to thrive in West End thoroughfares such as Oxford Street and Regent Street.[44] Not until March 1887, when the High Court of Justice ruled (in MacDonald vs. Lochrane) that the Newcastle Corporation bylaws on street trading were *ultra vires*, did the London SPCC's plan for national legislation win widespread notice. The court's opinion that juvenile hawking did not constitute an obstruction to traffic effectively invalidated most municipal regulations on the subject.[45] From Benjamin Waugh's perspective the ruling was fortuitous because it "cleared the field for action more direct and efficient." Writing in the *Contemporary Review*, Waugh argued that the society's bill aimed simply to uphold "the right of dependent children to endurable lives," a right long recognized by statute. Parliament already protected young workers in brickfields, mines, factories, and chimneys. Why not extend this protection to the children—Waugh estimated that there were as many as 200,000 of them—who made their livings in the streets?[46]

The other section of the bill that aroused Home Office sympathy dealt with neglect. Even before the founding of the society, Parliament had known about the need for more effectual punishment of neglectful parents. Joanna Hill, onetime Secretary to the Birmingham Boarding-Out Committee, told the Royal Commission on Reformatory and Industrial Schools that the powers of guardians to prosecute parents for willful child neglect were rarely exercised in her district. But even if these powers had been invoked more often, they would not adequately shield the young, reasoned John Watts, Chairman of the Industrial Schools Committee of the Manchester School Board. One sure way to curb juvenile crime, Watts believed, was to enforce parental duties:

I think it would be wise to enact powers to prosecute parents where . . . gross neglect has conduced to the offense of the child, and I would also give power to prosecute for habitual neglect of family, even where the neglect has not driven them to the union for relief; such an arrangement would allow the prosecution of a drunkard who is not technically disorderly, and of a gambler who spends his time recklessly and leaves his family without food, and of the idler who seeks to live upon his children when they ought to be at school.[47]

Reform sentiment fueled legislative action in 1880. In August of that year, MPs Charles Hopwood and John Thomasson introduced the awkwardly titled "Bill to Provide a Remedy by Law for Married Women Against Their Husbands Neglecting or Refusing to Maintain and Educate Their Children." Hopwood, who as we have seen would later oppose legislation to protect girls from sexual assault, was persistent (though unsuccessful) in pressing his bill. Introduced again in 1881 and 1883, it never reached a second reading. This measure, which would have permitted a married woman to obtain from her profligate husband "a sum of money proportionate to his means" for the support of their children under the age of sixteen, seemed to some MPs a "meddling interference with . . . the domestic concerns of life" and to others a threat "to those whom God had joined together."[48] Yet the concept embodied in Hopwood's bill found favor with other politicians, as evidenced by the passing in 1886 of the Married Women (Maintenance in Case of Desertion) Act. Though this law aimed to spare women the degradation of becoming inmates of a workhouse before their spouses could be forced to support them, it also allowed mothers to provide for their offspring without the intervention of Poor Law officials. As the *Child's Guardian* announced, "an unreasonable and unsuitable father is no longer sole guardian of the purse."[49]

Still, the 1886 Act applied to a narrow range of marital circumstances, leaving the problem of parental neglect of children largely unresolved. Guardians themselves were beginning to admit that the young needed special defense from dissolute mothers and fathers. In December 1887 a delegation from the Manchester Poor Law Conference urged the President of the Local Government Board, C. T. Ritchie, to permit guardians to retain custody of pauper children in cases where their return to parental control promised a resumption of ill-treatment. Although principally concerned with the ratepayer's investment in workhouse children, the delegation at least added an official dimension to the call for legislative redress.[50] As judicial statistics suggest (Appendix C, Fig. 2), per capita convictions of adults for deserting or neglecting to support their families rose substantially between 1866 and 1876.[51] Presumably guardians were responding to the 1868 Poor Law Amendment Act, section 37 of which stressed their duty to bring legal action against neglectful fathers and mothers.[52] But by the early 1880's proportionally fewer convictions were being won at a time when the issue of parental misconduct was under close review. Thus in 1888 a concerned Lords select committee studied proposals to curtail the custody of neglectful parents. Some boards went to great lengths to locate the parents of deserted children. The forsaken young meanwhile received education in district schools at the state's expense. Why, then, should long-absent parents be permitted to reclaim their off-spring once they reached wage-earning age? For that matter, asked Louisa Twining, a guardian of the Kensington Union, why should "ins-and-outs"—adults who tramped from one workhouse to another—be allowed to drag their young along? *

Under examination by a fellow society member, the Earl of Aberdeen, Waugh stressed that the London SPCC found little fault with the treatment of children by Poor Law personnel. Rather, the society regretted that the law appeared to invest guardians with sole responsibility for the prosecution of neglectful parents, while guardians themselves often seemed to be unaware of their duties in this matter. Since its founding, the London SPCC had uncovered 250 cases of child starvation, none of which had elicited any action from Poor Law authorities. In 25 of these cases the children died; in 35 the offenders went to prison for periods ranging from one month to fifteen years.[53] Citing the "startling" extent of child starvation disclosed by the society's work, the select committee recommended that the Local Government Board call the special attention of guardians to their powers and responsibilities under the 1868 Act. Accordingly, in a circular to the clerks of Poor Law districts dated December 31, 1888, the board once again impressed on guardians their duty to prosecute neglectful parents.[54] If the Lords committee had not actually endorsed the antineglect provisions of the society's bill, it had at least accepted the society's judgment.

---

* Lords Select Committee on Poor Law Relief, P.P., 1888, XV, QQ. 4999, 3037–39. For similar opinions by Poor Law guardians see QQ. 2830 and 5413. These sentiments were not new. Eighteen years earlier Florence Davenport-Hill had pleaded for "some change in the law, limiting, or even abrogating, the authority of parents over [workhouse] children." "The Family System for Workhouse Children," *Contemporary Review*, 15 (September 1870), 273.

This recognition must have cheered the society. Educating Englishmen about the problem of child abuse, after all, required public confidence in the society's methods. It also necessitated a high degree of public visibility. London SPCC members were exhorted to distribute propaganda to "magistrates, superintendents of police, guardians of the poor, relieving officers and district visitors, to gentlemen's and workingmen's clubs, . . . and to school teachers." Even the "little dead" came within the society's purview. "Make friends with your coroner," advised the *Child's Guardian*, "and ask [him] when a child inquest is held to telegraph . . . Childhood, London."[55] With only a token inspectorate—three men in mid-1887— the London SPCC depended on a cooperative public to refer cases. Thus supporters and staff distributed thousands of "reporting cards" throughout the Metropolis. Entitled "In Cases of Cruelty, What to Do," the cards explained:

Most persons witnessing cruelty are utterly at a loss what to do. First, make as sure as possible of all your facts; then write immediately to . . . 7, Harpur Street, Theobald's Road, London, W. C., and arrange them thus:— 1. Name and residence of the culprit. 2. Name and residence of the sufferer. 3. The place, time, date, and nature of the specific offence or offences. 4. The name or names of persons who witnessed it, or can give circumstantial evidence. 5. The name and address of the informant. Then all further steps will be taken, and all expenses paid by the London Society, and the informant's name will be strictly confidential.[56]

Where independent inquiry substantiated these reports, offenders received the society's Form XIV. Advising malefactors to "prevent the necessity for further proceedings," the form detailed the prison terms recently awarded to child abusers.[57] Faith in the efficacy of formal warnings derived from two assumptions. First, London SPCC leaders believed that the appearance of their officer at the offender's door fostered the idea of accountability. By "making crimes seem crimes, both in the culprit's mind and the mind, too, of his nobler neighbors," the society contributed to "an elevated moral tone." Second, as generally rational creatures, child abusers would desist from their cruel ways if confronted with the prospect of punishment. Even rough and uneducated brutes could understand the inexpediency of such behavior, "for they have sound brains in their heads, these wrong hearted men; and they are too contented with their freedom with pipes and glasses to recklessly throw it away." As proof of the deterrent value of prison, officials cited the "almost incredible fact" that during the society's first three years only one person had to be prosecuted twice. Still, the London SPCC sought security for its young clients. To prevent repeated cruelty, the society supplied relations and neighbors of victims with preaddressed forms. The inspectors too made supplemental visits, particularly to the homes of those who had served jail terms. Ideally, warnings to abusive adults, made credible by occasional prosecutions, would clip cruelty in the bud, obviate the necessity for separating parent and child, and so preserve English family life.[58]

This deterrence theory stemmed from an increasingly well-defined conception of cruelty. As noted, the society's initial attempt to explain the phenomenon of child abuse had contributed little to an understanding of the problem. But with greater case experience came a willingness to speculate about causes and conditions. In part, the social climate of late Victorian England seemed to promote the domestic mistreatment of children. London SPCC literature decried the rising tide of scientific materialism that appeared to have undermined the idea of spiritual obligation. Freed from a religious sense of duty to offspring, parents were, in the society's view, growing steadily more self-indulgent. This boded ill for children: "Plain as the sun at noon is it that eating well, and drinking well, and dressing well on thirty shillings a week is impossible where there are many mouths to feed and bodies to clothe."[59] Perhaps the most baleful product of the secularized conscience was a susceptibility to the "antipopulation creed." Manning, the Catholic patriarch, and Waugh, the proud father of eight children, pointed to the "crusade against families" as further evidence of the need for parliamentary legislation to buttress embattled religious precepts.[60] As we shall see, the child-savers' unyielding hostility to all forms of birth control would bring their cause added prestige in an era obsessed with racial decay.

But prevailing social fashion only exacerbated an ever-present problem. Whereas Frances Power Cobbe had assured her readers that "dangerous" wife-beating belonged almost exclusively to the artisan and laboring population,[61] the London SPCC vigorously argued that child abuse was unrelated to economic status. The true English savage often earned good wages; domestic squalor resulted not from his indigence but from his refusal to spend money on anything or anyone but himself. In an analysis of the 10,169 cases investigated between May 1889 and April 1891, the society could find only 396 instances of abusive families with weekly incomes below twenty shillings. Upwards of 3,000 cases revealed an average weekly family income of twenty-seven shillings, sixpence. Since British laborers earned an estimated average weekly wage of twenty-one shillings in 1890, it is obvious that London SPCC officials did not restrict their war on cruelty to those areas of the East End where high unemployment was chronic.[62] Nor, apparently, did mistreated children come from unusually large households. For the 258 cases investigated during 1886–87, the average family size was approximately 3.5. In 1891, on the basis of a much larger SPCC sample, families had on the average 2.78 children, or a total household size of 4.78, assuming a resident adult male and female to be typical. One modern demographer suggests that English families averaged only 4.34 members during the decade 1890–99.[63]

The London SPCC's careful separation of child abuse from economic conditions contrasted sharply with contemporary assumptions about the causes of most social ills. Fallen women "fell" because the wages of sin were comparatively lucrative. Adults turned to drink as an antidote to grinding poverty or took to the pub as an escape from the dreariness of subsistence living. Antivivisectionists aside, the RSPCA seemed to locate the bulk of its work among humans little elevated above the beasts they beat. The London SPCC's special vulnerability to charges of class antagonism no doubt made its unusual position expedient. But also, if mistreatment of the young really did pervade all social strata, then a preventive agency would merit the thanks—and generosity—of the entire population. Viewed in this light, the London SPCC was simply arguing for its indispensability.

Tactical considerations alone, however, do not suffice to explain the society's insistence on the theory of classless cruelty. Men and women who believed that economic deprivation caused mistreatment of the young would have been massively cynical to press for legal sanctions against offending parents. Rather, it appears that society officials, having gathered substantial evidence about the nature of child abuse, were beginning to note what modern studies of the problem continue to show—that cruelty to the young is so multicausal as to defy simple characterization. Though some recent investigations stress a strong positive correlation between poverty or subnormal education and mistreatment,[64] others point to parental tension arising from unstable marriages and social isolation, or, most broadly, to general societal expectations of obedience, submission, and uniformity from the young.[65] In any case, the ubiquity of child abuse became dogma for the society and was proclaimed at its annual meetings, echoed in its appeals, and transmitted to a wider public through sympathetic newspapers and journals.[66] If a major spur to reform had been fear of the brutal poor, child-savers soon found that brutality could also thrive amid plenty.

With confidence in their procedure, leaders of the society sought to enlarge their mission. Expansion made sense. For maximum impact upon Parliament, the call for legislative reform would have to be national. More immediately, the efficient investigation of provincial cases demanded the establishment of regional centers. As early as July 1886 the London SPCC's law committee complained about the difficulties of securing fair trials outside the Metropolis. This obstacle might be surmounted, the committee felt, by forming local branches. As the RSPCA's experience seemed to show, however, these branches should not be autonomous administrative units.[67] Not until 1870, nearly half a century after its founding, did the RSPCA move to impose organizational discipline on the animal-welfare movement. After that date, newly formed societies were permitted to claim the RSPCA title only if they agreed to defer to the parent body in all matters pertaining to finances and legal action. Thus, a kind of organizational crazy quilt took shape among animal lovers: local affiliates of the RSPCA coexisted with independent associations.[68] A member of both the London SPCC law and executive committees, RSPCA Secretary John Colam surely warned his colleagues about the disadvantages of haphazard growth.

According to the *Child's Guardian*, Bristol philanthropists found Waugh's "pathetic narratives" of tormented children so moving that they immediately voted to align themselves with the London SPCC as its earliest aid committee.[69] In fact, they demonstrated reluctance to accept London hegemony. On the evening of April 6, 1887, Waugh did indeed address the annual conference of the Children's Aid Union. Subsequently, however, the union decided to entrust child-protection work to the Children's Help Society, a Bristol charity devoted to providing cheap meals for the young. Only after a subcommittee of the C.H.S. declined to assume these additional duties did affiliation with London become acceptable.[70]

The pace of expansion quickened during the winter of 1888. In late January, T. F. A. Agnew joined with Waugh to promote the formation of an aid committee in Chester. Unlike the inaugural meeting at Bristol, the Chester gathering was carefully staged. With the Town Hall as a backdrop and the Mayor as the presiding officer, Waugh's lengthy and emotional address enjoyed official blessing. Anticipating objections that anticruelty societies usurped police functions, the Secretary insisted that whereas the constabulary sought to vindicate the law, the society gave first priority to the safety of the child. Waugh's rhetoric evidently struck a responsive chord, for amidst much applause the audience agreed to form an auxiliary to the London society. Within two months new aid committees were established in Bradford, Hastings and St. Leonards, Ipswich, Leeds, Norwich, and Scarborough. A formula for growth had evolved. Provincial enthusiasts should "first . . . interest a few leading citizens; then request the Mayor, or corresponding town authority, to convene in his parlour in the Council Chamber a hundred or two of the principal inhabitants, to hear a statement of the aims, methods, and results of the Society's work." [71] Sometimes, as at Leeds, an aid committee's first six months were tenuous. Doubtful citizens needed to be convinced that child abuse was prevalent in their own communities, yet prosecutions had to be judiciously managed in order to win over skeptical magistrates. [72] Regardless of local circumstances, however, a branch's subordination to London was absolute. "No man [can] serve two masters," the Bishop of Newcastle was told when he suggested that the proposed aid committee for his city be amalgamated with preexisting charity. [73]

By the spring of 1888, then, a rapidly expanding London SPCC, along with independent anticruelty agencies in Liverpool, Hull, and Birmingham, had transformed child protection into a major social issue. Largely because of their activity, the question of children's rights now permeated a broader public conscience. People unconnected with formal philanthropy were beginning to speak out. An Alfred Mager of Manchester called for a new Shaftesbury to wage a parliamentary war on the "selfish *laissez-faire*" theory of parental power. Ultimately, Mager admitted, an evil of the magnitude and complexity of child neglect required the intervention of state officials. He envisioned the creation of local tribunals similar to school boards, composed of wise and humane men, to deal with both juvenile delinquency and child abuse. These bodies might be supplemented on the neighborhood level by vigilance committees. [74] Still another writer held that "the mass of chronic poverty, of pauperism, disease, and crime which at this moment clogs the wheels of progress, and which forms one of the most insoluble problems of modern life, has its origins mainly in the refusal or neglect of the natural claims of children." This being the case, England urgently needed some sort of "Sustenance and Protection of Children Act."[75]

The Contest in Parliament

The time for reform seemed ripe. Joseph Chamberlain's haunting question, "What ransom will property pay for the security which it enjoys?," reverberated in the minds of politicians. The "unauthorized program's" promise of three acres and a cow to agricultural workers called for an urban equivalent.[76] In the interests of the "well being and happiness of their poorer and less fortunate fellow men," MPs from both parties gathered at Grosvenor House in late May 1888 to "turn into concrete facts some of the ideas which intelligent social reformers hold as convictions." Most pressing, argued Samuel Smith, were the issues of temperance and child welfare.* Other politicians agreed with him. After the death of Lord Iddesleigh, John Morley consented to sponsor the society's bill. Morley, one of the most respected of the Gladstonian Liberals, believed that the responsibility for administering reform legislation should rest with "local bodies," and his suspicion of a still more powerful central government probably disposed him to support the private policing activity of the London SPCC. It soon became apparent, however, that involvement in Irish affairs would prevent him from leading the society's delegation in Commons.[77] But at his urging A. J. Mundella, President of the Board of Trade in Gladstone's third government and a skilled parliamentary tactician, agreed to take charge of the bill. Mundella anticipated a fight. In a speech at the society's May meeting at the Mansion House, he predicted that "the moment this measure is introduced we shall hear a

---

* *Hospital*, May 26, 1888, pp. 117–18. This ad hoc committee, organized by the Earl of Meath, expressed interest in a wide range of contemporary issues. These included pauperism, workhouse reform, starvation wages, overpopulation, foreign immigration, colonization, emigration, pollution of air and water, prevention of infection, the drink and opium questions, overcrowding of dwellings, unsanitary buildings, prostitution, early closing; also industrial, technical, commercial, and physical education; public parks and playgrounds; factory, mining, and workshop legislation and inspection; and small holdings, allotments, and national insurance. The committee seems to have been short-lived.

great deal about the rights of parents and interference with the sacred rights of citizenship and liberty which all parents enjoy uncontrolled over their children." A few days later Mundella met with R. T. Reid, Q.C., MP (Liberal, Dumfries), to "harmonize" the bill with existing law, so "as far as possible not [to] shock the too-delicate sensibilities of our legislature."[78] Finally on August 10, Mundella moved in Commons that the Bill for the Better Prevention of Cruelty to Children be read a first time.[79]

Originally the London SPCC had planned to mount an intensive extra-parliamentary campaign. In April the *Child's Guardian* estimated that the society needed a minimum of £150 for the printing, postage, and manual labor necessary to "move Parliament from the outside."[80] The circulation of petitions would absorb most of this sum. Copies of the bill, together with printed testimonials and ruled paper for signatures, were distributed to subscribers. Once completed and sent to London headquarters, these petitions would be submitted en masse to Parliament at the appropriate moment. A barrage of newspaper publicity would further stimulate public support. Angela Burdett-Coutts did indeed write to *The Times* about eleven-year-old Louisa Eldridge, who had been forced by her mother to lie in the same bed with her dead father. Describing children as "infant citizens" of the state, inhabiting an "Empire within an Empire," she pleaded for the interest of all classes in the bill.[81]

But this was the only letter written by a London SPCC leader to appear in the London press. Nor did the society present a single petition to Parliament. For Waugh and most of his colleagues had quietly concluded that the bill as reconstructed was not worth promoting. In rendering the measure palatable for Parliament—by jettisoning such controversial provisions as allowing forcible entry into private homes for the removal of mistreated children, by compelling spouses to testify against one another in cases of child cruelty, and by dispensing with the oath requirements for all child victims of tender years—R. T. Reid had, in their view, eviscerated the bill. The society would have nothing to do with "statutory hypocrisy."[82]

Yet even in its comparatively conservative form the bill aroused strong opposition. Its penalty of up to £100 or six months in prison for any publican who sold alcohol to a child under ten enraged the liquor trade.[83] The same severe penalties for cruelty to or neglect of the young worried Home Office officials.[84] Cognizant of neither the society's nor the government's attitude, Mundella was taken by surprise when, on December 13, the Attorney General, Sir Richard Webster, objected to proceeding with a measure that contained "so much debatable matter."[85] Eight days later Mundella reluctantly withdrew his bill. In the society's view, of course, the mutant was happily stillborn.

With the close of the 1888 parliamentary session, London SPCC leaders decided to submit their original proposal. A new bill in any form seemed destined to be attacked by an unlikely triumvirate: the publican, the schoolmaster, and the Band of Hope movement. Most curious were the objections voiced by the last. A youth auxiliary of the temperance movement, this group feared that restrictions on the employment of children in public entertainments might jeopardize its penny readings, parades, and choir competitions. The London SPCC, in fact, sought only to discourage sending children to sing and dance in unwholesome environments (such as public houses); it had no wish to prevent performances associated with legitimate philanthropy. In theory, the Vagrancy Acts already rendered "every little door-to-door and street collector for a school treat or a missionary society" liable to arrest. What prevented this from taking place, the London society pointed out, was the common sense of the English bench.[86] Somewhat better founded was the fear among teachers that the bill would promote classroom anarchy by outlawing corporal punishment in schools. Not without reason did the *Schoolmaster* view the London SPCC as a threat. Six months earlier, after failing to prove its case against a Middlesex teacher, the society had announced ominously: "There is far too sturdy an idea of punishment in not a few of the institutions where the young people of England are taught. In all such places *we* intend to count for something. . . . It is to prevent the too confident exultation of the *stern* schoolmasters that are abroad, at whose hands delinquents fare grievously, that we venture on this note of warning. Let them beware."[87]

The idea of defining ill-treatment as anything "likely to cause . . . unnecessary suffering" seemed to some teachers a carte blanche for meddling philanthropists. But potentially most damaging was the hostility of the powerful Off-License Holders' National Federation. Publicans, like teachers, had good grounds for apprehension. To the liquor trade it seemed a subterfuge to drag the drink question into a measure "which on other points appeals to the sympathy of every human parent."[88] Here the child-savers yielded to expediency. At the urging of Sir Richard Webster, the society agreed to abandon the alcohol clause of its new bill. Thus on February 22, 1889, Mundella presented his fellow MPs with a fresh and in most respects even more radical measure for the protection of children.[89]

By heeding Webster's advice about the drink provisions of the bill, the society earned the support of a valuable ally—an advocate in the previously inaccessible Conservative camp. On March 15 Webster wrote to the Home Secretary suggesting that with some relatively minor revisions the bill might be supported by Her Majesty's government. Although still opposed to formal sponsorship, Matthews agreed that the government should express sympathy with the objects of the bill.[90] Translated, this meant that the Conservatives preferred a safe seat on the fence, ready to claim credit for encouraging important social reform if the bill passed, yet sufficiently detached to retreat gracefully in case the measure aroused stiff opposition. With the impediment of government opposition lifted, Mundella secured a second reading on April 4.

At last the society had something to sell. Its first step in rekindling reform sentiment was to distribute an explanatory letter, along with 10,000 copies of "Street Children," to every corporation in England. This tactic produced resolutions in favor of the bill from 87 municipalities. Two hundred public petitions containing more than 150,000 signatures were also presented to Parliament.[91] Probably most persuasive to individual MPs, however, was the receipt of the society's "army of facts"—a letter running to twelve foolscap pages, designed to defend the bill. At the suggestion of Webster, the letter included 32 case studies to illustrate the intended application of each subsection of the bill. In a mild and rather misleading statement of aims, Waugh noted that the proposal neither sought to make men moral by act of Parliament (which in fact it did) nor implied a condemnation of English parenthood. Rather, the "sole object of the Bill [was] to secure young children against odious wrongs."[92]

These public reassurances were necessary. By no means everyone concurred with *The Lancet*'s assessment of the bill as a "sensible and moderate endeavor to deal with what is at once a very pressing matter, and one which bristles with perplexing legal difficulties."[93] Predictably, the National Union of Elementary Teachers urged the government to modify the measure by excluding schools from its scope. Within the Home Office, the Assistant Under-Secretary, Godfrey Lushington, considered the bill's penalties for child abuse "simply monstrous." Also outrageous in the view of Lushington and some of his colleagues was the provision that enabled a court of summary jurisdiction to deprive a parent of his child once that parent had been convicted of any offense specified by the bill. Even the Commissioner of Metropolitan Police, generally sympathetic with the aims of the society, expressed serious doubts about aspects of the measure. Taking the example of an impoverished mother reduced to begging for survival, he noted that one clause would prevent her from employing her children as fellow mendicants; yet if she left them unsupervised in their wretched home during the day, she would run afoul of the bill's neglect clause.[94]

At the committee stage on June 19, therefore, both Webster and Mundella attempted to allay fears about a wholesale assault on family privacy. Webster assured his fellow MPs that Mundella "would be very sorry indeed, under cover of any bill of the kind, to interfere with the proper and legitimate control of the parent over the child." Mundella, in turn, observed that the amendments suggested by Webster would insure the preservation of parental prerogatives. As a conciliatory gesture Mundella accepted Webster's proposal to limit the bill's application to boys under fourteen and girls under sixteen. But as soon became clear to the House, neither man would accept any compromise that threatened the fundamental objectives of the bill. Walter McLaren, the Cheshire radical, found Webster adamantly opposed to altering the definition of ill-treatment from "in a manner likely to cause . . . unnecessary suffering" to the far more restrictive "in such a manner as to have caused suffering." John Kelly (Conservative, Camberwell North), representing the National Union of Elementary Teachers, encountered similar resistance when he suggested substituting the word "unjustifiable" for "unnecessary"—a distinction that, if allowed, would have made cruelty extremely hard to prove in the courts.[95]

The bill's antagonists were nearly as persistent as its defenders, however. When debate proceeded to the street trading provisions of the first clause, Kelly again led the attack, arguing that by prohibiting children from selling in public thoroughfares at night, the bill would deal a heavy blow to the honest poor. A costermonger, he pointed out, depended on his children to look after the animal pulling his cart, or, if he owned a stationary barrow, to help with selling until eleven or twelve on certain evenings.[96] The Conservative Member for Oldham, James Maclean, considered the clause repugnant not because it threatened the poor with economic hardship but because it represented a "perfectly unnecessary interference with freedom of trade and . . . individualism." Jumping to the bill's defense, H. H. Fowler, a prominent Liberal and a member of the society, replied that free trade had nothing to do with the proposal. Only "worthless, drunken, dissolute parents who live upon the earnings of their little children" would be inconvenienced. As to the charge of disregarding the working classes, Mundella claimed to have a singular "acquaintance with the poor in regard to the employment of their children." Having left school at the age of nine to work in a printing office, he insisted that his judgment carried considerable weight. Furthermore, the recent petitions from municipalities throughout the country attested to the widespread support of city fathers for restrictions on juvenile street trading. Ultimately the restrictionists prevailed, although not without concessions. Mundella accepted the Attorney General's amendment limiting the nontrading hours to 8 P.M. to 5 A.M. in the winter and 10 P.M. to 5 A.M. in the summer.[97]

Throughout the ensuing committee sessions of June 26 and July 3, the bill continued to draw fire. Though vociferous, the opposition was disorganized. Since the measure faced sporadic attack from MPs with individual grievances rather than continuous resistance from a centrally directed lobby, its proponents, backed by the society, had a strategic advantage. Some of the resistance reflected hostility to the London SPCC itself. To insure "that care is taken before allowing irresponsible people to undertake these [cruelty] cases," William Tomlinson (Conservative, Preston) proposed that only courts be permitted to institute prosecutions. John Kelly was more direct: "All over the country the Society is trying to get up these hole-and-corner inquiries, and to induce people, under the promise that the names of the informers shall be kept quiet, to bring all sorts of charges against a most deserving class of persons—the masters and teachers in our schools." Repudiated by an indignant Mundella, these attacks did little to foment opposition and may well have discredited their makers as quarrelsome malcontents.[98]

Perhaps the best illustration of inconsistent opposition attitudes was the stance taken by Edward Pickersgill, an "advanced" Liberal

called into existence an equally intractable pro-stage party. Two years before, Barlee's book had been criticized by that master of childhood fantasy, Lewis Carroll.[107] More prosaic but also more effective, London stage managers, led by Augustus Harris of the Theatre Royal, Drury Lane, now mounted a skillful campaign to discredit the antitheater faction as misguided puritans, insensitive to the economic value of child actors to their poor families.[108] Conceivably, Commons' opposition to this one provision could have imperiled the entire bill. When, therefore, the Attorney General moved on June 26 to exempt from the first clause "premises licensed for public entertainment," Mundella was prepared to accept his amendment. Other proponents of the bill chose to fight, however. H. H. Fowler insisted that the moral evil of stage life was "indescribable." Samuel Smith lashed out ungratefully against Webster: "I think it would be a shameful thing to introduce this Amendment, and I hope the country will take notice of those who are seeking to destroy one of the most salutary provisions of the Bill." To end this acrimony Mundella appealed for a vote, adding that the London SPCC itself had failed to unearth a single case of cruelty to child actors. But his call for compromise fell on deaf ears. Webster's amendment failed.[109]

This debate continued on July 10 before the whole House. L. J. Jennings (Conservative, Stockport) protested that the new outburst of reformist fervor threatened to destroy "many of the performances and plays which have been popular with the British people for generations." What, he asked, would *A Midsummer Night's Dream* be without its "little fairies"? Still unswayed, the Commons sustained its committee's stand, although by a much narrower margin—188 votes to 139.[110] To modern eyes the question of whether children should be permitted to act the parts of shrubs and water nymphs seems slightly absurd. Yet to late Victorians the issue embodied larger social questions, not the least of which was how far social reform should interfere with traditional patterns of recreation. Christmas pantomimes were, for example, a favorite spectacle of middle-class families. The issue cut across party lines. As *The Times* noted, the inveterate radical Henry Labouchere, "apparently to his astonishment," found himself voting with the Attorney General and Sir John Gorst against prohibition, while the stolidly conservative Sir Richard Temple joined Samuel Smith and Henry Fowler in the opposing camp.[111] But more important in the context of the bill was the diversionary role of the problem. With their attention occupied by the fate of young actors, MPs probably devoted less scrutiny to the measure's truly radical provisions. Despite unrelenting opposition from a few diehards, the bill received a third reading on July 13.

The society's hopes now rested with Lord Herschell. Brought before the Lords on July 15, the bill came up for a second reading one week later. Herschell was prepared. In what was for him an unusually impassioned speech, the former Lord Chancellor depicted the measure as crucial to the control of a widespread social problem.

I confess the more I have looked into the matter the more I have been astonished and alarmed at the amount of cruelty practised in this country. If my noble Lords should have doubts upon the subject, I would ask them to read the Report of a few years' work only of the Society for the Prevention of Cruelty to Children, and they will find enough there to show, even if they discard everything which has not stood the test of a Court of Justice, that there is an evil existing which urgently calls for a remedy.[112]

With this strong introduction the bill gained a second reading and went on to the Grand Committee on Law. Here Lords Fitzgerald and Thring challenged (respectively) provisions relating to the separation of parent and child and the abolition of the oath. Representatives from the society met privately with each, persuading them to withdraw their scheduled amendments.[113] Within the Chamber, Herschell continued to remonstrate with dubious Lords. During the committee debate of August 5, the Earl of Milltown took a stubborn stand against the bill's broad search provisions. Milltown had cause for concern. Clearly, the ability of a J.P. to authorize "any person . . . *bona fide* acting in the interest of any child" to enter a private home, accompanied by a police officer, and remove from it the young person specified in the warrant, did constitute a "most startling power." Hoping for some concession, Milltown urged that the hours of entry be restricted to the daylight and early evening. But Herschell stood firm. If the Commons, as representatives of the people, "consider that it was worth while to yield up a portion of the rights of the community . . . for the sake of securing . . . [an] important end," the Lords would do well not to "stand in the way." Chastised, the Earl finally abandoned his amendment.[114]

Despite Herschell's eloquence, the August 5 Lords' committee session forced a few alterations. The most prominent casualty was the theater employment clause. Extra-parliamentary opposition to this aspect of the bill had grown even more intense during the preceding weeks. Labor unions such as the East London Sugar Workers and the Amalgamated Society of Watermen and Lightermen of the River Thames thought that the prohibition of young children from stage work was likely to inflict "great hardship" on poor families. The Liberty and Property Defense League denounced the provision as an infringement on the freedom of the subject. Mary Jeune, supervisor of a home for fallen women, assured skeptics that the theater imposed a healthy moral discipline on girls.[115] Although supported on this issue by the Archbishop of Canterbury within the Lords and by *The Times* outside Parliament, Herschell recognized the wisdom of compromise. Reluctantly, therefore, he accepted Lord Dunraven's amendment allowing children between the ages of seven and ten to perform in theaters, provided that they were licensed to do so by a magistrate. Considerably more disappointing to the London SPCC was the Lords' rejection of the right to compel parents to serve as witnesses against each other. And lastly, the Upper House extended the time that a child hawker might trade in the streets to 10 P.M. on winter nights. So altered, the bill passed its third reading in the Lords on August 9.

Back in the House of Commons, advocates of the measure realized that protracted debate over these changes would block the bill's passage until the following session. Accordingly, the original leader of the revolt against exempting theater children from the bill, Henry Fowler, now begged his fellow MPs to accept the Lords' amendment. Fowler prevailed. Thus, on August 26, after an exhausting eight-week battle, the 1889 Act for the Prevention of Cruelty to Children received the Royal Assent.

For A. J. Mundella the job of guiding the bill through Commons had been exasperating. In mid-July he promised friends "I have had such laborious and incessant difficulties, such coaxings, wheedlings, and threatenings, such negotiations, conferences and complexities, that I am vowing I will never again, as a *private* member, attempt such a task." One month later Mundella reflected bitterly on what he saw as misplaced praise for the victory:

Stead has deliberately set himself to ignore all the labor and sacrifice of Lord Herschell and myself in reference to this important measure, and to call it *Mr. Waugh's* Bill, and assume that all Mr. Waugh had to do was to draw some vague and unworkable clauses and insert them in the "Pall Mall," and they would go through Parliament in a breath. I have rarely seen anything in such bad taste as what Stead and Waugh are doing. . . . This is the sort of new journalism of which Stead is the great pioneer, and Waugh and he are *bosom friends.* They keep up a certain prurient sensationalism betwixt them. They both pose everlastingly as Christians of a new type,—they call it unconventional X'tianity, and a pretty vulgar, . . . blasphemous muddle it is.[116]

Mundella was certainly justified in resenting Waugh's abrasive self-righteousness. And insofar as full extra-parliamentary support had been withheld from the 1888 bill, Mundella also nursed a legitimate grievance against the London SPCC. But, blinded by his indignation, he underestimated the shift in public opinion that had made the measure possible in the first place.[117]

The society, of course, was jubilant. Its "Children's Charter," as the Act came to be called, was England's first attempt to deal comprehensively with the domestic relationship between parent and child. Limitations on parental power over their offspring, previously vague if defined at all, were now made explicit in a single statute. No longer would local authorities be in doubt about the will of Parliament respecting treatment of the young. But the 1889 Act did more than create new crimes; it also specified new tools for combating them. Its search provisions, which the Earl of Milltown found so menacing, were essential for penetrating that "living tomb of ill and unwanted children," the home. Nor were the terms of the Act purely negative. If a parent was convicted of cruelty, the court could now order a change of custody for the child to a relative or other "fit person"—which meant industrial schools and charitable institutions. Yet even after a child had been removed from its home, the responsible parent was liable to contribute up to five shillings per week in maintenance fees. In theory at least, parental responsibility would not cease with the departure of the victim.[118]

Exactly two months prior to final Commons' approval of the bill, child-protection advocates in the Metropolis staged their own quiet coup. On May 14, 1889, the London Society for the Prevention of Cruelty to Children officially reconstituted itself as the National Society for the Prevention of Cruelty to Children. Ever since 1884 Benjamin Waugh had envisioned "one body with eyes and fingers everywhere to see and touch the cases." Now, five years later, his dream seemed the logical next step for an organization that controlled 32 provincial aid committees and was in the process of forming seven more. With ten inspectors to handle an ever-growing caseload, financed by nearly £4,000 gathered from 7,122 subscribers, the NSPCC was preparing to administer the law which it had brought before Parliament.[119] Across the Channel, French lawmakers had also just passed legislation designed to curb the power of parents whose misconduct threatened the safety, health, or morality of their offspring. The French law of 1889 was to be financed by contributions from the state, the departments, the communes, and private donors.[120] But in England neither central nor local government was to fund the highly sensitive task of policing family life. Left to bear the brunt of this work, the NSPCC would at times earn more criticism than thanks.

The Reverend Benjamin Waugh, chief administrator of the National Society for the Prevention of Cruelty to Children from 1884 to 1905. Under Waugh's supervision, the NSPCC became the world's largest child-protection agency. *Courtesy: NSPCC Archives.*

One of the many NSPCC placards posted throughout urban and rural districts. By 1900 the society had established 812 branches and aid committees in England, Wales, and Ireland. *Courtesy: NSPCC Archives.*

A "cruelty man" poses with a victim of severe parental neglect. Distinguishing between criminal neglect and the ravages of poverty was often difficult, making the NSPCC inspector's job a sensitive one. *Courtesy: NSPCC Archives.*

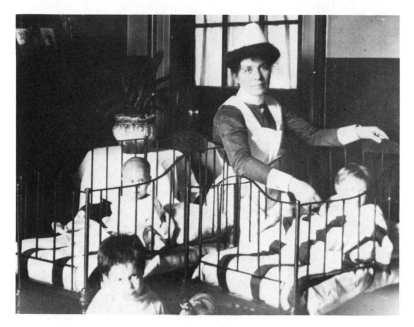

In the shelter of the Liverpool SPCC. Although England's anticruelty groups were reluctant to assume custody of injured children, a "place of safety" was sometimes essential for youngsters whose parents awaited prosecution. *Courtesy: NSPCC Archives.*

These sad-eyed Liverpool children testified to the urgency of anticruelty work. *Courtesy: NSPCC Archives.*

Before-and-after photographs, often used to advertise Dr. Barnardo's Homes, also figured in NSPCC propaganda. This particular pair appeared in the NSPCC's annual report for 1890–91. *Courtesy: NSPCC Archives.*

"THESE ARE *MY* JEWELS."

This 1890 cartoon from *Punch* dramatized one of the child-savers' most
frequent arguments: "Burial Insurance comes / As a boon unto the slums. /
The insurance love may fix / At five pounds, or even six; / A child's funeral
costs a pound, / And the balance means—drinks round!"

These Liverpool "street arabs" may have been too poorly educated to enjoy the *Boy's Own Paper* advertised behind them. *Courtesy: NSPCC Archives.*

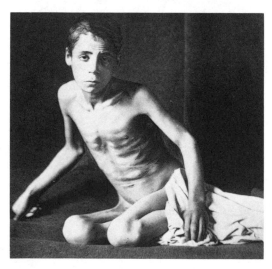

Aptly entitled "Famine," this NSPCC photograph was fashioned into a postcard and used to prick the public conscience. *Courtesy: NSPCC Archives.*

A Liverpool victim of parental assault. *Courtesy: NSPCC Archives.*

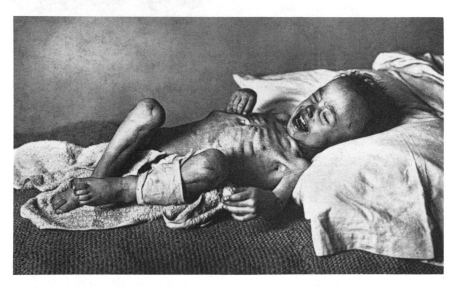

"From a Baby Farm" makes plain the hazards of professional adoption. *Courtesy: NSPCC Archives.*

SAVED FOR THE STATE.

HUMANITY. "GIVE THE CHILD TO ME."

Punch applauded the juvenile court system proposed in the 1908 Children's Bill. Edwardian legislators recognized that the protection of English children was a matter of national "efficiency."

CHAPTER 5

Philanthropy under Fire

Eнglish philanthropists concerned about child abuse derived moral as well as legal support from the 1889 Act. By its very presence on the statute books, the Children's Charter served to make legitimate what was still a controversial experiment in social reform. This aura of propriety cast by law upon the NSPCC's anticruelty campaign proved critically important throughout the 1890's, a period in which Benjamin Waugh's war on parental sin seriously compromised the child-protection movement. Danger threatened on two fronts. First, the NSPCC all but exhausted its fund of public goodwill by pressing an ill-conceived attack against the practice of child life insurance. Second, charges of administrative incompetence brought against the society by some of its own personnel called into question the organizational integrity of the whole anticruelty network. Though the advocates of child protection secured further legal safeguards for the young during the 1890's, too often the issue of children's rights was obscured by disputes over the style and method of reform.

The Politics of Mourning

Nowhere were the aims of the child-savers more thoroughly mired in debate over means than in connection with the insurance of young lives. When Waugh committed the London SPCC to abolishing "premiums on death" in 1888, he was resuscitating a debate that had raged sporadically for over forty years. This debate centered on what Edwin Chadwick called "the strongest and most widely-diffused feeling" among the English working classes, "the desire to secure respectful interment of themselves and their relations."[1] Chadwick's 1843 report on burial practices in towns set the pattern for bourgeois criticism of the working-class celebration of death. The poor, it seemed, spent far too much on their funerals. According to the information obtained by Chadwick and his fellow investigators, the cost of an adult artisan's funeral averaged about £4. This sum generally provided for a good, strong elm coffin, bearers to carry the corpse to the grave, a pall, and fittings for mourners. Additional charges for ground and burial fees could drive the total figure up to £5, more than a great many laboring men earned in a month.[2] That large numbers of the poor tried to avoid this potentially ruinous expense by subscribing to burial clubs was, middle-class critics allowed, prudent in the abstract. But burial insurance did nothing to counteract the wanton extravagance of the funeral rites themselves. Samuel Smiles, the Victorian high priest of thrift, cited John Wesley's will as a model of common sense in the face of death. If, like Wesley, the English worker adjured his family to permit "no pomp, except the tears of those that love [him]," then the cost of respectable burial would not require insurance in the first place.[3]

The poor, of course, were not unique in their fondness for elaborate funerals. Phillipe Ariès's characterization of the nineteenth century as an era of "hysterical mourning" applies particularly well to Victorian England.[4] Due in part to the idealization of family life and in part to lengthened life expectancy, survivors came to accept the deaths of friends and relatives with greater difficulty than in the past. Thus during the nineteenth century a perceptible shift in the social view of death became generalized to the extent that even where genuine sorrow did not exist, the convention of public grief encouraged people to stage lavish funerals. The obsequies of the Victorian elite hardly dampened public enthusiasm for conspicuous mourning; few of the estimated one and a half million people who gazed upon the Duke of Wellington's ten-ton bronze and silver funeral car could have interpreted the show as a plea for simplicity.

At the opposite end of the social scale, death rites carried no less symbolic weight.[5] A working-class family that dispensed with black mourning dress invited neighborhood censure. Even the absence of black crepe trim on shawls and bonnets could be interpreted as disrespect for the dead, or worse, as a niggardly attempt to economize on the occasion of a family's most important public ceremony. Among the poor, the state of mind called "mourning" was perfectly

compatible with—indeed often demanded—some show of household generosity such as a funeral feast held directly before or after
the burial.[6] Above all else, however, one aim obsessed those of
slender means—to avoid a pauper's funeral. Not only "the power of
Mrs. Grundy," as Samuel Smiles put it, but also the determination
to secure some scrap of independence underlay the funeral pomp of
the poor. "Rattle his bones over the stones, / He's only a pauper
whom nobody owns." Thomas Noel's formula stressed that to die
bereft of a caring community was the ultimate badge of failure.[7]
Moreover, the fate that pauper corpses met in some of England's
old city graveyards reinforced this aversion to burial by the parish.
In mid-century London, slum houses looked out on cemeteries
where bits of pauper skull, scalp, and clothing protruded from
earth that felt greasy because of the mass of putrefying flesh it held.[8]
The custom of insuring against burial expenses was, therefore, a rational attempt to introduce an element of dignity into working-class
lives.

Children, though less expensive to bury than adults, required
their own form of funeral insurance. Coverage for children could be
obtained through the same clubs in which their parents were enrolled. However, the notorious financial instability of these clubs
encouraged parents to buy multiple policies, particularly on the
young, for whom insurance premiums might run as low as a penny
per week. To Edwin Chadwick and many social critics after him, it
seemed that duplicate policies on the lives of children earned re-
imbursements that were greater than the actual cost of a funeral,
thereby sweetening the "temptation for evil." In extreme cases—for
example, the Manchester man who enrolled his baby in nineteen
different burial societies—Chadwick cautioned that the reward for
a child's death could serve as "a bounty on neglectual infanticide."[9]
Middle-class sentimentality about the deaths of children clearly
prejudiced some reformers against "infantile assurance"; indeed, a
generation that had anguished over the fates of Little Nell and Paul
Dombey would naturally have regarded the admixture of profit and
tragedy as repellent. The occasional real-life horror story only substantiated prejudices against this form of working-class self-help.
Appended to Chadwick's 1843 report was a long letter from Henry
Coppock, the Town Clerk of Stockport, detailing two cases of parents tried for killing their liberally insured offspring. On exhuma-
tion, the body of Robert Standring's teenage daughter showed clear

signs of arsenic poisoning. Despite this damning circumstantial evidence, Standring went free. Less fortunate was Robert Sandys, a mat maker who was transported for life after a postmortem proved that his two little girls had likewise been poisoned.[10]

Shaken by the "appalling facts" unearthed in Stockport, Dr. Lyon Playfair undertook an investigation of 232 burial societies. The financial records of these societies revealed that adults had received an average of £8 12s. toward funeral expenses for each enrolled child, as against an average interment cost of £2. The death of a working-class child was so commonly a source of surplus cash, Playfair found, that an expected death was often brought forward as a plea for delay in the collection of rates.[11] John Clay, the outspoken prison chaplain at Preston, also feared for the safety of insured children, but unlike Playfair, he was not content to quote statistics. Just as Clay never ceased vilifying publicans as the archenemies of working-class respectability, so he maintained that "in hundreds of thousands of instances" the prospect of burial money created "direct and powerful inducements to parental neglect and cruelty."[12] Clay was skilled at kindling public outrage. In the autumn of 1848, for example, English newspaper readers learned of the so-called Essex poisonings. *The Times* was particularly disturbed to find that the murder of children for their burial premiums could occur outside the conurbations of Lancashire.

We are forced to admit the existence of a state of things in real life more terrible than the imaginative horrors of the modern school of French novelists. . . . As you pass through a country village in England, and see the children playing in the sunshine, can the mind admit the conviction that in many instances they are predoomed to a lingering and painful destruction; that the blooming cheek must soon grow pale, the rounded form be worn down by an emaciating fire from within, and the changing expression of childhood give way to the monotonous aspect of death, and all this will be the work of their parents' hands?

In a soothing note to *The Times*, Tidd Pratt, since 1829 the Chief Registrar of Friendly Societies, assured citizens that no insurance could legally be purchased on the life of a child under six years old. Pratt's words might have calmed public concern about a secret slaughter of the innocents had Clay not countered with an anxiety-provoking gem. Recounting such heinous acts as that of John Rodda, the Yorkshire "wretch" who spoonfed his baby sulphuric acid,

Clay's long letter of January 18, 1849, intensified the infant insurance scare.[13]

As new exposés of parental malignity came to light, the case for legislative action grew stronger. In mid-1848, Mary May, convicted of poisoning her brother, reportedly mounted the scaffold at Chelmsford muttering "If I were to tell all I know, it would give the hangman work for the next twelve months." Since Mrs. May had produced fourteen children, all of whom died after sudden illnesses, this allusion made hideous sense. England's lawmakers evidently agreed with Joseph Kay "that a great part of the poorer classes [had] sunk into . . . a frightful depth of hopelessness," for in August 1850 Parliament passed legislation (13 & 14 Vic., c. 115) that prohibited burial insurance in excess of £3 on any child under the age of ten.[14] More importantly, the Act stipulated that all death benefits be paid directly to the undertaker. The sensationalist approach to social reform seemed to have borne fruit.

But the gains of the early campaign against child life insurance proved fleeting. The legislation of 1850 was experimental, intended to stay in force for one year only. Soon Clay was back lobbying politicians to approve a permanent ban.[15] Unfortunately, this renewed assault on burial insurance suffered from a dearth of solid evidence. When in 1854 the House of Commons requested a list of persons tried during the previous decade for the murder of children who were members of burial societies, MPs found that neither the Record of Trials nor the Clerks of Assize could supply the desired information. Not only were the documented cases involving parental mistreatment for profit rare, but even some of the celebrated horror stories were irrelevant to the issue. At the time of Mary May's trial, for instance, there were no burial clubs near her home in Essex that admitted children under fourteen as members. A monster she may have been; but she did not profit from the deaths of her young.[16]

Still, political luminaries such as Lords Palmerston, Stanley, and Shaftesbury were sufficiently disturbed by continuing allegations of foul play in connection with burial clubs that Parliament in 1854 appointed a select committee to review a proposed friendly societies bill. Testimony taken by this committee revealed two particularly sensitive issues. Burial society representatives insisted that a maximum coverage of £3 on a child's life would preclude decent working-class burials. For this reason, they argued, laboring men should be allowed to insure their offspring in more than one society, or else the maximum coverage should be increased, both of which options struck reformers as invitations to mayhem. Furthermore, friendly society spokesmen stressed the hostility of England's working classes to the proposed "undertaker's clause." Legislation that barred the poor from conducting the last rites for their own children was insulting, and would, these spokesmen predicted, result in a mass defection of laborers from provident institutions.[17] Both these objections to the stricter regulation of child life insurance implied that the proponents of control were insensitive, even hostile, to traditional working-class culture. Clay and like-minded critics had softened their case by emphasizing the unconscious predisposition of parents to neglect their insured children; but they had no ready response to the charge of class hostility. Not surprisingly, the select committee concluded that the murder of children was not demonstrably linked with burial insurance, and so recommended only minor modifications in the law.*

What neither the defenders nor the critics of life insurance for children could know was that their quarrel had only begun to take shape. Following passage of the 1855 Friendly Societies Act, the mainstays of the prohibition movement—Chadwick, Playfair, and Clay—retreated into comparative silence on the subject.[18] In their place arose a less prominent although probably more influential coterie of reformers, nearly all of them medical men. The Lancet assured doctors in 1861 that the "excited cupidity" of parents who had entered their children in several burial clubs remained a "large and perpetually active cause of infant mortality." England's leading medical journal left no doubt that the fatal effects of policies on children were "very palpable and horrible."[19] Yet doctors too conjured up evil from exceedingly thin evidence. "Is there not a temptation for certain persons to enter their children at a dozen societies?" asked one medical correspondent. The answer was, of course, yes; and further, for multiple coverage to benefit a poor parent, death "must cease to be a speculation—it must be a certainty."[20] Presumably at some point of potential gain the nurturing

* Section ten of the Friendly Societies Act of 1855 (18 & 19 Vic., c. 65) raised the legal coverage to £6 for a child under five, and to £10 for a child between five and ten. The requirement that burial payments could not be made without a death certificate signed by a qualified medical practitioner gave the reformers their only cause for encouragement.

instinct had to give way to a brutal preoccupation with hard cash. That very few examples could be adduced to confirm such suspicions did little to check the vehemence of some doctors. A *Lancet* article of 1865 denouncing child insurance dwelt on the case of Mrs. James Brown of Plymouth. So eager was she to collect the £14 burial policy on her husband that she had placed the starved but still breathing man in a coffin. Luckily his feeble cries alerted a lodger before Mrs. Brown could nail down the lid. The implication of the case was clear: if spouses could kill one another for financial gain, they could surely be tempted to kill helpless children.[21]

The pronouncements of English doctors helped fuel periodic attacks on juvenile burial insurance during the late 1860's and early 1870's. Tenuous as the evidence may have been, medical men were correct to point out that haphazard certification of death gave wide scope to the commission of violence against the young.[22] Of more immediate interest to laymen, however, was the knowledge that the burial societies themselves were undergoing a troubling transformation. At the beginning of the century, local friendly societies had defrayed funeral costs either by making irregular contributions to survivors or by providing a fixed sum taken from a central fund. Where friendly societies limited their functions to providing burial benefits, they often teetered on the edge of insolvency.[23] Larger clubs, administered by professionals rather than working men, promised greater stability. As a result, mid-Victorian England witnessed the rise of burial societies wherein the mutual-aid ideal gave way to an obsession with growth and profit. By the late 1860's even some of the local burial societies enrolled between twenty and fifty thousand members, many of them children.[24] But working men bent on avoiding the disgrace of a pauper funeral were turning to still larger institutions known as collecting societies. A few of these, most notably the Royal Liver and the Liverpool Victoria Legal, claimed well over a hundred thousand members, were national in scope, and remunerated their managers handsomely. Many collecting societies, according to Tidd Pratt, dragged their feet when it came to settling disputed claims. And nearly all such institutions gathered subscriptions and solicited new members by sending paid agents, aptly called "touts," from house to house on a regular basis.[25]

Large burial and collecting societies thus fell far short of the benevolent ideal. Gladstone, when Chancellor of the Exchequer, felt obliged to offer the working classes a sounder insurance scheme.

Distressed by the high proportion of policies that lapsed because their holders received no schedule of payments from the issuing companies, he pressed Parliament in 1864 to pass a bill allowing the Post Office to administer life insurance. Although the resulting plan (27 & 28 Vic., c. 43) eliminated commission-hunting collectors, it failed to attract laboring men because its minimum policy (£20) was too dear.[26] Four years later Lord Lichfield introduced a bill in the Upper House that struck directly at the burial societies themselves. Perhaps most sweeping was the bill's third section, which barred children under seven from membership in a friendly society. The reaction from the private sector was shrill. Accusing the government of "a cunning attempt . . . to rob the poor of their independence," Liverpool's great burial societies turned collectors into propagandists and besieged Parliament with well-paid lobbyists.[27] Lord Lichfield eventually withdrew his bill, but sufficient doubt had been cast on the operation of funeral insurance to render the issue a major concern of the Royal Commission on Friendly Societies, appointed in 1870.

Significantly, it was Sir Stafford Northcote who presided over the royal commission's three-year study. Having developed a keen interest in child welfare through his association with the reformatory and industrial schools movement, this eminent Tory now confronted a problem whose dimensions could not be accurately gauged through statistics.[28] Instead, judgment had to be based on inference. That the mortality rate for children in heavily insured Liverpool jumped inexplicably during the second year of life, "precisely within the year when infants can first come into full insurance benefit," thus impressed the commissioners as strong circumstantial evidence against such policies. To err on the side of public safety seemed most prudent.[29] As a result, one of the 46 recommendations urged by Northcote and his associates was the prohibition of insurance on the lives of the very young. But largely because of renewed pressure from burial societies, this guideline emerged in the Friendly Societies Act of 1875 (38 & 39 Vic., c. 60) as ceilings of £10 and £6 on the lives of children under ten and five respectively. Plainly the impact of such a law would be modest; depraved parents still had some incentive to destroy their offspring.[30]

For a decade following the 1875 Act, child life insurance drew intermittent fire from critics. George Sims, a London journalist with an eye for the sensational, contributed an unusually imaginative version of the road to domestic hell. In his fictional account, Mrs. Joyce, the wife of a mechanic, places a bottle of "linerment" next to the bed of her youngest. At the ensuing inquest a verdict of accidental poisoning is returned, and the family pockets £6 of the £10 insurance award. Some months later Mrs. Joyce shoves her drunken husband down a flight of stairs, nets £20, and uses the money to start a greengrocery business. Fanciful as Sims's tale seems now, it had the ring of plausibility about it at a time when the practice of child life insurance was spreading.[31] This was in large part due to the phenomenal growth of "industrial assurance," a field dominated by one firm, the Prudential. A joint stock company and, therefore, excluded from friendly society status, the "Pru" by 1886 nevertheless had 7,111,828 policies in force, producing an annual income in excess of £3,000,000. At least 25 percent of its policies covered children under the age of ten.[32] Although thorough bookkeeping and comparatively efficient supervision of collectors had earned the Prudential a reputation for sound management, the very scale of its business was a source of concern for the child-protection movement.

The interests of child-savers and burial societies collided with full force in mid-1888. Benjamin Waugh and the London SPCC provoked this collision, confident that a large reservoir of reform sympathy stood ready to be tapped.[33] Among anticruelty groups the Liverpool SPCC had been the first to focus on the problem. In February the society's executive appointed a thirteen-member committee, headed by T. F. A. Agnew and Clarke Aspinall (the Liverpool city coroner), to investigate rumors of insurance-related abuse. Although it would not go so far as a nearby medical officer of health in branding collectors "death men," the committee found that a disturbingly high proportion of children suffocated by their parents had been insured.[34] The London SPCC exercised less restraint when it aired its views in May. The society's *Fourth Annual Report* rued the inability of law to control "this gambling in little human things." To counter the impression "that moneymaking out of children is safe as well as a right . . . thing," the London SPCC attached to its omnibus anticruelty bill a clause specifying double prison terms for convicted child abusers with direct monetary interests in the death of their young.[35]

Aggressive as these pronouncements were, the storm did not break until midsummer. On July 11, while testifying before the

Lords' Select Committee on Poor Law Administration, Waugh observed that child life insurance was "simply ruining the country." Shortly afterward the London SPCC leader warned that a thousand children were murdered every winter in London. This totally undocumented claim was the fruit of frustration rather than an attempt to mislead. Informed by the Earl of Strafford that the society's anticruelty bill probably would not pass during the current parliamentary session, Waugh had simply lashed out with the most arresting "fact" he could muster.[36] Unfortunately, many people construed his claim literally. The *Pall Mall Gazette* questioned his "process of deduction." Other journals, particularly those tied to the insurance business, were far less charitable. Mincing no words, the *Insurance Guardian* demanded "evidence . . . in the name of the thrifty parents amongst the industrial classes . . . upon whom this foul aspersion has been thoughtlessly cast."[37]

Prior to the passage of the Children's Charter, anticruelty groups could not devote their full energies to the life insurance fray. But support from without nevertheless helped to blunt attacks on Waugh and his society. No less an authority than the Chief Registrar of Friendly Societies, J. M. Ludlow, assured Parliament that the prospect of burial money "dangled" before parents served to intensify infant mortality.[38] Periodicals such as the *Hospital* piqued public interest by castigating the "monsters" who killed their children and the "tempters" who made it profitable to do so. Letters to *The Times* told of homicidal mothers and unscrupulous collectors, one of whom allegedly swooped down on a Berkshire village during a measles epidemic.[39] The London SPCC was in fact sufficiently impressed with the strength of public sentiment that it announced in October 1888 its commitment to the total abolition of insurance on young lives.[40]

The opposition, however, proved fierce. At their most conciliatory, insurance journals admitted the existence of rogue collectors or blamed drink as the cause of rare abuse.[41] More often they sought to humiliate critics. How could a charge of wholesale murder be levied against England's self-sacrificing working class, asked the *Insurance Guardian*. After all, "Baby is [the poor woman's] only treasure, and on it she lavishes a wealth of affection that is a beautiful illustration of the finer emotions . . . common to humanity." As for those who assailed child insurance, they were either sensationalist fools or, like Waugh, possessed "ill-balanced minds."[42]

What mattered most about these attacks was not the invective itself but the weight of opinion behind it. Certainly the government wanted no part of a campaign against the rich insurance industry.[43]

Because such powerful vested interests were involved, the 1889 select committee on industrial insurance companies asked its witnesses to give evidence under oath. Waugh was hamstrung. Having gleaned his data from inspectors' reports rather than from attendance at trials and inquests, he could only state the London SPCC's "impressions." Thus Waugh testified that neighbors rarely gave evidence against parents because "bad cases [took] place where the people [were] all much-of-a-muchness"; and those who insured their young for unethical purposes tended to be "loafers."[44] According to his enemies, Waugh had proven himself utterly incompetent. Yet unconvincing as he may have appeared, the select committee did not dismiss the possible hazards of burial insurance. On the contrary, the carelessness with which some doctors granted death certificates—occasionally several for a single child—encouraged foul play by parents. At the very least, medical certificates of death should specify the ages and illnesses of all insured children.[45]

Some legislators could not wait for the select committee's report. On May 23, A. D. Provand introduced a bill to ban all juvenile policies issued by industrial assurance companies. Cosponsored by six other MPs, including London SPCC advocates Samuel Smith and Sir Robert Fowler, this rather crude cure never gained a second reading.[46] A more carefully organized reform effort might have succeeded, however, for growing numbers of medical men and judges were lending their prestige to the cause.[47] Among the converts, none was better known than William Magee, the Bishop of Peterborough. Nineteen years earlier Magee had incensed the temperance movement when he declared it was "better that England should be free than . . . compulsorily sober." A second controversy greeted an 1879 speech in which he defended the practice of vivisection. No sane man could call him sentimental, and only a fool would deny his political acumen. Magee was, therefore, the ideal person to take charge of the NSPCC's child life insurance bill.[48]

Brought before the Lords on May 20, 1890, this measure took direct aim at the burial societies. It not only limited death payments on boys under fourteen and girls under sixteen, but also required that monies be paid directly to the person conducting the funeral. For knowingly accepting bogus death certificates or making excessive payments, burial societies risked £50 fines, and their agents faced prison terms of up to three months.[49] Some of the NSPCC's allies balked at the prospect of supporting such a severe bill. The *Lancet*, for one, predicted that the funeral clause would only encourage collusion between parents and undertakers. Scottish anticruelty groups attacked the measure for failing to differentiate adequately between friendly and collecting societies, while, even closer to home, the NSPCC's own Leeds branch committee felt that the amounts allowed for child burial were too small.[50] Yet in London, Waugh's conviction that the death merchants would be toppled in "an avalanche of doom" had blinded reformers to these cracks in their base of support.

Increasingly, backers of the NSPCC's child insurance bill pinned their hopes on Magee and his oratorical power. In a lengthy speech of June 16, Magee waxed dramatic: "Parents have been heard more than once to say of a dead or dying child, 'Now we shall have a little funeral and a big drink.' My Lords, I state the whole case for the Bill in that one sentence. I want to stop these little funerals and big drinks."[51] After its second reading, however, the measure went before a select committee, of which Bishop Magee as chairman could do little besides ask leading questions. As in previous parliamentary probes, some of the testimony cast doubt on the safety of the child insurance system, particularly with regard to the conduct of collectors. Paid a commission on the weekly premiums they brought in, plus a bonus for every new policy sold, the touts had never enjoyed much social esteem; even well-managed burial societies admitted to prizing persistence over "intelligence and education" in their agents. "Making a book" demanded a great deal of door-to-door drudgery and might also involve physical risk, since, as in Liverpool, ambitious men sought new members among the "most squalid, unhealthy, and dangerous" neighborhoods. But once compiled, an agent's book served as his financial map. Sir Stafford Northcote's Royal Commission on Friendly Societies had found that books surveying large working-class districts could fetch sums as high as £1,000.[52] Given these stakes, agents from rival companies sometimes went beyond persistence in their work. The chief constable of Rotherham noted that local touts paid wet nurses and midwives in order to get early notice of prospective customers. Agents in many areas failed to make proper medical inquiries before accepting a child, or misled their companies about its state of health. And even

where collectors abided by the law, one judge insisted, their unwholesome equation of childhood and death could not fail to "de-
moralise" poor parents.[53]

Balanced against the glaring sins of some collectors was the reality that burial insurance for working-class children had become a
norm. As of the 1881 census, there were 6,668,260 children under
the age of ten in England and Wales. Of this number the Prudential
alone insured 2,099,369, or nearly one-third of the age group. De-
ducting roughly 25 percent of the 1881 census figure "for children
belonging to classes who would not insure," the Prudential's Man-
ager, T. C. Dewey, estimated that of the remaining 5,000,000, a
total of 4,149,369 were enrolled in some death benefit plan. Dewey's estimate was inflated to the extent that it did not allow for
multiple policies on a single life. Even so, his point held: when a
working-class child died, surprise should have been expressed only
if it was found to be uninsured.[54] Some burial societies did pander
to "the dissolute." True also, parents occasionally received small
"goodwill" payments even when their offspring had died before
coming into benefit. These gratuities served the burial firms, Waugh
argued, "as ribbons and dresses in his window [served] a draper."[55]
But what were the alternatives? As more than one witness predicted, ending the system of child insurance would only revive
"friendly leads" and "slate clubs" whose hit-or-miss hat-passing
often took place over beer in local pubs.[56]

What emerged most clearly from the evidence was the depth of
working-class hostility to Magee's bill. Ever since the 1840's the di-
rectors of burial societies had played upon Parliament's concern for
the "mood" of the respectable poor. Now laboring men were making their own angry sounds. On June 16, representatives of the Ancient Order of Foresters, a benevolent body claiming nearly two
million members, sent their strongly worded protest to the Upper
House.[57] Soon thereafter the select committee learned that the
undertakers' clause had enraged laboring men in Lancashire. Magee pressed witnesses to explain why his bill should be deemed a
"slander" on the industrious poor, a tactic that elicited only evasive
answers in committee and redoubled opposition from friendly societies and labor clubs on the outside.[58] How much this working-
class protest was shaped by the great burial societies is difficult to
judge. The Child's Guardian asserted that "legions" of touts had
gone "house to house canvassing against the Bishop's bill, misrepre-

senting him and his supporters and objects; and . . . getting up class meetings."[59] Few links between the interests of big capital and working-class self-expression could have been more effective than the insurance agent. The Prudential alone employed at least 10,000 collectors; overall as many as 16,000 of these "pushing, active men" combed poor neighborhoods each week.[60] What portion of time agents spent proselytizing parents and whether they personally arranged local protest meetings are not clear from published records. Unquestionably, however, the resulting din from working-class districts forced Magee to withdraw the undertaker's clause.

By midsummer 1890, the Lords' select committee still had not finished its deliberations. Magee's bill had run out of time, but the door remained open for its reintroduction in the next parliamentary session. Publicly at least child-savers expressed confidence in the moral vision of the electorate.[61] But to hasten the predicted outpouring of social conscience, NSPCC strategists thought it wise to print a special supplement to the *Child's Guardian*. Featuring four closely printed pages of testimony from doctors, coroners, judges, Poor Law officials, and policemen, all of whom were critical of child life insurance, the supplement seemed to distill the essence of expert opinion. Appended was a grim cartoon from *Punch* showing an evil hag gloating over the death throes of her two offspring. The cartoon and the testimony fed one another; "fact" and melodrama coalesced around the figure of the hollow-cheeked child. As the insurance press had correctly noted, however, most of the NSPCC's experts offered impressions rather than facts. For example, when a coroner began to view insurance money as a possible motivation for child abuse, his inquests could become interrogations. Subjected to a barrage of leading questions, a mother who had accidentally overlain her baby might well hesitate to discuss its burial arrangements. To the coroner, however, her reticence simply confirmed his tendency to see cause and effect. Thus reinforced in his opinions, the coroner would warn local health and law enforcement officials of the "menace" threatening their community.[62] And since both doctors and laymen were already embarrassed by what they regarded as an excessive infant mortality rate, such a warning offered a convenient focus for their reform energies.[63]

It took a concerted effort by England's insurance lobby to slow the momentum of reform. An article published in the *Fortnightly Review* late in 1890 did considerable damage to the child-savers'

cause. Captain Pembroke Marshall, with obvious but unacknowl-
edged help from the Prudential, attacked the reformers at their
most vulnerable point—Waugh and his wild rhetoric. To classify
goodwill payments on lapsed policies as "dead-baby bait" was
grossly misleading, Marshall pointed out; after all, the Prudential
realized a slim 2 percent profit on its juvenile insurance trade. Nor
did statistics bear out the much-discussed link between insurance
and high infant mortality rates. The alleged "universal impression"
of coroners, doctors, and judges notwithstanding, young children
covered by Prudential policies died *less* frequently than the standard life tables would predict. But worst of all, both Waugh and his
hardheaded Bishop had made fools of themselves before the Lords'
select committee. On one occasion, Marshall observed, Magee had
become so muddled in his questioning of T. C. Dewey that the other
committee members felt obliged to clear the room.* Spurred on perhaps by Marshall's example, other insurance companies mounted
their own, more local campaigns. At Accrington the Pearl Insurance
Company's district superintendent cited Waugh's now-infamous
"slanders" as reason enough for barring the NSPCC from that part
of the north.[64] What the society needed at this point was a convincing defense.

That defense never materialized. In the first place, Waugh's retort
to Marshall was less than persuasive. Perhaps, he asserted, juvenile
policies really did "pay" if they helped Prudential agents to recruit
entire households. Similarly, even if the Registrar General's figures
did not show a correlation between insurance and high infant mortality, the correlation could still exist. Without any doubt, however,
Marshall's remarks had been "unjust and unmanly," written at the
bidding of great commercial interests.[65] Next, a new Lords' select
committee, appointed in January 1891 to weigh the society's re-
vived bill, did more harm than good to the reformers' cause. The

* Pembroke Marshall, "Child Life Insurance: A Reply to the Rev. Benjamin
Waugh," *Fortnightly Review*, n.s. 48 (December 1890), 839, 845, 847. Precisely
why Magee, a man renowned for his hatred of exaggeration and misdirected enthusiasm, should have allied himself with Waugh is puzzling. A letter written to J. C.
MacDonnell on June 25, 1890, hints that Magee saw the child insurance dispute as
his opportunity for regaining the political center stage. After defeating the Earl of
Beauchamp on a matter of committee procedure, he declared: "First round. B—
knocked out of time, & a good omen for the future. . . . But I must be very cautious
and courteous. . . . 'Noble lords' do not like other 'noble lords' being sat upon by
bishops." John Cotter MacDonnell, *The Life and Correspondence of William Connor Magee, Archbishop of York* (1896), II, 288–89.

NSPCC hoped that the testimony of several former collecting society touts would at last validate most of the assertions for which Waugh had been blasted. Edwin Niness, once a Prudential agent in Leeds, began auspiciously. He assured the committee that insurance had tended to promote child neglect in "hundreds of cases within his experience." More impressive still, Niness could state that unscrupulous doctors sometimes falsified death certificates at the request of agents. He himself had procured such a document. The committee was momentarily stunned. Niness had all but accused a physician of criminal malpractice; he would, therefore, have to give evidence under oath. When the ex-agent balked at this requirement, Magee had no choice but to strike his evidence from the record. Faced with similar treatment or, worse, with the prospect of a trial for perjury at which the "whole Bar" would be ranged against them, three more ex-agents changed their minds about testifying.[66] The NSPCC's cause was not to be vindicated. When Magee, now Archbishop of York, died on May 5, his bill died with him. The suggestion that Waugh should stop playing Don Quixote among insurance windmills seemed good counsel.[67]

Although the parliamentary inquiries of 1890–91 had seriously undermined the NSPCC's case against child insurance, the society kept its fight alive for another four years. Certain sections of the English public still looked to Waugh and his society for leadership in this campaign. Worried by reports of doctors granting illegal death certificates, the medical press favored legislative action both as a boon to child life and as a new tool with which to police the profession.[68] If the NSPCC wanted to press still another bill, however, something would have to be done to silence the cries of class prejudice. Conveniently enough, the society disclosed a "striking fact" in its next annual report: "that, amongst those working men who insure for their children's burials in their own mutual clubs, the Society has not had *one single case* of cruel treatment of an insured child. Yet of those persons who insure in the collecting societies it had last year to interfere in 5,509 cases."[69] What distinguished these two systems, the NSPCC argued, was the size of the prize on a child's death. Well-established affiliated orders such as the Odd Fellows, the Foresters, and the Hearts of Oak, typically granted average maximum payments of £2 for each child under ten years of age. The great collecting companies, by contrast, were pleased to pay the legal limit of £6, provided that parents had kept current with their weekly premiums. Perhaps if the Prudential and its competitors could be forced to conform to the "mutual" custom in this respect, child neglect would diminish appreciably.

England's Lord Chief Justice, Sir Richard Webster, was sufficiently impressed with this logic to sponsor the NSPCC's third child insurance bill. Presented to the Commons in May 1895, the measure had a predictably chilly reception. This time the reformers' threat to "well established and wealthy . . . offices," as the insurance lobby described itself, warranted a public address to the infantry. "This is a crisis," declared one trade paper, "in which the industrial agents throughout the country should arouse themselves as one man to oppose so monstrous a 'fad.'"[70] Both the touts in the field and the lobbyists in London heeded this call to arms, for the resulting furor caused Sir Richard to withdraw his bill, convinced Home Office officials that legislation on the subject was foolhardy, and, finally, persuaded the NSPCC that the battle could not be won.[71]

During the 1896 parliamentary session, separate measures dealing with friendly societies (59 & 60 Vic., c. 25) and industrial insurance (59 & 60 Vic., c. 26) left the law on children's policies virtually unchanged. Unencumbered by new restrictions, the large collecting societies kept on growing rapidly until, by 1905, England's three largest firms had approximately two million members apiece. The Prudential likewise maintained its near-monopoly of industrial insurance. According to Seebohm Rowntree's census of York in 1899, 40 Prudential men, 35 agents of other collecting societies, and 10 part-time touts canvassed a wage-earning population of approximately 51,000.[72] Doctors and public health workers, at the same time, continued to warn of a causal tie between burial policies and chronic child neglect. But these early twentieth-century reformers, like their Victorian predecessors, accomplished very little. Having brought remedial measures before Parliament 64 times in the years 1875—1905, the foes of child insurance were remarkable above all for their doggedness.[73]

The NSPCC's obsessive interest in the problem requires some explanation. Other hazards to child life, hazards with clearer statistical dimensions, were waiting to be addressed. The Registrar General's annual reports, for example, showed an alarming increase in the number of babies suffocated in bed. Between 1881 and 1890, the number of infants under one year old who suffocated rose from 130 per 1,000,000 live births to 174. Surely the NSPCC could have used its reform energies more profitably by tackling the problem of overlying? Yet infant suffocation, "an obviously preventable form of death" according to one medical expert, could not easily be separated from the broader subject of parental drunkenness, and the temperance issue was a morass from which the society had so far kept a safe distance.[74]

The child insurance issue was compelling because it seemed reducible to simple terms: rich burial societies dangling gold in front of poor parents, resulting in misery and death for children. Waugh and his backers had not been the first to take this view, nor were Englishmen unique in debating the dangers of burial money. Industrial insurance came to the United States in 1875, when John F. Dryden organized the Prudential of America. In America, as in England, this business grew fast, with fifteen companies holding a total of twelve million policies by 1902.[75] And with the rise of industrial insurance went demands for its prohibition in the case of children. In 1884 and 1889 the governors of Massachusetts and Pennsylvania, respectively, called for legislative interference on behalf of the young. Anticruelty groups in several states kept the controversy alive through the mid-1890's, though only in Colorado did reformers succeed in abolishing child insurance.[76] Acutely aware that their fight was both historic and transatlantic, the NSPCC was encouraged to pursue the burial societies with a vigor that far outstripped its supply of evidence.

But at base, this uncompromising assault on corporate "evil" betrayed an insensitivity to working-class culture that colored much of the social rehabilitation attempted by voluntary effort. The great insurance firms capitalized on what well-to-do Victorians viewed as the extravagant response of laborers to death within their families. Few reformers understood that as late as 1901 one person in five could expect a pauper's burial.[77] Although NSPCC spokesmen never faulted the funeral rites of the poor, Waugh and his backers plainly underestimated their symbolic importance and overestimated the ease with which working-class mothers and fathers might be tempted into barbarism. Having declared that cruelty was classless, the child-savers launched a decade-long campaign to publicize an exception to this rule. Here and in other articles of its faith, the NSPCC would continue to find that its theory often did not mesh with the evidence.

Administrative Crisis

While locked in its losing battle against child life insurance, the NSPCC was also undergoing rapid and sometimes painful growth. The society's leadership faced an organizational dilemma. Determined to preserve the ideal of "one army and one crusade for wronged children, under one head," Waugh and his staff at headquarters could not allow branch committees to form their own policies.[78] This inevitably gave rise to provincial resentment, which in turn helped fuel a crisis that very nearly brought the child-savers to their knees.

English philanthropic bodies received at least £5,000,000 annually during the 1890's, and on this scale late Victorian child-protection activity appears relatively modest.[79] But the NSPCC's imaginative approach to getting and spending was of vital importance to the society, and an examination of this area shows why the administrative crisis of the mid-1890's was so serious.

With respect to fund raising, the NSPCC enjoyed three advantages over most moral reform groups. First, it rigidly maintained its nonsectarian status. During the late 1880's and early 1890's, Protestant-Catholic religious rivalry infected a great deal of the child-rescue work undertaken in England's large cities. Previously, aid to neglected and destitute Catholic children had been limited largely to the provision of orphanages. Realizing finally that Protestant charities were succoring and, worse, sometimes converting Catholic youths, Catholic leaders such as Bishop Vaughan in Manchester and Salford and Cardinal Manning in London began to strike back. Manning would not wait for his waifs and strays reclamation plan to stem the proselytizing tide; where a child's faith was imperiled, it might be necessary to override agreements between Catholic priests and Protestant philanthropists.[80] Dr. Barnardo, for one, found these tactics so repugnant that he went beyond attacking the Cardinal in print to accusing the London SPCC of giving preferential treatment to the children of Rome. In addition to placing Catholic young with foster parents or in asylums run by their coreligionists, the society saw to it that those in its Harpur Street shelter recited Catholic prayers morning and evening and attended mass each Sunday in the company of a lady appointed by the local priest.[81] It did not console Barnardo that Protestant and Jewish children received equivalent treatment. Late in 1889 he therefore withdrew from the NSPCC. Although he rejoined in February 1892, he continued to scold the society for being pro-Catholic.[82] Nevertheless, by the early 1890's it was obvious to the great majority of potential contributors that their money would go to a cause that served children of all religious faiths.[83]

England's chief child-protection agency also continued to draw impressive support from the upper classes. Although some of the society's aristocratic friends did no more than grace its membership lists, their names alone could generate potent propaganda. When the Queen agreed to become a patron in 1890, NSPCC literature declared proven "the constitutional principle that the Crown is the guardian of all the children of the land."[84] Similarly, it was "a tribute to the satisfactoriness of the Society's public conduct" that the Marquis of Salisbury subscribed £10 and thereby earned a life membership late in the next year. With the leader of the Tories in their camp, the society's parliamentary strategists must have breathed easier, for the Children's Charter had been won largely with help from Liberals.[85] Moreover, a substantial number of the society's prominent members played active roles in its routine work. Powerful women, such as Lady Willoughby de Eresby, Lady Iddesleigh, and Baroness Burdett-Coutts, kept close watch on children sheltered at Harpur Street; others, such as Lady Ancaster, helped plan the formation of new branch committees.[86] At the local level, too, the rich and well-connected made their presence known. Late in 1895 a series of charity bazaars held throughout England netted the society nearly £32,000. At York, the Duke of Cambridge, the Marquis and Marchioness of Ripon, and Viscount Halifax coaxed town mayors to attend in their colorful robes, supervised the setting up of tea rooms, and persuaded railway companies to offer special fares for visitors within sixty miles of the bazaar.[87]

Other organizations—for example, the RSPCA—could boast equally prestigious memberships. But few late Victorian campaigns for moral reform enjoyed the NSPCC's unity of purpose. The older and richer animal-protection movement never successfully resolved its internal debate over the proper scope of humane activity. Noting that "some strange things are occasionally done by the aristocratic patrons" of the RSPCA, one journal went on to describe how Colonel Howard Vincent, an MP and member of the society's council, appeared on the platform of the Sporting League at Sheffield to urge the perpetuation of rabbit coursing, stag hunting, and pigeon shooting. Even ardent animal lovers sometimes performed acts that contradicted their words. It was most disconcerting that, while awarding prizes at an RSPCA ceremony, the Duchess of York wore an "aigrette" in her hat, "that is, a plume torn from a heron at the nesting season—the most horrible of the many horrible trophies of murderous millinery."[88] Equally, temperance groups never achieved a consensus on the key issue of prohibition versus restriction of drink. Advocates of child protection, however, gave the NSPCC leadership full power to create and execute policy. Individual council members who proposed changes in the society's work typically withdrew their motions as soon as a member of the executive committee expressed reservations. This reluctance to challenge established procedure owed less to a tyrannical central executive than to a widely shared trust in the NSPCC leadership and an appreciation of the complexity of anticruelty work.

Despite its attractiveness to the benevolent, the NSPCC expanded faster than its income throughout the early and mid-1890's. Passage of the Children's Charter had presented NSPCC leaders with the legal leverage essential for effective intervention between parent and child. As a comparison between pre-enactment and post-enactment statistics indicates, the society was quick to exploit this new tool (see Table 5). By September 1890 the Harpur Street organization was reaching seven times as many children as its par-

TABLE 5
NSPCC Application of the 1889 Act

Persons affected	Sept. 1, 1888, to Aug. 31, 1889	Sept. 1, 1889, to Aug. 31, 1890
Children	869	10,522
Offenders warned	270	2,423
Offenders prosecuted	148	857
Offenders convicted	115	779

SOURCE: NSPCC 7th Annual Report.

ent body in Liverpool, while the other independent groups located south of the Scottish border (in Hull and Manchester) operated on minuscule scales.[89] And though the society's subscription lists had also grown impressively—from 225 names in its first year to 1,700 by mid-1890—this increase did not meet the needs of an organization determined to spread "vitalised limbs over all the land."[90] NSPCC propaganda often referred to "suffering childhood," conjuring up images of an aggregate pool of cruelty; if enough new preventive centers were established, perhaps this pool could be drained. Thus the eighth annual report took great pride in announcing the formation of 41 branches in the year ending in April 1892, an expansion that signaled the spread of NSPCC influence "from one-quarter to one-third of the population."[91] By this date anticruelty organizers had crossed the sea to form Irish branches in Dublin, Belfast, and Cork. As their network spread, so did the reach of their propaganda. The monthly circulation of the *Child's Guardian* rose from five thousand to over twenty thousand copies between 1888 and 1892, and it emerged as a philanthropic standard sold at the bookstalls of W. A. Smith and Sons.[92]

Haunted by the thought that theirs was a race against time to save tortured children, NSPCC leaders often rode roughshod over rival groups. The notion of "one army" so captured Waugh and his backers that they regarded the independent societies in Liverpool and Manchester as pockets of resistance. Over protests from "many principal citizens," the NSPCC opened its own branch in Manchester in 1893. Subsequent experience seemed to justify this encroachment; whereas up to 1893 one inspector had sufficed for the indigenous society, by 1895 the NSPCC's branch was employing five. That the young of Manchester might have benefited equally from an enlargement of the old organization did not occur to NSPCC officials.[93] Nor did they tread more lightly in Liverpool. Here the nation's oldest child-protection agency had been pleased to cooperate with the NSPCC, even assisting the larger group with its parliamentary lobbying costs. But when Liverpool's executive committee refused to be absorbed by the NSPCC in 1895, T. F. A. Agnew resigned as Chairman of the body he had founded to become Treasurer of a new NSPCC branch. Although two years later these groups reached an agreement giving the Liverpool SPCC exclusive jurisdiction within the city and the borough of Bootle, local resentment of the national society died hard.[94]

To control its rapidly growing empire the NSPCC developed an ever more elaborate central office staff. By mid-1893 Waugh's responsibilities as Honorary Director had grown so heavy that an assistant was needed. This post went to Mary P. Bolton, a woman about whom the society's records yield little information. Having entered the society's service in 1891, Miss Bolton obviously treated child protection more as a calling than a job. Since she superseded Waugh as the central office's speaker at many branch annual meetings, she must have spent nearly as much time in trains, cabs, and railway stations as she did at home in London. Besides these two executive officers, there were no fewer than 25 clerks assigned to various departments, eight people whose only job was addressing and packaging NSPCC literature, and two porters. From the central office one passed through a door to an adjoining building that housed the shelter, with its matron and her staff of seven. Immaculate and cheerfully decorated, the shelter's dormitories, dining room, and play yard bore no resemblance to the warren-like office, one of whose rooms displayed various "instruments of torture"— iron bars, pokers, leather straps—used to assault the young.[95]

From these Harpur Street headquarters flowed a stream of correspondence to the branch committees scattered throughout England, Wales, and Ireland. Waugh was far better as an administrator than as a witness. His flair for philanthropic salesmanship, combined with his gift for reducing complex issues to Manichean terms, made him a valued adviser to provincial anticruelty workers. Asked by the newly formed Birmingham branch where to set up its office, Waugh offered three very practical suggestions: that it should be located in a thoroughfare frequented by the town's "best people"; that it should occupy the ground floor, because "what the eye does not see the heart does not feel"; and that a shelter need not be built so long as the local Poor Law authorities smiled on the society's work.[96] Occasionally, Waugh and his staff made administrative concessions to keep provincial centers content. By waiving the rule that headquarters always selected inspectors for the localities, for example, London built up a large fund of goodwill with the luminaries of the Leeds branch.[97] What such diplomacy could not mask, however, was that until 1894 the NSPCC remained a creature of London philanthropists. So long as subscribers living in the Metropolis dominated its public meetings, and, more importantly, so long as the 30-member central executive committee framed policy and appointed officers, talk of a "national" crusade to combat child abuse rang hollow. Already under attack for its stand against burial insurance, the NSPCC executive could not risk disaffection among the more than two hundred branch committees. It was in a spirit of preemptive housecleaning, therefore, that the executive proposed a new constitution. Ratified on May 7, 1894, the revised rules gave the society's council—a body composed of two representatives elected by the subscribers in each branch committee area—ultimate power within the organization.[98] In theory, the NSPCC became democratic. In practice, the central executive's continued supervision of day-to-day affairs gave its wishes disproportionate weight at the biannual council meetings.

The receipt of a Royal Charter of Incorporation in 1895 seemed to confirm the society's organizational integrity. Like its new constitution, however, the charter conferred strategic as well as symbolic benefits. Incorporation allowed the NSPCC to hold property in its own right. Formerly, all assets had been vested in the society's trustees, among whom Baroness Burdett-Coutts was preeminent. Now 81 and openly critical of the NSPCC's expansionist gospel, the Baroness was no longer an ideal guarantor.[99] Also, the society could now initiate law suits. As RSPCA officials would not discover until 1925, it was sometimes better to adjudicate libels than to ignore them.[100] Lastly, the charter made the NSPCC eligible for a grant from the Exchequer. Receiving a government subsidy would be perfectly reasonable, the leaders of the society contended, because the NSPCC was "accomplishing the objects of Parliament embodied in its statutes on behalf of those subjects of the Crown who, by their tender years and the conditions of their life, are all and wholly unable to accomplish those objects for themselves."[101] But to the society's keen disappointment, a government grant never materialized. Presumably the Exchequer withheld funds on the assumption that child-savers would retrench if faced with a true financial crisis.

Yet many anticruelty workers felt that their mission should not be shaped by the whims of supply and demand. The suffering of little children was inelastic, so retrenchment in the interests of good business seemed a betrayal of the young. Vowing that it would never refuse to investigate a complaint of cruelty, wherever the case, NSPCC propaganda could go on to make a virtue out of indebtedness. To keep the Children's Charter and its amending Act of 1894 from becoming a mere "phantom of justice," new inspectors had to be trained and new branch committees founded to oversee their work. Unfortunately, branch committees typically spent £100 more than they raised during their first year, and about £50 more in their second.[102] NSPCC administrators did experiment with cost-cutting devices. Throughout 1890 the *Child's Guardian* carried three extra pages of advertisements for baby food, homes for lost dogs, and the Metropolitan Drinking Fountain and Cattle Trough Association ("the only Society providing free supplies of water for man and beast in the streets of London"). Similarly, for a brief period in 1894 only annual subscribers of £1 or more received the *Child's Guardian* free. Though both these expedients resulted in small savings, neither was thought conducive to a healthy public image. Thus for most of the 1890's growth and solvency seemed incompatible.

In large measure the society's financial strains stemmed from the unpredictable nature of philanthropic giving (see Appendix C, Fig. 3). Like all voluntary groups, the NSPCC could count on receiving only the sum pledged by its subscribers; and a long subscription list meant teaching Englishmen to regard the support of child protection as an annual habit. This latter process took time. The fourteen hundred NSPCC subscribers in 1889–90 gave an average of twenty-four shillings to the cause. More than 80 percent of the society's income in this year had to come from additional donations, some of which, such as Mrs. Frank Morrison's gift of £2,000, were very large.[103] Though by 1899 forty-six thousand subscribers were annually contributing at least five shillings each, this broadening of the NSPCC's economic base was not won with ease. On the contrary, periods of severe financial drought such as the winter of 1892–93, when expenses outran income by as much as £400 per week, placed a premium on opportunism. Making use of aristocratic and royal friends not only ingratiated the society with blue bloods but also provided ideal settings for appeals. The death of young Viscount Drumlanrig in 1895 produced a memorial fund of £2,000, and Victoria's Diamond Jubilee occasioned an all-out drive to commemorate the Queen's concern for her "least and most miserable" subjects.[104] Nor did the NSPCC spurn more sustained fund-raising techniques. As early as 1890 Waugh advocated establishing a reserve fund to give the society ballast at times when trade depressions, strikes, and news of philanthropic frauds cut short the flow of public largesse. Although periodic financial crises slowed the accumulation of a reserve, by mid-1896 approximately £32,000 had been banked for this purpose.[105] Indeed, few causes were so relentless in pursuit of fuel for their fires.

As the NSPCC grew, it increasingly relied on two elements for its financial health. First was the loyalty of its local militia, the lady collectors. Branches of the society adopted several methods to insure that subscriptions were renewed. In some cases the central office furnished a branch treasurer with a list of local subscribers, whereas in other cases the treasurer did this task unassisted. More effective than either of these methods, however, was the system, constantly recommended in NSPCC literature, of leaving the renewal of subscriptions to a special branch committee of lady collectors. Many major cities and several smaller towns were carefully subdivided into districts so that these women could make door-to-door calls. Before actually soliciting funds, they saturated both rich and poor neighborhoods with an assortment of leaflets, including "Form XX," the card for reporting alleged cases of assault or neglect. A day or two after this literature had been distributed, the ladies were urged to call on "well-off people" in the hope of securing a subscription. By mid-1897, nearly six thousand upper-middle-class women were engaged in this promotional campaign across England, Wales, and Ireland.[106]

The NSPCC's lady collectors seem to have been both efficient and enthusiastic. Although canvassing door-to-door was hard work, it offered genteel women the excitement of prowling strange districts without compromising their reputations.[107] Lady collectors found, moreover, that they could serve a crusade for the promotion of domestic peace while enjoying a respite from their own household chores. NSPCC literature left no room for doubt on the subject of female duty:

Much is said and written to-day concerning women's rights. Zealous upon the Platform and in the Press, uttering their furious indignation against being deprived of votes at Parliamentary elections, and of standing for election to public bodies, all, too, of the pride and malice of a man. But, happily, a far larger number of women are capable of indignation at the masses of helpless children [and at the] wrongs which inflict on their tender years fearful sufferings and life-long injury to their health. This is the sphere in which we should ask women to labour. . . . Of their own citizenship and rights true women can think little and say nothing till the citizenship and rights of children are established.

"True women" as defined by the society were plentiful in late Victorian and Edwardian England.[108] The NSPCC's second key to economic survival was its method of centralizing funds raised throughout the country. When lady collectors gave their proceeds to the nearest branch treasurer, the latter sent the money directly to headquarters. Then, before a branch committee could make any expenditure of over £1, it had to submit a request to London. NSPCC accountants thereupon scrutinized the request and passed it along to a financial and general purposes committee for approval or rejection. If, at the end of the financial year, a branch had spent more than it had raised, headquarters almost always made up the deficit. Despite the fact that this system soon required committee action on over nine thousand separate accounts each year, the society's insistence on "one pocket and one paymaster" meant that anticruelty work seldom fell prey to local prejudices.[109] Branch committee minute books show that after initial misgivings, most provincial child-savers were content to let the central authority ration resources.[110] Yet a handful could not abide London's financial and administrative control, and these few malcontents set in motion a controversy that pushed their movement to the brink of scandal.

Branch officials at Grimsby drew first blood in what became a bitter debate over the NSPCC's management. In May 1895 this anticruelty outpost in Lincolnshire sent a memorandum to the central executive committee citing a long list of administrative ills. For a start, the Grimsby officials judged headquarters irresponsible for having continued to expand rapidly while compiling a massive debt (£7,071) during 1893–94. Such imprudence allegedly marred many of the NSPCC's administrative policies. With respect to prosecutions, the society had spent over £3 per case in 1894. Since the RSPCA had conducted 7,548 prosecutions for an average of less than twenty-five shillings per case during the previous year, it seemed that child-savers should allow the police to assume a greater share of the caseload. Also irritating to the dissidents was their discovery that not all the branches received equal treatment from London. Whereas most provincial centers, Grimsby included, had to raise or guarantee £150 before an inspector would be sent to them, at least two new branches had recently been allowed agents without raising the stipulated sum.[111]

The society's finance and general purposes committee countered with a point-by-point defense more notable for its length than for the cogency of its reasoning. Cost-cutting measures had not been implemented during the disastrous 1893–94 season, NSPCC defenders said, because resources had not evaporated until the final quarter. Nor was the society's defense of its costly prosecution procedures—namely, that dogs and children warranted different grades of protection—entirely satisfactory.[112] The Grimsby officials felt that glaring problems had been glossed over; whitewash must not be allowed. Thus, Thomas Porteous, Grimsby's Honorary Secretary, now dropped all pretense of discretion. Porteous hinted that the society's financial ills were almost inevitable so long as Waugh remained at the helm, for it was the NSPCC's Director—now drawing a salary of £800 per year, enjoying unrestricted travel expenses, and maintaining a stranglehold on the central executive committee—who had steered the society toward financial ruin. As editor of the *Child's Guardian* as well as principal architect of the annual reports, Waugh was ideally stationed to smother opposition. To Porteous, the most striking illustration of Waugh's ability to do this was the shroud of silence that he had drawn around the departure of Angela Burdett-Coutts from the central executive committee.[113]

At first Waugh could afford to ignore this thorn in his side. He had already warned his colleagues to stay "stone deaf to the multitude of [ill-informed] letter writers" who questioned the society's methods; and all but a handful of NSPCC officials gave Waugh complete support in his skirmish with the Grimsby branch.[114] But soon the dispute became an extramural matter. On March 5, 1896, the London *Echo* carried a front-page article entitled "A Study in Philanthropic Finance." Written by "M.," the article berated NSPCC administrators for their "extravagant methods and unbusinesslike expenditure." It was bad enough that the society had spent £6,519 on printing and postage during 1894–95, but worse still that the sale of its publications had realized only £17. What need had a child-protection agency for a specialist on bazaar orchestration, or eight salaried packers? The interests of abused children had been subordinated to those of a philanthropic bureaucracy, and Benjamin Waugh was responsible for this perversion.[115] Both the NSPCC and its Director would have to seek public vindication.

The society went on trial one year later. Thomas Porteous had continued to harass headquarters, going so far as to suggest that the paysheets of Waugh and Miss Bolton should be scrutinized.[116] More disquieting, the article by "M." had driven friends as well as enemies to debate the NSPCC's administration in print. In mid-March 1897, therefore, the society asked Sir Matthew White Ridley, the Home Secretary, to direct a government investigation of its finances and general management. When Ridley denied this request, the society turned to Lord Herschell, whose status as a former Lord Chancellor seemed to place him above bias. Significantly, however, in obtaining the services of Lord Herschell, NSPCC officials rejected the Charity Organisation Society's offer to conduct the probe. Further affronted when Herschell declined a C.O.S.-nominated assistant, the C.O.S.'s Secretary C. S. Loch resolved to go ahead with a study of his own.[117] Here was Loch's chance to embarrass a group he viewed as growing fat off the public conscience.

Loch's report made matters worse for the NSPCC. The C.O.S.'s inquiry department took very seriously its role as the self-appointed policeman of English philanthropy. Both fraudulent and mismanaged charities came within its purview.[118] And by C.O.S. standards, the NSPCC seemed seriously mismanaged. Analyzing the society's balance sheet for 1895–96, Loch found that £18,248, or approximately 36 percent of the society's total outlay, went to cover the costs of administration and expansion. Though such a sum appeared "excessive" even when due allowance was made for "reasonable expenditure in propagandism," the C.O.S. did not dwell on this flaw. Far more troubling were the failings attributable to a director "who showed no disposition to submit to control." Waugh allegedly appointed and dismissed inspectors at will, evaded committee supervision by paying over half the society's expenses from a petty cash fund, and drank spirits with Miss Bolton, charging the cost to an NSPCC account. The C.O.S. painted a confidence-shattering portrait of megalomania and deception,[119] from which there could be but one conclusion: "Until these . . . faults have been remedied the Charity Organisation Society recommend the public to withhold support from the National Society for the Prevention of Cruelty to Children, and they are strongly of opinion that the first step in reform ought to be a complete reorganisation of the staff at the central office." The C.O.S. circulated this report to its district committees throughout England, advising them to redirect all reports of child abuse to local police.[120] The NSPCC had been excommunicated well before Lord Herschell could complete his probe.

If Herschell's inquiry had corroborated Loch's, the largest child-protection agency in the world would have suffered irreparable harm. As it happened, however, this second and far more searching study exonerated the society on all but some relatively minor issues. Because he did not share Loch's long-standing contempt for work that thrived on "harrow[ed] feelings," Herschell was prepared to be open-minded.[121] Over a six-week period he and his two assistants, a barrister and a banker, examined witnesses, studied account books, and solicited opinion from auditors and law enforcement officials. The closely printed, 28-page report that resulted is one of the most detailed contemporary analyses of a late Victorian philanthropic organization ever attempted. What the three investigators soon discovered was that a very large proportion of the charges leveled against NSPCC officials could be traced to one individual, a Mr. Hodge, formerly chief clerk in the society's prosecution department. Hodge had been a valued employee since 1888, the only blot on his record being a bout of drunkenness in 1890. But he had taken to the bottle again early in 1897, when a mere "boy" was added to the prosecution department's staff at a salary equal to Hodge's. The older clerk felt so betrayed by his superiors that soon after he went to the Attorney General and urged that the society's Royal Charter be revoked. Of the many rumors fostered by Hodge, two were positively scandalous: that Waugh and Miss Bolton swilled brandy while working and were lovers while traveling. On cross-examination Hodge denied that he had any knowledge of a liaison between the NSPCC's two top administrators. As for the alcohol, Waugh, acting on his doctor's orders, did take a small amount of brandy mixed with milk each morning. Miss Bolton followed Waugh's morning habit, and drank a brandy and water at teatime as well. Although the investigators clearly frowned on Bolton's choice of refreshment, their only explicit criticism was that the alcohol had been charged to the society.[122]

No doubt the NSPCC's management could have stood improvement. Lord Herschell and his assistants felt that a budget statement prepared at the beginning of each year would aid in anticipating lean times. Tighter controls on the amount of printed matter distributed to the branches and greater reliance on public prosecutors in court cases would help reduce costs. Lastly, it was preferable that the central executive committee have sole responsibility for hiring and firing inspectors, and that no paid officer of the society, including the Director, sit on any of its committees.[123]

But by and large the NSPCC won much-needed praise. Granted, the administrative machinery at Harpur Street was large and expensive; yet this rigorously centralized system was probably the cheapest way of running such a complex organization. One auditor, who regularly examined the accounts of some 64 charities, described the NSPCC's books as models of accuracy—again, a virtue attributable to centralization. Given the large number of branch committees, some friction was bound to develop between provincial centers and the staff in London. That more branches did not follow Grimsby's lead only confirmed the NSPCC's fundamentally sound administration. Finally, Herschell's team came to Waugh's defense. Though Waugh may at times have used language "too impetuous and vehement," it was rare for "the zeal and enthusiasm which can promote a great cause . . . [to be] combined with a philosophic calm."[124] For thirteen years the moving spirit behind his organization, Waugh earned every farthing of his salary.

The NSPCC was not the only philanthropic target at this time. Mid-1897 also saw the National Life-Boat Association's executive attacked for alleged profligacy. However, a review of its management demonstrated that shipwrecked sailors, like battered children, were being well served.[125] In both cases the press had taken a deep interest, and newspapers expressed undisguised relief when these mainstays of English philanthropy were exonerated.[126] The *British Medical Journal* observed that the NSPCC's vindication was "a matter of national importance," because few reform groups had so effectively led "the wealthier and happier classes . . . to think of the poor and suffering." So "gigantic"—to use *The Lancet*'s word— had child protection grown by the late 1890's, that any blow to the cause reverberated throughout the world of private charity, shaking the faith of the comfortable in their ability to civilize industrial society.[127]

The NSPCC nevertheless paid a price for its vindication. In some provincial centers, committee meetings and fundraising efforts ceased, pending publication of Herschell's report. Lady Portman, President of the Dorchester branch, not only counseled caution while the parent body was on trial but also threatened to drop her anticruelty work altogether if the suggested reforms were not quickly implemented. Even after the report became available, Reading's Honorary Secretary felt that some charges had been papered over.[128] Lingering doubts about alleged improprieties on the part of Waugh and his staff, coupled with the postponement of festivities designed to commemorate the Queen's "reign for children," produced an estimated loss of £15,000 in contributions. Nor did Herschell's favorable report keep NSPCC leaders from feeling rebuked. Benjamin Waugh's letter of resignation, submitted to and rejected by the central executive committee in late October, was not an empty gesture. Mary Bolton fared worse. Because the investigators recommended that the office of Assistant Secretary be filled by "a gentleman of financial business capacity," Miss Bolton was entrusted with duties deemed less "unsuitable for a lady." [129]

Old Wars, New Battles

Excoriated for its stand against child life insurance and criticized for alleged mismanagement, the NSPCC scarcely needed more controversy. Yet England's anticruelty leaders did not hesitate to join another old and difficult fight, the campaign against baby-farming. It would have been service enough if the society had supplied case data to the champions of more stringent infant-life protection. Instead, the NSPCC wielded its empirical knowledge as a club, contending that experience with unwanted children entitled it to dictate the shape of legislation. Overly eager to transform sentiment into law, Waugh and his colleagues further jeopardized their claim to authority in matters concerning the young.

Ever since Margaret Waters's sensational murder trial in 1870, the supervision of children put out to nurse had been regarded as a police matter rather than as a job for the public health authorities. Except in London, where the Metropolitan Board of Works and, after 1888, the London County Council had struggled to enforce its provisions, the 1872 Infant Life Protection Act never dented the baby-farming trade. Those few cases that did reach the courts snared only the most careless practitioners, leading critics to conclude that many more crafty "nurses" worked beyond law's reach. Doctors were particularly angry. Although the Infant Life Protection Society did not survive the 1870's, some veterans of the earlier agitation continued to denounce what they saw as a catastrophic social ill. Ernest Hart, still editor of the *British Medical Journal*, could not forgive those who had "maimed" the I.L.P. bill. In 1883, while Josephine Butler's crusade against the Contagious Diseases Acts was at its peak, Hart noted caustically: "There is at present, thanks to the disturbing vigilance of certain ladies who constitute themselves the advocates of liberty of the baser members of their sex, great facility to commit systematic manslaughter amongst . . . helpless infants." *The Lancet* was more restrained. Regarding the true hazards of professional adoption, both the courts and public opinion stood "in need of a little common-sense enlightenment." [130]

Medical men were not alone in their concern. Rescue workers such as J. W. Horsley of the Church of England Waifs and Strays Society warned that newspaper advertisements for adoption should be treated with extreme caution. He thought it suspicious that a mother would contemplate paying four shillings per week to an unknown nurse when his society offered to place children with carefully selected foster parents whose homes remained under "proper and continuous supervision." However, Horsley neglected to mention the strings attached to his service. If children were illegitimate, their mothers had to show that they had fallen but once and had "a reasonable prospect of amendment"; mothers had to promise to pay a weekly sum for child maintenance; and the children had to be Protestant. [131] It was, after all, precisely the bastard, at law *filius nullius* ("nobody's child"), who remained in greatest danger. The solution seemed straightforward to some reformers. According to one of them, the Industrial Schools Acts set a clear precedent for state adoption of illegitimate children, since these laws had already recognized the principle of finite parental custody. [132] In another view, the key to infant salvation lay entirely with the gentle sex. Once women ceased trying "to openly arrogate man's authority" through their "screaming and shrieking" for the vote, more than enough moral force would be freed to steer Parliament toward legislative action. [133]

As it happened, Lord Salisbury's Tory government did not need maternal suasion to press for amendment of the 1872 Act. The facts spoke only too clearly for themselves. In the autumn of 1888, wide publicity greeted the trial of Mrs. Arnold of Wolverton, whose enterprise as a foster parent rattled even the Home Office. For four years Arnold had been seeking children to adopt. Soon after an infant arrived, accompanied by a lump sum of between £20 and £40, she passed the child on to another woman with a much reduced fee. This system of rapid turnover the *British Medical Journal* dubbed "baby sweating"; thanks to the "supineness" of local authorities, Mrs. Arnold had sweated away at least 25 infants during her brief career.[134] Hard on the heels of Mrs. Arnold came the equally grim story of Jessie King, aged 27, who farmed young children in Stockbridge, near Edinburgh. King and her paramour, a part-time gardener, might have continued to take illegitimate babies at a £2 or £3 fee if they had been more circumspect. Having suffocated her first charge and placed it in a closet, King soon found the stench of rotting flesh so strong that she wrapped the body in a towel and dumped it in a vacant lot. Unfortunately for the murderess, some neighborhood boys unwrapped the package and alerted the police. When they arrived to search her home, the police found a second dead child, whom King later admitted smothering as it choked on the whiskey she had poured down its throat.[135] Jessie King was hanged on March 11, 1889, but well before that date the shock waves from these two cases had provoked official action. Early in December 1888 the Home Secretary, Henry Matthews, sent a circular letter to the corporations of England requesting opinions about the need for a new bill. As a result of the data elicited, Matthews brought before the Commons a government-sponsored remedy in February 1890.[136]

Unlike the related problem of child abuse, baby-farming had a well-defined legislative history. Because the government could work with a long-standing statute, it was for once willing to enter the hazardous arena of family law. NSPCC officials should have been relieved. Spared the onus of spearheading yet another fight against convention, the society could have limited its action to providing the Home Secretary with corroborative data. Initially, child-savers did give priority to the collection and publication of baby-farming facts. A private donation of £250 earmarked for just this purpose allowed the society to air the plight of cast-off infants in much greater detail. For shock value, few of its early baby-farming cases surpassed that of the Swindon couple, George and Mary Hayes, against whom prison terms of nine months and two years respectively were won. In a bare, filth-encrusted room, twelve feet square, the Hayes had kept seven children, ranging in age from twenty months to five years. When rescued, all were nearly naked and severely emaciated, their hair matted with one another's excrement.

The youngest was so weak that he had to be carried to a workhouse on a pillow—an image later used in some of the NSPCC's most arresting photographs.[137] Not satisfied with simply compiling case data, however, the society's officers resorted to the old tactic of answering adoption advertisements in a variety of newspapers. Although this time-consuming process netted few hard facts—in no instance was an advertiser tracked to her home—Waugh assured the public that the stream of infants flowing from procurer to receiver was "prodigious." He added that the same person's advertisements had been found as far north as Sunderland and as far south as Eastbourne, suggesting, somewhat contradictorily, that a fairly small number of procurers cast very wide nets.[138]

Ignoring that Parliament already had before it a government measure on the subject, NSPCC leaders in May 1890 sent their own infant-life protection bill to the Home Office. Visions of starving babies had apparently blinded NSPCC strategists to political reality, for their bill was draconian. By its terms no person could keep for profit another's child under the age of twelve, unless the keeper's house was registered with the local authorities. Failure to observe these guidelines could result in a fine of £100 and/or a prison term of six months.[139] Much less severe, the government's bill was still sufficiently controversial to demand examination by a select committee. The case for extending the 1872 Act to cover all homes that took in one or more children under the age of five years was no doubt strong. Samuel Babey, for example, noted that between 1878 and 1889 only 13 percent of the infants kept for fees in his area of London came within the Act's purview. But imprecision in the wording of the government's bill, together with fears that rescue work for unwed mothers might be curtailed, led to the bill's dismemberment by the select committee.[140] Fortunately for anticruelty workers, the NSPCC's more stringent measure was not served up to the same body.

The refusal of Parliament to place tighter controls on baby-farming in 1890 only amplified the calls for reform. A few voices, notably those associated with Henry Salt's Humanitarian League, urged "sisterly" help to poor girls and their illegitimate children in place of persecuting baby-farmers.[141] But as the list of heinous deeds lengthened, such broadmindedness became very rare. The NSPCC's conviction of Alice Reeves for manslaughter helped fan public fears about systematic child-murder. Of the twelve infants traced to Mrs.

Reeves's Lambeth home between September 1890 and March 1891, eight subsequently died the "lingering, horrible death" of starvation. In an attempt to milk as much anxiety from the case as possible, the *Child's Guardian* first identified Mrs. Reeves as but one of "hundreds of traders in baby slaughter," and then added that three hundred children's garments had been found in her basement. Perhaps most unnerving of all was the element of cold calculation involved. For Mrs. Reeves and her husband, a lawyer, had been plying their trade while living next door to a constable, "the only man who could never interfere with his neighbour."[142] Other organs followed the society's lead. *The Lancet* commented at length on the 1891 trial of Joseph and Annie Roodhouse, through whose hands at least 35 children and £219 in fees had passed. Even more zealous was the *British Medical Journal*, which, by 1894, was informing its readers that there were no fewer than six hundred baby farms in England.[143] Outside medical circles, groups as disparate as the Women's Liberal Federation and the Coroners' Society of England and Wales joined the reform chorus.[144]

Understandably, neither Tory nor Liberal party leaders were eager to promote a new infant-life protection bill, only to watch it die in committee. But, wondered the society, was government initiative now so vital? Having paraded a series of "human butchers" before the public eye, NSPCC leaders were hoping that Parliament would at last seize the chance to right a glaring wrong. Optimism turned to anger, however, when in the spring of 1893 philanthropists found MPs too engrossed in their "cock-pit" to grant the society's revised bill a hearing.[145] Two years later, Lord Onslow, acting on behalf of the London County Council, brought before the Upper House a scheme very similar to the ill-fated government bill of 1890. Yet Onslow's measure was "so hacked and chopped about" that its sponsors withdrew their "mutilated offspring." Eventually, however, persistence paid off: in 1896 the Earl of Denbigh secured a second reading and a select committee for an identical bill. Among the groups pressing for reform, only the NSPCC protested. Well-meaning as the London County Council might have been, it had overlooked two critical issues, the society held. Experience showed that an adopted child required supervision well beyond the age of five. And further, to exempt from regulation those cases where a mother handed her bastard to her relations made no sense. After all, sympathetic parents might be particularly willing to eliminate their daughter's source of shame. These flaws in Lord Denbigh's bill prompted the society to introduce its own more stringent measure.[146] Thus, the 1896 select committee found itself with two private members' bills on a most difficult subject.

Although the committee's subject was adoption for payment, its deliberations took place within a wider context of concern about infant life. Both lay and medical witnesses deplored the growing number of advertisements that hawked nostrums for removing female "obstructions" and "preventing large families." At the very least, such notices suggested a booming trade in quack medicine; at the worst, they heralded a heavy traffic in criminal abortion.[147] Advertisements for gynecological cures, lying-in homes, and baby-farming merged in many reformers' minds, the sum of these symptoms being a homicidal subculture that fed on a late nineteenth-century erosion of parental (and specifically maternal) "feeling." Behind most reformers' zeal lay a fear that this perversion of parental feeling might spread, disease-like, if statutory controls were not forthcoming.

As the select committee soon learned, even conscientious enforcement of the 1872 Act was not enough. Within the limits of that law, the London County Council's Public Control Department ran an "almost perfect" inspection system. Since April 1894 the P.C.D. had employed three persons to visit registered homes, seek out violations, and counsel nurses on proper sanitation and infant care. One of the three was a woman, Miss Isabel Smith, who, in addition to her other duties, answered adoption notices, as the handwriting of a female was thought more likely to disarm suspicion. By tracing such advertisements and by keeping in touch with police, relieving officers, and registrars of births and deaths, the P.C.D. inspectors were well positioned to know of infants kept for cash.[148] Yet through this net slipped a large number of children. In all of London only 41 houses appeared on the P.C.D.'s registration lists. Outside the Metropolis the statistics were even less encouraging; 29 chief constables in major towns across England and Scotland reported just two registered homes, one each in Manchester and Bath.[149]

In Benjamin Waugh's view the solution to this problem lay in a stricter law, enforced by child-protection specialists. Both parts of his formula made sense. The Public Control Department's Samuel Babey testified that he had not encountered a case of child neglect for some time, while in 1895 alone the NSPCC had been forced to "interfere" in approximately 250 cases of nurse-children taken for profit. Quite possibly the society's 137-member inspectorate was better equipped than local authorities to supervise adopted infants.[150] But Waugh's infamous gift for hyperbole soon undermined his case. Attempting to dramatize the ease with which nurses could kill their charges, he announced, "I could baby-farm a million a year in this country and never be convicted, and make a good fortune." In the end Waugh's rhetoric only antagonized a tribunal already ill-disposed toward the NSPCC bill.[151]

The committee was dubious of even the more moderate measure before it. How, Lord Thring wanted to know, would the proposed law affect children under five whose parents in India wanted to have them kept by friends in England? Similarly, might not the London County Council's bill pose difficulties for philanthropic groups that boarded out their young with foster parents? Nearly 30 percent of Dr. Barnardo's children were under the age of five, for example. Ultimately, though, the committee worried most about the bureaucratic machine that would be created. If the 1872 Act were to be amended as proposed, the Bishop of Winchester observed, infant-life protection would assume a "gigantic scale," with nearly every street in London coming under the inspector's lens.[152] Thus, fearing that its bill might be savaged once more, the London County Council decided to compromise. If the measure were to cover all nursed children under five years of age, the council would abandon its efforts to bring single-child houses under inspection.[153] Compromise was the answer. Ten months later, after minor committee modification, the new Infant Life Protection Act (60 & 61 Vic., c. 57) became law.

The 1897 Act was poor recompense for eight years of sustained reform agitation. Perhaps because the London County Council had never expected much from Parliament, it was pleased to win some added security for adopted children. A number of doctors also greeted the Act with "qualified welcome."[154] But in the eyes of those who had taken the strongest stand against baby-farming— Ernest Hart, Benjamin Waugh, and their allies—Parliament had forsaken its most needy constituents. What the House of Lords had done was "sickening and unjust," declared the *Child's Guardian*.[155] Certainly their lordships had been willfully meek, for, by empowering boards of guardians to inspect registered houses without making such inspection obligatory, the 1897 Act all but guaranteed that boards in cost-conscious districts would forgo this duty. Those Poor Law unions that chose to exercise their new power could handpick inspectors from large numbers of interested men and women. The Kingston Union sorted through 177 candidates before selecting a surgeon's widow to take the post and its £100-per-year salary. But such unions were few; and soon after the Act took effect social critics resumed their warning that England was falling even further behind France and Germany in her care for the adults of tomorrow.[156] For the NSPCC, considerations of national pride paled beside the far deeper problem of injustice to the young and indifference to the advice of their guardians.

It would be wrong to argue that the English child-protection movement was disintegrating during the 1890's. On the contrary, anticruelty workers won some major legislative concessions. For example, NSPCC leaders and factory medical inspectors together helped to defeat an effort to relax the 1878 Factory and Workshops Act. This law had set three conditions for a child's admission to the workforce: the child must be of proper age, must have sufficient schooling, and must be physically fit. As insurance that the young were indeed healthy enough for labor in factories and workshops, no child could start such a job without a certificate of fitness obtained from a medical man appointed under the Act. Yet in the spring of 1891, Henry Matthews, the Tory Home Secretary, brought before Commons a bill that sought to dispense with medical certification. More than a few philanthropists thought that this idea was "astonishing," a reversion "to the ethics of the wolf and the crocodile." Indignation acquired substance, however, only after the NSPCC publicized details of cases in which frail or sick children had been spared suffering by the refusal of a physician's certificate.[157]

Far more significant was the refinement of the Children's Charter. Many regarded the 1889 Act as a classic illustration of legislating morality by act of Parliament, or, in the words of a prize-winning essayist, as proof that the "wakening conscience of the masses" could be "nourished and fostered by penal laws."[158] Unquestionably the society's executive believed this to be so. By the winter of 1893, therefore, the NSPCC had prepared a new anticruelty bill to plug the loopholes in its first Act. Immediately after Sir Richard Webster presented this corrective to the Commons, Waugh began pressing H. H. Asquith, now Home Secretary, for support from the Liberal front bench.[159]

In principle, Home Office officials agreed that the Children's Charter could stand repair. But what the NSPCC had in mind involved a great deal more than gap filling. In the first place, by redefining certain terms, the whole intention of the law would be altered. The expression "child," for instance, was henceforth to mean both boys and girls below the age of sixteen, whereas the 1889 Act applied to boys fourteen and under. As a London police court magistrate pointed out, this change seemed at variance with the common view that a male of fourteen was very nearly independent of his parents, and thus presumably capable of looking out for his own welfare.[160] Equally, expanding the phrase "injury . . . to health" to cover not only physical harm but also "any mental derangement" signified a vast broadening of the accepted idea of child abuse. "Children have painful and deadly sufferings to endure which have only the brain as their sphere," contended the NSPCC. Beyond these fundamental redefinitions, the bill would force poor parents to obtain parish aid for their ill offspring, set stiffer penalties for convictions, bring about major changes in search and arrest procedures, and place new restrictions on the employment of the young as street traders and acrobats. Interestingly, Asquith and his advisers were most critical of the society's plan to separate "alcoholic insanity" from deliberate brutality by allowing courts to sentence drunken abusive parents to a year's detention in a retreat for inebriates rather than send them to jail.[161]

Waugh was pleased to let Asquith make minor improvements in the wording of the bill, but flatly refused to abandon or dilute any of its major provisions. Given such intransigence, it was hardly surprising that the NSPCC's "new morrow for unhappy children" never gained a third reading.[162] Yet one year later virtually the same measure was presented to Parliament. This time fellow anticruelty spokesman James Grahame maligned the proposal, noting that in his native Scotland "at least we regard these [child-protection] Societies as ameliorative, educational and preventive more than punitive."[163] But as in 1889 with A. J. Mundella, the NSPCC possessed a powerful friend on the parliamentary inside. Sir Richard Webster was so convinced by the society's arguments that he impressed on Asquith how "extremely anxious" he was for the bill's success. This combination of persuasion from within and pressure from without proved decisive. Early in June the bill passed unscathed through Commons, whereupon the Cabinet allowed Lord Herschell to steer it through the Upper House. By late August this bold new law was on the statute books.[164]

The NSPCC had carried its case on virtually every point. If the Children's Charter made cruelty to the young a crime, the 1894 Act established it as a positively hazardous practice. Henceforth adults who intentionally ill-treated or neglected children risked a prison term of up to six months. As the habitual drunkards' clause demonstrated, however, deterrence was not the society's sole aim. By stipulating that parents who abused their offspring while under the influence of alcohol must consent to the alternative sentence, the Act sought to rehabilitate offenders and promote long-term healing of family wounds. The stress placed by NSPCC literature on the responsibilities of parenthood found expression in the clauses requiring a doctor to be called when needed for a sick child and increasing from five to twenty shillings the maximum contribution courts could impose on parents whose behavior forced their children to be placed in new homes. Where parents simply could not afford adequate care for their offspring, workhouses now had to accept such children if they had room. Finally, the Act greatly facilitated the rescue of endangered children by empowering policemen to remove suspected victims from their houses without a court order.[165]

There can be no denying that the NSPCC excelled at its specialty, the orchestration of public concern for the physical well-being of the young. But throughout the early and middle 1890's the society overextended itself. As the shapers of late Victorian England's most arresting moral reform, NSPCC zealots lapsed into the practice of condemning without adequate proof, and as administrators of a fast-growing philanthropic network, they tended to promote expansion as a goal unto itself. On both rocks the child-protection movement foundered dangerously. That the anticruelty cause did not suffer permanent damage was due to the few individuals who drew much of the hostile fire upon themselves. Benjamin Waugh, and to a lesser extent Mary Bolton, were easy targets for those who remained suspicious of the society's assault on parental prerogatives. In deflecting controversy from their cause, Waugh and Bolton paid a price. From late June through September 1898, Waugh was

forced by failing health to holiday in Switzerland. Shortly afterwards, Miss Bolton suffered a physical collapse that left her bedrid-
den for three weeks, prompting the executive committee to send her
on a cruise to Natal.[166] Although they returned to full-time service,
neither Bolton nor Waugh would again show the kind of fanatical
intensity that had inspired both admiration and resentment from
their peers.

CHAPTER 6

In the Light of Experience

HOME AND FAMILY were perhaps the most cherished idols of Victorianism. Although by the close of the nineteenth century England faced stiff competition in the realms of industry and empire, middle-class writers still found comfort in the belief that "the home part of our life bears a greater proportion to the whole, than that of any other people."[1] Since domestic harmony remained the "sheet anchor of the nation's greatness," it followed that national "betterment" had to begin within the family. And no feature of family life could so materially influence England's future health as the welfare of children. Useful citizens were the products of clean, tasteful homes, where sternness gave way to unselfishness in domestic government and "no loud, harsh tones are ever heard."[2] Such prescriptive literature recognized implicitly that some English children in fact grew up with dirt, hunger, and blows. Some parents were deaf to the advice of penny tracts; for them, a more potent reformatory influence was needed.

The child-protection societies of late Victorian and Edwardian England offered precisely such an influence in the form of their inspectors. The use of agents by voluntary groups to supervise the care of children was not peculiar to the NSPCC. The Metropolitan Association for Befriending Young Servants arranged monthly meetings between its "lady inspectors" and the maids over whom it cast a maternal eye. The Girls' Friendly Society not only assisted young domestics but also made periodic checks on females resident in workhouses.[3] Charities that specialized in finding homes for the homeless, such as the Church of England Waifs and Strays Society and Dr. Barnardo's group, sent their agents every year on unannounced calls to visit the families that had taken in their children.

The long-established Reformatory and Refuge Union found that reaching juvenile delinquents before they became hardened criminals required the use of "Boy's Beadles" to patrol city streets and assist public authorities in extracting contributions from parents whose offspring were sent to corrective institutions.[4] But no children's philanthropy could compare with the NSPCC in terms of the size or the sophistication of its inspectorate. From a single officer in 1884, the society expanded its private police force to 163 in 1900, and to 250 in 1910. More importantly, by the close of the nineteenth century NSPCC agents had become neighborhood institutions in many English towns—highly visible reminders that parental misuse of the young now constituted unacceptable behavior. To working-class children the school attendance officer was "the punishment man"; to young and old alike the NSPCC's blue-uniformed inspector was "the cruelty man."[5]

Who were the cruelty men? What was their mission, and how successfully did they translate the society's aims into action? To what extent did the NSPCC's explanation of child abuse grow out of the experience of its inspectors? Wealthy England associated the child-protection movement with disturbing case studies, aggressive parliamentary lobbying, and notices of fundraising fêtes in *The Times*; but poor families thought first of private policemen knocking on their front doors. Whether the NSPCC's domestic "espionage" could be justified was a favorite debating point for the comfortable classes. Laboring men and women were more apt to worry about what a visit from the inspector would do to their reputation in the neighborhood.[6] Ultimately, both concerns hinged on the conduct of the society's agents.

The Cruelty Men

For its community militia the NSPCC preferred men who had been trained to follow orders. If one compares a sample of 100 candidates recruited by the society between 1889 and 1908 with a sample group hired by the RSPCA between 1880 and 1890, one sees that the two agencies valued similar kinds of experience (Table 6).[7] England's two largest humane agencies competed for the services of ex-policemen, but, with 29 occupational categories represented in the NSPCC sample, its inspectorate seems to have been the more diverse group.[8] Cruelty men tended to be middle-aged

TABLE 6
Major Occupational Backgrounds of NSPCC and RSPCA Inspectors

Former occupation	NSPCC (N = 95)		RSPCA (N = 97)	
	Number	Percent	Number	Percent
Policeman	44	46.3%	38	39.2%
Army	8	8.4	38	39.2
Clerk	7	7.4	1	1.0
Insurance agent	4	4.2	0	—
Farmer	2	2.1	4	4.1
School attendance officer	2	2.1	0	—
Railway employee	1	1.0	6	6.2
Other and unknown	27	28.4	10	10.3

SOURCES: NSPCC *Record Book of Inspectors* (1889–1910); RSPCA *Record of Inspectors*, I (July 1851–September 1896).

when they joined the society: according to the same samples, NSPCC inspector-trainees were on average 36.7 years old, as compared with 31.2 years old for RSPCA recruits.[9] Maturity and willingness to abide by regulations were two marks of "steadiness," perhaps the NSPCC's most sought-after characteristic. Also highly valued was temperance. An assessment of drinking habits was standard procedure in selecting new inspectors. Thirty of 83 men from the sample were described as "total abstainers"; and all NSPCC agents learned that tippling was antithetical both to the gospel of self-control spread by the cruelty men and to the coolheadedness that intervention between parent and child so often demanded. Further, "inspectors must not frequent public-houses, or bad company, or bet, or gamble," for cruelty men were expected to be ambassadors of respectability with long-term assignments.[10] For the 26 men in the sample who remained NSPCC employees for ten years or more, the average posting lasted 7.8 years. By contrast, 42 RSPCA agents with equivalent seniority remained in one locality for an average of only 2.4 years. Child-protection leaders recognized that winning the confidence of neighbors—persuading them to use the cruelty man as an instrument of community justice— took time.

Although not handsomely paid, NSPCC agents were more comfortably off than the majority of the parents whom they counseled. By the mid-1890's inspectors received twenty-eight shillings per week throughout their six-month probationary period and thirty shillings on promotion to the regular staff. Cruelty men with outstanding records might hope to attain a salary of fifty shillings per week in the field—still less than half of what junior factory or mine inspectors earned.[11] The job carried other compensations, however. At the turn of the century between 80 and 90 percent of the agents and their families lived in the NSPCC's local offices. Resident inspectors sometimes paid no rent, though more often they contributed five shillings per week for their rooms and in return got a weekly allowance of one shilling and sixpence for coals, gas light, and a charwoman. All the cruelty men were obliged to participate in the NSPCC's endowment life insurance scheme and to contribute jointly with the society toward a sick-pay fund.[12]

Yet these material inducements alone could not have sustained many agents in a job whose demands were prodigious. In 1907 Mary Loane, a district nurse serving London's East End, described the inspector who called on her as "a short, strongly-made man, whose appearance and manner reminded me simultaneously of a soldier, a sailor, a policeman, a home missioner, a father of a large young family, and an Irishman with a genuine love of 'a bit of a shindy.'"[13] Loane's description probably held true for many a cruelty man since the NSPCC acknowledged that it sought candidates in whom "tenderness" was tempered by a "righteous" anger over misuse of the young. True believers in the society's cause, not "luminous jelly fishes," were needed; moral pugnacity might be controlled, but it could not be created.[14] The late Victorian mind perceived such a personality as intensely male, and, indeed, the first NSPCC agents saw themselves as belonging to a fraternal elite that included the regional supervisors, the training staff at headquarters, and Benjamin Waugh himself.[15]

When the society found a promising "children's servant," it subjected him to a rigorous training in law and public relations. A 62-page handbook, the *Inspector's Directory*, stressed the crucial importance of tact in dealing with parents on their own turf. Gaining entry to the home of a mistreated child might require no more than a perfunctory rap on an open door; and once across the threshold an agent could ask inoffensive questions while he scanned the interior for signs of trouble.[16] But a cruelty man was not to take cooperation for granted: "Mere officialism or bounce will unlock no door either of house or heart. . . . Courtesy in a man with authority and power behind him has a wonderful effect. You may destroy the need for a prosecution by showing to the accused the nobleness of your calling. Two can generally play at the game of bounce, and the owner of the house plays it with all the odds on his side."[17] Nor should the agent ever assume that a parent was guilty of wrongdoing. On the contrary, since by 1900 about 5 percent of all complaints proved to be groundless, the agent must be prepared to "retire gracefully." Where the evidence did point to a problem, agents had to ascertain such facts as family size, income, and religion, determine whether the victim was insured, arrange for a qualified medical examination, and, if headquarters decided that prosecution was necessary, engage a local solicitor to work up the case. Following either a warning or a successful prosecution, there remained the delicate task of making supervisory visits to the offender's home. And while he juggled his roles as diplomat and policeman, the agent was to act as an interpreter of the young. "Besides listening to what little children say, learn what by such sayings little children mean. Get at *what* it is they call stealing, and telling stories, and being naughty. . . . What the starved child calls 'stealing' may not be stealing; yet as his parents call it stealing, the child calls it so, too. . . . Never take a frightened, ill-treated child's *names* for its actions; find out, in particular, what those actions were."[18]

Tutored in the art of family fact-gathering, cruelty men stayed under close observation after taking up their posts. Save for cases involving imminent danger to a child's life, NSPCC agents always consulted their branch secretaries before dismissing a complaint, issuing a warning, or passing on details to headquarters. This procedure slightly reduced agents' field time, but it served the vital function of sustaining local philanthropists' interest in and generosity to the cause.[19] If an agent's supervision by branch officials tended to be pro forma, the evaluation of his work by unannounced visitors from London was not. Anticruelty leaders had long been sensitive to charges that the NSPCC manufactured statistics to dramatize its mission, and one by-product of this sensitivity was an unbending insistence that agents record in detail each complaint investigated.[20] An agent could be admonished not only for carelessness in the preparation of case reports but also for major disparities between his case statistics and those of the "average" inspector. For example, an unusually low ratio of convictions to cases investigated might suggest that some cases had been invented "for show." Although the information available suggests that such behavior was rare, it is nevertheless true that agents felt pressured to unearth cases. Assuming, as the officials of the society did, that child abuse was endemic throughout England, it followed that efficient agents could be expected to deal with a rough quota of cases per month. If an agent's case load remained conspicuously small, he might be transferred to another branch, where, his superiors hoped, the fresh environment would inspire greater zeal.[21]

As contemporaries remarked, the NSPCC earned an impressive return on its training investment.[22] By the 1890's an agent could not carry out his primary task of investigating complaints without performing a wide range of related chores: finding work for unemployed parents; helping men keep their jobs by speaking to their employers; arranging for the adoption by boards of guardians of misused offspring; obtaining clothes for ill-clad children; supplying fireguards; and seeing that the rent was paid while a breadwinner remained in jail.[23] When an inspector lived at the society's local office, he (or his wife) would have been expected to care for an injured child until more permanent arrangements could be made. Like local authorities in Britain and America today, an NSPCC cruelty man often kept in close contact with hospitals for information that might reveal an abusive adult. A few agents were even sufficiently well versed in family law to conduct simple prosecutions.[24] Eventually the NSPCC appointed specialists to cover coroners' inquests, visit charitable institutions where it had sent victims, and observe canal boat children while their floating homes waited for the locks to fill. But at no time prior to the Great War did these specialists appreciably lighten the cruelty man's work load.[25]

The need to patrol immense areas complicated an already complex job. When Inspector W. Payne arrived at the assize town of Stafford in 1903, he was confronting a district of some five hundred square miles. It took Payne several days of cycling to survey the terrain of farms, small towns, and colliery villages surrounding his branch office.[26] Densely populated urban areas presented equally daunting challenges. The society declared it "a fact of experience" that one inspector could not deal effectively with an urban population greater than 100,000. It would be interesting to learn how "experience" had dictated this particular limit, but child-protection literature did not elaborate. The NSPCC did admit, however, that as late as 1907 sixteen branches retained only one agent each to patrol areas with more than 250,000 inhabitants.[27]

Regardless of district size, it was inevitable that some cruelty men would encounter violent hostility to their surveillance work. Yet if NSPCC propaganda is to be believed, assaults on agents seldom took place. In 1888, having pursued 760 complaints, the society noted that only once had an inspector been attacked. Standing orders to its officers to "treat offenders with great respect" and injunctions to avoid "all appearances of fuss and meddlesomeness" had allegedly produced this happy result.[28] On but two other occasions between 1888 and 1910 did NSPCC literature mention specific assaults: in 1891 a Preston man struck an agent with his fist, and in 1908 a Londonderry father applied a sledgehammer to his interrogator. In both cases the society had already taken the assailant to court. Surely there were similar incidents that the NSPCC chose to conceal for fear of fanning controversy over its methods.[29] We do know that cruelty men sometimes sought police escorts for their own safety. Referring to his interview with Mr. Knaggs, a wine-merchant's cellarman, York's Inspector Walter Jackson wrote: "His whole face trembled with passion when conversing with me, and had I not had P. C. Searle there to keep the peace I should not have been here to tell the tale."[30]

Under trying and occasionally hazardous conditions, therefore, cruelty men tried to stir a sense of parental duty in the adults they cautioned. Given how methodically the NSPCC's inspectorate approached the problem of child abuse, the society should bulk large in any history of English social casework. Instead, the group has been ignored. Social casework, according to one recent definition, is "a specialised *personal* service provided in a disciplined manner by a social welfare organisation for families and individuals who require help, both material and emotional, with problems of social adjustment."[31] The Charity Organisation Society is often accepted as the best late Victorian exemplar of the case method. Although the C.O.S. did not invent home visiting and committee deliberation of cases, it certainly applied both techniques with unprecedented rigor. Moreover, the C.O.S. came to recognize the need for training its home visitors in the theory and practice of casework, a recognition that sprang from Octavia Hill's experiences with rent collecting among the tenants in her model dwellings.[32] Yet in some respects the NSPCC was an even more thoroughgoing champion of the social casework method. Whereas the C.O.S. began formal training for home visitors in 1896, the NSPCC had adopted an intensive training course for its "probationers" at least six years earlier. The C.O.S. employed a mixture of salaried and voluntary visitors; paid professionals investigated all of the NSPCC's cases (32,787 in 1901, as compared with 14,000 for the C.O.S.).[33] Unable to locate any of the NSPCC's original case records, Young and Ashton concluded that cruelty men rarely saw "the wider implications of their material or reflected on their methods." This assumption, fresh evidence suggests, is misleading.[34]

Much to the poverty of social historians the NSPCC routinely destroyed its old case records. The cramped conditions at headquarters, first in Harpur Street and later in Leicester Square, required that tens of thousands of detailed family studies be burned. Perhaps because they were misplaced, however, a tiny handful of reports—64—from the society's York branch have survived. With one exception these reports were compiled between March 1898 and August 1903 by Inspector Walter Jackson, an assistant schoolmaster before he joined the NSPCC in 1894.[35] Each of his reports is about 30 pages long and includes data on the victim(s) and the accused, medical examiners' letters, neighbors' testimony, correspondence with headquarters, Jackson's assessment of the emotional interaction among family members, and reports of his follow-up visits. The obvious care with which this information has been gathered might seem to indicate that Jackson was an atypically thorough agent. Yet the sole report of the 64 not prepared by him is equally comprehensive.[36] One might assume also that because 53 of the 64 cases went to court (the usual ratio of prosecutions to investigations was then one to ten),[37] Jackson had taken atypical care in their compilation. But here again a review of the records suggests that York's cruelty man did not reserve his best investigatory work for courtroom consumption.

If Walter Jackson can be taken as roughly representative of NSPCC agents, the same cannot be said of his district. At the turn of the century York contained roughly 15,000 houses and 75,812 persons, of whom Seebohm Rowntree estimated that 28 percent lived in poverty.[38] Additionally, Jackson's district extended eastward into the Wold country, south nearly to the River Humber, and northwest as far as Ripon. In all, the area's population of about 450,000 made it one of the largest single-agent posts in the NSPCC system.[39]

What first strikes the reader of Jackson's reports is the degree of personal concern he had for his clients. Inured as he must have become to family violence, he nonetheless retained a capacity for moral outrage. "A more revolting and disgusting case of ill-treatment it is impossible to imagine" was his comment on the plight of eleven-year-old Richard Prentice, a boy whose female cousin had not only terrorized him into incontinence, but also forced him to eat his own excrement.[40] He found George Headly, a groom, a "lazy, drunken, beastly scamp," and Florence Simpson, wife of a railway guard, a "dirty, filthy slattern." Both offenders deserved to be "well punished" for grossly neglecting their families.[41] But more often the inspector was prepared to overlook parental failings where any hope of reformation remained. A month in prison for child neglect had been hard enough on Mary Connor. Shortly after her release Jackson visited Mrs. Connor: "I was prepared to close my eyes to anything irregular as long as I could find the woman sober in order that by moral suasion and advice, I could get her to do right for right's sake." Similarly, he passed the residence of Mrs. Ellen Bruce almost daily, but usually refrained from approaching the neglectful mother as she lounged about the entry to Ebor Buildings. If unharassed, perhaps she too would undergo that "transformation" in parental feeling about which Jackson delighted to write.[42]

York's cruelty man thus assumed the sometimes discordant duties of "seeing through brick walls" and convincing citizens to use him as an arbiter of domestic justice.[43] Shouldering both these responsibilities meant that Jackson enjoyed very little privacy of his own. In September 1898, the *Child's Guardian* printed a sample schedule for one agent who had purportedly worked 92 hours in one week for the society, including eleven and a half hours on Sunday.[44] Jackson's experience suggests that such labor may not have been rare. News of a serious case sent him into the streets at any time between dawn and midnight. More time-consuming still was the personal assistance he gave: searching for a mother who had deserted her home; buying milk for malnourished children; interceding with the pawnbroker to return a family's last blanket.[45] Indeed, despite the NSPCC's heated denial that it was a charity, child-protection officials knew their work could not be wholly divorced from the granting of material aid. Agents like Jackson passed on both used clothing and money to families in which one parent had been jailed for harming a child. In local emergencies cruelty men might even turn to organizing public relief. When widespread unemployment in the local ironworks coincided with the end of free lunches to children during a school holiday, Inspector Payne set up a soup kitchen that eventually fed two thousand needy scholars.[46] NSPCC agents probably had fewer doors slammed in their faces because they came calling with a reputation for goodwill toward the neighborhood.

The Patrolled

Walter Jackson's York case reports show that the prevention of cruelty to children elicited a wide range of behavior from offenders and their communities. Middle-class observers were right to stress the reluctance of the poor to inform on their neighbors. In Arthur Morrison's turn-of-the-century Jago, London's most fearsome slum, feuding factions might fall on each other with knives and jagged bottles, but carrying a tale to the police was unthinkable. "Thou shalt not nark" was the slum's sole commandment.[47] Similarly, informing against a child abuser might violate the hallowed norm of neighborhood self-sufficiency. To "put oneself forward" in this way, Mary Loane explained, was to risk ostracism. Moreover, some working-class parents worried that once summoned, the "N-Spectre" might turn from berating the genuinely brutal party to harassing the informer for slapping his disobedient child.[48] When an accused parent returned home to await trial, an informer's initial anger might melt into remorse at having brought on the prosecution or into fear at the prospect of eventual retribution. For these reasons, the witness might refuse to testify against the accused.[49]

If a cruelty man appeared overly censorious, particularly in cases where outright brutality was not at issue, he could alienate local opinion. Stephen Reynolds and his co-authors, two fishermen, offered this unflattering portrait of an NSPCC agent on the prowl.

Look what the National Cruelty 'spector did for Mrs. Sherwill. 'Twas a shame, I reckon. Her's so hard-working a woman as anybody, an' clean too, and her's often and often gone short for to give they kids o' hers enough. They'm so happy as any chil'ern I knows of, for all they 'am poor. Well, somebody tells up a parcel o' chatter an' down comes the 'spector 'long wi' a policeman. In they goes, wi'out any warrant as I've heard of. The 'spector asks her if her's married to her man. Says Mrs. Sherwill, "Do 'ee thinks I'd be bothered wi' a family o' chil'ern like mine if I wasn't!" But her refused to show 'em her marriage lines, not if her burnt 'em or went to prison for't. Up goes the 'spector an' turns over all the bedclothes an' feels the beds wi' his hands, like so. *They* was clean, he said. Down he comes again, an' turns up the chil'ern's hair, an' pokes his nose into cupboards an' everywhere; an' when Mr. Sherwill, coming home, asks 'en what he wanted there, he says, "None o' your cheek, my lad!"[50]

Walter Jackson also scoured children for evidence of body and scalp lice. Occasionally, as in the case of five-year-old Benjamin Thompson, he found skin so riddled with vermin bites that the undergarments were bloodstained.[51] Even the presence of a few fleas earned a lecture from York's cruelty man. Trained by middle-class superiors to wage war on dirt in all its forms, Jackson and his fellow agents no doubt were prone to interpret a lack of cleanliness in house and offspring as evidence of parental neglect. At school verminous children were isolated from their peers in a "small sanitary cordon of humiliation"; at home it was their fathers and mothers who ran the risk of reproof.[52]

Verbally abusive or intemperate parents likewise brought out the scold in Jackson. Elizabeth Winspear referred to her five children as "blasted little bastards." George Appleton habitually called his house-bound stepdaughter "nothing but a whore in the streets." Their case reports indicate that Jackson was swayed to recommend prosecution partially on account of such "unnatural" language.[53] The inspector could be equally stern where drink was a central issue. One evening, nine months after Mrs. Elizabeth Kendale's trial for neglect, Jackson stopped at her house to check on her battle against beer. He had just finished an examination of the children when their mother and father returned from a temperance meeting. Greeting Mrs. Kendale with the observation that her young ones could be cleaner, Jackson was not made welcome. "I suppose she thought I ought to be satisfied," he wrote in a tardy flash of insight.[54]

Despite what at times may have seemed "incredible impertinence" on the part of NSPCC agents,[55] the fact remains that England's working classes did confide in the cruelty men. Of the 64 cases documented by Jackson, 47 stated the source of the complaint, and in 55 percent of these, the source was the general public. Concerned citizens stopped Jackson in the streets, found him at home, or sent letters to his office. Salaried officials (most notably policemen), Poor Law relieving officers, schoolmasters, and truancy agents accounted for 36 percent of the complainants. Jackson himself discovered only two (4 percent) of the cases. Nor were York and its environs unusual in this respect. Of the 23,124 cases reported to the society in 1896–97, 58 percent of the complaints emanated from the general public, 24 percent from salaried officials, and 18 percent from the personal investigations of cruelty men. A decade later the proportion of cases unearthed by NSPCC agents had fallen to less than 10 percent.[56]

Gradually, therefore, the society's inspectors were accepted as the legitimate guardians of ill-used children. Robert Roberts recalled that in Edwardian Salford, "whenever my mother heard of a heinous case, as with the women who boasted in the shop, 'My master [husband] allus flogs 'em till the blood runs down their back!' she quietly 'put the cruelty man on.'"[57] It was possible for Mrs. Roberts to alert the local inspector "quietly" because the NSPCC held to its policy of preserving the confidentiality of all informants. Only in very rare cases, where it was obvious that an allegation had been prompted by malice, would child-savers divulge the name of their source. For example, in 1903 a schoolmistress suffered such embarrassment over her alleged cruelty to a pupil that Waugh revealed the identity of her false accuser—a member of the society's own local committee.[58] The York records contain only one case in which a termagant put Jackson onto her neighbor out of pure spite. Such grudge-motivated resort to NSPCC agents may have been more common, though close questioning of the informer often would have unmasked the lie—as in the York example—before any action was taken.[59] Generally, private citizens provided facts that were well-intentioned, if not always accurate. Anonymous tips gave the greatest scope for malicious misinformation. In 1901 NSPCC statisticians found that 105 of 1,000 complaints had been made anonymously; yet 83 of these proved to be "well-founded." In 1908 a similar study revealed that 89 percent of the society's anonymous complaints had a factual basis.[60]

Many people turned to Inspector Jackson because they had already tried and failed to discourage the ill-use of a neighbor's children. Investigating a complaint of assault against a farmer living near Stamford Bridge, Jackson found Mrs. Sykes, the resident of an adjacent farm, only too eager to talk: "Now mister, I is only a poor woman, but I have had many a sleepless night, and shed many tears over the poor lass. I have prayed God morning and night to deliver her, and now my prayer is going to be answered." Similarly, a shoemaker living in York's Hungate slum confessed that seeing Mrs. Appleton drag her daughter by the hair across the cobbled courtyard "made my blood boil." Although he "went out and shooed her off the bairn," the shoemaker knew that only a prolonged surveillance of Mrs. Appleton's behavior could afford any protection to the daughter.[61]

By the close of the nineteenth century England's county police had nearly suppressed "stang-riding," "rough music," and most other forms of popular justice.[62] Hindered from exercising traditional sanctions against those who were perceived as social deviants, some working-class communities apparently accepted cruelty men as surrogate instruments of coercion. A characteristic feature of working-class culture in late Victorian and Edwardian England was its hostility to state-sponsored welfare programs such as compulsory vaccination.[63] Though NSPCC inspectors were also imposed on communities, they were much more likely to be regarded as useful allies in the struggle of the poor to maintain neighborhood respectability. Significantly, Jackson's informants often described the actions of brutal parents as "shameful." One witness moved because she could no longer bear the screams of the battered children living next door.[64]

Allegedly even those whom the NSPCC chastised sometimes smiled on the cruelty men. Child-protection literature abounds with testimonials from erring adults who thanked the society for showing them the path of true parenthood. Mary Loane, too, noted that uneducated fathers and mothers who had been warned, fined, and jailed rarely held grudges. One normally pugnacious mother reduced an inspector to "helpless laughter" when she declared publicly, " 'He's been as kind to me as a father!' "[65] But for other adults the society's glare must have seemed less than benign. Ellen Bruce plainly felt persecuted. Summoned to appear before the York city bench for neglecting her three children (on more than one occasion she had pawned the family blankets as well as most of its clothing to buy drink), Mrs. Bruce fled rather than face prison and separation from her young ones. From Leeds she wrote movingly to her estranged husband, a glass blower then living in London:

Dear Husband

I write a few lines hoping it will find you well as I am glad to say we are all right & we are in good lodgings. I have been hear a week to day & have kept the children all right so far. Please write back by return of Post & send me what you can by Saturday morning. I am going to stay hear for a week or two or until the time you send for me as I don't intend going back to York. I would sooner die in the streets. I am doing my best for the children and I am sure it would be much better for us all to be to gether than be as we are. They say they would sooner be hear than in York. They are amused with the Electric light. It is very miserable being far from you. Excuse me this time. With our best love & wishes.

Your Aff
E Bruce
good by & God bless you
xxxxxxxxxxxxxxxxxxxxxxxx
don't forget to write

Mrs. Bruce was apprehended in Leeds, brought back to York, and sentenced to three months with hard labor. Her children were placed in the workhouse.[66]

Thus, some adults feared the society's intervention in their domestic lives not because, as in New York City, child-savers had a reputation for snatching the offspring of the poor, but rather because the NSPCC seemed so relentless in applying its code of good parenthood.[67] Based on parliamentary law, this code was not itself procrustean. Nor did the society often hold parents accountable for violations of anticruelty law when these violations seemed to be the unavoidable product of want. But at what point did a parent become morally as well as legally culpable for his child's suffering? The laborer whose young stayed malnourished while a trade depression kept him out of work would probably get NSPCC aid rather than a reprimand. However, the same man, if he balked at taking an available job, might well incur the wrath of an inspector. It was in such morally ambiguous circumstances that the reformers' class bias showed most clearly.

How English children themselves viewed the society and its work is harder to judge. The NSPCC's assertion that cruelty men were "popular" with the boys and girls they met on their rounds should be received with caution. Surely there were times when the sight of an inspector at a door brought to the children within some hope of relief from the kicks, cuffs, or starvation that they had endured. But equally, there must have been occasions when children regarded the arrival of a cruelty man as a distinct threat to family unity. "As a rule," noted one observer, "the working classes show remarkable loyalty to the memory of their parents, and seem convinced that 'they done their best.'"[68] The young who confided in Walter Jackson sometimes added that a difficult parent was harsh only when vexed or drunk, implying, first, that they thought it *their* responsibility to gauge the parent's mood and react accordingly, and second, that they did not see the parent as cruel by nature. Although these offspring seemed to welcome the sobering influence of a visit from Jackson, they did not want their parents punished or, worse, taken away.

What happened to the children whose parents were imprisoned? Even when jailed for severe neglect or assault, offenders usually returned to their young—closely watched, of course, by cruelty men. Thus NSPCC leaders not only spoke and wrote about preserving the family but also worked to honor this ideal. Of the 754,732 children on whose behalf the society intervened between mid-1889 and mid-1903, only 1,200—far less than 1 percent—were removed from parental custody.[69] Magistrates placed a few of these children with relatives, but sent most on to orphanages, industrial schools, and, as a last resort, workhouses. Impersonal as such new homes may have been, the boys and girls settled in them through NSPCC action were at least safe from physical harm.

Rethinking the Problem

The great majority of NSPCC cases involved children who had been mistreated by their parents. Although national statistics on the relationship between victims and offenders were not usually published, Jackson's experience in York is suggestive. Eighty-seven percent of his case reports cited parents or stepparents as the culpable parties. A cousin, an aunt, and a grandmother accounted for three more cases. Only five of the York area offenders were unrelated to the children whom they had reportedly misused.

Dr. Barnardo himself gave voice to the common belief that stepmothers were frequently abusive:

It is, perhaps, too much to expect that the second wife of a working-man should have the same affection towards her husband's children by a former wife as towards her own; but case after case has come before us in which the jealousy of a step-mother has led to the most cruel treatment of the little folks committed to her charge. . . . Maternal affection is jealously exclusive, and degenerates, in numerous instances, into a hatred that results in many a tale of long-continued cruelty.[70]

Barnardo was probably exaggerating the havoc wreaked by working-class stepmothers. Some years later Mary Loane remarked that stepchildren so often became the concern of interfering neighbors that a stepmother "dares not inflict the most reasonable and necessary punishment." Based on the evidence gathered in an extensive oral survey, Paul Thompson hinted that stepfathers better fit the stereotype of severity. But NSPCC data conjure up a different image. For the year 1891–92 the society found that only 4 percent of its 8,324 cases involved stepchildren.[71] In the York district, eight of the 64 families investigated by Jackson contained stepparents: four stepfathers, three stepmothers, and one family where each spouse had children by a former marriage. Though the York sample is far too small to permit confident generalization, it is noteworthy that in five of the eight households with stepparents *both* man and wife were charged with neglect or physical violence; and in only one case did a stepparent appear to be unilaterally responsible for causing "unnecessary suffering." More damning was the evidence against single-parent offenders. Eighteen (28 percent) of Jackson's cases involved men or women who seemed unable to cope alone with their offspring. Taken as a group, widowers (six), widows (five), and wives separated from their husbands (seven) posed a greater threat to the well-being of their young than stepparents.

If the York data supported headquarters in its rejection of the wicked stepmother theory, there was less accord over the economics of cruelty. In the beginning, as we have seen, child-protection literature flatly rejected any link between poverty and child abuse. The average earnings of offending parents were described as "very good" or "high."[72] As the NSPCC gained in both reputation and experience, however, it grew more cautious about such pronouncements. Once certain that their cause had taken firm root among philanthropists, Waugh and his staff were prepared to admit that the collection of statistics by branch societies lacked uniformity. Charles Booth's revelation of mass poverty in the East End of London may also have given NSPCC leaders pause. After all, child-savers could not ignore Booth's discovery, based on a systematic street-by-street search, of neighborhoods typified by "brutality within the circle of family life."[73]

Possibly, too, the society's own records may have forced a rethinking of its position on poverty. Here Jackson's data provide some interesting clues. The range of family income among York offenders was very wide, from an annual salary of nearly £200 for a senior clerk with the North East Railway Company, to no regular wages at all for an unemployed laborer with four children. Plainly, the presence of such extremes renders the averaging of family incomes unfruitful. Variations in the cost of living between urban and rural districts pose further obstacles to comparison. Fortunately, Seebohm Rowntree's meticulous survey of poverty in York offers a standard for gauging the urban data. Rowntree divided York's 75,812 inhabitants (as of late 1899) into seven economic and residential groups. By applying Rowntree's standards to Inspector Jackson's 38 city cases with household income data, one sees at once that Jackson's cases do not form a balanced economic cross section.[74] Whereas 4 percent of Rowntree's city-wide population fell into "class A"—those who were chronically ill-housed, ill-clothed, and underfed—42 percent of the families visited by Jackson lived at this level. Residential addresses confirm that a substantial part of the cruelty man's casework was in the poorest and most overcrowded areas of York. "Hungate," "Hope Street," "Bedern," and "Skeldergate"—all colored purple (for slums) on Rowntree's city map—were the scenes of most of Jackson's work. Given that York in 1899 was "fairly representative of the conditions existing in many . . . provincial towns," it seems probable that the NSPCC looked for and found much of its work in the "low districts" of major urban centers. Child-protection officials could still maintain that cruelty was "classless," but they found it increasingly difficult to deny that poverty was a strong contributory factor.[75]

The society's public stance on drink changed even more dramatically. Apart from the unexamined link between brutality and intemperance set forth in its *First Annual Report*,[76] the London SPCC would not isolate drunkenness as a cause of parental misconduct. In mid-1889 anticruelty spokesmen were still arguing that those "who perpetrated these crimes [against children] were not drunkards; they were callous people, cold and calculating."[77] Neither did the society at first favor legislation to shield boys and girls from the influence of pubs. C. A. V. Conybeare in 1886 brought before the Commons a controversial bill designed to keep the holders of liquor licences from "knowingly" selling any alcoholic beverage—for consumption on the premises—to a child under thirteen.[78] An incensed Waifs and Strays Society declared that children of tender years "in almost incredible numbers" were compelled by their lazy parents to fetch drink from beer houses and gin shops, thus exposing the innocents to "object lessons" that undermined every value taught in schools. A Bristol census conducted in 1881 established that over a four-hour period on a single Saturday night 12,000 children entered 900 drinking houses. A similar situation existed in London. Surely then "all lovers of children" together with "all who desire the future stability of the State" would support Conybeare's plan?[79] But London SPCC leaders regarded the original bill and the statute that evolved from it as flaccid, likely to deter no one. And they were right. December 1887 saw pubs such as the Bedford Arms in Kensington with provocative signs in their windows: "A Monster Christmas Tree within. Whatever child brings a jug on Thursday, the 28th, shall receive a handsome present."[80]

However, it was over this issue of selling drink to the young that anticruelty workers began to change their minds about the link between alcohol and child abuse. Throughout the 1890's temperance advocates hammered home the depths to which publicans stooped in luring children to their establishments. Poor parents were motivated to send their offspring in search of beer by the "long pull," an extra measure of liquor drawn free into a jug. Then, to attract young carriers, publicans gave away an assortment of toys, fruit, and sweets. Probably best known was the toffee whistle whose toots filled city streets on Sunday. The Chief Constable of Manchester found that during August 1897 63 percent of the 1,764 local pubs serving liquor to children also offered them some small favor. Such inducements went far toward explaining why in certain London districts between 10 and 16 percent of public house customers were children, some of them "tiny mites."[81]

Further, boys and girls supposedly risked acquiring a taste for drink by sipping from the containers they carried home. England's juvenile temperance groups warned their members about the "hereditary predisposition to alcoholism," a trait thought by some doctors to be as transmissible as physical or mental characteristics.[82] Nor was this danger exclusive to the offspring of low-living parents. The Royal Commission on the Liquor Licensing Laws learned that some women who would not enter pubs still sent their children to buy drink at nearby grocers.[83] When in 1896 and 1897 Merseyside magistrates successfully enforced the law against serving alcohol to children under thirteen, the NSPCC at last closed ranks with temperance workers. The society's branches were urged to petition borough officials and JPs for strict observance of the 1886 statute.[84] Soon thereafter Waugh and company gave their full support to legislation aimed at prohibiting alcohol sales for any reason to children under fourteen. To NSPCC leaders it was now plain that children should be shielded from the "base and shameful sights and sounds" of public houses. Thus, although the Act of 1901 (1 Edw. VII, c. 27) eliminated "sipping" as a danger by forcing publicans to cork and seal all vessels sold to young messengers, it did not go far enough to suit the society.[85]

By the turn of the century NSPCC leaders were also shedding their reluctance to equate cruelty with drunkenness. Beer was the laboring man's staple beverage. Since five shillings per week could buy as many as 24 pints of beer, some working-class fathers who came home to a quarrelsome wife or fractious children may have been primed to restore domestic peace by force rather than reason.[86] But what most worried middle-class observers was the apparent rise in intemperance among women. Rowntree and Sherwell noted that although England's criminal statistics did not necessarily support this assumption, the Registrar General's data on deaths due to alcohol abuse gave good cause for concern; whereas the ratio of mortality from excessive drinking had increased 43 percent among males between 1877 and 1896, it had increased 104 percent among females. Public officials in Liverpool felt that the "long pull" encouraged heavy consumption at home. Likewise, liquor sold at the back doors of public houses promoted female drinking during the daytime. However they got their liquor, drunken women constituted a hazard to the children with whom they spent so much time.[87]

It was primarily to help alcoholic mothers that the NSPCC sought special powers to deal with habitual inebriates. By the early 1890's English public opinion was warming to the idea of compulsory detention of chronic drunks in government-approved retreats. At least one reformer had gone so far as to urge the removal of children from women with three convictions for drunkenness.[88] Though medical activists continued to press for a major overhaul of public policy toward alcoholic disease, the society in its 1894 amending Act did win for drunken parents convicted of offenses against their young twelve months' detention in a licensed inebriates' retreat as an alternative to prison. Sometimes only prolonged isolation could cure "drink despotism," the society felt. This held especially true for women, who, being "more excitable, less subject to the control of motive and more to the promptings of impulse," clung more tightly to their besotted ways.[89]

Required to gain an alcoholic parent's consent to committal, and burdened with the full costs of institutionalization, the NSPCC was slow to exercise its new power. Between 1894 and 1898, during which time the society dealt with 2,084 cases involving habitual drunkenness, only a dozen adults entered retreats. With the advent of compulsory institutionalization under the 1898 Inebriates' Act, however, child-savers could be more systematic in this phase of their work. By late 1902 over a hundred parents per year were being placed in retreats. "Wrecked mothers of wrecked families" received very careful attention. At the end of six months in a retreat, the convalescing woman received a photo of her now-healthy children to stir her "maternal feelings"; to help restore a firm marital bond, the husband was urged to keep up a loving correspondence; and on her release, the mother found a sympathetic lady volunteer to befriend her. Although the rate of relapse among these women tended to be high, NSPCC literature argued that any progress in the war on alcoholism was a boon to children.[90]

Once it had become a vocal supporter of inebriates' homes, the society could hardly deny that alcohol was a prime factor in parental misconduct. In 1898 cruelty men W. H. Mason and George Luff offered some striking testimony to the Royal Commission on Liquor Licensing Laws. Mason estimated that roughly half of all NSPCC cases were attributable to drink, and Luff declared that fully two-thirds of the complaints made to him involved chronic intoxication.[91] The York case records reinforce these impressions. Jackson's reports show that 53 percent of alleged offenders were frequently drunk, and this figure excludes those listed simply as "drinkers." Since York's ratio of pubs and off-licenses to population was not unusually high for a major city, the figure becomes even more striking.[92] Yet NSPCC officials could still reject the inference that cruelty to children was merely a facet of the temperance question, for both the society and its allies depicted the drunken parent as generally neglectful rather than willfully harsh. More often, it seemed, overt cruelty was the province of sober, calculating brutes. The man who pawned his family's bedclothes for beer money or the woman whose slavery to drink pushed her young ones to the brink of starvation might be reformed by assaulting their drinking habits.

But "ingenious and fiendish" parents would continue to demand scrutiny by specialists in child welfare.[93]

According to some contemporary observers, working-class parents in prewar England rarely administered severe corporal punishment. In all Mary Loane's experience among the poor, she could recall no more than twelve cases of physically abused children, and not a single instance of persistent ill-treatment. More recently, Paul Thompson has interpreted his oral survey data to mean that Edwardian parents did not often use physical force because their authority was rarely challenged.[94] Thompson may be right that grand thrashings were comparatively rare events, but his assumption that parental authority usually went unchallenged needs qualification. Children in poor families were often far from compliant. Impudence and swagger in the very young were frequently either ignored or met with bribes of sweets.[95] But precisely because domestic discipline could be lax during a child's first years, the attempt by parents to assert their authority at a later stage in the child's development sometimes required real severity. This disciplinary pattern may help to explain why middle-class investigators often described slum children as either spoiled or brutalized.[96] In comfortable working-class homes the administration of corporal punishment was probably more frequent though less extreme than among the desperately poor.[97]

The NSPCC's records show that by the opening years of the twentieth century a great majority of its cases involved neglected rather than physically abused children. Whereas assaults on the young constituted roughly half of the society's complaints in four of its first five years, by 1900 these cases made up only an eighth of its total work. And after a quarter century of experience, the NSPCC found that a mere 7 percent of its complaints could be attributed to "violence" (see Appendix C, Fig. 4). An obvious explanation for this change is that severe beating of children is apt to be noisier and therefore more likely to draw attention than, say, gradual starvation. As a result, in its early days the society naturally heard most often about public outrages; as its reputation and inspectorate grew, the discovery of child neglect grew correspondingly. However, NSPCC literature continued to dwell on acts of parental violence long after they had ceased to form a large proportion of the society's case load, a preoccupation that seems to have stemmed in part from the shock value of such behavior.

Reformers liked to think that a "manly and judicial bench" and the Children's Charter had deterred English parents from resorting to the most extreme cruelties. The NSPCC's eighth annual report implied, for example, that there was a direct relationship between its advertising the prison terms imposed on offenders and the virtual disappearance of the poker as an instrument of torture. It was "curious," though, that the "milder torture" of lighted matches held to a child's hands and nostrils made its debut in the same year.[98] The society also took heart from what seemed to be a drop in the frequency of child suicide. Here anticruelty workers were assuming that punishment, whether experienced or anticipated, was the single most important factor in driving children to take their lives. Yet the long-term trends in the statistics for child suicide, unreliable as they are, show no diminution of suicide for the ten- to fourteen-year-old age group until after 1900.[99] Nor was the steadily declining percentage of NSPCC cases ending in death a clear-cut victory, for again it was predictable that as the society became better known life-threatening incidents would be reported more promptly than in the past.[100]

Even the growing resort to warnings in lieu of prosecutions cannot be construed as proof of the society's inhibitory effect on parental misconduct (see Appendix C, Fig. 5). The sensitivity of child-protection leaders to the criticism that they spent too much on legal fees would have made them moderately court-shy, particularly after Lord Herschell presented his cost-cutting recommendations in 1897.[101] Moreover, as the movement continued to gain in public stature, the importance of self-justifying prosecutions diminished correspondingly.

It is also hazardous to compare the incidence of child abuse in the late Victorian and Edwardian era with more modern figures. In the middle of the twentieth century, it was estimated that between 6 and 7 percent of English children were at some time during their childhood so neglected or ill-treated, or became so "maladjusted," as to require the help of the NSPCC.[102] A study published in 1972 drew the troubling conclusion that eighteen of 100 selected cases of physical injury to children had been misdiagnosed cases of child abuse.[103] Recent American studies paint an equally grim picture. Extrapolating from a 1965 survey of 1,520 respondents, David Gil suggested the possibility of as many as 4.1 million cases of child abuse per year for the United States. Richard Light has reinterpreted Gil's data to find a minimum annual figure of 200,000 cases of physical abuse of children under the age of eighteen, with an upper figure of 500,000 cases. Taking into account an estimated additional 465,000 cases of neglect and maltreatment, the resulting total would mean that approximately one American child in every hundred is physically abused, sexually molested, or severely neglected. Obviously, how one chooses to define "abuse," "neglect," or "maladjustment" will in large part determine the size of the estimated population at risk.[104] Insofar as the first anticruelty groups interpreted such labels more narrowly than latter-day experts, it is safe to assume that the NSPCC's published case statistics appreciably understate the extent of childhood suffering.

The Appeal of the Crusade

The NSPCC was obsessed with expansion precisely because it viewed child abuse as a social problem whose depths had yet to be plumbed. Sounding the sea of cruelty required instruments more complex than England then possessed. But given sufficient funding and continued support from right-minded citizens, the NSPCC felt confident that it could reshape the idea of parental prerogative. Most humane activists indeed shared the view that cruelty was "unnatural," an aberration of human nature. RSPCA propaganda generally depicted the desire to inflict pain as a learned depravity. Cruelty could be extinguished, animal lovers liked to think, by removing its stimuli. Hence the RSPCA advocated banishing all slaughterhouses to the thinly populated rural districts, and attempted to inculcate in children a reverence for animal life by promoting humane essay competitions in elementary schools.[105] Similarly, the Humanitarian League, founded in 1891, believed that cruelty "in nine cases out of ten" was the result of a defective imagination; the brutal man is brutal because he cannot put himself in the place of those who suffer. Henry Salt, the league's most active spokesman, went on to argue that the fostering of a sympathetic imagination was possible only when society recognized the universal brotherhood of sentient creatures. It followed, therefore, that all action tending to diminish such universal sympathy—corporal punishment of criminals, vivisection, flesh-eating—was unjust.[106]

NSPCC supporters saw intentional abuse of the young as symptomatic of a pathological impairment in the natural affection of parent for child.[107] Sometimes cruelty resulted when adults lost a "sense of proportion" in dealing with their offspring. A drunken cook's admission that she struck her daughter with boots, pans, and carving knives because she could not "bear the sight of her" prompted the society to suggest that "the motive of cruelty is often the cruel person's own self-loathing. . . . Generally speaking, the faults with which children are credited by cruel people are the illusions of bad minds. Hating the child, hateful things are seen in it. The devil in *them* sees a devil in the *child*."[108] Mary Loane described a twelve-year-old girl who was severely thrashed by her mother when she accidentally broke a jug. The daughter's behavior had been misinterpreted as an act of overt hostility, an attempt to do personal injury to her mother. Thus the parent was seeking revenge.[109]

The overly demanding parent could construe the most trivial incidents as proof of a child's ill will. Inspector Jackson noted that a boy's cowed expression and a baby girl's crying had been enough to spark outbursts of fury in two families. Equally, petty thefts of sugar from the table or coppers from the purse could set certain parents on a rampage.[110] One Edwardian physician ventured the opinion that highly strung parents who were "well up in the doctrine of heredity" seemed especially prone to treat their naughty children as hateful reflections of themselves.[111] Taken together, these observations by prewar advocates of child protection pointed to what later theorists would call the "role reversal" phenomenon. Whether or not abusive adults encountered physical degradation as children, recent studies maintain, they share a common heritage of intensely demanding and critical mothers and fathers. Excessive and premature parental expectations breed in their offspring feelings of inadequacy. On becoming parents themselves, these ego-impaired individuals tend to rely on their own children for emotional support, and when the young prove unable to supply this anticipated gratification, they respond punitively.[112]

The NSPCC also subscribed to an important variation on the theory that abusive adults suffered from low self-esteem. This variation maintained that some parents, possessed of "a sullen, ill-conditioned temperament," found the affliction of pain on helpless beings somehow gratifying. These adults most nearly fit Frances Power Cobbe's model of the "heteropath."[113] In Benjamin Waugh's typology such adults were simply cowards; and since cowards responded most sharply to fear, the threat of punishment could work wonders. This formulation, wrote W. T. Stead, was rather like the Calvinistic idea of innate depravity, combined with a modified doctrine of reprobation: "For those lost souls, for whom the society prepares scorpions and tread-mills, although given over to the possession of a foul spirit, are not wholly lost. Given the lack of pipe and beer, and a long enough period of reflection on the bread and water of affliction, many of them can be reclaimed." [114] Thus physical deprivation could steer wayward souls back to the path of true parenthood. But for a lasting reformation in behavior to take hold, the cruel or neglectful parent must actively want a better life for his family. And the chief agent in tapping hidden springs of "parental feeling" was the former victim.

It is the mystic power of a child, the warm flesh of a child, the sweet smile of its eyes, its clean new print frock in which you return it to the ex-prisoner, which makes him often find himself more sensible of shame and pride and good resolves than he cares to confess, which nonetheless on that account tend towards, at least, a less base life . . . in the future. A child's happiness is a power over a man; and even when he is not subject to its influence at the moment of his release from prison, he has still a chance to feel that passion for a child which gives colour and warmth to the six month's supervision of the child which follows its return to him. [115]

What NSPCC case data do not reveal is the extent to which prosecuted parents resumed their brutal ways, perhaps sometimes vindictively. Child-savers never missed a chance to herald their impressive ratio of convictions to prosecutions. After twenty years the NSPCC had achieved a success rate of about 97 percent in the cases it brought to trial. But unlike the advocates of prison reform, child-protection leaders kept no close track of recidivism. This is not altogether surprising, for at the local level even a conscientious inspector could not watch old offenders forever. In his York district Walter Jackson sometimes spread his supervisory visits over several years. Ultimately, however, Jackson depended on the vigilance of neighbors; and with the passage of time his informers might move and be replaced by new families more reticent about "narking" on local tyrants. [116] Modern studies of family violence suggest that the rebattering of children is an all-too-common phenomenon. In light of these findings the historian must wonder if an unintended result of the NSPCC's campaign was to drive cruel parents to inflict pain with greater stealth. [117]

Although the English child protection movement failed to propound a coherent etiology of child abuse, it unquestionably succeeded in depicting its work as both urgent and hopeful. The cause was urgent because if left to fester, cruelty would spread, infecting the next generation of adults just as it had the present.[118] Many of the ill-used children discovered by the society were very young; 43 percent of the 109,364 boys and girls assisted during the NSPCC's first decade, for example, were six years of age or under. The sooner intervention between young and old came in these sad cases, therefore, the better off the community would be.[119] The cause was hopeful, too, because the child-protection crusade promised explicitly to save "infant citizens" from unnecessary suffering and implicitly to succor adults in an age of high anxiety.

After all, it was during the late Victorian period that man's kinship with the beast became a matter of particular concern. By the 1880's Tennyson's view of nature as a battleground "red in tooth and claw" had gained wide currency, and to laymen the social implications of a biology that equated survival with struggle were profoundly troubling. If man was merely an animal assigned to a contest in which strength invariably prevailed over sensitivity, trust in the nobility of the human mind became difficult. Some members of England's social and intellectual elite thus tried to save the mind from the advance of godless science by demonstrating that human intellect transcended its corporeal shell. In 1882, for example, a group of scholars, scientists, and religious leaders, with the distinguished Cambridge philosopher Henry Sidgwick at their head, founded the Society for Psychical Research. Officially dedicated to empirical investigation of all reported paranormal phenomena, the society in fact served as a vehicle through which its members hoped to amass incontrovertible proof of the immortality of the mind.[120] Psychical research appealed to those who felt that a thoroughly materialist conception of mental activity reduced man to a bestial level, thereby precluding the possibility of an afterlife.

Another and very different approach to the problem of redefining human nature in the wake of the Darwinian revolution was to concede man's kinship with animals while exalting the nature of the latter. This view often entailed a reliance on highly anthropomorphic imagery. As evidenced by the popularity of Edwin Landseer's canine portraits, English preoccupation with the protohuman qualities of animals antedated the emergence of antivivisectionist sentiment.[121] NSPCC propaganda depicted animals not so much as unique beings with varying mental and moral qualities but as repositories of instinctual virtue. Founders of the society, it was subsequently claimed, felt that bad parents needed to be reshaped more like animals than saints, for "it is to instincts, which men share with the beasts of the field, that we must look to remove and prevent the calamities to offspring's lives."[122] In his own tracts, the blunt Benjamin Waugh usually dispensed with animal imagery, preferring instead to confront directly the "increasing tendency to regard human beings as protoplasm [and] . . . to account for human life by molecules." Clearly, however, child protection, like other humane causes, did provide the public with a concrete program for improving society. Against a background of growing concern about the survival of religiously based values, this opportunity to participate in moral reclamation was particularly welcome.[123]

At the same time, the prevention of cruelty to children appealed to philanthropists as a practical investment in social stability. To many members of the late Victorian political elite, the prospect of molding a stable working class must have been comforting. The 1884 Reform Act brought Britain closer to universal male suffrage, enfranchising an additional two million voters. Now that working-class sons had become "the future masters of the political situation," it was doubly important that they be shielded from character-warping influences.[124] By aiming to save the child from mistreatment in his own home—in effect, to regulate the shaping of personality—the NSPCC presented a method for rendering the next generation of adults more tractable without requiring sweeping changes in the economic organization of society. The NSPCC, of course, disavowed any objective other than defending the young:

Though it is true that to do right to a child and to secure its welfare, is to do right to the community and to secure the welfare of the community, we have not been working for the community. . . . In the yearly swelling number of voices lifted up in praise of our work we recognize another than our own key-note. . . . The politician speaks of our future voters, and asks with horror what they will become if nurtured in brutal homes. The political economist asks what charges upon taxes and rates must follow the growth of emaciated childhood up into muscularly-ruined manhood, to meet its crime and pauperism. The commercial mind cries out against unfitness of boys and girls for juvenile labour, by the cheapness of which our factories can compete with the Continent. For this work children must be healthy.

The educationalist demands their proper feeding, or he cannot teach his rule of three. . . . All these are facts; . . . but, as the vital motive of our work, they are none of them worthy. They are, indeed, all comparatively ignoble, and selfish, and base.[125]

That the society felt obliged to reject such motives as legitimate incentives for child protection testifies to the strength of their attraction. Moreover, by carefully listing these "base" arguments before dismissing them, the NSPCC was serving notice that its work *ought* to attract the hard head as well as the soft heart.

Indeed, the child-protection movement of late nineteenth- and early twentieth-century England might seem to constitute a classic case of philanthropy as a tool of social control. NSPCC leaders certainly left little to chance. The cruelty men were trained to persuade adults—most of them poor—to honor a new and complex set of regulations on domestic conduct. Further, to insure continuing support from the comfortable classes, the NSPCC sought allies among the children of these classes. The idea of a youth auxiliary, modeled on the RSPCA's Band of Mercy, seems to have been broached at a Richmond branch meeting in 1891. By December of that year the *Child's Guardian* was calling for ten thousand young workers "to get money and to give it, because it costs money, a great deal of money, to make cruel people do right." The resulting League of Pity made no attempt to disguise its class orientation. Each member was expected to give five shillings to the parent body and asked to secure three more five-shilling donations each year. All participants received a medal, a badge, and ranking as an associate of the society; and those who collected the requisite sum became NSPCC members for one year.[126] Such a scheme offered obvious economic advantages: middle-class children not only made effective canvassers but also, in the long run, were likely to become mainstays of the society as adults. To this end the *Children's League of Pity Paper*, first published in August 1893, entreated its young readers to show unselfishness and sacrifice for their "sad and suffering small brothers and sisters."[127]

Some contemporaries found the society's appeal to privileged children reprehensible. Louisa Twining, well known for her writing on pauperism and the workhouse system, decried the increasing use of the young as "touters" by charities, protesting that a free and happy childhood would "vanish before all this premature initiation into . . . knowledge, fitted only for riper years and a later period of life." No organization deserved censure more richly than the League of Pity, she thought, for here children were asked to confront the horrors of domestic brutality.[128] Yet attacks by Twining and like-minded critics left the NSPCC relatively unscathed. The league's *Paper*, although honest in depicting parental misdeeds, never treated cruelty with the kind of graphic candor characteristic of the *Child's Guardian*.

Privileged boys and girls were taught that by "giving up" something they could materially improve the lives of their poor contemporaries. On joining the League of Pity, members received collecting cards with which to record all acts of self-denial. As proof that these children were absorbing the lesson of sacrifice, Mary Bolton cited some typical entries:[129]

CARD A

Instead of Chocolate .... 6d.

Not taking sugar in my tea .... 4d.

Uncle Jack gave me .... 1s.

CARD B

Instead of Toffy .... 1d.

For getting the Lesson Books ready .... 9d.

Saved in Farthings .... 4d.

For not making holes in my stockings .... 10d.

Nearly one-third of the £4,887 contributed to the society in 1902–3 by 11,560 members of the league came from such personal savings. Beginning in the late 1890's NSPCC officials arranged for members to witness the fruits of their labor. Usually this meant Christmas parties given for children on whose behalf the society had intervened during the previous year. It would be interesting to discover what percentage of the parents that the NSPCC warned or prosecuted allowed their offspring to attend these fêtes. We do know that in London, on December 20, 1899, six hundred former victims were picked up at their doors by NSPCC vans and driven to King's Hall, Holborn, there to sip tea, eat sweets, and be serenaded by Dr. Barnardo's boys' band. The event was a paean to noblesse oblige, for members of the League of Pity sat in the galleries "riveted by the delightful sight of the joy they had given, and on which they were looking down."[130]

Despite such determined wooing of future middle- and upper-class patrons, however, support for child protection was not invariably genteel. This, indeed, must be the first objection to the argument that the NSPCC was primarily an agency of social control. Conspicuously present at the society's seventh annual meeting was Tom Mann. One year later his fellow Dockers' Union leader Ben Tillett addressed the Mansion House gathering.[131] No doubt these highly publicized occasions were orchestrated to convey the impression of multiclass backing for the NSPCC; but equally, neither Mann nor Tillett would have graced the NSPCC's platform had he regarded the society as a tool of class coercion. Significantly, by 1903 212 workingmen's cooperative societies were regular contributors to the cause.[132] This was undeniably impressive support, given the resentment that many laborers must have felt toward the NSPCC for its war on child life insurance. Benjamin Waugh and his associates lectured not only to blue-blooded ladies at tea parties but also to cloth-capped audiences at Toynbee Hall and the People's Palace, for if the campaign to win children's rights failed to take root among "the masses of the people themselves," it would prove utterly ineffectual.[133]

If the "controllers" were not a unified elite, neither were the "controlled" passive, malleable subjects. Cruelty men such as Walter Jackson may have tried to wean poor parents from living in dirt, speaking in vulgarities, and drinking themselves into a stupor, but it is doubtful that they succeeded very often in creating "conventicles of respectability." [134] In its *First Annual Report*, the London SPCC had noted the importance of overcoming slum dwellers' fear of losing face because of informing on cruel neighbors.[135] Subsequently, philanthropists faced with an ever-growing case load concluded that "moral cowardice" among the masses was being routed. In drawing this conclusion they were overestimating their powers of persuasion and underestimating the rationality of the poor.

People were not mystified by the first man who put on a wig, observes E. P. Thompson about the rule of law in eighteenth-century England. "If the law is evidently partial and unjust, then it will mask nothing, legitimize nothing, contribute nothing to any class's hegemony. The essential precondition for the effectiveness of law, in its function as ideology, is that it shall seem to be just. It cannot seem to be so without upholding its own logic and criteria of equity; indeed, on occasion, by actually *being* just." [136] Analogously, the residents of mean streets in late Victorian and Edwardian times were not cowed into helping an NSPCC agent when he came knocking on their doors. The cruelty man found common folk prepared to inform on their neighbors because he was the personification of a legal structure that had an aura of equity about it. In York, neither the Catholic headmistress who flogged little Arthur Galpine nor the senior clerk who attacked his teenage son with a whipstock could escape a humiliating trial once the NSPCC decided to prosecute.[137]

Indeed, the latter case, that of Robert King, shows how the society sometimes alienated its own patrons by pursuing genteel offenders. King earned almost £200 a year in the architect's office of the North East Railway Company, and he was determined to see that his fifteen-and-a-half-year-old son followed in his footsteps. The boy, however, dreamed of being a sailor rather than a clerk. When King found some letters his son had received from the Navy, he erupted. Vowing "I'm going to teach you the first order in the Navy—obedience," the father tied a dog collar around his son's neck, attached a chain to the collar, then used the chain to secure the boy to the door of a backyard coal house. For the next fifteen minutes neighbors on two sides of the King property watched helplessly as whipstock and walking stick rained down blows on the boy. One day later a doctor noted that on the boy's "left forearm there is a wound, also a livid mark two inches across. . . . There are a number of livid marks running across his left shoulder blade & back. A portion of skin has been removed from the back on the right-side. . . . The whole of the outside of the left thigh is green. . . . In my opinion his father lost all control over himself when chastising the lad. It was a most brutal assault & has caused the boy much unnecessary suffering."

When these facts reached London, the NSPCC's legal office decided that King must face the bench. In preparation, Waugh wrote to the society's solicitor in York, asking him to stress both that the NSPCC "does not interfere with parent and child in lawful punishment" and that "the Society found . . . very considerable provocation was given by the boy in the case," thus justifying some form of correction. Nonetheless, King had far exceeded his parental right.

Before the father went to court, however, his friend and physician, Dr. Hinton Bateman, tried to persuade the society to drop the

case. "As a member for several years, and I believe, a large subscriber for the district of the Royal [sic] Society for the Prevention
of Cruelty to Children, I am writing to ask you to stop the action
now pending against Mr. Robert King." Dr. Bateman explained
that his own examination of the boy ten days after the thrashing
showed no skin bruises and only one cut mark. In sum, this loyal
backer of the NSPCC felt strongly that it would "inflict . . . vindic-
tive punishment on a worthy man to be brought into Court on a
criminal charge." But the society would not back down. King was
convicted of assault and fined £5 plus court costs.[138]

Similar incidents took place elsewhere. Bishop Cramer-Roberts,
President of the society's Blackburn branch, resigned when the society pushed ahead with its prosecution of a Blackburn curate's wife
for flogging her servant girl.[139] Again, it was the NSPCC that drew
national attention to the barbarities of two highly connected ladies—Mrs. Montagu, who literally beat her daughter to death, and
Mrs. Penruddocke, who scoured her child's face with nettles.[140]
What C. F. G. Masterman called "the dreary life of the ghetto" did
draw a disproportionate share of the society's attention. But this
was true in part because poor people themselves summoned the
eyes and ears of a body whose first concern seemed to be children,
not class. The NSPCC could argue convincingly that it led "a movement towards a juster civilisation."[141]

CHAPTER 7

Voluntary Effort and the State

B Y THE EARLY twentieth century, acute public concern about the health and safety of children was forcing the state to assume greater responsibility for the welfare of its youngest citizens. Among the reforms passed by Liberal governments between 1906 and 1908, those providing for the feeding and medical inspection of school-children, the early notification of births, the probation of young offenders, and the establishment of a juvenile court system were important because they signaled a clear perception of children as England's most precious natural resource. Few would argue, however, that the Liberals deserve all the credit for these measures. To take an obvious example, it was the fledgling Labour Party that made school feeding a major parliamentary issue. Nevertheless, recent studies of the "new," "progressive," or "radical" Liberalism in Edwardian politics leave the impression that social reform aimed at the young flowed mainly from a "collectivist" mentality.[1] To the extent that lawmakers and civil servants, some of them Liberals, were seeking "to replace the rôle of political economy by a form of moral economy," this impression is accurate.[2] But if we are to understand the genesis of most Edwardian legislation for children, we must look beyond party politics to the philanthropic experts whose mission had long been the defense of "suffering childhood."

Conversely, it is misleading to suppose that voluntary effort in late Victorian and Edwardian England was necessarily hostile to state-sponsored social remedies. Many philanthropists believed with the Charity Organisation Society that indiscriminate almsgiving undermined rather than nurtured a spirit of self-reliance among the poor. It does not follow from this, however, that the C.O.S.'s dogmatic individualism was typical of private welfare work, or even that C. S. Loch and his group were recognized as the principal authorities on family assistance.[3] The world of Edwardian philanthropy by and large mirrored broader doubts about England's ability to compete with her industrial and imperial rivals; and as national attention turned following the Boer War to the alleged physical decay of the race, many children's charities came to welcome the idea of government aid for their clients. Interestingly, a few voluntary groups, most notably the NSPCC and the State Children's Association, began to urge a larger state share in child welfare work before "national efficiency" emerged as an English catchphrase in 1902. Accustomed to advancing controversial views on the rights of the young, NSPCC leaders felt comfortable voicing early support for state aid to pauper, vagrant, and delinquent children. Yet it is significant that the society's pronouncements at the turn of the century touched off far less controversy than those it had made a decade earlier. The difference was more than a matter of acquired credibility: expectations of the young were themselves changing.

New Champions of the Child

In the spring of 1893, the *Spectator* attributed "a very large increase of respect, and even love for children" to the NSPCC's work, "for neither respect nor love can grow in a mind full of its own self-importance, and fattened into a sort of grossness which extinguishes the very possibility of sympathy with weakness."[4] True in part, this analysis ignores the more fundamental fact that the last years of Victoria's reign saw a progressive lengthening of childhood. The advent of compulsory education had provided an institutional confirmation of the idea that preadolescent boys and girls lacked certain intellectual and physical powers necessary to cope with the adult world. Each child needed a training period—the school years—during which these powers might be refined without interference from the harsh demands of the marketplace. In 1890 the normal school-leaving age was ten; by 1900 it had been statutorily raised to fourteen.[5] This prolongation of dependency occurred in part because the sentimental view of childhood, originally a hallmark of middle-class culture, had been embraced by many working-class parents who no longer relied on their offspring to supplement family income. Among such parents, juvenile precocity was falling into disfavor by the end of the century. "We make the great mistake of expecting too much of our children," observed Martha Mosher in 1898. "The moral faculties evolve slowly, and overstimulation will have reaction. A boy of eight or ten years, who never transgresses, never needs correction, is lacking in physical or mental vitality."[6] Books, museums, and public gardens had their place in educating town children, Helen Dendy allowed, but all these were "tainted by the same leaven of artificiality, and subordination to the little uses of man." A true love of nature, through which a child learned to revere creatures both large and small, could best be instilled by exposure to rural life. Mary Loane remarked in 1905 that city boys now treated animals with much greater kindness than formerly. Since few of these youths had tasted country ways, their humanity may have been a product of newly attentive parents who guided without browbeating.[7]

Late Victorian children were theoretically entitled to love and esteem from their elders. Surely the most public expression of parental pride was the baby show. The first show to gain wide attention took place in North Woolwich in the summer of 1869. *The Lancet* was not charmed:

Infants are exhibited for a prize as if they were so many pigs or dogs, and this seems to us a degrading thing to do; and for a row of mothers to suckle their babes in public, exposed to the gaze of every on-looker, is to our minds simply indecent. Poets may sing of the . . . dimples of childhood; but a Baby Show, composed of fatigued and perspiring mothers, nursing infants of all ages, in a large, hot, and ill-ventilated tent, with all the aggravated odours of an overcrowded nursery, puts infancy in another and very disagreeable aspect. The triplets were painfully puny, ugly, wrinkled little creatures; and there did not appear to us to be much to choose between the pulsating brain of one bald-headed infant and the hairy scalp of another.[8]

During the 1890's baby competitions grew very popular, particularly in poor districts. Handsome prizes such as the cart offered by the *Strand Magazine* for the best overall child in an 1897 event would have tempted many an East End mother to display her infant. But the lure of reward alone cannot explain the appeal of late Victorian baby shows. Their popularity may also suggest an intensification of maternal attachment to the very young, though this inference rests on thin evidence.[9] There can be no doubt, however, that by the outbreak of the First World War incubator charities, dramatic improvements in the quality and supply of fresh milk, and large-scale health visiting schemes had contributed to reduced infant mortality rates, thus encouraging poor women to make a greater emotional investment in each child.[10]

Increasingly valued during infancy, children were also becoming the focus of scientific attention. British delegates to the International Educational Conference at Chicago in 1893 came home impressed with Dr. G. Stanley Hall's work in the new field of child study. Shortly thereafter groups dedicated to analyzing the "natural history" of childhood were formed in Edinburgh, London, and six provincial centers. Organizations with kindred aims (such as the Childhood Society, founded by Sir Douglas Galton, a relative of the great eugenist) sprang to life in the late 1890's.[11]

This interest in the developmental aspects of childhood helped to generate a heightened self-consciousness about family government. Tracts painting sweet pictures of parents ennobled by their offspring continued to be written. "It is only when the children come that life becomes real, and that parents begin to learn to live," gushed one such study.[12] More often, however, prescriptive literature now acknowledged that some parent-child conflict within the family was normal. The question of how to make parental discipline effective thus assumed new importance. One broad school of thought maintained that fathers and mothers must exercise a "necessary autocracy" over their young. Perhaps most vital, parents should be scrupulously consistent in dealing with children: "Make no promises which you cannot fulfil; threaten no penalties which you do not exact." Sometimes punishment was needed to check "such acts [as would] cause the child to suffer later in life much harder consequences." When administering physical pain, though, the parent should show indignation rather than anger, for anger could breed dangerous resentment.[13] The competing view of domestic order urged a kind of family democracy wherein children generally behaved well because they had a say in the decisions that affected them. Charlotte Mason, well known for her essays on home education, went so far as to argue that "a single decision made by the parents which the child is, or should be, capable of making for itself, is an encroachment on the rights of the child, and a transgression on the part of the parents."[14] Where this egalitarian system failed to prevent disobedience and some form of punishment seemed essential, parents were reminded that the application of brute force seldom taught respect for law and for the rights of others.[15]

Both the democratic and autocratic views of family government were in agreement, however, that corporal punishment was a tactic best used sparingly. A few contemporaries rued this advice, and held the NSPCC partly responsible for what appeared to be a new generation of uncontrollable youth. One writer, rather carried away with indignation, charged that the growing disrepute of whipping children, sending them to bed, and making them stand in the corner left genteel households with no respectable forms of chastisement apart from reproving looks, lectures, or, in extreme cases, deprivation of some promised treat.[16] Occasionally, NSPCC workers counseled greater lenience in the correction of children. Mary Bolton, for example, berated "strict disciplinarians" in an article published by the *Sunday Magazine*; fractious boys and girls staying at the society's Harpur Street shelter, her readers learned, suffered no punishment more harsh than the loss of pudding. Yet in its casework the NSPCC routinely dismissed complaints about mild beatings administered "to intensify the child's hatred of wrong." [17]

Anticruelty leaders clearly approved of whipping as an alternative to jail terms for juvenile delinquents. The Juvenile Offenders Amendment Act of 1862 (25 & 26 Vic., c. 18) had provided that on summary conviction for certain crimes boys under fourteen could be sentenced to a maximum of twelve strokes with a birch rod in lieu of imprisonment. Subsequent legislation allowed magistrates to choose birching for older youths and also for boys convicted of various indictable offences.[18] But despite this and other discretionary options—principally releasing first offenders on the promise of good behavior and committing youths to industrial schools—magistrates were still sending hundreds of children to jail during the 1890's (see Table 7). Having proposed a system of juvenile courts as early as 1873, Benjamin Waugh was especially keen to keep the young separate from hardened criminals throughout the penal process. Because the NSPCC had at first very few backers in the agitation for juvenile courts, however, it used the issue of whipping to dramatize the evils of incarceration for children.[19]

The results of this stand proved doubly ironic. By supporting controlled corporal punishment rather than prison for all crimes by youths save homicide, the society found itself charged with "cruel, barbarous, and retrogressive" thinking. Henry Salt was the most ve

TABLE 7

Number of Youthful Offenders Sent to Prison, 1893–1900

Year	Under 12 years of age		Over 12 and under 16 years of age	
	Male	Female	Male	Female
1893	134	16	2,512	262
1894	82	2	1,942	227
1895	54	1	1,735	178
1896	59	1	1,336	102
1897	57	1	1,541	89
1898–1899	42	1	1,586	93
1899–1900	18	1	1,193	60

SOURCE: Home Office Records (P.R.O., HO45, 10157/B23010C).

hement critic of court-ordered whipping, and Salt's Humanitarian League led the outcry against the practice.[20] Although Lord James steered bills permitting whipping through the Upper House in 1899 and 1900, the forces of what the Howard Association called "nominal humanitarianism" blocked both measures in the Lower House. NSPCC strategists felt understandably irate that their progressive views on juvenile justice had been so thoroughly misunderstood.[21] The second irony of the NSPCC's stand was not as immediately evident. John Gillis has shown that in Oxford the NSPCC's efforts to reduce arbitrary treatment of young offenders had the effect of curbing traditional police practices such as on-the-spot punishment with a constable's stick. Left increasingly little latitude, policemen brought children before regular courts, thereby expanding the pool of delinquents from which some youths were sent to jail.[22]

Some late Victorian champions of a thoroughgoing system of juvenile justice also tried to halt the breeding of crime in workhouses and in the streets. For more than half a century, middle-class moralists had denounced "street arabism," arguing that children swarming in city thoroughfares not only smacked of social disorder but also bred contempt for authority.[23] As we have seen, the Children's Charter of 1889 restricted the hours during which the young could sell goods in public areas and set penalties for parents who caused their offspring to beg. Nonetheless, by the early 1890's it was disconcertingly clear that not all towns shared London's success in discouraging juvenile hawking.[24] Liverpool in particular was beset by a small army of juvenile hawkers, many of whom used newspapers and matches to mask their real profession as beggars. During the twelve months ending on September 29, 1892, Liverpool police brought 976 children before courts of summary jurisdiction for hawking-related offences; 9 percent of them were committed to industrial schools. Given these conditions, Liverpool philanthropists hit on the idea of requiring each young hawker to carry a license and wear a brightly colored badge.[25]

First in Liverpool, then later in Bradford, Halifax, Scarborough, and Southport, city fathers won from the Home Office permission to license male hawkers under fourteen and female hawkers under sixteen. Civil servants saw this step as "a new departure in legislation," since the Home Office was loath to allow local variations on national law. But the problems faced in several northern cities seemed to demand special action. Soon Liverpool devised a scheme whereby special belts and badges were used to distinguish children who were exempt from compulsory school attendance. All applicants deemed "sickly, blind, deaf, dumb, deformed, or mentally deficient" were refused licenses.[26] Compassion for young hawkers was by no means the only spur to the adoption of such codes. English cities in 1900 were generally cleaner and more orderly places than they had been half a century before, and the spectacle of half-clad urchins shouting, gambling, and begging in public seemed all the more discordant. Unfortunately, neither the indignant nor the compassionate citizen found much solace in the hawking regulations adopted by some northern towns. Thomas Burke, an administrator of Liverpool's new local code, wrote that the code could never hope to control the vagaries of the labor market, much less to modify the home lives of children. He agreed with the NSPCC that only by enforcing parental responsibility through statute could juvenile hawking be stopped.[27]

Many of the arguments brought against juvenile hawking were also used to attack juvenile vagrancy. As defined by the Poor Law authorities, a "vagrant" was any person who lacked both a permanent residence and a place of settlement, and who sought temporary relief in a workhouse.[28] More popularly, vagrancy was associated with the wandering life, even when such an existence cost the ratepayers nothing. Thus, George Smith's decade-long struggle to bring van dwellers under the sanitary and education codes was aimed at a "class" of people who, though economically independent, were suspected of the same guile and sloth that was believed to typify the occupants of casual wards. He was especially perturbed about Gypsy culture, that "last prop of English heathenism," and the rearing of an estimated eight thousand Gypsy children in an atmosphere of "lying, begging, thieving, cheating, and every other abominable, low, cunning craft that ignorance and idleness can devise."[29] By 1894 Smith's clumsy assault on movable dwellings had so alienated the defenders of "liberty and property" that the Gypsy issue could not be pursued.

Other reformers demonstrated more subtlety in tackling the problem of tramping children. Unlike Gypsies, tramps did burden ratepayers. But both populations shared the important distinction of being extremely mobile—a frightening characteristic in a society where even respectable workers were thought to harbor latent impulses toward wandering.[30] The Vagrancy Act of 1824 had made it illegal to "wander abroad and lodge in barns, tents, the open air, &c, not having visible means of subsistence and not giving a good account of one's self," and had set a maximum penalty of three months in prison for conviction under the statute. But this early nineteenth-century law gave no thought to the care of tramping children while their parents or guardians remained in jail. Two generations later philanthropists began searching for a solution. One reformer reasoned that since the state was ethically "the father of the fatherless," local authorities should be allowed to sweep wandering children into special state homes, there to be cared for and educated until they could be trained as soldiers, sailors, or agricultural workers.[31] Airing similar views were the Poor Law guardians, school board members, and representatives of private charity who met in 1899 to discuss the issue of tramping juveniles. This 23-member group pieced together a bill empowering constables to arrest any apparently unemployed adult found wandering with a child younger than sixteen. If convicted, the adult might receive up to six months' imprisonment with hard labor; the child would be maintained in a workhouse or certified industrial school, primarily at the expense of local county councils. What the Home Office judged a drastic measure some MPs thought compelling enough to bring before the House of Commons later that year. John Burns, formerly a socialist agitator and champion of the London Dock Strike, was one of the bill's co-sponsors. For Burns, the objection that the law might be used oppressively against poor laborers roaming the countryside in search of work dissolved when weighed against the harm that could befall the offspring of vagrants.[32] Defeated in 1899, the bill, with only minor modifications, reached Parliament again in 1900, 1903, 1904, and 1906. Despite support from prominent Liberals and Tories, however, it failed to pass.

No doubt the case for protection would have been strengthened by NSPCC support. But the society was reluctant to back punitive legislation for two reasons, neither of which struck contemporaries as entirely persuasive. In the first place, child-savers maintained, the object of their work was to ease the distress of suffering children. Removing juvenile vagrants from the casual wards of workhouses might be desirable in the abstract; but only where wandering had caused or was apt to cause "unnecessary suffering or injury to health" could NSPCC agents legitimately intervene. This jurisdictional precision in fact made a virtue of necessity, for the rescue of tramping children had always been costly. Indeed, by 1899 the society was so concerned about being saddled with the maintenance of young vagrants that cruelty men were barred from applying to magistrates to get such children committed to industrial schools.[33] More comforting, perhaps, was the society's second reason for not backing punitive legislation—the claim that children who entered casual wards were already the objects of special surveillance by its agents. Starting in the mid-1890's, cruelty men kept "tramp registers," detailed notes on the condition of all vagrant children and their adult companions. The nearest district workhouse master as well as the neighboring cruelty man were then warned by letter or telegraph of approaching vagrants, thus permitting nearly continuous observation of these people. Workhouse officials would, in turn, alert NSPCC agents when a tramping family left the casual wards. Convinced that this intelligence system had reduced the number of vagrant women with children in East Anglia, a Local Government Board inspector, T. C. Murray-Browne, urged other guardians to adopt the same system. The resulting expansion of the tramp register program, together with the money contributions it received from some boards of guardians, led the society to conclude that fewer boys and girls were now roaming through the English countryside, and that those who did enter casual wards were on the whole healthier than ever before.[34] Again, child-savers were probably too optimistic, since it is far from certain that the reduced juvenile population of casual wards had not been offset by greater numbers of children seeking shelter with their parents in common lodging houses or under bridges and hedges. Plainly too, the NSPCC's assertion that it was improving the lot of young tramps did little to mollify those who had called for the total prohibition of juvenile vagrancy.[35]

The voices urging state custody of juvenile vagrants and street-sellers often belonged to people who had already attacked the Poor Law provisions for the young. In Victorian England the failings of public relief for pauper and orphaned children were most palpable at the workhouse level. Here, efforts to render indoor relief as unappealing as possible for able-bodied adults had sometimes fostered malnourishment and disease among workhouse inmates of all ages. Obviously victimized by the strictures of "less eligibility," workhouse children became the only segment of the pauper population to receive state relief in foster homes. This system of "boarding out" originated in the parish of St. Cuthbert's, Edinburgh, in 1843. Regular inspection of these children by Edinburgh's parochial authorities belied predictions that the experiment would subject the young to ill-treatment at the hands of their foster parents, and provided a model for the English boarding-out system, started in 1870.[36] Despite lingering fears that the provision of foster homes might tempt poor parents to desert their offspring, the Local Government Board allowed guardians to place children both within and beyond the borders of their Poor Law Unions. Florence Davenport-Hill was overly sanguine when she wrote in 1889 that "systematic and continued cruelty is virtually impossible with the checks of private and public inspection, neighborly observation, and our Argus-eyed and ubiquitous press." [37] But she was right in believing that a private home was vastly preferable to a workhouse for rearing the wards of the state.

Unfortunately, by no means all pauper children could be boarded out. Many more had to endure life in workhouse wards where, Miss Davenport-Hill insisted, children "whose parents may have kept [them], as far as possible, from the knowledge of evil" were forced to mingle with "idle and vicious" adults.[38] The attack on Poor Law care of the young launched in the mid-1890's was far better organized than any previous protest. The men and women who joined together to found the State Children's Aid Association, though they too advanced the "pauper taint" critique, typically anchored their case in a wealth of carefully mined facts. Reformers such as Canon and Mrs. Samuel Barnett, Sidney Webb, Ernest Hart, Samuel Smith, and Mrs. Francis Rye, all of them members of the SCAA's original executive committee, were predictably cool to the idea that only the Local Government Board and the Poor Law guardians could properly assess England's system of public relief for the young.[39] It did not take a civil servant, for example, to see that "barrack" schools fell far short of even very modest educational ideals. Mrs. Barnett, a long-time member of the Forest Gate School's board of management, granted that her institution had been gradually "humanized" through allowing toys and encouraging play periods. But large barrack schools (the establishment at Sutton housed 1,541 children in 1894) could never serve adequately the needs of their inmates, and as a result, critics held, adolescents left them untutored in the skills needed to keep respectable jobs.[40]

At first Mrs. Barnett resented England's preoccupation with the NSPCC and its work. After all, she asked, "How could the evils of the system [of crowding in barrack schools] which robbed children of freedom, joy and individuality be brought home to an indifferent public, who care only for physical suffering?" Tragically, Poor Law education soon earned national notice when fire and later poisoned meat ravaged inmates at the Forest Gate School. Mrs. Barnett's brother-in-law, Ernest Hart, used the *British Medical Journal* to amplify demands for a full-scale study of Poor Law education.[41] The departmental committee on Poor Law schools, organized in 1894, was a direct result of pressure from Hart, Sir John Gorst, and Mrs. Barnett. Sifting through the evidence of 73 witnesses, this committee issued a report in 1896 confirming the suspected existence of chronic ophthalmia as well as abysmal ignorance among the young educated en masse at Poor Law schools. Late that same year the SCAA was formed "to obtain individual treatment of children under the Guardianship of the State."[42] But the new group's aim was broader still. As reflected in the parliamentary debates it annually staged during the discussion of Local Government Board estimates, the SCAA sought greater state aid for all neglected children.[43] The Poor Law Act of 1899, partly a product of SCAA lobbying, gave boards of guardians control over the offspring of paupers deemed mentally or morally unfit, and extended guardians' authority over orphans chargeable to the rates.[44] Ultimately, the patchwork quality of the Poor Law itself, many of these reformers thought, guaranteed inferior care for disadvantaged youth.

Well before the specter of "physical deterioration" became a national obsession, therefore, philanthropists were calling for sweeping state action to salvage physically and mentally damaged children. Foreign models spurred discussion of a "Department of State Children." Two decades earlier, for example, Massachusetts had vested a Board of Health, Lunacy, and Charity with power to oversee the care of all destitute, neglected, and criminal youths under the age of eighteen. Later, South Australia and New South Wales established state children's councils to provide for the same population.[45] Mindful of these precedents, the SCAA as early as 1897 condemned England's dividing up of the responsibility for state children among the Local Government Board, Home Office, and Education Department. Twelve years later the famous minority report of the Royal Commission on the Poor Laws would make precisely the same point.[46] In their analysis of "children under rival authorities," Beatrice Webb and her three co-authors drew on a critical tradition bred in the world of late Victorian philanthropy.

Child Protection and National Efficiency

Historians have written much about the impact of the Boer War on English social policy. It is now beyond dispute that the high proportion of recruits rejected as physically unfit for service in South Africa sparked intense concern about the health of the laboring population in general, and of working-class children in particular. Edwardian strategies to combat "physical deterioration" in the young were part of a wider quest for "national efficiency," a quest that G. R. Searle has defined as "an attempt to discredit the habits, beliefs and institutions that put the British at a handicap in their competition with foreigners and to commend instead a social organization that more closely followed the *German* model."[47] As we have seen, the notion that sickly and unfit children were a drain on England's wealth was neither new to the twentieth century nor bound up with envy of German efficiency. George Smith, the heavy-handed patron of Gypsy and canal boat children, was echoing still earlier sentiments when he wrote to the Home Secretary in 1871 that young lives damaged physically and morally "deteriorate the national life." Similarly, appeals for children's country holidays and for improved medical care of elementary school students had been couched in terms of lost productivity.[48] But Sir Frederick Maurice's

"Where to Get Men," published in the *Contemporary Review* in January 1902, signaled the start of a truly national preoccupation with the social costs of child neglect.

This preoccupation grew rapidly. A year and a half before the Inter-Departmental Committee on Physical Deterioration issued its troubling August 1904 report, Sir John Gorst was clamoring for a streamlined system of education on the grounds of economic survival: "If it is true that the international rivalry of the future will be one of commerce and manufactures, the uninstructed nations will have to reconcile themselves to be the menial servants of the rest of the world, and to perform the lower and rougher operations of modern industry; while all those which require taste, skill, and invention, gradually fall into the hands of people who are better taught." [49] The Inter-Departmental Committee's subsequent report, although it tried to allay fears about racial decay, only compounded them. What had caused physical degeneration, however, was uncertain. One scholar has characterized the debate among the expert witnesses brought before the Inter-Departmental Committee as revolving around two "not precisely contradictory" points of view, the "medical" and the "Darwinist." Proponents of the latter view believed that constitutional weaknesses were rife among the masses because genetically inferior individuals had propagated faster than the genetically superior; as long as this pattern obtained, little could be done to improve England's overall racial stock. Most medical men, by contrast, refused to believe that the race was degenerating; if the poor were to receive better health education and children regular medical inspection at school, future generations would be stronger and smarter. [50]

The advice of a few eccentric but very visible physicians may have confused some laymen. R. R. Rentoul, a prominent member of both the Royal College of Surgeons and the London Medico-Legal Society (and several times a witness before parliamentary committees), was adamant that steps should be taken to prevent the decay of the race resulting from the "disgusting system of inducing certain mentally and physically diseased persons to marry." If these persons could not be forcibly sterilized—an idea that found many advocates—they could at least be taught to abstain from intercourse during pregnancy, lactation, and menstruation (including the week after all menstrual flow had ceased). Abstinence at these times, Rentoul maintained, would reduce the danger of harming an unborn or very young child.[51] Generally, though, medical testimony presented to the Inter-Departmental Committee encouraged more reformers than it discouraged. John Spargo drew from the committee's evidence a conclusion of "tremendous sociological significance," namely, "that each generation gets practically a fresh start." Spargo, an American socialist and author of a widely read book on poverty and childhood, explained why he felt inspired.

I had long believed and had promulgated the opinion that the great mass of children of the poor were blighted before they were born. The evidence given before the British Interdepartmental Committee, by recognized leaders of the medical profession in England, pointed to a fundamentally different view. According to that evidence, the number of children born healthy and strong is not greater among the well-to-do classes than among the very poorest. The testimony seemed so conclusive, and the corroboration received from so many obstetrical experts in the country was so general, that I was forced to abandon as untenable the theory of antenatal degeneration.[52]

The year following the publication of the report saw a rush of philanthropic planning as doctors and laymen cooperated to found or revivify race-strengthening programs. Best publicized was the National League for Physical Education and Improvement, a London-based group organized in June 1905 by a "galaxy" of scientific and social luminaries to aid several smaller societies already working in the field.[53]

The verdict of England's child-protection specialists complemented this outburst of voluntary effort. Soon after Maurice's first article appeared in the *Contemporary Review*, the NSPCC began its own study of the physical condition of London schoolchildren. On the basis of the preliminary findings of this study, Benjamin Waugh exuded what the *Glasgow Herald* termed "a convinced and almost buoyant optimism" concerning the health of English youth. As of August 1903 it appeared that the majority of boys and girls were tolerably well nourished, though the fact that the average London child weighed less than his New York City counterpart gave some cause for worry.[54] The study in its final form rested on the labor of Dr. C. T. W. Hirsch, who measured and weighed 6,500 London schoolchildren. Hirsch's results showed to be still valid the twenty-year-old standard on which the NSPCC based its definition of child neglect, the tables in Melmouth Tidy's *Legal Medicine*. "If the Society has been at a little expense," one member declared, "this only gives further proof of its passion for justice, and its absolute refusal to take advantage of any standard that is not perfectly fair, even to the brutal parent." More to the point, of course, Hirsch's data showed that no perceptible decay in the physical stature of London youths had taken place. The Royal College of Surgeons officially accepted these NSPCC findings and passed them on to Balfour's Tory government. "Scientific" social reform had been validated.[55]

Indeed, the NSPCC was becoming a much less controversial body than it had been even five years before. This was true partly because the society had at last acquired the look of a properous and well-run business. In 1902 a gift of £10,000 from William Waldorf Astor made possible a move from the warren-like Harpur Street building to larger quarters in Leicester Square. Significantly, the new building had no shelter attached to it, nor were NSPCC shelters active anywhere in Britain after 1902. Since the 1894 Act for the Prevention of Cruelty to Children had obliged guardians to accept all boys and girls brought to them under that law, there was now little need for the society to maintain costly refuges. By 1905 the NSPCC's 200,000 subscribers knew that their money was going to support work with one overriding aim: the enforcement of parental duty.[56]

Just as importantly, the tone of the society's propaganda had softened from acerbic to merely assertive, thanks to the retirement of Benjamin Waugh. Since 1884, Waugh, with his flair for the melodramatic, had been the child-protection movement's lightning rod. First as an unpaid Honorary Secretary and, after 1895, as the professional head of a corporation, he had been ridiculed by commercial interests, sued for both abduction and libel, and slandered as an adulterer. By early 1904 Waugh was on the brink of physical collapse. Hoping that an extended holiday might revive him, the NSPCC council sent him on a cruise to New Zealand for half a year.[57] While he was away the affairs of the society were managed by Robert J. Parr. Parr had come from Torquay in 1899 to be an NSPCC staff speaker; two years later he became the society's Assistant Secretary. Like Waugh, Parr was an absorbing speaker, although he relied more heavily on precision than on emotion. Methodical where Waugh was impassioned, Parr seemed to be the kind of pilot the society would one day need at its helm. His skills were tested sooner than expected, however, for Waugh never fully recovered. On March 27, 1905, Waugh, then aged 67, wrote to Lord Ancaster, chairman of the NSPCC council, formally resigning from the society's service.[58]

Under Parr's guidance the NSPCC continued to provide the public with abundant evidence of childhood trauma. "The tale of pitiful suffering, of appalling brutality, of almost fiendish cruelty, must be told again and again" as "the only remedy against indifference."[59] But Parr also recognized that England's obsession with racial degeneration could prove useful to the society. Certainly the ease with which the 1904 Prevention of Cruelty to Children Amendment Act (4 Edw. VII, c. 15) passed through Parliament augured well.[60] Since 1899 child-savers had been pressuring the Home Office to approve a further refinement of family law. Some of the proposed changes left civil servants very uncomfortable. The NSPCC's contention that it should be a criminal offense to leave children alone in a room with an uncovered fire plainly threatened a great many poor mothers with prosecution for an action they could not always avoid. Equally unsettling was Waugh's wish to punish those who "terrorized" their offspring. Here Waugh was thinking of instances in which a man's drunken rage had so frightened his children that they sought shelter outdoors, cold, wet, and cruelly anxious. Yet what assurance could there be, wondered the Home Office, that only truly brutal parents would be affected by this new definition?[61] Though Lord Alverstone's amending bill of 1904 contained neither of these provisions, it did facilitate the enforcement of maintenance orders against wayward parents, dispensed with the need for injured children to appear in court, and allowed greater flexibility in prosecuting adults charged with carnally assaulting the young. Alverstone, then Lord Chief Justice, and the NSPCC's lieutenant in the Commons, H. D. Greene, won these concessions from a legislature deeply worried about racial degeneration.

The much-discussed theme of degeneration was not, however, the only source of anxiety for race patriots. Troubling too were reports of a falling birthrate. Doctors and sanitary specialists had often remarked on the dramatic drop in national fertility, but not until the early Edwardian period did speculation about the causes of this drop fix on the evil of birth control. The Registrar General's statistics (see Table 8) begged for speculation. Contemporaries knew that the 26.6 percent fall in female fertility between 1876–80 and

TABLE 8
The Birthrate in England and Wales, 1876–1905

Quinquennia	Rate per 1,000 females aged 15 to 45 years	Percentage change over previous quinquennium
1876–1880	153.3	—
1881–1885	144.3	−5.9
1886–1890	133.4	−7.5
1891–1895	126.8	−4.9
1896–1900	118.8	−6.3
1901–1905	112.5	−5.3

SOURCE: Report of the Registrar General for 1907.

1901–5 stemmed from several causes, among them a rise in the age of women at marriage, a decline in the marriage rate, and a steady drop in the absolute number of illegitimate births. Yet far more important, some said, was "the deliberate and voluntary avoidance of child-bearing on the part of a steadily increasing number of married people, who not only prefer to have but few children, but who know how to obtain their wish." By 1907 Reginald Bray's lament seemed commonplace: "We are now beginning to suffer from that wild orgy of individualism into which the nineteenth century plunged with all the reckless abandonment of desperate and insensate folly."[62] Apparently the rich had begun this orgy, for if the birthrate in posh Kensington was any test, London's "idle and luxurious" classes were ahead of their East End counterparts in practicing deliberate restraint. Perhaps, now, the poor were succumbing to this Malthusian madness as well. Some working-class newspapers had started advertising birth control devices, from which Thomas George Cree, Honorary Secretary of the Church Penitentiary Association, somehow deduced that girls younger than sixteen were using them.[63] A few health reformers ventured to say that if less frequent childbearing meant improved care of fewer offspring, then perhaps this demographic trend was not the disaster it seemed. Yet England's lower birthrate was being mirrored throughout the white Empire, casting doubt on the vitality of British settlers in Australia, New Zealand, and Canada. Much as in ancient Rome, it appeared, the mother country could not supply her children with new blood, and the children themselves were unable to grow without a transfusion.[64]

Abroad and at home race patriots had two duties. Most urgently, they were obliged to intensify their attack on all behavior that led to the lower birthrate. Mere denunciation of contraceptives and criminal abortion might not be sufficient; women would have to be shown that these social abominations also posed grave personal risk. Precisely this spirit informed Samuel Hemphill's *The Murderess of the Unseen*, a tract that assured its readers that "nervous enfeeblement, impaired mental vigor, fibrous tumours, ovarian diseases, uterine cancer, and other dreaded complaints, in more than three cases out of four coincide with practices of restriction, and can justly be attributed to them." As for the females who submitted to illegal abortions, Hemphill declared, about 50 percent die, and most of the survivors "lose their health permanently." [65] Hazardous to the women who sought them, these operations made a mockery of the rights of the unborn child. T. Arthur Helme, Honorary Physician to the Northern Hospital for Women, Manchester, was one of several Edwardian doctors to agitate for improved prenatal care. Helme was troubled that the death rate from "premature birth" had not begun to rise until the overall birthrate began to drop. At a time when the potential value of the life of the child *in utero* was increasing, therefore, proportionally more women were having miscarriages or delivering fatally defective infants. Several factors gave rise to this alarming trend, and most of them, Dr. Helme believed, could be reduced through a combination of maternal, medical, and state effort. Mothers might be taught to reduce their consumption of alcohol during pregnancy; doctors should use therapeutic abortion only as a last resort to save a woman's life; and the state ought to provide hospitals for pregnant women, as well as prohibit the employment of women during pregnancy.[66] All these recommendations had been urged before, but their advocacy in the name of fetal rights was new.

Furthermore, it was the duty of loyal citizens to give every possible help to the children who survived birth. Whereas the general death rate in England and Wales had fallen 17 percent during the final quarter of the nineteenth century, the infant mortality rate remained the same. Only after 1900 did the infant mortality rate begin to creep downward, and even then the alarming frequency with which newly born children perished during their first weeks of life gave added weight to demands for improved postnatal care.[67] By 1906 the combined evils of a falling birthrate and an unacceptably high level of infant mortality moved John Burns, then President of the Local Government Board, to preside over the National Conference on Infantile Mortality. Burns demonstrated more than polite interest in this event. During his opening address he strongly objected to women working within six months of giving birth, and he opposed crêches on the grounds that they might encourage women to return to work too quickly.[68] The two-day meeting was noteworthy both for its official standing—the King and Queen acted as patrons—and for the scope of its deliberations, which ranged from maternal alcoholism to the old issue of baby-farming.[69] G. F. McCleary, at the time Medical Officer of Health for Battersea, later described the conference as the dawn of a new era for mother and child: "Infant welfare became not only popular but fashionable. It had 'news value' for journalistic purposes, and was a favorite subject for addresses at drawing-room meetings. . . . Voluntary health societies sprang up all over the country and did valuable service in spreading abroad information on the essentials of successful infant nurture."[70] McCleary was too modest. His work and that of like-minded reformers created the familiarity with infant health problems that made a national conference seem essential.

The NSPCC played an important if often overlooked role in this process of public education. England's first coherent system of health visiting started in the Midlands when the Ladies' Health Society of Manchester and Salford, formed in 1862, began hiring respectable working-class women to counsel new mothers in their homes. In 1890 the Manchester Corporation gave its approval to the scheme by paying some health visitors and ordering the city's medical officer of health to supervise their work. Carrying simply worded leaflets on the care and feeding of babies along with small cans of disinfectant powder, Manchester's sixteen female inspectors were visiting 14,424 houses per year by 1905.[71] One wonders if the women employed by other towns were as effective, for health visiting could too easily become an exercise in condescension. As Emilia Kanthack wrote: "You will understand them [poor mothers] right enough if you take an amazing interest in them as human beings, and you must be *very* fond of them *as a class*, even including the rather horrid, dirty individuals. Always think of the dreadful pity of it all!"[72] Whatever their sympathies, health visitors turned to the NSPCC when they came across cases of neglect or abuse. But as a group determined to prevent childhood suffering, the NSPCC felt compelled to promote infant welfare more directly. Thus, when the

Local Government Board refused in 1896 to grant the society's wish that registrars of births and deaths be ordered to distribute cards about methods of feeding infants, NSPCC leaders launched a "mothercraft" campaign of their own. At the turn of the century, then, cruelty men and lady collectors were annually distributing thousands of copies of the society's booklet *How to Bring Up a Baby*; and though comparative statistics are not available, as many mothers may have been exposed to the rudiments of proper infant care by NSPCC personnel as by health visitors.[73]

The society's interest in experiments such as the Huddersfield plan for early notification of birth suggests that anticruelty workers saw their mission as tied to, rather than at odds with, the war on excessive infant mortality.[74] On at least one issue, baby-farming, NSPCC concerns were identical with those of race patriots. Following the passage of the flimsy 1897 Infant Life Protection Act, child-savers had reluctantly suspended their fight against unregulated adoption, while continuing to prosecute heartless foster parents.[75] From several papers read at the Third International Congress for the Welfare and Protection of Children, however, it appeared that a fresh reform effort might at last yield legislation with teeth. Edward de M. Rudolf, Secretary of the Waifs and Strays Society, posed an interesting question when he asked why private children's asylums should be exempt from official inspection; it was not unknown for self-styled philanthropists to mask greed with honeyed words.

But it was Miss Frances Zanetti who struck the most forceful note at the 1902 congress. Zanetti was an inspector for the Chorlton (Manchester) Poor Law Union, appointed under the 1897 Act, and her experience in this post had shown that it was folly to exempt single-child nursing operations from supervision. Previously, most of the women to appear before select committees investigating baby-farming had been matrons of homes for the "fallen." Rescue work would be ruined, these ladies had testified, if all homes for the offspring of unwed mothers were subjected to inspection. Zanetti believed, by contrast, that the "better class" of foster mothers would not mind inspection performed with tact.[76] Rescue workers remained skeptical. The Reverend G. Astbury, of King's Norton, even proposed that schoolchildren of thirteen and fourteen be required to attend lectures that would explain "very minutely and very clearly" the social consequences of sin. Public sex education,

Astbury and his allies hoped, would so reduce illegitimacy that the compulsory inspection of foster homes might cease to be an issue.[77]

Naturally, the reemergence of the baby-farming issue in 1902 was linked to doubts about national efficiency. For all their dire predictions, the foes of compulsory inspection could not deny that England lagged behind France and America in the care of foster children. Through application of the *Loi Roussel*, the French had been particularly successful in reducing mortality among illegitimate offspring. Could England afford unfettered philanthropy if the cost of such freedom was the death of even a few of its children?[78] The NSPCC would not press for strict control of baby-farming by preying upon fears of physical degeneration, but it could assure rescue workers that discrete inspection of homes was possible. "Many a scandal, small and great, has it been in our power to make from the . . . correspondence found in . . . miserable nurseries for unwanted children," announced the society. Yet nothing of the sort had ever occurred because the infants themselves, not their parentage, concerned child-savers. Similarly, state supervision of all children raised apart from their natural parents would be undertaken solely with the safety of the young in mind.[79] Rather more persuasive was the empirical evidence that NSPCC officials amassed between January 1903 and June 1907. During this time the society documented 2,101 charges of neglect and ill-treatment brought against persons keeping one child for profit. Cheered by the public's growing concern for infant welfare, the NSPCC built a factual base upon which the adoption clauses of the 1908 Children Act would soon be argued.[80]

Even more than infant-life protection, the issue that stirred controversy among child welfare advocates in the Edwardian era was the state feeding of schoolchildren. To focus reform energies on the care of the newly born was vital; but once they had weathered infancy, the young still faced grave health hazards. Of these, none seemed so intractable as chronic hunger. The ideal that every English citizen should start his working life equipped with at least an elementary education ran headlong into the reality that some children were too undernourished to learn. As early as 1889 a committee of the London School Board had turned its full attention to this subject. On the basis of circulars returned by teachers, the committee estimated that of the 341,495 children in average attendance at board schools, 12.8 percent were habitually "in want of food." Although London at that time boasted six large charities and numerous small ones that specialized in providing cheap meals, the distribution of meals was so uneven that children in some districts never saw a penny dinner. As a result new groups (notably the London Schools Dinners Association) were formed, while older charities heard stern words from the C.O.S. for allowing wasteful overlap.[81]

By the late 1890's some reformers had grown openly critical of the assumption that voluntary effort could cope with "necessitous schoolchildren." Sir John Gorst suggested in 1899 that teachers be required to keep detailed records on the condition of their pupils, thereby allowing education authorities to identify neglectful parents as soon as possible.[82] Appalled five years later when the Inter-Departmental Committee on Physical Deterioration learned that children still attended class half-starved, Gorst and three companions made their famous "descent" on Lambeth's Johanna Street School. When twenty boys there were found to bear the marks of debilitating hunger, the incensed quartet first marched into a meeting of the Lambeth guardians, demanding that these children be fed immediately, and soon thereafter harassed the Local Government Board into conceding that all genuinely hungry children were entitled to prompt relief from the Poor Law authorities, regardless of the status of their parents.[83] Although little change resulted from the order of April 1905 permitting guardians to relieve undernourished pupils, the demand for state feeding could not now be silenced. If socialists remained alone in fueling this agitation, the Countess of Warwick argued, then they alone would deserve thanks for serving "the practical interests of the race." Although the Countess—one of Gorst's associates in the Johanna Street School raid—was a socialist, many other champions of state feeding of undernourished schoolchildren were simply pragmatists who believed that the scope of "collective parenthood" should be enlarged to succor the adults of tomorrow.[84]

Historians have noted that the Education (Provision of Meals) Bill of 1906 aroused fierce debate because contemporaries viewed the measure as the thin edge of a collectivist wedge. Edwardian reformers like Reginald Bray approved. Under the resulting Act, Bray wrote, "All are taxed, for the benefit of all; the State takes men's money and spends their money better than they do themselves. This principle of collective spending admits of considerable develop-

ment, and is merely an expression of that broadening of human relations and that deepening of the sense of common interests and
common responsibilities which are the most characteristic features
of a progressive civilization."[85] Indeed, Asquith's Liberal government translated "the principle of collective spending" into old-age
pensions in 1908 and health and unemployment insurance in 1911.
The Act of 1906, in Bentley Gilbert's words, "recognized that poverty was of itself a danger, and that if it could not be prevented it
must be alleviated."[86]

Yet by no means all those who opposed the state feeding of
schoolchildren were troubled primarily by creeping collectivism. To
be sure, the C.O.S. lashed out instinctively against any legislation
that encroached on the domain of voluntary action. Far more telling to contemporaries, however, was the opposition of the NSPCC.
"Is it wise," asked Mary Loane, "to reject the testimony of a great
Society which solemnly assures us that it has dealt with scores of
thousands of children . . . deprived of necessary food not by their
parents' poverty but by their ill-will?" Philanthropists believed that
the NSPCC had done much to reform negligent parents just by
warning them of the penalties they faced. Might not an extension of
this procedure serve both children and ratepayers better than universal feeding of children in the elementary schools?[87] NSPCC
spokesmen argued that if shown "the practical demands of the
State," most fathers and mothers would mend their mistaken ways.
Robert Parr clung to this line of reasoning when he appeared before
a select committee on school feeding in April 1906. In 30,977 (96
percent) of its neglect and starvation cases for 1905, Parr explained,
the society had witnessed marked improvement in parental care. Of
course, brute poverty had been found to cause malnourishment in
some cases; and children in such circumstances must be fed by any
means at hand. But if the NSPCC were empowered to investigate all
the "hunger" cases then being reported to education authorities,
Parr assured the select committee, the need for indiscriminate feeding would vanish. Since an estimated 250,000 boys and girls fit this
category, Parr's plan assumed working-class compliance on a vast
scale.[88] Though the committee's chairman seemed startled by Parr's
optimism, neither he nor his fellow members were surprised that
Parr should have offered his society as the mechanism for so ambitious a scheme.

The select committee's report showed that NSPCC cooperation

in any public feeding program was deemed essential. School canteen committees, the units proposed to oversee the distribution of meals, were advised to recruit a representative from the nearest NSPCC branch. More significantly, where it seemed appropriate to take legal action against parents who refused to contribute toward the cost of their children's meals, only the NSPCC or the guardians would be allowed to prosecute.[89] Parr and his society lost their case against rate-assisted feeding in the schools. But their opposition, a key plank in the wider antifeeding campaign, was based on the apparent success of private persuasion rather than on a fear of collectivism.[90] The 1906 Education (Provision of Meals) Act was permissive, virtually guaranteeing that its implementation would be slow. Where local authorities made this harbinger of the welfare state work, however, they did so with the help of child-savers from the NSPCC.

Private Voice, Public Sphere

By 1908 the economist B. Kirkman Gray could write that a "co-partnership" had been established in the English home between parents and the state, with the latter growing "ever more active and masterful." "This is a result," he added, "which is calculated to give satisfaction to the socialist, but it was brought about by philanthropic individualists."[91] Perhaps slightly puzzling to later generations, Gray's assertion made perfect sense at a time when the central government was at last assuming responsibility for the protection of children within their families. Throughout most of the late Victorian and Edwardian period, the overwhelming majority of civil servants had been relieved that philanthropists were defining and administering domestic justice; just as the decision of husband and wife to become parents was a voluntary one, so also the regulation of parental duty seemed the province of voluntary effort.[92] In attempting to patrol family life, however, the NSPCC had of necessity created a large, centralized bureaucracy that functioned very much like a state department. Thus, when Herbert Samuel announced the Liberal Party's decision to sponsor a comprehensive child-protection law, anticruelty specialists were pleased by the prospect of some state assistance. NSPCC leaders had opposed the weakening of philanthropic control over the feeding of schoolchildren, but by and large they looked forward to augmenting their resources with help from the central government.

At the neighborhood level, as we have seen, the NSPCC found citizens willing to inform on brutal or negligent parents, partly because the society seemed genuinely committed to obtaining domestic justice for the young. True, NSPCC justice was highhanded at times.[93] Whereas after 1898 parents with authentic "conscientious objections" could obtain a release for their children from the vaccination laws, the society gave no quarter to those whose religious scruples exposed offspring to physical harm. Parents belonging to the "Peculiar People" could not, for example, satisfy both their theological precepts and the NSPCC's demands. To their sick, these faith healers gave food, warmth, and love, but not, in deference to James 5 : 14 – 15, medical treatment. The judgment in Reg. v. Wagstaffe (1860) had been that such parents were innocent of culpable homicide in the event that their young died.[94] But as soon as the 1889 Children's Charter received royal assent, NSPCC strategists began hauling "Peculiar People" into court, charging them, and frequently convicting them, of causing "unnecessary suffering" to their offspring.[95] By the Edwardian era "unnecessary suffering" had become such an elastic notion that child-savers could wield it to force the proper setting of broken limbs. Probably its most extreme application came in the Russell case of 1906, when the NSPCC brought neglect charges against an admittedly kind mother because it wanted custody of her eight-year-old son long enough to arrange for a fifth operation on his lame left leg.[96]

Such flagrant tampering with parental prerogative was often dismissed as the pardonable excess of an otherwise noble cause. Underlying public tolerance of the society was the assumption that voluntary child-protection work staved off collective responsibility for the young. The burden of supporting and training children rested squarely on their parents, Henry Sidgwick reasoned, "since it would obviously be the gravest interference with an individual's freedom of action to compel him to contribute to the support of an indefinite number of his neighbour's children."[97] Compulsory elementary education had already curbed the ratepayer's "freedom of action" two decades before Sidgwick wrote The Elements of Politics, but there was hope that the advance of state action could be halted there. Similarly, Herbert Spencer regarded child-savers as

performing a duty that government might legitimately have performed, but that, happily, voluntary effort had reserved to itself.
Several times an NSPCC subscriber, Spencer was neither insensitive
to human suffering nor unconcerned with social obligations, as
some scholars have implied.[98] Yet in his eyes the proper role of government remained narrow: "to defend the natural rights of man—
to protect person and property—to prevent the aggressions of the
powerful upon the weak—in a word, to administer justice." That
the society had assumed some of these state obligations struck
Spencer as wholly to the good, for philanthropists would, he
thought, be less apt than civil servants to promote the growth of
government.[99] In fact, Spencer plainly underestimated the degree to
which the NSPCC's mission would impel it to seek partnership with
the state.

Of all contemporary analysts, Kirkman Gray had perhaps the
clearest understanding of the relationship between anticruelty work
and the state. The state's response to voluntary social service, he reasoned, might assume one of six forms: first (and most obtrusively),
"annexation" of once private work; second, "partition" of duties;
third, "co-operation"; fourth, "supervision"; fifth, "co-ordination";
and sixth, "delegation." This last relationship, wherein the state
was "unwilling to be its own executive," described the position of
the NSPCC. Given the government's obligation to the society, Gray
concluded, it ought to receive state compensation for its work.[100]
But, of course, this had been the child-savers' refrain for fifteen
years.

Like animal-protection groups, the NSPCC early on forged a
symbiotic relationship with the police. Following an order issued in
late 1886, New York City police routinely reported all cases of
child mistreatment as well as all arrests of persons under sixteen to
the New York SPCC.[101] Eager for similar aid, London SPCC leaders
had set out to avoid jurisdictional disputes with the Metropolitan
Police. This did not prove difficult, for the London constabulary,
already hard pressed to deal with the capital's young pickpockets,
prostitutes, and street toughs, welcomed cruelty men as specialists
who could save them considerable labor. Official recognition of the
society's role as a crime prevention auxiliary came in March 1889,
when the Commissioner of Metropolitan Police, James Monro, issued instructions very like the earlier New York City order. Not
even the RSPCA enjoyed such close cooperation. Henceforth, po-

licemen would afford the society "every information and assistance within their power" in suspected cases of mistreatment, and would also remand children arrested under the Vagrancy Act directly into the society's custody.[102] By the end of the Edwardian period most large urban constabularies had set similar if less formal guidelines for their officers. Child-savers smugly observed of Nottingham, where the police continued to prosecute parents independently of the society, that the conviction rate was woefully low.[103]

A few police departments even donated bazaar or entertainment proceeds to the NSPCC, but more often direct financial aid came from Poor Law Unions. Guardians of the Highworth and Swindon Union set the precedent in this regard, voting unanimously on September 24, 1888, to give the society £25 "in recognition of the great public service rendered . . . in prosecution of the man and woman [baby-farmers] Hayes." In 1889 the Sunderland guardians went further when they resolved to bear the cost of all future court actions undertaken by the NSPCC.[104] These grants were especially meaningful because prior to 1904 they had to be disguised as part of the local board's regular operating budget—for example, as costs "for collecting and preparing information."[105] Educational authorities in some areas began to follow suit after 1900, awarding grants to the NSPCC for its help in reporting cases of underfed or verminous schoolchildren. Yet the central board refused to compensate child-savers for the extra work thrown on them by the Education (Administrative Provisions) Act of 1907.[106] That a voluntary organization already obliged to support itself should also have to pay for prosecuting lawbreakers seemed anomalous. At the very least, W. Clarke Hall argued, the direct legal expenses incurred in convicting a parent of neglect or assault should be borne by the nation. His reasoning made sense, since without the society to compel parental duty, state reformatories and industrial schools would swell in size and, therefore, cost.[107]

But if anything, the NSPCC's well-wishers underrated the second service it rendered, that of technical adviser to the state. On three occasions between September 1905 and May 1906, Robert Parr was asked to testify before government or parliamentary committees. As noted, Parr explained to the select committee on school meals why his society thought rate-financed feeding of the young would be inexpedient. A departmental committee on vagrancy also called Parr as an expert witness, and learned from him that, contrary to reputation, many tramp children were well looked after, and thus as a class should not be torn away from their parents.[108] The Royal Commission on the Care and Control of the Feeble Minded, by contrast, heard Parr urge the compulsory removal of all child imbeciles from their homes. NSPCC case experience proved that such children were often the victims of incest and sexual assault. To prevent these evils, the state should maintain them in special institutions.[109]

Perhaps the greatest tribute to Edwardian philanthropy, however, was the Children Act of 1908. This cumbersome statute, a tangle of 134 clauses, touched on every child-related issue from baby-farming to juvenile smoking. It is sometimes cited as a milestone of Liberal social reform in the prewar era, and is generally conceded to be the triumph of Herbert Samuel, then Parliamentary Under-Secretary at the Home Office. Both views need qualification. The Liberal Party clearly did give the bill every assistance as it lumbered through Parliament. H. H. Asquith, in his budget speech of 1907, had anticipated such legislation when he described the appeal of the child as "irresistible," reminding his fellow MPs that "the State . . . cannot pass by that appeal with folded arms." In justifying further social reform to safeguard England's "raw material," Asquith employed the rhetoric of national efficiency in a manner palatable to every political taste.[110] As Herbert Samuel would later recall, the bill emerged from Parliament without a single division on a point of principle because "men of all parties were eager to help [it] forward." If the Act of 1908 bore a collectivist stamp, it was collectivism by consensus, not the characteristic mark of New Liberals.[111]

Samuel's contribution to the bill is likewise misunderstood. There is no reason to doubt that the idea of an omnibus statute occurred to him after an interview early in 1907 with Mrs. M. K. Inglis, a Scotswoman who advocated the formation of a government ministry for children.[112] What both Samuel's and most later accounts obscure is the extent to which Samuel had fashioned his bill from existing law. The NSPCC's anticruelty statutes of 1889, 1894, and 1904, for example, had already placed severe restraints on the liberty of the parent; with respect to child protection, the 1908 Act was chiefly a consolidating measure. This applied also to its provisions for reformatory and industrial schools. Here the need for consolidation was plain, since, prior to 1908, these institutions were regulated by seventeen separate statutes for Ireland, Scotland, the

Isle of Man, the Channel Islands, England, and Wales. The comprehensive form of the Act would serve as a model for children's legislation passed in 1933 and 1948, but Samuel's handiwork was itself largely derivative.

Still less understood is Samuel's debt to nongovernmental groups for whatever novelty his Act did possess. The Home Office files for 1907 and 1908 bulge with resolutions from trade associations, public health workers, and philanthropists, but the evidence of extra-parliamentary pressure is most abundant in connection with the issues of children's courts and infant-life protection. Baby-farming, of course, was a subject that aroused nearly as much feeling in the Edwardian years as it had in the early 1870's. By the time that civil servants began sorting out this controversy in 1907, the bulk of philanthropic opinion was in favor of abolishing the clause in the Act of 1897 that freed from inspection persons who took in children with a lump-sum payment of more than £20.[113] But the debate surrounding the inspection of homes that received only one baby at a time in return for weekly payments raged on. Pressing hard for inspection were the NSPCC, the State Children's Association, and the Association of Poor Law Unions; ranged against them were the London County Council, the Reformatory and Refuge Union, the London Diocesan Society for Rescue and Preventive Work, and a host of smaller magdalene groups.[114] Samuel leaned toward the proponents of inspection, but "in view of the strength of the opposition" he opted to postpone a decision until after yet another select committee had allowed both sides to air their cases. The report of this committee, published in April 1908, found the NSPCC's massive case documentation too compelling to dismiss.[115] Thus, lone nurslings should be—and subsequently were in Samuel's bill—brought under the eye of English law.

NSPCC labor also helped to bring about the establishment of children's courts in 1908. In 1897 the Metropolitan Asylums Board established remand homes in London for the accommodation of juveniles awaiting sentencing; after the passage of the Youthful Offenders Act four years later, these homes, rather than workhouses and police cells, received nearly all such juveniles under sixteen.[116] By 1905 the society was "very pleased" with the progress of "the movement in favour of dealing with the delinquencies of children in a less arid and pedantic and a more humane and reasonable manner." Juveniles were being spared not only the trauma of incarceration, but also, in some districts, the "contamination" of mixing with hardened criminals in court. Complying with a Home Office order, police courts in London saw to it that charges against children were heard first each morning, before any adult prisoners appeared. Birmingham reserved Thursday mornings for juvenile cases, at which time the young, accompanied by their parents or guardians, waited in one of two rooms (one for minor, the other for more serious offences) and then appeared individually before the magistrate. Although the NSPCC applauded these innovations, it would accept nothing less than a national network of juvenile courts administered by special magistrates and tied to a unified probation system.[117] Once again, the society cast envious eyes on an American model, New York City's Children's Court. There, "paternal" judges in chambers no longer "poisonous with crime" tried to prevent the young offender "from ever taking another false step and to save him to the State." Significantly, the court's chief parole officer, E. Fellows Jenkins, was also superintendent of the New York SPCC, and his inspectors compiled reports on the conduct of paroled youths at school, work, and home.[118]

When Parliament passed the Probation of Offenders Act in 1907, therefore, NSPCC leaders welcomed the appointment of cruelty men as children's probation officers. Because the agents so appointed were already trained social investigators, their reports proved particularly useful to magistrates in making decisions about young offenders' futures.[119] Moreover, the experience gained by the NSPCC in this new field gave greater credence to its recommendations on children's courts. Combined with pressure from the State Children's Association and the Church of England's Waifs and Strays Society, these recommendations did much to shape the fifth section of Samuel's bill.

It was fitting that Samuel should have been the NSPCC's featured speaker at its 25th annual meeting. He came to the Mansion House on May 24, 1909, to be thanked by grateful philanthropists. But just as important, he came to offer thanks of his own. Samuel admitted that he owed a "very special obligation" to Parr and his staff for their aid in framing the 1908 Act, and to the society as a whole for portraying the child in such a way that few now dared practice cruelty.[120] Here was hyperbole worthy of Benjamin Waugh himself. Few of the well-heeled patrons present could have imagined that the war on parental sin was over. Perhaps some of the better informed ladies and gentlemen even harbored doubts about those sections of the 1908 Act that created new sins: overlying a baby while intoxicated; allowing one's offspring to be burned by an uncovered fire; and sending children to fetch liquor and tobacco.[121] Nevertheless, Samuel's flattery contained a solid core of truth. State responsibility for the treatment of children at home was growing in an atmosphere of intense expectation.

Benjamin Waugh did not live to hear this tribute. Frail ever since retirement, he died on March 11, 1908. Cruelty men he had helped train bore his body to a grave in Essex. Four years earlier this "useful combination of the fanatic and the man of business" had assured the *Daily News* that he never cared about public opinion. "Public opinion," he noted, "condemned Christ to crucifixion." Then, in characteristic self-contradiction, he added: "You must know how it [public opinion] has been aroused, who has moved it, and why. Sometimes I am pessimistic. But I feel that our work and ways will win conviction in the end."[122] He was subdued at the time because his cruise to the antipodes had revealed that child-protection groups in New Zealand and Australia were straying from the example of the NSPCC by rescuing children without trying to cure their parents. That his society had inspired imitation in Germany, Italy, Spain, and India, as well as in the South Pacific, did not ease his frustration. Waugh never lost his Victorian faith in the transforming power of moral reform. Rightly run—along the lines he had laid down—the battle against parental cruelty might one day be won. It was merciful that Benjamin Waugh did not achieve extreme old age.

The "Discovery" of Child Abuse

M EDICAL EXPERTS typically date the "discovery" of systematic child abuse from the mid-1950's, when American radiologists began to note a connection between skeletal lesions in infants and parental mistreatment.[1] Widespread medical concern about the abuse of the young did not, however, materialize until 1962. In that year, C. Henry Kempe, a pediatrician at the University of Colorado School of Medicine, and several of his colleagues published an article in which they spoke of a "battered child syndrome." Kempe's charge that physicians had long been emotionally unwilling to believe that parents could attack their offspring seemed to trigger a shift in medical thinking, for there followed in both Britain and America a spate of writing on the subject.[2] At the same time that Kempe's article appeared, the *Journal of the American Medical Association* ventured: "It is likely that the battered child syndrome will be found to be a more frequent cause of death than such well recognized and thoroughly studied diseases as leukemia, cystic fibrosis, and muscular dystrophy, and it may well rank with automobile accidents and the toxic and infectious encephalides as causes of acquired disturbances of the central nervous system."[3]

Since then American and British psychiatrists, sociologists, social workers, and journalists have joined doctors in producing a steady stream of literature on child abuse. Although a consensus regarding the etiology and incidence of the problem has not yet emerged, the number of cases of trauma in children diagnosed as the consequence of battering continues to rise.

One result of this recent interest in cruelty to children has been a foreshortening of historical perspective. Viewing the battered child syndrome as a mid-twentieth-century discovery, social scientists have tended to belittle earlier child protection work. Victorian medical men, modern experts pointed out, puzzled over "obvious" cases of child-beating without recognizing the true causes of the trauma. On April 13, 1888, for example, Dr. S. A. West described to colleagues at a meeting of the Clinical Society of London a strange swelling associated with the long bones of both arms and one leg of a five-week-old infant. Even more curious was the fact that three of the infant's four siblings had experienced similar symptoms at early ages. Since there was no history of syphilis in the family, West and his fellow physicians surmised that a heretofore unknown form of rickets, possibly intrauterine in character, might have produced the symptoms. The proper diagnosis, we are told to-day, would have been injury resulting from parental assault.[4]

What modern experts overlook, however, is that private philanthropy, not the medical profession, was directing the late nineteenth-century campaign against child abuse. In America, particularly in New York City, it is true that early anticruelty workers tried to remove children from physical harm without much thought to reforming their parents. Convinced that institutionalization was best for suffering boys and girls, the New York SPCC payed little attention to the problem of family breakup and less still to the causes of child abuse. But one cannot level these criticisms at the NSPCC. For Benjamin Waugh and his allies not only acted on the belief that most threatened children could be helped within their homes, but also gave much thought to the pressures that shaped "unnatural" parents.

Vast improvements in the quality and availability of medical services, combined with the proliferation of central and local government bodies alert to violence against children, have produced a screening system far more effective than anything the NSPCC assembled. Further, modern mass communication has publicized the problem of child abuse with a thoroughness unimaginable even three generations ago. And yet, despite the intense scrutiny to which the phenomenon of intrafamily violence has been subjected, we know only marginally more about what motivates parents to harm their young than did reformers in late Victorian times. To patronize their concern for the safety of the child would be presumptuous.

There remains to be explained the curious decline of public interest in child abuse between 1914 and the early 1960's. No doubt the material and psychological wounds of two world wars and protracted economic crisis tended to divert humane attention on both sides of the Atlantic. But other, more uniquely national, issues were also at play. In America, the readiness of anticruelty societies to separate parents and children began to draw fire from the new professions of social work and child psychology. Particularly after the 1909 White House Conference on Children reaffirmed the ideal of family unity, SPCC leaders saw their old methods roundly criticized.[5] A very different problem took shape in England, where widespread faith in the NSPCC's ability to enforce protective legislation bred dangerous complacency.

Indeed, by the 1920's some English writers had concluded that child abuse was "extinct" in the "higher walks of life," and rapidly vanishing "amongst the roughest and most uncivilized classes."[6] Government officials, too, were optimistic. Noting that English courts had prosecuted 2,052 persons for assaults on or neglect of children in 1921, as against 4,106 in 1900, the Home Office asked rhetorically if there had been a "permanent improvement during the last fifteen or twenty years in the sense of responsibility of parents toward their children?" This happy trend apparently sprang from several "active influences": better education, medical attention in schools, decreasing drunkenness as a result of shortened pub hours, and, not least important, the zeal of the NSPCC. Moreover, the philanthropic engine that Waugh and Parr had built showed no signs of wear, for the NSPCC's work still seemed inappropriate for a state agency.[7]

Yet, forty years later, NSPCC leaders would find themselves berated for pursuing policies that had once won praise. Even before pediatric specialists in America helped rekindle public concern over mistreatment of the young, a few Englishmen attacked the society for its "lady-like" response to parental violence.[8] Such criticism grew more frequent in the wake of publicity about the battered child syndrome; having achieved what seemed to be a wise balance between protection of the young and preservation of the family unit, the NSPCC was now forced to reckon with a new, militantly interventionist climate of opinion. Today, two decades after the rediscovery of child abuse as a major social sore, voluntary effort in Britain receives less blame for "missed" cases because a confusing array of government departments and local authorities share this responsibility. As all interested parties agree, however, a key goal of future social policy must be to refine methods for identifying children at risk—those whose home environments are most apt to generate mistreatment. What Victorian moral reformers liked to call "the cry of the children" may never be hushed. But perhaps, given close cooperation between state and private bodies, more parents can be helped to wield their power with discretion.

Child-Welfare Legislation, 1870-1908

Date	Title	Subject Matter
1870	33 & 34 Vic., c. 75	Elementary Education.
1871	34 & 35 Vic., c. 112	Children of Criminal Mothers.
1872	35 & 36 Vic., c. 21	Elementary, Industrial, and Reformatory Schools.
1872	35 & 36 Vic., c. 38	Infant Life Protection.
1872	35 & 36 Vic., c. 77	Metalliferous Mines.
1872	35 & 36 Vic., c. 93	Pawning by Children.
1872	35 & 36 Vic., c. 94	Selling Drink to Children.
1873	36 & 37 Vic., c. 12	Custody of Infants.
1873	36 & 37 Vic., c. 67	Agricultural Children.
1874	37 & 38 Vic., c. 44	Factories.
1874	37 & 38 Vic., c. 47	Industrial Schools.
1874	37 & 38 Vic., c. 62	Infants.
1875	38 & 39 Vic., c. 17	Gunpowder not to be Sold to a Child.
1875	38 & 39 Vic., c. 39	Metalliferous Mines.
1875	38 & 39 Vic., c. 60	Infant Life Insurance.
1875	38 & 39 Vic., c. 70	Chimney Sweepers' Regulations.
1875	38 & 39 Vic., c. 90	Apprentices.
1876	39 & 40 Vic., c. 22	Infant Life Insurance.
1876	39 & 40 Vic., c. 32	Registration of Births.
1876	39 & 40 Vic., c. 61	Child's Settlement (Poor Law).
1877	40 & 41 Vic., c. 60	Canal Boats.
1878	41 & 42 Vic., c. 16	Factories and Workshops.
1878	41 & 42 Vic., c. 19	Divorce—Custody of Children.
1878	41 & 42 Vic., c. 40	Industrial Schools (Scotland).
1879	42 & 43 Vic., c. 34	Dangerous Performances.
1879	42 & 43 Vic., c. 49	Summary Jurisdiction.
1880	43 & 44 Vic., c. 15	Industrial Schools.
1880	43 & 44 Vic., c. 23	Education—Poor Relief.
1880	43 & 44 Vic., c. 25	Education—Metropolis.
1880	43 & 44 Vic., c. 45	Indecent Assault—Consent.
1882	45 & 46 Vic., c. 75	Liability of Married Woman.
1883	46 & 47 Vic., c. 53	Factories and Workshops.
1884	47 & 48 Vic., c. 68	Matrimonial—Custody.
1885	48 & 49 Vic., c. 69	Criminal Law Amendment.

Date	Title	Subject Matter
1886	49 & 50 Vic., c. 27	Infants—Guardianship.
1886	49 & 50 Vic., c. 52	Married Women—Desertion.
1887	49 & 50 Vic., c. 56	Sale of Drink.
1887	50 & 51 Vic., c. 25	First Offenders.
1887	50 & 51 Vic., c. 58	Coal Mines.
1888	51 & 52 Vic., c. 43, s. 96	Minors May Sue.
1889	52 & 53 Vic., c. 44	Prevention of Cruelty.
1889	52 & 53 Vic., c. 56	Pauper Children.
1891	54 & 55 Vic., c. 3	Custody of Children.
1891	54 & 55 Vic., c. 23	Reformatory and Industrial Schools.
1891	54 & 55 Vic., c. 75	Factories and Workshops.
1891	54 & 55 Vic., c. 76	Public Health—Workshops.
1892	55 & 56 Vic., c. 4	Betting—Infants.
1892	55 & 56 Vic., c. 62	Factories—Shop Hours.
1893	56 & 57 Vic., c. 67	Factories.
1894	57 & 58 Vic., c. 27	Prevention of Cruelty.
1894	57 & 58 Vic., c. 33	Education—Industrial Schools.
1894	57 & 58 Vic., c. 41	Prevention of Cruelty.
1895	58 & 59 Vic., c. 39	Married Women—Separation.
1897	60 & 61 Vic., c. 52	Dangerous Performances.
1897	60 & 61 Vic., c. 57	Infant Life Protection.
1899	62 & 63 Vic., c. 12	Reformatory Schools.
1899	62 & 63 Vic., c. 13	Elementary Education—School Attendance.
1899	62 & 63 Vic., c. 32	Elementary Education—Defective and Epileptic Children.
1900	63 & 64 Vic., c. 21	Mines.
1900	63 & 64 Vic., c. 53	Elementary Education.
1901	1 Edw. VII, c. 20	Youthful Offenders.
1901	1 Edw. VII, c. 22	Factory and Workshops.
1901	1 Edw. VII, c. 27	Intoxicating Liquors.
1902	2 Edw. VII, c. 10	Immoral Traffic (Scotland).
1902	2 Edw. VII, c. 16	Pauper Children (Ireland).
1902	2 Edw. VII, c. 28	Licensing.
1902	2 Edw. VII, c. 42	Education.
1903	3 Edw. VII, c. 13	Elementary Education—Defective and Epileptic Children.
1903	3 Edw. VII, c. 24	Education (London).
1903	3 Edw. VII, c. 45	Employment.
1904	4 Edw. VII, c. 15	Prevention of Cruelty.
1906	6 Edw. VII, c. 10	Education of Defective Children (Scotland).
1906	6 Edw. VII, c. 57	Education (Provision of Meals).
1907	7 Edw. VII, c. 10	Factories, Workshops, and Mines.
1907	7 Edw. VII, c. 17	Probation of Offenders.
1907	7 Edw. VII, c. 40	Notification of Births.
1907	7 Edw. VII, c. 43	Education (Administrative Provisions).
1908	8 Edw. VII, c. 45	Punishment of Incest.
1908	8 Edw. VII, c. 67	Children Act.

Sample Case Record

The original spelling and syntax have been retained. Italic type indicates printed matter; roman type indicates handwritten material.

Date of Complaint
 June 1ˢᵗ '98

CHILD—Name, Age, and Address of
 Anne Purcell, 13½ yrs.
  2 Underwood's Buildings.
  Regent Sᵗ
  York

What Religious Persuasion? Prot.	*Is child insured?* Yes
Relationship to Accused? Child of	*For how much?* 1ᵈ pr week
Are parents living? Father only	*In what Society?* Prudential
Is child illegitimate? No	*Where child is?* above a/d

OFFENCE—

Nature of Illtreatment & Assault
Time of May 17ᵗʰ & June 1ˢᵗ '98.
Locality of Regent St.

ACCUSED—

Name Geo. Purcell
Address above
Family (5)
Occupation Bricklayers Labourer *Income* 28/-

WITNESSES—Names and Addresses of

Anne Purcell.	Underwood's Bldgs.	Regent S.
Mrs Ridley.	" "	"
Mrs Prince.	Regent St.	York.
Mrs Hudson.	"	"
Insp. Hare.	Boro Police	"
Dr Reynolds.	St. Saviourgate	"
Insp. W. Jackson.	N.S.P.C.C.	"

ACTION taken— Summoned to appear before City Bench, on Monday
June 13th at 11 a.m.

Result Defendant convicted & sentenced to 2 calendar months impt.
with h. l.

How child dealt with Children to go to workhouse

Inspector W Jackson

Date June. 3. '98.

June.1.98.
Mrs Annie Hudson states
I live at N° 53 Regent Street, York. I have known the Purcell family for
about four months. For two months I lived four doors from them and Cissy
Purcell used to, and does still, play with my child Ruth. They now live in
Underwood's Yard, Regent Street.

Mr Purcell is a widower and has three children living with him, Cissy
aged 13 yrs, a girl about 3 years, and a baby 10 months. Mr Purcell does
not come home to my knowledge till 11 p.m. Three nights this week Cissy
has been in my house till that time, waiting for her father to come home.
Sometimes I have let Ruth stop with her until 10.30 p.m.

To-night between 8 & 9 pm I went up Regent Street and I saw Cissy
Purcell crying, with the baby in her arms, and a crowd round her— I went
up to her and asked her what was the matter— She replied—"Father has
been thrashing me with a strap with a buckle on"— A woman in the crowd
showed me the child's arm. It looked frightful, bruised, & showing marks
where the buckle had caught it.

Cissy has told me that she is afraid of her father— She said on Monday
night when in my house, "Mrs Hudson I am afraid of my father coming
home tonight,—if he's drunk he thrashes me so and I'm so frightened."

June.2.'98

Dr H. W. Reynolds states
I am a duly qualified medical practitioner and live at 28 St. Saviourgate, York.

The bruises I found on Anne Purcell, especially that on the left fore arm are very bad indeed and great violence must have been used to produce them. The child's story that they were produced by a strap with a buckle on is quite consistent with the marks I found. It is a pity the magistrates could not see her to-day.

June.2.98

Insp. Hare states
I am an Inspector of the York Police force.

At the request of Insp. Jackson, I accompanied him, for his protection, to the house of George Purcell, 2 Underwoods Buildings, Regent St. I saw Anne Purcell and the bruises upon her. That on the left arm must have been caused by great violence.

After waiting five minutes Mr Purcell came home to dinner. Insp. Jackson then told him who he was and that he had examined his child and warned him that the consequences of a repetition of the offence would aggravate the case against him. Insp. Jackson said no more than this. As we were leaving Purcell said "I beat her with a strap because she did not do as I told her." We neither of us made any reply.

June.2.'98

Mrs Ridley states
I live next door to Mr Purcell but I have never seen him hit Cissy or heard her scream, but I see the poor child working and carrying the baby about all day and I am sure she is not strong enough for she is so bow-legged that she is almost a cripple. The man ought to have a woman to look after his home and children. I saw the child's arm last night where he beat her, but I did not see or hear him do it.

June.2.'98

Mrs Prince states
I live next door to Mr Purcell and did in his wife's lifetime.

He is a most violent tempered man. I have seen him chase his wife round the yard with a razor in his hand— I once interfered and he gave me a black eye.

All the neighbours know how hard the child works but we none of us dare go up against him. We never hear Cissy scream she dare not and he never lets us see him hit her—but she is very much afraid of him as you see.

He has taken up lately with a woman of light character and she professes to come and do for him, but she only turns up at the end of the week when he takes his money.

He drinks a little at the end of the week but never breaks time to drink.

June 2.'98

Anne Purcell states

I am 13½ years of age and live with my father at 2 Underwoods Buildings, Regent Street, York.

My mother died a year ago next month.

Father is a Bricklayer's labourer, he goes to work at 6 a.m., and leaves work at 5.30 p.m. He comes home to dinner at 12.10 p.m.

I have been left school for a long time now and keep fathers house for him and mind my brother, Charlie, aged 6 yrs, Lucy 3 years, and the baby 13 months. I cook the dinner and do all the work of the house, but father makes his own bed.

Mrs Camidge comes at the end of the week and bakes the bread and does the washing— Sometimes she comes on Thursdays, but mostly on Fridays.

Father only takes drink at the end of the week.

I am very much afraid of my father. He swears and shouts at me and hits me with his hands. On Tuesday May 17th, between 6 & 7 pm, my brother who had come from soldiering asked for a handkerchief— I said there was one in the drawer but could not find it. My father then hit me with his hand, and when my brother had gone out, my father beat me with the strap he wears round his body and bruised my arm. The strap has a buckle to it.

Last night about 5.30 pm father came home. I took baby off the couch and my father saw it had dirtied on it. He took a towel and hit me with it, and when I put baby in the chair, he took off his strap and beat me as hard as he could over my arm & back with the buckle end of it— I did not scream out— I dare not for he would have hit me more. He hit me three or four times. My arm hurts me now, and nursing the baby makes it worse.

When he went out last night, after beating me, he said when he came back he would thrash me with a stick that would make me feel. I sit up late at night as I do not like to go to bed until father gets home.

After you and the policeman had left this dinnertime, my father asked me who I had told about him beating me— I said "The neighbours"— He then put his fist in my face and said—"If you go out this afternoon I'll cut you in two." He swore at me and said "You are going away you little B——. and a B——y good job."

My arm is in great pain now.

June.3.'98

Sir [Honorary Secretary of the York Branch]

This is a case of alleged Illtreatment and Assault by a man named George Purcell a Bricklayer's Labourer, living at N° 2 Underwoods Buildings, Regent Street, York, on his daughter Anne Purcell, aged 13½ years. The man is a widower, his wife having died 12 months ago. He has four young children

Anne, aged 13½ yrs

Charles "   6   "

Lucy   "   3   "

Baby   "   13 months

and for the last three or four months the eldest child Anne has acted as housekeeper to her father, and mother to the other children.

Just lately, for the last week or two, a woman named Camidge has come to the house at the end of the week and done the washing and baked the bread, but, say the neighbours, this is not the primary object of her visits.

The man is earning 28/– a week, and although he indulges in drink at the end of the week he does not neglect his work for it. It is as a sober man that he is most violent. He has, says Mrs Prince, a most violent and uncontrollable temper as I have reason to know for once when trying to shield his poor wife from his violence he struck me a violent blow on the eyes.

This then is the character of the man. The whole neighbourhood are afraid of him, and judging from the extreme nervousness of the child Anne and the distress she was in yesterday because I had called, and her father must hear of it, I am quite convinced that the two assaults spoken to, and which she declares are the only assaults by no means truly represents his general treatment of her. She is afraid to speak out, and so are the neighbours. I think therefore now that we have caught him after the committal of a most brutal Assault, is our opportunity to punish him for a long course of continued illtreatment, the knowledge of which is kept back through the fear of both victim and neighbours.

The child is exceedingly short for her age, and so bow-legged to be almost a cripple. To see and hear this child, and to note her anxiety as to the consequences to herself of anything she tells against her father, is most distressing to the onlooker. I sincerely hope something may be done for her.

I am Sir
Yours Obediently,
W. Jackson
Insp

REPORT OF SUPERVISION

No. of Plaint 643

Date of Visit Janry. 18.'99

Name of Officer
making enquiry W Jackson.

Name and Address of family
Supervised:
   Geo. Purcell
   18 Portland Place
   Layerthorpe.

Sir

   This is the man we prosecuted on June 13th 98—for a brutal assault on his child Anne & he received 2 months imprisonment with H.L. After his release I could not find out where he was living but as I was entering Portland Place today I saw him enter N° 18 & followed. I found a beautiful home well arranged & Purcell in no way resented my visit. He stated he was very comfortable & that Anne was a good housekeeper to him. The condition of the home does great credit to the girl.

Yrs. Obdtly,

W. Jackson

Insp

Figures

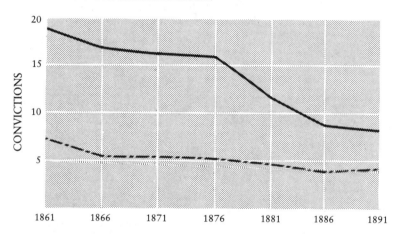

—— Convictions per 100,000 population, aged 15 and older

-- — Convictions for aggravated assaults against women and children as a percentage of convictions for all common assaults

Fig. 1. Convictions for aggravated assaults against women and children, 1861–91. (Source: Judicial Statistics for England and Wales.)

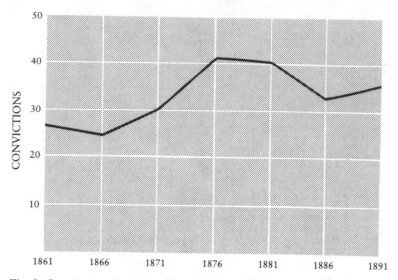

Fig. 2. Convictions for neglecting or failing to support one's family,
1861–91. (Source: Judicial Statistics for England and Wales. Convictions
are per 100,000 population, aged 20 and older.)

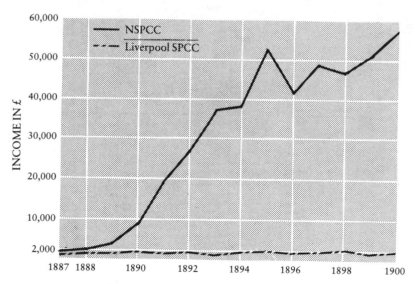

Fig. 3. Annual income of the NSPCC and Liverpool SPCC, 1887–1900.
(Sources: NSPCC 26th Annual Report; Liverpool SPCC *Jubilee Report*.
The years refer to the calendar years ending on March 31.)

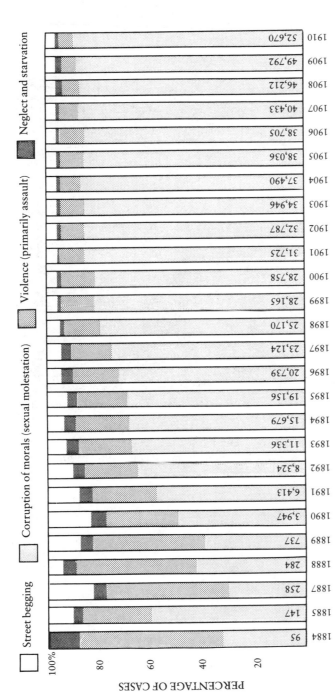

Fig. 4. Nature of the complaints investigated by the NSPCC, 1884–1910. (Source: NSPCC 26th Annual Report. From 1888 on, the years refer to the calendar years ending on March 31. The data for 1884 are for six months only; the data for 1885 are for the full calendar year; and the data for 1887 are for the fifteen months ending on March 31, 1887. The numbers given within the bars are the total numbers of cases investigated.)

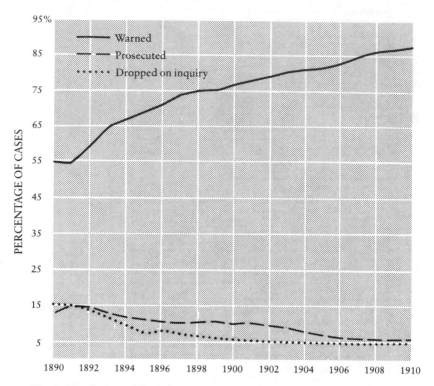

Fig. 5. Resolution of the NSPCC's cases, 1890–1910. (Source: NSPCC
26th Annual Report. The years refer to the calendar years ending on
March 31. The NSPCC's case load grew from 3,947 in 1890 to 52,670
in 1910.)

Notes

Complete authors' names, titles, and publication data for works cited in short form in the Notes are given in the Bibliography, pp. 280–308. The following abbreviations are used in the Notes:

B.M.J.   *British Medical Journal*
C.G.   *Child's Guardian*
DNB   *Dictionary of National Biography*
Hansard   British parliamentary debates
HO   Home Office
I.L.P.S.   Infant Life Protection Society
N.A.P.S.S. National Association for the Promotion of Social Science
NSPCC   National Society for the Prevention of Cruelty to Children
P.M.G.   *Pall Mall Gazette*
P.P.   Parliamentary Papers
P.R.O.   Public Record Office
R.C.   Royal Commission
RSPCA   Royal Society for the Prevention of Cruelty to Animals
S.C.   Select Committee

Chapter One

1. *The Times*, April 6, 1860, p. 9.

2. *Ibid.*, April 13, 1860, p. 10.

3. Mill, p. 107.

4. Harris, p. 359.

5. Macaulay, II, 418–19; Hobbes, p. 210.

6. On the development of kindness to animals in England, see Fairholme and Pain; also Moss. More recently, James Turner has studied the prevention of cruelty to animals as an Anglo-American phenomenon.

7. Hood, p. 60.   8. Coveney, p. 115.

9. Browning, pp. 247–50.   10. Pattison, pp. 72–74.

11. *Notes & Queries*, 3d ser., 1 (January 11, 1862), 39; Young and Ashton, p. 164.

12. Stone, pp. 163–64.

13. *Ibid.*, pp. 174–75; Elyot, I, 32.

14. Powers, pp. 165–66.

15. Goodsell, p. 346; Bayne-Powell, p. 1.

16. De Mause, pp. 42, 51; Bogna W. Lorence, "Parents and Children in Eighteenth Century Europe," *History of Childhood Quarterly*, 2 (Summer 1974), 24.

17. Trumbach, pp. 244–46.

18. Plumb, p. 70; Stone, p. 468; Bayne-Powell, p. 149.

19. Stone, pp. 467, 666–69, 677–78; Wesley, as quoted in Sangster, p. 75.

20. Barker, pp. 8, 45, 50. Cf. Degler, pp. 90–91.

21. Place, pp. 34, 62.

22. D. Roberts, "Paterfamilias," pp. 64–65, 72.

23. *Ibid.*, pp. 68, 77.

24. Blackstone, I, 440. Emphasis added.

25. Dunlop and Denman, pp. 255–57; George, pp. 226–32. Seventeenth-century London apprentices sometimes did sue their masters as a result of cruel usage; see S. R. Smith, pp. 152–53.

26. *Appeal to Humanity.*

27. Jonas Hanway, *A Sentimental History of Chimney Sweeps in London and Westminster*, in *Improving the Lot of the Chimney Sweeps* (New York, 1972), p. 14.

28. 32 Geo. III, c. 2.

29. 7 & 8 Vic., c. 101; 14 Vic., c. 11. See Hansard, 3d ser., 114 (March 12, 1851), col. 1297, for the rationale behind the 1851 Apprentices' and Servants' Act.

30. Bill for the Protection of . . . Domestic Servants and Apprentices, P.P., 1863, II, 15–17; Bill for the Better Protection of Children, Servants, and Apprentices, Hansard, 3d ser., 193 (June 29, 1868), col. 300.

31. The Carter case received six separate notices in *The Times*. See especially February 15, 1877, p. 5; July 5, 1877, p. 9.

32. As quoted in Driver, pp. 42–44. England abolished its slave trade in 1807, but not until 1833 was slavery eliminated by statute in British colonies.

33. Ward, p. 51; Oastler, "A Letter to . . . Millowners," in *Richard Oastler*. As originally formulated in 1832, the Ten Hours Bill aimed to prohibit employment of children under the age of nine in all manufacturing work, to limit daily labor for persons between nine and eighteen to ten hours (eight on Saturdays), and to forbid night work for all persons under the age of 21.

34. S.C. on the Labour of Children in the Mills and Factories, P.P., 1831–32, XV, QQ. 496–97, 506–7, 241–43, 1079–82. Spinners some-

times employed—and beat—their own children. For contrasting modern accounts, see E. P. Thompson, *Making*, pp. 336–39; and Smelser, pp. 275, 278–79.

35. Hansard, 3d ser., 11 (March 16, 1832), col. 367; John Brown, especially pp. 33–39. *The British Labourer's Protector and Factory Child's Friend*, October 26, 1832, p. 44; January 11, 1833, pp. 133–34.

36. Hansard, 3d ser., 11 (March 16, 1832), col. 358; First Report on Employment of Children in Factories, P.P., 1833, XX, 31; Fielden, p. 40.

37. Wing, pp. vi, xxxv; Gaskell, pp. 97–98.

38. Head, p. 190.

39. Ure, pp. 290, 300.

40. McKendrick, p. 162. On child-labor legislation as social insurance, see [Anthony Ashley Cooper,] p. 180.

41. Lord Ashley, quoted in Hartwell, p. 406.

42. S.C. on Juvenile Offenders and Transportation, P.P., 1847, VII, Q. 101.

43. Worsley, p. 140; S.C. on Criminal and Destitute Juveniles, P.P., 1852, VII, QQ. 1557, 2091, Appendix No. 3, pp. 427–28.

44. Sidney Turner, p. 406.   45. See Stack, pp. 311–12.

46. Carpenter, p. 74.   47. May, "Innocence," pp. 7, 29.

48. Jeune, "Innocents," p. 355.

49. *Ragged School Union Quarterly Record*, April 1877, p. 60; *Dens of London*, p. 16; Collins, p. 96.

50. Dickens, *Nickleby*, chap. 8. Dickens to Miss Coutts, quoted in Pope, p. 166.

51. Dickens, quoted in Collins, p. 102.

52. Return Relating to Charges Preferred Against Male Persons for Assaults on Women and Children, P.P., 1854, LIII, 23.

53. *Ibid.*, pp. 7, 21.

54. In the 1860's Hippolyte Taine observed that public fighting was a favorite spectacle among the poor. The sound of brawling in Shadwell brought "the population of neighbouring 'lanes' . . . pouring into the street . . . as if a human sewer were suddenly clearing itself." Taine, p. 29.

55. Reports . . . on the State of the Law Relating to Brutal Assaults, P.P., 1875, LXI, 22–63, 149–65. Biting, wounding with dangerous weapons, and kicking with clogs or metal-tipped boots constituted the greatest dangers to women according to chairmen of the Quarter Sessions.

56. Cobbe, "Wife-Torture," pp. 80, 82. Noting that "sensational cases of cruelty [to women] . . . were of almost daily occurrence," Lord Penzance successfully introduced an amendment to the 1878 Matrimonial Causes Bill (later 41 Vic., c. 19) that enabled wives to live apart from abusive husbands. Hansard, 3d ser., 239 (March 29, 1878), col. 191.

57. Cobbe, "Wife-Torture," pp. 65–66, 70; Cobbe, *Life*, pp. 593–94.

58. Judicial Statistics for England and Wales, P.P., 1862, 1867, 1872, 1877, 1882, 1887, 1892; census figures for 1861, 1871, 1881, and 1891. Population estimates for census midpoints were calculated using the geometric mean.

59. Bill for the Better Protection of Women and Children . . . from Crimes of Violence, P.P., 1882, VI, 755–75.

60. Gatrell and Hadden, p. 374.

61. Tomes, p. 340.

62. Evans, pp. 116–17; Alford, p. 506.

63. Kenny, p. 154; E. P. Thompson, "'Rough Music,'" p. 297. Michael Anderson cites one case of neighborhood outrage against a father who threw his sons into a canal; see M. Anderson, p. 104. But far more frequent are the accounts of charivaris aimed at wife-beaters. E.g., *Notes & Queries*, 2d ser., 10 (September 29, 1860), 258; 10 (October 20, 1860), 319; 10 (December 15, 1860), 476-77; 5th ser., 6 (December 9, 1876), 463.

Chapter Two

1. *Saturday Review*, August 5, 1865, p. 161. For a more detailed discussion of this subject, see Behlmer, pp. 403–27.

2. H. R. Jones, p. 43; Criminal Statistics of England and Wales, for 1977, P.P., 1978, Cmnd. 7289, p. 136.

3. *Lancet*, November 1, 1862, p. 491.

4. *Morning Post*, ca. September 22, 1863, clipping in *Infanticide Memoranda* (Harvard Law School, n.d.).

5. *Lancet*, October 10, 1863, pp. 426–27. Cf. Lowndes, pp. 591–93.

6. *B.M.J.*, October 14, 1865, p. 409; *Transactions of the N.A.P.S.S.*, 1864, p. 583.

7. R.C. on Capital Punishment, P.P., 1866, XXI, QQ. 410, 3197–3200, p. l. See also the Society for the Abolition of Capital Punishment's *Analysis and Review of the Blue Book*, pp. 18–20.

8. P.P., 1866, III, 311; P.P., 1867, IV, 467.

9. *The Times*, August 2, 1865, p. 9.

10. *Life and Trial*.

11. "England—Infanticide Amongst the Poor," *The Nation*, 1 (August 31, 1865), 270–71.

12. Greenwood, *Curses*, pp. 22–23. The Home Office commuted Winsor's capital conviction to penal servitude for life. She died in prison at age 76.

13. E.g., *Lancet*, March 23, 1861, pp. 294–95; *B.M.J.*, July 18, 1857, p. 606; *B.M.J.*, November 9, 1861, p. 509. See also Forbes, p. 355.

14. *B.M.J.*, October 24, 1903, pp. 1104–5.

15. *Medical Press and Circular*, June 13, 1866, p. 627.

16. Walkowitz, p. 81.

17. Ledbetter, pp. 121–22.

18. Behlmer, pp. 424–25.

19. Walkowitz, p. 84; Peterson, p. 16.

20. *DNB*, Supplement, II, 396–97.

21. Peterson, p. 196. The Harveian Society itself was founded in 1831 "by a few zealous medical men anxious to improve their own knowledge and to advance the status of medicine." Sir D'Arcy Power, ed., *British Medical Societies* (1939), p. 91.

22. Curgenven, "Infanticide," pp. 461–63.

23. *The Times*, January 29, 1867, p. 8; P.R.O., HO45, O.S. 8040, marginal notes on letter to Walpole.

24. *P.M.G.*, February 9, 1867, p. 10.

25. Curgenven, *Waste*, p. 1.

26. *Social Science*, 1 (May 17, 1867), 259–60.

27. Similar practices had been criticized for many years. In *Moll Flanders* (1722), Defoe's heroine attacked "those women who consent to . . . disposing their children out of the way, as it is called, for decency sake." Daniel Defoe, *Moll Flanders* (Penguin edn., 1979), p. 173. More than a century later Dickens wrote of the child "farm" run by Bartholomew Drouet in Tooting, where 150 pauper children died of cholera; see Brice and Fielding, pp. 229–31.

28. *P.M.G.*, September 25, 1867, p. 1; Greenwood, *Curses*, pp. 24–25.

29. *B.M.J.*, October 19, 1867, p. 343; *The Times*, December 17, 1867, p. 5.

30. *B.M.J.*, January 15, 1898, pp. 176–77; O'Neill, pp. 273–75.

31. S.C. on Infant Life Protection, P.P., 1871, VII, QQ. 18–26, 30, 44; *B.M.J.*, January 15, 1898, pp. 178–79. Accounts of the investigation occasionally conflict. Hart himself misinformed the select committee when he stated that his advertising ruse took place in January 1866.

32. *B.M.J.*, January 25, 1868, p. 75.

33. *P.M.G.*, January 31, 1868, p. 5.

34. *The Times*, April 8, 1868, p. 10; *The Public Health: A Record & Review of Sanitary, Social, & Municipal Affairs*, November 1868, pp. 298–99. Lady Petre's crèche may have been modeled on the Nassau Street Nursery, opened in March 1849. See *Public Nurseries*; and Hewitt, pp. 161–62.

35. Wood; W. S. Gilbert and Arthur Sullivan, *H.M.S. Pinafore* (Boston, 1879) [first produced in London on May 25, 1878], pp. 29–30.

36. Hansard, 3d ser., 193 (July 28, 1868), cols. 1896–97.

37. Little, pp. 124, 182, 214; *B.M.J.*, August 8, 1868, p. 144.

38. S.C. on Infant Life Protection, P.P., 1871, VII, Q. 64.

39. Curgenven, *Baby-Farming*, pp. 6, 9. According to the official fig-

ures, 44,691 illegitimate children were born in 1869, of whom, by Curgenven's calculation, some 29,764 would have gone to professional foster parents. Thirty-Second Annual Report of the Registrar-General, P.P., 1871, XV, 28.

40. Hansard, 3d ser., 197 (July 13, 1869), cols. 1739–40.

41. *The Times*, June 16, 1870, p. 12; June 21, p. 10.

42. *The Times*, July 2, p. 11; July 4, p. 9; July 7, p. 12; July 28, p. 11; September 24, p. 9.

43. *Daily Telegraph*, October 12, 1870, p. 4; Dickson, pp. 325–26.

44. Curgenven, *Prospectus*, pp. 1, 3; *B.M.J.*, October 22, 1870, pp. 443, 451.

45. Curgenven, *Prospectus*, p. 1.

46. *Ibid.*

47. *The Times*, November 11, 1870, p. 6.

48. P.R.O., Mepo. 3/92, misc. reports. See also the letter of "A.B." in *The Times*, July 14, 1870, p. 4.

49. P.P., 1871, II, 483–88. See also Curgenven, *Bill*, pp. 2–4.

50. *B.M.J.*, February 22, 1896, p. 489; Blackburn, pp. 101–8.

51. "Day nursing" was a standard practice in the factory towns and villages of Lancashire; see Hewitt, pp. 129–34.

52. *Infant Mortality*.

53. Curgenven, *Reply*.

54. Curgenven, *Laws of France*, pp. 13–14.

55. *Sessional Proceedings of the N.A.P.S.S.*, April 16, 1868, pp. 265–78; McHugh, p. 44.

56. *B.M.J.*, July 9, 1864, p. 42.

57. *The Times*, April 1, 1871, p. 11; Hansard, 3d ser., 206 (May 5, 1871), col. 320; Hammond, pp. 182–88.

58. S.C. on Infant Life Protection, P.P., 1871, VII, QQ. 219–20, 234, 256–58, 1190–98, 1239–44, 1325.

59. *Ibid.*, p. iii; QQ. 2017, 2022, 2164–65, 2371–74.

60. *Ibid.*, p. iii; QQ. 597–98, 1118–22. James Greenwood pointed out that though many unmarried domestics and factory girls could not have afforded the services of baby-farmers, much less retained a Mrs. Hall, their seducers may sometimes have been willing to pay to avoid exposure; see *Curses*, pp. 28–29.

61. S.C. on Infant Life Protection, P.P., 1871, VII, 229–34.

62. *Ibid.*, Q. 633, p. vii.

63. *The Times*, January 18, 1872, p. 8; January 30, p. 4.

64. Hansard, 3d ser., 209 (March 6, 1872), cols. 1486–89.

65. Briggs, pp. 322–23.

66. Report of the Metropolitan Board of Works for 1872, P.P., 1873, LVI, 50; *The Times*, January 3, 1873, p. 8.

67. *B.M.J.*, March 25, 1876, p. 388.

68. Lords S.C. on the Infant Life Protection Bill, P.P., 1896, X, Q. 24; S.C. on the Infant Life Protection Bill, P.P., 1890, XIII, QQ. 336–38, 341–46; Reports of the Metropolitan Board of Works for 1878–80.

69. *The Times*, May 23, 1877, p. 7; September 12, 1879, p. 5; September 25, p. 9; October 13, p. 9; October 16, p. 11. *Lancet*, October 25, 1879, p. 622; *B.M.J.*, February 28, 1880, p. 340.

70. *B.M.J.*, April 5, 1873, pp. 378–79.

71. This despite the Royal Sanitary Commission's view that registration of stillbirths would contribute to appreciably reduced infanticide and criminal abortion; see Second Report of the Royal Sanitary Commission, P.P., 1871, XXXV, 58. See also the Manchester Statistical Society's *Memorial* to the Home Office (May 1867) and that of the Liverpool Northern Medical Society (June 1, 1869); P.R.O., HO45, O.S. 8044.

72. Hansard, 3d ser., 215 (May 14, 1873), cols. 1981–87; 221 (July 28, 1874), col. 846; Report on the Homicide Law Amendment Bill, P.P., 1874, IX, QQ. 236, 302; *Lancet*, May 22, 1875, pp. 734–35; Fyffe, p. 594.

73. Bill for the Protection of Children, P.P., 1873, I, 171–74.

74. As quoted in Armytage, p. 79.

Chapter Three

1. T. W. Preyer, *The Mind of the Child*, trans. H. W. Brown (New York, 1898); Kanipe, pp. 212, 246.

2. Gillis, *Youth*, p. 107; *Lancet*, November 20, 1880, p. 823. There is a large literature on flogging in nineteenth-century schools. For an unusually detailed account of brutality by a headmaster, see Hopley; also see *Annual Register* (1861), pp. 58–60.

3. Armstrong, pp. 6–7, 13; *B.M.J.*, February 9, 1884, pp. 279–80; *Lancet*, June 21, 1884, pp. 1132–33.

4. Teale, p. 11; Hansard, 3d ser., 281 (July 16, 1883), cols. 1465–73; Robertson, pp. 316–19; Duffy, p. 74.

5. John Ruskin, "Of Queens' Gardens," in *Sesame and Lilies* (1928), p. 59.

6. The 1880 Act (43 & 44 Vic., c. 23), introduced by A. J. Mundella, required school attendance of all children between the ages of five and ten, and also from ten to fourteen, unless exemption could be gained on grounds of educational attainment.

7. MacLeod, "Social Policy," pp. 104–5.

8. J. B. Brown, p. 47.

9. Booth, "Occupations," p. 319.

10. Musgrove, pp. 79–82.

11. T. Guthrie, p. 524; G. S. Jones, *Outcast London*, p. 13.

12. "Juvenile Criminals," p. 31; [Anthony Ashley Cooper,] "The Second Annual Report of the Ragged School Union," *Quarterly Review*, 79 (December 1846), 127–28.

13. Worsley, p. 81.

14. M. Anderson, especially pp. 62–70, 135–36.

15. G. S. Jones, "Working-Class Culture," p. 466.

16. Symons, pp. 8–9.

17. Howell, p. 995.

18. Hennock, p. 68; *'Light and Shade': Pictures of London Life* (1885), as quoted in Mearns, p. 12.

19. Census of England and Wales, 1881, P.P., 1883, LXXVIII, p. xv; R.C. on the Housing of the Working Classes, P.P., 1884–85, XXX, Q. 13, 454. At this time only Paris, of major European cities, had a higher population density than Liverpool; see Weber, p. 468.

20. T. Baines, p. 676; R.C., Housing of the Working Classes, QQ. 13, 454.

21. S.C. on Artizans' and Labourers' Dwellings, P.P., 1882, VII, QQ. 3485–91, 3579; S.C. on Habitual Drunkards, P.P., 1872, IX, QQ. 2017, 2124, Appendix B, pp. 332–33; Tobias, p. 156.

22. McCabe, pp. 15–16.

23. [Shimmin,] pp. 14, 54; Hume, p. 29.

24. Hocking, pp. 13–15. The lawless behavior of these slum poor must have struck civic leaders as particularly troubling in view of the fact that Liverpool already possessed a comparatively large and well-trained police force; see Midwinter, p. 153.

25. Muir, pp. 304, 306.

26. Collier, p. 537. For an overview of Liverpool philanthropy, see Simey.

27. During one week in mid-April, no fewer than ten cases of suffocation of infants came to light. G. Y. Tickle wrote a macabre poem in praise of Clarke Aspinall, the city coroner who had undertaken the investigation of children "Crushed, blackened, choked, in helpless agony, Beneath a mass of vile maternity." *Liverpool Mercury*, April 22, 1881, p. 5.

28. *Liverpool Mercury*, April 28, 1881, p. 6.

29. *Ibid.*, May 28, 1881, p. 15; see also June 1, 1881, p. 8.

30. Shaftesbury to Staite, n.d., as quoted in Morton, *Early Days*, pp. 6–7.

31. The sixth son of Sir Andrew Agnew, MP, a vigorous promoter of Sabbatarian legislation, Thomas Agnew (1834–1924) was born at Blackheath, but grew up in Scotland. After completing his education at Edinburgh University, Agnew went to Liverpool where he joined a firm engaged in the East India trade. He became a specialist in commercial finance and,

in 1889, was appointed agent to the Bank of England in Liverpool. Agnew, pp. 1–3.

32. The New York SPCC was formed on December 15, 1874, and received its charter of incorporation on April 21, 1875. See its *Manual*. The society owed its establishment to an 1874 case involving a little girl who had been beaten by her foster parents. When both police and charity officials refused to intervene, a social worker consulted Henry Bergh, founder of the New York Society for the Prevention of Cruelty to Animals. The "myth of Mary Ellen" states that since Bergh could find no legal justification for wresting custody of the child from her foster parents, he decided to treat the case as an act of cruelty to an animal. Thus, wrapped in a horse blanket, Mary Ellen was carried to court, where Bergh won a conviction against her tormentors. Allen and Morton, pp. 15–16. The facts of the case are less colorful. Bergh petitioned for a writ *de homine replegiando*, on the strength of which he obtained a special warrant to bring Mary Ellen before the court. Eventually she was committed to an orphan asylum. See M. P. Thomas, pp. 308–9.

33. Ross, pp. 51–52.

34. New York SPCC, *First Annual Report*, p. 26.

35. See Coleman, pp. 65–88.

36. Gerry, p. 68.

37. S. Smith, *Life-Work*, pp. 89–90. An ardent temperance advocate, Smith (1836–1906) was particularly concerned about "children ... maimed by their drunken parents" (p. 126).

38. Agnew, pp. 6–7.

39. Liverpool SPCC, *Report for 1883*, pp. 9–10; *Ragged School Union Quarterly Record*, January 1884, pp. 13–15.

40. Liverpool Obituary Notices, 1883–1929, Liverpool Record Office; "Society," p. 597. One of the twelve men on the executive committee could not be identified.

41. *Report for 1883*, p. 4.

42. *Ibid.*, pp. 3–4.

43. Liverpool SPCC, Ex. Comm. Mins., June 27, 1883.

44. *Jubilee Report, 1883–1932* (Liverpool, 1932), p. 16.

45. S. Smith, "Social Reform," p. 902.

46. Owen, pp. 413–15.

47. *Baroness Burdett-Coutts*, pp. 70–82. Her early support of the Liverpool society was characteristic of a mind that "caught from afar the first influences of coming change"; see C. C. Osborne's unpublished biography, B.M. Add. MS. 46405, p. 179.

48. *The Times*, December 8, 1883, p. 9.

49. *Ibid.*, November 27, p. 3; November 29, p. 3; December 12, p. 4. See also December 15, p. 4.

50. *Ibid.*, December 17, 1883, p. 10.

51. *Ibid.*, January 8, 1884, p. 3. Hesba Stretton (1832–1911) achieved literary prominence with the publication in 1866 of *Jessica's First Prayer*, the story of a girl waif's religious awakening. *DNB*, 2d Supplement, III, 346.

52. *P.M.G.*, January 8, 1884, p. 3.

53. *B.M.J.*, January 19, 1884, p. 122.

54. Trench, p. 77.

55. Rossiter, p. 568; *Ragged School Union Quarterly Record*, October 1877, pp. 151–58.

56. *Annual Report of the East End and Juvenile Mission* (1885), p. 402.

57. *Night and Day*, November 1881, p. 204; September 1882, p. 96.

58. Barnardo, *A Year's Work*, p. 18. See also *Our Waifs & Strays*, September 1886, p. 2.

59. *Night and Day*, February-March 1882, pp. 32–34.

60. Collier, p. 538.

61. *Child's Guardian*, Benjamin Waugh Centenary Number (February 1, 1939), p. 11; *Yorkshire Post*, February 23, 1939.

62. R. Waugh, pp. 26, 31.

63. *Southport Visitor*, September 29, 1973.

64. As quoted in R. Waugh, p. 36.

65. Hinchcliffe Higgins, "The Rev. Benjamin Waugh: The Apostle of Childhood," *The Quiver*, May 1907, p. 591; *DNB*, 2d Supplement, III, 620.

66. "To the Voters of the Greenwich Division," handbill (1870), Waugh Papers.

67. R. Waugh, p. 54.

68. As quoted in L. Huxley, II, 353.

69. [B. Waugh,] *The Gaol Cradle*, p. 4.

70. *Ibid.*, p. 86.

71. *Ibid.*, p. 4. Not until 1908 did the concept of children's courts gain legislative approval in England.

72. *Ibid.*, p. 183.

73. Howard Association, *Annual Report for 1874–75* (1875), p. 4.

74. As Waugh told his eldest daughter, "We are followers of Jesus Christ when we are useful; for he went about *doing good*: That is what we should all try to do. It is so pleasing to Him and so pleasing for everybody." Letter to Bertha Waugh, March 18, 1878, Waugh Papers.

75. *Sunday Magazine*, 1882, p. 206.

76. The attraction of socially and politically prominent members could be vitally important to the success of voluntary organizations in Victorian England. Certainly one explanation for the decline of the Social Science Association in the early 1880's, for example, was the loss of "name" supporters such as Brougham, Russell, and Shaftesbury. See Ritt, pp. 303–11.

77. *The Times*, June 30, 1884, p. 11.

78. *Animal World*, September 1884, p. 132.

79. *Lancet*, July 12, 1884, p. 73. No one present voiced the *Spectator*'s fear that "There could be no worse service done to a child, who will have many hardships to undergo, than to teach him to think himself greatly aggrieved by their occurrence." "The Protection of Children," p. 910.

80. London SPCC, *First Annual Report* (1885), pp. 3–4. As Brian Harrison observes, "A nineteenth century reform movement does, after all, set its 'tone' by the names it includes among its vice-presidents and officials, and these are the men who control policy." "State Intervention," p. 322.

81. RSPCA, *61st Report* (1884), pp. 7–8, 106–7; *Zoophilist*, August 1, 1885, p. 260.

82. For Dr. Barnardo's Homes, see *Annual Report of the East End and Juvenile Mission*, pp. 399, 401; for the C.E.W.S.S., see *Our Waifs and Strays*, September 1885, p. 8; for Dr. Stephenson's Home, see Heywood, p. 55. The percentage of London SPCC members then engaged in all forms of philanthropy for children was, no doubt, much higher.

83. Election results in *The Times*, November 30, 1870, p. 5; December 1, 1870, p. 3; December 11, 1872, p. 10; December 2, 1876, p. 6; November 29, 1879, p. 6; November 24, 1882, p. 7.

84. United Kingdom Alliance, *Annual Report* (1885); Church of England Temperance Society, *Annual Report* (1885), pp. 2–5; National Temperance League, *Annual Report* (1884); Central Association for Stopping the Sale of Intoxicating Liquors on Sunday, *Nineteenth Annual Report* (Manchester, 1886), pp. 3–6. It is plain that extremist teetotal sentiment was rare among the founding members.

85. Moral Reform Union, *Fourth Annual Report* (1886), pp. 16–21; for the National Vigilance Association, see Coote, pp. 7, 15–17; Social Purity Alliance, *Annual Report* (1884), p. 31; London Committee for Exposing and Suppressing the Traffic in British Girls, *Fourth Report* (1885), pp. 4–5.

86. Only five of these women were unmarried.

87. Heasman, p. 13.

88. Schupf, p. 96; Heasman, p. 83.

89. K. S. Inglis, p. 83. On the difficulty of identifying evangelical traits in the late Victorian mind, see Meacham, "Inheritance," pp. 100–103.

90. See Hodder, *Shaftesbury*, III, 456.

91. London SPCC, *First Annual Report* (1885), p. 2.

92. Hesba Stretton, "The Prevention of Cruelty to Children: The Appeal of the London Society," *Sunday Magazine* (Christmas number, 1884), pp. 778–79.

93. RSPCA, *87th Annual Report* (1910), p. 164.

94. London SPCC, *First Annual Report*, pp. 23–29; RSPCA, *61st Report* (1885), pp. 15–34. Colonel Sir Francis Burdett, the brother of Angela

Burdett-Coutts, and R. Ruthven Pym, an employee of Coutts & Company, were two of the RSPCA's three trustees. These men, along with the Baroness herself, were three of the four London SPCC trustees. Pym also served as the London Society's Treasurer and Chairman of its executive committee.

95. *Animal World*, September 1884, p. 131. The patterns of influence within the Anglo-American humane community were reciprocal. It was Colam who, in 1865, described the activities of the RSPCA to Henry Bergh, then a member of the American Legation in St. Petersburg. On returning to the United States, Bergh founded the New York Society for the Prevention of Cruelty to Animals, and, as we have seen, subsequently helped to publicize the problem of child abuse. Moss, p. 30.

96. Harrison, "Animals," pp. 805–6. The RSPCA was least successful in retaining the allegiance of the antivivisectionists. See French, pp. 80–86.

97. Moss, p. 30.

98. *Our Waifs and Strays*, January 1885, p. 3.

99. Liverpool SPCC, *Report for 1884*, p. 13.

100. London SPCC, *First Annual Report*, p. 7.

101. Liverpool SPCC, Ex. Comm. Mins., September 29, 1884; C.O.S., *16th Annual Report* (1884), p. 201.

102. London SPCC, *First Annual Report*, p. 15.

103. Liverpool SPCC, Ex. Comm. Mins., May 7, 1885.

104. London SPCC, *First Annual Report*, p. 7.

105. *Ibid.*, pp. 19–20; Hansard, 3d ser., 297 (May 4, 1885), cols. 1491–92.

106. See *The Times*, January 6, 1885, p. 5; January 8, p. 10; January 10, p. 10; January 13, p. 4.

107. London SPCC, *First Annual Report*, pp. 5–6.

108. *Ibid.*, p. 13.   109. *Ibid.*, p. 8.

110. *Ibid.*, p. 6.   111. *P.M.G.*, July 11, 1885, p. 1.

112. Wohl, "Sex," pp. 206–7.

113. As early as 1874 the Home Office knew that English girls were being held in Continental brothels. Typically, working-class girls would be promised "a situation" in Holland or Belgium, with the understanding that they could return to England if the job did not suit them. P.R.O., HO45, 9546, Metropolitan Police Report, October 10, 1874. The "decoy" system came to public notice in 1880, and the following year a select committee of the Lords began to examine this problem. In its final report, the Lords committee recommended, among other changes, the enactment of penalties to discourage white slavery, and the raising of the age at which carnal knowledge of a woman became felonious from thirteen to sixteen. S.C. on the Protection of Young Girls, P.P., 1882, XIII, p. iv. Criminal law amendment bills embodying similar provisions passed the Lords in 1883 and 1884, but died in the Commons. See Terrot, pp. 127–31.

114. P.R.O., HO45, 9547, report of the London SPCC Deputation.

115. Hansard, 3d ser., 300 (July 30, 1885), cols. 579–82; Gorham, p. 366.

116. Hansard, 3d ser., 300 (July 30, 1885), cols. 588–89.

117. *Ibid.* (July 31), cols. 754–62.

118. *P.M.G.*, August 1, 1885, p. 1.

119. [W. T. Stead,] "Two Champions of the Children," *Review of Reviews*, American ed., 4 (January 1892), 696.

120. Hansard, 3d ser., 300 (August 7, 1885), cols. 1970–74.

121. *Law Times*, 79 (August 29, 1885), 304.

122. *P.M.G.*, August 24, 1885, p. 4. Cf. Gorham, pp. 365–66.

123. B. Waugh, *Stead*, p. 7; Hopkins, pp. 336, 338.

124. See W. T. Stead, pp. 3, 12.

125. On the founding of child protection agencies in Scotland, see Edinburgh SPCC, *Preliminary Report* (Edinburgh, 1884), pp. 11–17; *First Annual Report of the Glasgow Society for the Prevention of Cruelty to Children* (Glasgow, 1885), pp. 5–6; *Report of the Children's Aid and Refuge and Stockbridge Day Nursery* (Edinburgh, 1886), p. 3.

126. *Night and Day*, November 1885, pp. 149–52. For more on philanthropic abduction see J. Parr, pp. 62–72.

Chapter Four

1. B. Waugh, *Public Policy*, p. 3.

2. Colam, p. 9.

3. Stewart's opinion corresponded with that of the old Poor Law Board. See the Twenty-First Annual Report of the Poor Law Board, P.P., 1868–69, XLIII (Lords), Appendix A, p. 62.

4. Liverpool SPCC, *Report for 1883*, pp. 23–24.

5. P.R.O., HO45, 9547, L.G.B. Asst. Sec. Adrian to HO Perm. Under Sec. Liddell, August 5, 1884; HO departmental notes, 12 and 13 November, 12 and 15 December.

6. Manning and Waugh, p. 699.

7. E. Fellows Jenkins, "The Law, the Child, and the Societies," in Sir William Chance, ed., *Report . . . of the Third International Congress for the Welfare and Protection of Children* (1902), p. 47. "Cruelty" to young acrobats had also received serious attention in England. In 1879, the Children's Dangerous Performances Act (42 & 43 Vic., c. 34) banned the employment of persons under fourteen from participating in any public amusement that might endanger life or limb. But because it made no provision for regulating the training of child acrobats, the Act became a "motionless monument of amiable inefficiency." Hall, *Queen's Reign*, p. 68. Late in the parliamentary session of 1883, Lord Shaftesbury reintroduced

the subject after reading an account in *The Times* of the "human serpent"—a little girl trained to bend over backwards and put her head between her legs. To "save the country from exhibitions so disgusting, to every sense of humanity," Shaftesbury urged that apprenticeship for the gymnastic profession be absolutely forbidden. Hansard, 3d ser., 282 (August 3, 1883), cols. 1462–64. Despite his efforts, however, the law remained unchanged until 1894.

8. R. Waugh, p. 163. As Colam explained to the Chief Commissioner of Metropolitan Police, Sir Edward Henderson, the London SPCC was particularly anxious to supervise the homes of brutal parents recently released from prison. P.R.O., HO45, 965, Asst. Commissioner of Met. Police to Under Sec. of State, April 8, 1886.

9. Liverpool SPCC, Ex. Comm. Mins., March 18, 1886; *Report for 1885*, p. 6.

10. See above, p. 42.

11. S. A. Barnett, pp. 284–85. Cf. Pringle, p. 92.

12. *C.G.*, January 1887, p. 1; *Tortured Children* (London SPCC 3d Annual Report, 1887), p. 17.

13. *C.G.*, January 1887, p. 4.

14. *The Echo*, July 7, 1887, p. 1; *C.G.*, September 1887, p. 71. The charge against Waugh stemmed from his unsubstantiated assertion that most of the London children who died from suffocation were in fact murdered.

15. *St. James's Gazette*, December 23, 1887, pp. 3–4; *C.G.*, December 1887, p. 94.

16. Benjamin to Bertha Waugh, November 10, 1886, Waugh Papers. The two crusaders apparently enjoyed one another's company both on and off the field of battle. Waugh and his wife occasionally dined at the Steads' Wimbledon home.

17. *P.M.G.*, January 23, 1886, p. 3; September 23, p. 7.

18. *The Times*, January 8, 1887, p. 7; January 15, p. 6; January 20, p. 10. Nor did Stead's paper show much compassion for the disgraced couple: "The only consolation is that the brutal doctor and his no less abominable wife are now stamped and branded as child torturers before all the world." *P.M.G.*, January 6, 1887, p. 3.

19. *Statements, Illustrations, and Pleas* (London SPCC 2d Annual Report, 1886), p. 20.

20. *C.G.*, April 1887, p. 25. Referring to first-year statistics, Baroness Burdett-Coutts offered as "striking proof both of the prudence and necessity of the society's action that in no instance has the prosecution failed." *The Times*, December 19, 1885, p. 9. For 1887–88, the conviction rate was 96 percent. *P.M.G.*, May 8, 1888, p. 6.

21. *P.M.G.*, January 5, 1888, p. 7.

22. Hansard, 3d ser., 317 (July 22, 1887), cols. 1760–61; 318 (July 26), cols. 30–31; 320 (September 2), cols. 908–9. C.G., October 1887, pp. 75–76.

23. *Tortured Children*, pp. 18–19.

24. P.R.O., HO136, entry book no. 137, Matthews to Waugh, December 3, 1887; C.G., June 1887, p. 47.

25. *P.M.G.*, July 18, 1885, p. 7.

26. *The Times*, May 30, 1885, p. 13. The cheapest ticket for this entertainment cost a half guinea.

27. McClelland, p. 199.

28. Manning, *Temperance Speeches*, p. 22.

29. Dingle and Harrison, pp. 498–99; quotation from Manning's diary, August 1, 1890, in McClelland, p. 20.

30. B. Waugh, "Manning," p. 188.

31. Selby, pp. 406–7.

32. Manning and Waugh, pp. 687–89.

33. P.R.O., HO45, 9764, Waugh to Matthews, January 24, 1887.

34. Waugh began to solicit Herschell's support for protective legislation in 1885, when the eminent barrister was still sitting in the Commons for Durham City. Herschell recalled some years later: "I confess at times that I thought him a bore, but it was no use getting rid of him on one day, for I knew that I should only have to [see] him . . . on another." C.G., July 1898, p. 83.

35. P.R.O., HO45, 9764, Charles Stuart-Wortley to Waugh, May 6, 1887; printed memo, "Draft Bill for the Prevention of Cruelty to Children."

36. Ribton-Turner, pp. 303–4.

37. P.R.O., HO45, 9366, misc. correspondence; Coleman, p. 84.

38. H. Bosanquet, *Social Work*, pp. 240–41.

39. S.C. on the Law Relating to the Protection of Young Girls, P.P., 1882, XIII, QQ. 98–99. Nugent claimed that, "At the very least, in a day, I could count from 200 to 300 girls in certain localities in Liverpool, under 14 years of age trading on the streets" (Q. 112).

40. 42 & 43 Vic., c. 78. The Act defined casual employment as "employment for the purposes of gain in streets or other places in vending or exposing for sale any article whatsoever."

41. Report of the S.C. on Police and Sanitary Regulations, P.P., 1882, XII, p. v, and Appendix No. 3, p. xi; P.R.O., HO45, 9970, departmental memorandum.

42. *Statements, Illustrations, and Pleas*, p. 15.

43. C.G., March 1887, pp. 18, 22.

44. *Hospital*, January 15, 1887, p. 257. The society's report for 1886–87 frankly admitted defeat: "In an attempt to suppress the milder forms of cruelty practised in sending out young children as street-hawkers your

Committee has been bravely supported by the Mansion House. It has told off a special officer, directing him to patrol the little victims' beats at night. It has done its best; the magistrates have done their best; and the attempt is a failure. The expedients it has had to resort to—having to charge *children* and not parents, landing them at the police station, and sometimes in the lockup for the night, were all base and abominable. Almost everything your Committee had to do was neither straightforward nor fair; and it has given it up." Not once during the society's first three years did a policeman bring a child hawker to its shelter. In contrast, the Liverpool SPCC's shelter accepted 386 street children from constables during 1886–87 alone. *Tortured Children*, pp. 14–15.

45. *Justice of the Peace*, March 19, 1887, pp. 180–81, October 1, pp. 129–30; C.G., May 1887, p. 39.

46. B. Waugh, "Street Children," pp. 825–27, 832.

47. R.C., Reformatory and Industrial Schools, P.P., 1884, XLV, QQ. 7465, 5780. The Howard Association went even further, arguing that the rights of industrial and reformatory school children "should be rendered paramount over the justly forfeited claims of their vicious relatives." P.R.O., HO45, 9617, Howard Assoc. to Under Sec. Hibbert, November 20, 1884.

48. Hansard, 3d ser., 259 (March 16, 1881), cols. 1214–15.

49. 49 & 50 Vic., c. 52; C.G., March 1887, p. 23.

50. *The Times*, December 9, 1887, p. 5.

51. In 1881 only 0.13 percent of all married males and 0.71 percent of all married females were below the age of 20.

52. Webb and Webb, *Poor Law*, p. 180.

53. Lords S.C. on Poor Law Relief, QQ. 5853–58.

54. Eighteenth Report of the Local Government Board, P.P., 1889, XXXV, Appendix A, p. 150.

55. C.G., March 1887, p. 20; June 1887, p. 42.

56. *Tortured Children*, p. 71.

57. *A Fourth Year's Work* (London SPCC 4th Annual Report, 1888), p. 19.

58. *Five Years with Cruelty to Children* (London SPCC 5th Annual Report, 1889), p. 25; *Tortured Children*, p. 21; *A Fourth Year's Work*, p. 20.

59. C.G., June 1887, p. 41.

60. Manning and Waugh, p. 693.

61. Cobbe, "Wife-Torture," p. 58.

62. *New Law and Life for Children* (NSPCC 7th Annual Report, 1891), p. 34; Bowley, p. 133.

63. *Tortured Children*, pp. 15–16; *New Law and Life for Children*, p. 34; Wrigley, pp. 186–87.

64. See, for example, Skinner and Castle, p. 4.

65. Selwyn M. Smith, et al., "Social Aspects of the Battered Baby Syndrome," *British Journal of Psychiatry*, 125 (December 1974), p. 568; Erlanger, pp. 73–83; Gil, "Child Abuse," p. 351.

66. *Hospital*, January 15, 1887, p. 257; *The Times*, May 13, 1887, p. 13.

67. R. Waugh, pp. 180–81.

68. Moss, p. 193.

69. C.G., May 1887, p. 36.

70. E. N. Tribe, typescript notes to NSPCC Director William Elliott, 1935, NSPCC Archives. Tribe was present at the original conference.

71. C.G., February 1888, pp. 14–15; June 1888, p. 50.

72. Leeds Branch, Min. Bk., I, May 8, 1888; November 20, 1888.

73. C.G., June 1888, p. 51.   74. Mager, pp. 6–7, 11, 17.

75. Tabor, pp. 412, 414.   76. McGregor, p. 155.

77. C.G., January 1893, p. 3; Morley, "Liberalism," p. 3.

78. Mundella to the Leaders, August 21, 1889, NSPCC archives, item no. FXIII-23 (copy from the Leader Correspondence, Sheffield University Library).

79. Co-sponsoring the bill with Mundella were Morley, the late Lord Iddesleigh's son, Sir Stafford Northcote (Conservative, Exeter), Sir Henry James, Samuel Smith, Sir Robert Fowler, R. T. Reid, and F. A. Channing.

80. C.G., April 1888, p. 30.

81. *The Times*, October 27, 1888, p. 6; *Hospital*, November 3, 1888, p. 65.

82. C.G., September 1889, p. 155.

83. C.G., November 1888, p. 109.

84. P.R.O., HO45, 9764, C. E. Troup to Charles Stuart-Wortley, November 29, 1888. Home Office officials were aware, of course, that certain American states had enacted stringent laws to protect the young. In Massachusetts, a parent could be fined $200 or spend six months in prison for causing his child to beg or peddle without a license.

85. Hansard, 3d ser., 332 (December 13, 1888), col. 76.

86. C.G., January 1889, p. 130. See Shiman, pp. 49–74.

87. C.G., August 1888, pp. 67–68; January 1889, p. 130.

88. *Ibid.*, October 1888, p. 96.

89. Alverstone, p. 181. Other than the substitution of Sir Albert Rollit (Conservative, Islington South) for R. T. Reid, the sponsors for the new bill remained the same.

90. P.R.O., HO45, 9764, Webster to Matthews, March 15, 1889; Matthews to W. H. Smith, March 15, 1889.

91. C.G., September 1889, p. 155.

92. B. Waugh, *Bill for the Better Prevention of Cruelty to Children* [printed letter to A. J. Mundella] (April 5, 1889).

93. *Lancet*, May 11, 1889, p. 949.

94. P.R.O., HO45, 9764, Resolution from NUET, April 25, 1889; Lushington to Stuart-Wortley, April 11, Monro to Lushington, May 2.

95. Hansard, 3d ser., 337 (June 19, 1889), cols. 227—34.

96. *Ibid.*, cols. 248—50. Costermongering did tend to be a family enterprise. Henry Mayhew had observed that "when, as is the case with many of the costermongers, . . . the parents and children follow the same calling, they form one household and work, as it were, 'into one another's hands.' The father can buy a larger, and consequently cheaper quantity, when he can avail himself of a subdivision of labour as inexpensive as that of his own family—whom he must maintain whether employed or unemployed—in order to vend such extra quantity." Mayhew, I, 479.

97. Hansard, 3d ser., 337 (June 19, 1889), cols. 251—63.

98. *Ibid.*, 337 (June 26, 1889), cols. 838—39; (July 3), cols. 1381—85.

99. *Ibid.*, 337 (July 3, 1889), cols. 1365—68, 1371; G. D. Nokes, "Evidence," in R. H. Graveson and F. R. Crane, eds., *A Century of Family Life* (1957), pp. 147—48, 161—62.

100. R. Waugh, pp. 148—49.

101. Barlee, p. viii.

102. *Ibid.*, pp. 3, 18, 22, 50—56, 74—83.

103. See, for example, Mitchell, *Rescue*, p. 71.

104. *A Fourth Year's Work*, p. 22. The *Lancet* agreed that theatrical employment entailed a "considerable" health risk for children; see November 10, 1888, pp. 926—27.

105. Final Report, R.C. on the Elementary Education Acts, P.P., 1888, XXV, 110. The Commissioners based their recommendation on the testimony of Mrs. Fawcett and on the testimony of Charles T. Mitchell, a barrister and member of the N.V.A. See the Third Report of the R.C., P.P., 1887, XXX, 305—20. For the most important letters to *The Times* on this subject, see January 28, 1889, p. 7; February 5, p. 10; February 7, p. 12; February 8, p. 8; February 9, p. 16. Note also Mrs. Fawcett's "Employment of Children."

106. *The Times*, April 16, 1889, p. 12; May 17, p. 10; June 15, p. 8.

107. "Children in Theatres," p. 108.

108. Jeune, "Children in Theatres," p. 12. Virtually the same controversy was beginning to take shape in New York. See Dailey, p. 385.

109. Hansard, 3d ser., 337 (June 26, 1889), cols. 806—20.

110. *Ibid.*, 338 (July 10, 1889), cols. 6—38.

111. *The Times*, July 11, 1889, p. 9.

112. Hansard, 3d ser., 338 (July 22, 1889), col. 950. "Consummately skillful in command of apt legal words, ingenious turns of sentence, and all the other arts for stopping one hole without opening another," Herschell was ideally suited to steer the bill through the hidebound Lords. Morley, *Recollections*, I, 360.

113. *C.G.*, September 1889, p. 157.

114. Hansard, 3d ser., 339 (August 5, 1889), cols. 306–11.

115. P.R.O., HO45, 9764, T. M. Kelly and Frederick Wigington to Matthews, July 2, 1889; Liberty and Property Defence League, *Report of Proceedings and Speeches* (1889), p. 41; *The Times*, August 5, 1889, p. 4.

116. Mundella to the Leaders, July 13, 1889, as quoted in Armytage, p. 276; Mundella to the Leaders, August 21, NSPCC archives, item no. FXIII-23.

117. Equally myopic was the anonymous Conservative spokesman who implied that the 1889 Act owed its passage to the "industry of the Government." C.M.C., pp. 3, 8–9.

118. *Our Sixth Year's Work for Unwanted & Ill-Used Children* (NSPCC 6th Annual Report, 1890), pp. 46–47. To characterize the 1889 Act as "a tiny inroad into the all-powerful rights of parents" is to superimpose twentieth-century expectations on nineteenth-century possibilities; see Berger, p. 160.

119. Morton, *Early Days*, p. 13; *Five Years with Cruelty to Children*, p. 46; *Lancet*, June 28, 1890, p. 1434.

120. Donzelot, pp. 83–84; Barrett, p. 7.

Chapter Five

1. Edwin Chadwick, A Supplementary Report on the Results of a Special Inquiry into the Practice of Interment in Towns, P.P., 1843, XII, 55.

2. *Ibid.*, p. 48.

3. Smiles, pp. 276–77.

4. Ariès, *Death*, p. 66.

5. Morley, *Death*, p. 63. At the turn of the century Arthur Morrison's East End poor were still obsessed with burying their loved ones in style. "'When I lost my pore 'usband,' said the gaunt woman, with a certain brightening, 'I give 'im a 'ansome funeral. 'E was a Oddfeller, an' I got twelve pound. I 'ad a oak caufin an' a open 'earse. There was a kerridge for the fam'ly an' one for 'is mates—two 'orses each, an' feathers, an' mutes; an' it went the furthest way round to the cimitry.' 'Wotever 'appens, Mrs. Manders,' says the undertaker, 'you'll feel as you've treated 'im proper; nobody can't reproach you over that.' 'An' they coundn't; 'E was a good 'usband to me, an' I buried 'im respectable.'" Morrison, *Tales*, p. 163.

6. Curl, p. 12.

7. Smiles, p. 274; Blackley, p. 32.

8. Board of Health, Report on a General Scheme for Extramural Sepulture, P.P., 1850, XXI, 13–28. I owe this reference to Dr. Norris Pope.

9. Chadwick, A Supplementary Report, pp. 63–64.

10. *Ibid.*, pp. 235–38; S.C. on Friendly Societies Bill, P.P., 1854, VII, QQ. 494–95, 500; "Cemeteries and Churchyards," p. 457.

11. Second Report of the Commissioners for Inquiring into the State of Large Towns and Populous Districts, Appendix, Part II, P.P., 1845, XVIII, 71.

12. Clay, pp. 493, 497.

13. *The Times*, September 20, 1848, p. 4; September 22, p. 5; January 18, 1849, p. 3.

14. Kay, I, 438–39, 447. The hanging of Mary May, aged 38, drew "an immense multitude" to Chelmsford on August 14, 1848. It had been ten years since an execution had taken place there, and forty since a woman was hanged. *The Times*, August 15, 1848, p. 5.

15. Clay, pp. 541–48.

16. Return of the Number of Persons Tried in England and Wales in Each of the Last Ten Years, 1844 to 1853 Inclusive, for the Murders of Children Under Ten Years of Age, Who Are Members of Burial Societies, P.P., 1854, LIII; S.C. on Friendly Societies Bill, QQ. 1033–36, p. 72; Kay, p. 438.

17. Hansard, 3d ser., 133 (May 10, 1854), cols. 95–97; Hodder, *Shaftesbury*, II, 465–66; S.C. on Friendly Societies Bill, QQ. 586, 1099, 1101–2, 1155–65, 1232, 1234, 1541.

18. Clay, the most persistent mid-Victorian critic of child life insurance, died in 1858.

19. *Lancet*, September 28, 1861, p. 299.

20. "Bar Sinister," p. 24.

21. *Lancet*, October 21, 1865, pp. 461–62.

22. In mid-Victorian Salford, perhaps as many as 25 percent of the death certificates of working-class children were issued by druggists rather than doctors. Nearby, in Manchester, even physicians sometimes issued certificates without having seen the child alive. S.C. on Infant Life Protection, P.P., 1871, VII, QQ. 2127–28, 2225, 2234–35. See also *The Public Health: A Record and Review of Sanitary, Social, and Municipal Affairs*, November 1868, p. 300; *B.M.J.*, June 12, 1875, pp. 784–85.

23. Gosden, *Friendly Societies*, p. 59.

24. Hardwick, p. 27.

25. John Tidd Pratt, "Observations on Friendly Societies for Payments at Death, Commonly Called Burial Societies" (1868), P.R.O., HO45, O.S. 8157, pp. 8–9; Gosden, *Self-Help*, pp. 72, 115.

26. Masterman, pp. 218–19; Gosden, *Self-Help*, pp. 132–33.

27. Report of the Registrar of Friendly Societies in England, P.P., 1867–68, XL, 78; Fourth Report of the Commissioners Appointed to Inquire into Friendly and Benefit Building Societies, P.P., 1874, XXIII, Part I, p. cxxvi.

28. A. Lang, I, 126–27.

29. Fourth Report [on] Friendly . . . Societies, p. cxxxvii. English public

opinion generally agreed that the young needed more stringent safeguards. See "Reports of the Royal Commission," pp. 217–18; *B.M.J.*, June 12, 1875, p. 785.

30. Reports of the Chief Registrar of Friendly Societies, for the Year Ending 31st December 1875, Part I, P.P., 1876, LXIX, 22.

31. Sims, *Kaleidoscope*, pp. 116–21; *The Times*, September 29, 1884, p. 12; *Lancet*, October 4, 1884, p. 602.

32. Gosden, *Friendly Societies*, p. 215; Wilkinson, pp. 209–10.

33. See, for example, Clotten, p. 17.

34. Liverpool SPCC, Ex. Comm. Mins., February 20, 1888; Liverpool SPCC *Annual Report* for 1888, p. 6; Vacher, pp. 212, 246–47.

35. *A Fourth Year's Work*, pp. 20–22; B. Waugh, "Street Children," p. 834. In its final form, the Children's Charter provided fines of up to £200 for convicted child abusers who were "interested in any sum of money . . . payable in the event of the death of the child."

36. Lords S.C. on Poor Law Relief, P.P., 1888, XV, QQ. 5965–66, 1570.

37. *P.M.G.*, July 17, 1888, p. 4; *Insurance Guardian*, August 1, 1888, p. 254.

38. S.C. on Friendly Societies, P.P., 1888, XII, QQ. 14, 20–21, 64, 92, 162–63, 234.

39. *Hospital*, August 11, 1888, p. 311; February 23, 1889, pp. 323, 334. *The Times*, September 26, 1888, p. 13; September 28, p. 10; October 6, p. 8.

40. *C.G.*, October 1888, pp. 90–91.

41. *The Insurance Agent and the Insurance Review*, February 1, 1889, pp. 24–25; *The Review*, October 3, 1888, p. 611.

42. *Insurance Guardian*, September 1, 1888, p. 266; December 1, 1888, p. 304. *The Review*, December 19, 1888, pp. 826–27.

43. P.R.O., HO45, 10069, Matthews to W. H. Smith, January 17, 1889. Godfrey Lushington, Permanent Under-Secretary at the Home Office, was "sure" that the law on infant insurance needed strengthening, but feared the burial societies' "Parliamentary resources." Lushington to Stuart-Wortley, April 25, 1889, *Liverpool Poisoning Case* ("confidential," 1887), p. 3.

44. S.C. on Friendly Societies Act, 1875, P.P., 1889, X, QQ. 3746, 3802–3, 3836, 3847, 3885, 3943. The select committee would not admit into evidence shorthand notes taken by the London SPCC's inquest officer. *C.G.*, July 1889, p. 122.

45. *Insurance Guardian*, June 1, 1889, pp. 73–74; *The Insurance Agent and the Insurance Review*, July 1, 1889, pp. 104–5; S.C. on Friendly Societies Act, pp. xi, xviii; Hicks, pp. 3–7, 13.

46. Hansard, 3d ser., 336 (May 23, 1889), col. 908; 339 (August 8, 1889), col. 872.

47. *B.M.J.*, July 13, 1889, p. 83; B. Waugh, "Child Life Insurance," pp. 46, 48.

48. Magee, p. 120; MacDonnell, II, 113–14. Cf. B. Waugh, "Reminiscences of Dr. Magee," *Sunday Magazine* (1891), pp. 456–57.

49. *New Law and Life for Children*, pp. 169–71.

50. *Lancet*, June 14, 1890, p. 1316; S.C. of the House of Lords on Children's Life Insurance Bill, P.P., 1890, XI, 131–33. See also *Minute Book* of the Glasgow SPCC, April 2, 1890, pp. 157–58.

51. Hansard, 3d ser., 345 (June 16, 1890), col. 967.

52. *The Insurance Agent and the Insurance Review*, February 1, 1890, p. 19; Fourth Report [on] Friendly and Benefit Building Societies, P.P., 1874, XXIII, p. cxi; Baernreither, p. 193.

53. Lords S.C. on Children's Life Insurance Bill, 1890, QQ. 884, 1278, 1305, 1851.

54. *Ibid.*, QQ. 2792, 2797, 2805.

55. *Ibid.*, QQ. 218–20, 323–25, 1075, 1249, 1270; B. Waugh, "Child Life Insurance," p. 54.

56. Lords S.C. on Children's Life Insurance Bill, 1890, QQ. 2275, 4036–37.

57. *Daily Chronicle*, June 18, 1890, p. 5.

58. Lords S.C. on Children's Life Insurance Bill, 1890, QQ. 2556, 2615–17; *The Times*, July 24, 1890, p. 4; July 28, 1890, p. 4; *Insurance World and Monetary Record*, July 30, 1890, p. 3.

59. *C.G.*, August 1890, p. 41.

60. Wilkinson, p. 299; S.C. on Friendly Societies Act [1889], Q. 4446.

61. *C.G.*, August 1890, p. 41.

62. Berdoe, p. 560.

63. See, for example, Paget, pp. 67–68.

64. *Insurance Guardian*, February 1, 1891, p. 18.

65. B. Waugh, *Child-Life Insurance*, pp. 7, 11–13.

66. *The Times*, April 24, 1891, p. 10; *C.G.*, May 1891, p. 42.

67. Marshall, p. 946.

68. See, for example, *B.M.J.*, December 12, 1891, p. 1276; *Lancet*, January 19, 1895, pp. 166–67, June 29, 1895, p. 1653.

69. *The World of Forgotten Children* (NSPCC 9th Annual Report, 1893), pp. 50–51.

70. *Insurance Guardian*, June 1, 1895, pp. 76–77.

71. *C.G.*, July 1895, p. 101; Birmingham Branch, Ex. Comm. Min. Bk., II, March 8, 1902; P.R.O., HO45, 10069, "Memorandum," June 7, 1907.

72. Gosden, *Self-Help*, p. 141; B. S. Rowntree, pp. 1, 26, 364–65.

73. W. G. A. Robertson, *Manual of Medical Jurisprudence, Toxicology, and Public Health* (3d ed., 1916), p. 195; P.R.O., HO45, 10069, Runciman to Chalmers, May 9, 1907; *B.M.J.*, January 14, 1905, p. 102.

74. H. R. Jones, pp. 40–43, 71; Charles Templeman, "Two Hundred and Fifty-Eight Cases of Suffocation of Infants," *Edinburgh Medical Journal*, 38 (October 1892), 322–29. Cf. Todd L. Savitt, "Smothering and Overlaying of Virginia Slave Children: A Suggested Explanation," *Bulletin of the History of Medicine*, 49 (Fall 1975), 400–404.

75. Hoffman, p. 4.

76. *Ibid.*, pp. 14–16; *Lancet*, April 20, 1895, p. 1024; Frederick L. Hoffman, "Medico-Legal Aspects of Child Life Insurance," *Medico-Legal Journal*, 13 (1895–96), 284–85.

77. Laslett, *World*, p. 213; Lewis, p. 77.

78. *Justice to Children: A Ten Years' Review* (NSPCC 10th Annual Report, 1894), pp. 51–52.

79. Harrison, "Philanthropy," p. 353.

80. *The Times*, June 10, 1889, p. 3; Snead-Cox, pp. 264, 403, 411; Bready, *Barnardo*, p. 188.

81. [Crawford,] pp. 1–2; B. Waugh, "Prevention," p. 141.

82. *C.G.*, February 1891, p. 12; February 1892, p. 16.

83. The NSPCC was so scrupulously nonsectarian that it avoided prayer at the start of its meetings. R. Waugh, p. 236. Waugh's own latitudinarianism must have helped set this tone. Although he remained devoutly Free Church, Waugh's wife turned Catholic, and one of his sons became a Catholic priest. *The Planet*, May 4, 1907, NSPCC Archives, Box III.

84. *Our Sixth Year's Work*, p. 31.

85. *C.G.*, December 1891, p. 131.

86. Waugh to Lady Iddesleigh, September 30, 1892, NSPCC Archives, Box III; Lady Willough de Eresby to Executive Committee, n.d., NSPCC Archives, Box FXXIV-IB. Despite Waugh's willingness to court the highborn, he never fully trusted their intentions: "I really fear this crowd of the great: They may become the rulers of the Society; then it will become a plaything for their bit of humanity." Waugh to his wife, May 10, 1895, Waugh Papers.

87. *C.G.*, December 1895, p. 165; September 1896, p. 122.

88. *Humanity*, July 1895, p. 33.

89. *New Law and Life for Children*, pp. 37–39.

90. *Our Sixth Year's Work*, pp. 33–34.

91. *The Crown and the Child*, p. 49.

92. *C.G.*, November 1892, p. 142.

93. *Justice to Children*, pp. 51–52; *Civil Rights of Children, Being the Report for 1894–95* (NSPCC 11th Annual Report, 1895), p. 49. The Manchester SPCC amalgamated with the National Society's branch in 1895.

94. Liverpool SPCC, *Annual Report* for 1892, p. 7; Liverpool SPCC, Ex. Comm. Mins., October 1, 1894; *Annual Report* for 1895, p. 8; *Annual Report* for 1897, pp. 4, 8.

95. *The World of Forgotten Children*, pp. 64–65; Tuckwell, pp. 134–35; *P.M.G.*, November 23, 1900, p. 2.

96. Birmingham Branch, Ex. Comm. Min. Bk., I, November 6, 1891.

97. Leeds Branch, Min. Bk., I, February 6, 1891.

98. *C.G.*, June 1894, pp. 73–75; October 1894, p. 121.

99. As early as 1889 the Baroness had argued against nationalization on the grounds that the society's base of support was peculiarly metropolitan. See C. C. Osborne's unpublished biography, B.M., Add. MS. 46405, p. 157.

100. Moss, p. 194.

101. *C.G.*, March 1895, p. 29. See also *Justice to Children*, pp. 52–53.

102. *Lancet*, January 18, 1890, p. 143; *The Times*, January 8, 1890, p. 3; *C.G.*, February 1892, p. 13.

103. *Our Sixth Year's Work*, p. 34.

104. *C.G.*, June 1899, p. 71; *The World of Forgotten Children*, p. 42; *Civil Rights of Children*, pp. 28–29; *C.G.*, February 1897, p. 18.

105. *C.G.*, December 1896, p. 159; *Justice to Children*, pp. 47–48.

106. *C.G.*, July 1893, pp. 89–90; October 1895, p. 141; June 1897, p. 65. By 1909, 15,000 ladies were helping to circulate NSPCC literature.

107. Harrison, "Philanthropy," p. 360.

108. *C.G.*, October 1895, p. 133; Harrison, *Spheres*, pp. 55, 91.

109. *The Power for the Children, Being the Report for 1895–96* (NSPCC 12th Annual Report, 1896), p. 35. With respect to legal proceedings, NSPCC headquarters charged branch committees for the court costs incurred in local action. However, headquarters paid for all prosecutions of exceptional cost, particularly test cases, as well as for all appeals against decisions.

110. E.g., Leeds Branch, Min. Bk., I, April 30, 1890.

111. NSPCC Council Minutes, May 13, 1895, pp. 2–3; *Report* of the Finance and General Purposes Committee, October 7, 1895, NSPCC Archives, Box FII-501, pp. 3, 5, 8.

112. *Report* of the Finance and General Purposes Comm., pp. 2, 6.

113. Grimsby Branch Executive Committee, "To Messrs. Adam & Whitbread and the General Purposes Committee and Council of the NSPCC," December 6, 1895, NSPCC Archives, Box FII-501.

114. *C.G.*, January 1895, p. 1; August 1895, p. 110.

115. *Echo*, March 5, 1896, p. 1. Bazaars were in fact vital to the maintenance of much philanthropic work. See Prochaska, "Charity Bazaars," pp. 62–84.

116. *C.G.*, July 1896, p. 97.

117. C.O.S., "Private and Confidential," *A Report upon the Finances and General Management of the NSPCC* (April 1897), pp. 2–4, NSPCC Archives, Box II.

118. H. Bosanquet, *Social Work*, p. 106.

119. *A Report upon the Finances and General Management of the NSPCC*, pp. 6, 8–10. Cf. Huxley, *Social Diseases*, pp. 55, 94.

120. *A Report upon the Finances and General Management of the NSPCC*, p. 16; *C.G.*, July 1897, p. 80.

121. H. Bosanquet, *Rich and Poor*, p. 158.

122. *Report of Lord Herschell's Inquiry into Charges Preferred Against the NSPCC* (July 27, 1897), pp. 2–4, 13, NSPCC Archives, No. 501.

123. *Ibid.*, p. 26.

124. *Ibid.*, pp. 7, 23, 27.

125. *C.G.*, August 1897, p. 95.

126. *St. James's Gazette*, August 6, 1897, p. 5.

127. *B.M.J.*, August 21, 1897, p. 480; *Lancet*, May 15, 1897, p. 1356.

128. Dorchester Branch, Ex. Comm. Min. Bk., April 24, 1897; October 2, 1897; November 6, 1897.

129. *The Society: Its Policy and Triumphs, Being the Report for 1897–98* (NSPCC 14th Annual Report, 1898), pp. 56–57; *C.G.*, December 1897, p. 153.

130. *B.M.J.*, January 13, 1883, p. 69; *Lancet*, July 12, 1884, p. 69.

131. *P.M.G.*, October 19, 1885, p. 2; Lords S.C. on the Infant Life Protection Bill and Safety of Nurse Children Bill, P.P., 1896, X, QQ. 860–62, 876, 878–79, 882–83, 927.

132. Jeune, "Innocents," p. 355.

133. Clotten, p. 32.

134. *B.M.J.*, October 13, 1888, p. 825.

135. *P.M.G.*, November 13, 1888, p. 6; *B.M.J.*, March 23, 1889, p. 667; *The Times*, February 19, 1889, p. 11.

136. Lords S.C. on the Infant Life Protection Bill and Safety of Nurse Children Bill, QQ. 35–36; P.R.O., HO45, 10361, outline of infant life protection legislation, 1872–96, n.d.

137. *Five Years with Cruelty to Children*, pp. 37, 49–50.

138. *Our Sixth Year's Work*, p. 48; B. Waugh, "Baby Farming," pp. 701, 704. The society's investigation also revealed that adoption advertisements were relatively abundant in newspapers serving resort areas, both in England and on the Continent.

139. *New Law and Life for Children*, pp. 172–76.

140. S.C. on the Infant Life Protection Bill, P.P., 1890, XIII, QQ. 355–56, 624–25, 1257–58.

141. *R.J.*, p. 52.

142. *C.G.*, April 1891, p. 31; Lords S.C. on the Infant Life Protection Bill and Safety of Nurse Children Bill, QQ. 1583–85.

143. *Lancet*, May 16, 1891, p. 1114; April 2, 1892, p. 701. *B.M.J.*, August 4, 1894, p. 274; February 22, 1896, p. 489; May 30, 1896, p. 1347. The *B.M.J.* conceded, however, that some of these 600 establishments were kept by "humane and honest persons."

144. *B.M.J.*, June 5, 1891, p. 1264; P.R.O., HO45, 10458, Hicks to Ridley, June 26, 1896.

145. *The World of Forgotten Children*, p. 51; *C.G.*, August 1893, p. 111.

146. Newman, p. 283; *B.M.J.*, March 7, 1896, pp. 617–18; *Good Hope for Children, Being the Report for 1896–97* (NSPCC 13th Annual Report, 1897), pp. 52–53; *C.G.*, June 1896, p. 88.

147. In 1896 alone, the Chrimes brothers spent nearly £2000 advertising abortifacients. Later they tried to blackmail the women who had ordered their products. See McLaren, pp. 232–35.

148. *B.M.J.*, February 29, 1896, p. 543; Lords S.C. on the Infant Life Protection Bill and Safety of Nurse Children Bill, QQ. 10, 361, 366, 1027–28.

149. Lords S.C. on the Infant Life Protection Bill and Safety of Nurse Children Bill, QQ. 68, 71, and Appendix B; *B.M.J.*, March 21, 1896, p. 747.

150. Lords S.C. on the Infant Life Protection Bill and Safety of Nurse Children Bill, QQ. 638–39, 1559, 1726–27, 1760–61. What Waugh did not add was that, if so empowered by statute, his society would surely get the government grant it had been seeking.

151. *Ibid.*, QQ. 1595, 1597–98; *Lancet*, September 12, 1896, p. 762; *Insurance Gazette*, June 1896, pp. 302–3.

152. Lords S.C. on the Infant Life Protection Bill and Safety of Nurse Children Bill, QQ. 271–75, 1156, 1966, 1970–71.

153. *Ibid.*, Q. 3073.

154. *Lancet*, September 11, 1897, p. 675.

155. *C.G.*, September 1896, p. 121.

156. *B.M.J.*, October 1, 1898, p. 1017; *Hospital*, August 27, 1898, p. 365; Low, pp. 280–81. Some boards of guardians requested NSPCC inspectors for service under the Act. Although the society turned down these requests, feeling that voluntary effort should not relieve the state of its rightful duties, it did continue to cooperate with Poor Law authorities informally. Morton, *Directorate*, p. 11.

157. Hansard, 3d ser., 350 (February 26, 1891), cols. 1720–21; *Hospital*, March 28, 1891, p. 374; *C.G.*, March 1891, pp. 17–18, April 1891, p. 30; *The Crown and the Child*, p. 53. Cf. Manning, "Child Labour," pp. 794–96.

158. R. Anderson, p. 82; H. R. Jones, p. 3.

159. P.R.O., HO45, 9764, Waugh to Asquith, March 3, 1893.

160. P.R.O., HO45, 9764, Bridges to Lushington, March 11, 1893.

161. *C.G.*, September 1894, p. 113; P.R.O., HO45, 9764, "Memorandum on Bill to Amend the Prevention of Cruelty to, and Protection of, Children Act," n.d., p. 4.

162. P.R.O., HO45, 9764, Waugh to Herbert Gladstone, June 16, 1893.

163. P.R.O., HO45, 9764, HO minutes for April 2, 1894; Grahame to Russell, April 6, 1894.

164. P.R.O., HO45, 9764, Webster to Asquith, May 16, 1894; *C.G.*, July 1894, p. 95.

165. Additionally, 57 & 58 Vic., c. 27, expanded the field in which children might give evidence without taking an oath.

166. *C.G.*, February 1899, p. 21; R. Waugh, pp. 243–44. In February 1901 a recurrence of "profound nervous exhaustion" obliged Miss Bolton to give up work for the society. *C.G.*, October 1901, p. 120.

Chapter Six

1. Greenhough, p. 133.

2. Mitchell, *House and Home*, p. 16; Miller, pp. 102–7; Greenhough, p. 137.

3. Davenport-Hill, pp. 122, 128.

4. C.E.W.S.S., *Handbook for Workers, Part II* (1895), p. 5; Reformatory and Refuge Union, *Fifty Years' Record of Child Saving and Reformatory Work* (1906), p. 20.

5. Loane, *Neighbours*, p. 182.

6. *Hospital*, April 24, 1897, p. 57; *Insurance Guardian*, January 1, 1894, p. 11.

7. The NSPCC sample consisted of the first 100 recruits listed in the society's *Record Book of Inspectors*. For five men, no occupational data was given. The RSPCA sample included the first 100 men hired after 1880. Three of the latter entries did not list job experience. Both samples contained men who had served on a police force as well as in the army.

8. Cf. Harrison, "Animals," p. 797. In the late 1950's the NSPCC was still drawing a majority of its inspectors from the armed services and police constabularies. See Leis, pp. 106, 109–10.

9. By 1900 the average age of all NSPCC inspectors was 45. *C.G.*, February 1900, p. 20.

10. *Inspector's Directory* (1901), p. 13.

11. NSPCC *Register of Inspectors* ("A"); *Whitaker's Almanack* (1899), pp. 158–59.

12. NSPCC *Local Office and Inspector's Register*, especially "Local Premises Return Form" for the Darlington Branch; *Inspector's Directory*, p. 14; *C.G.*, July 1896, p. 98.

13. Loane, *Next Street*, pp. 210–11.

14. *C.G.*, March 1889, p. 42.

15. *Inspectors' Quarterly*, September 29, 1913, title page. The Liver-

pool SPCC experimented with female agents as early as 1886, but it was not until 1948 that the NSPCC appointed its first "lady visitors." Liverpool Ex. Comm. Mins., December 6, 1886; March 7, 1887; May 9, 1887.

16. S.C. on Friendly Societies Act, P.P., 1889, X, Q. 3771.

17. *Inspector's Directory*, p. 12. Cf. "Entering Private Premises," RSPCA *Rules & Instructions* (1906), p. 12.

18. *Inspector's Directory*, pp. 10, 25, 37–39, 49–50.

19. Burton Branch, Min. Bk., November 2, 1899; Halifax Branch, Min. Bk., April 6, 1904.

20. *Register of Inspectors* ("A"), pp. 1, 179; *Our Sixth Year's Work*, p. 43.

21. Birmingham Branch, Ex. Comm. Min. Bk., II, December 3, 1902; C.G., July 1909, p. 82; *From Strength to Strength* (NSPCC 23d Annual Report, 1907), p. 43.

22. E.g., E.C., pp. 28–29.

23. *"250": A Year's Work of the NSPCC* (NSPCC 26th Annual Report, 1910), pp. 21–24; Loane, *Next Street*, pp. 216–17.

24. Manchester Branch, Ex. Comm. Min. Bk., I, October 30, 1901; *Our Sixth Year's Work*, p. 33; Birmingham Branch, Ex. Comm. Min. Bk., I, November 2, 1898; C.G., December 1898, p. 144.

25. S.C. on the Children's Life Insurance Bill, P.P., 1890, XI, Q. 2151; C.G., February 1904, p. 18; *The Silver Lining* (NSPCC 25th Annual Report, 1909), p. 19; R. J. Parr, *Canal Boat Children*, p. 18.

26. [W. Payne,] pp. 12–13.

27. *Our Inspectors: A National Duty to Provide More* (NSPCC 16th Annual Report, 1900), p. 54; *From Strength to Strength*, pp. 27–29.

28. *A Fourth Year's Work*, pp. 24–25.

29. C.G., October 1891, p. 110; January 1908, p. 4. NSPCC patrons never knew, for example, that in late 1897 Inspector Uphill was charged with assaulting a man named Sherwood. Although the Kidderminster magistrates dismissed all charges against this agent, Benjamin Waugh's summation is intriguing: "The case will, I hope, teach Uphill not to interfere with people at public houses about what he has no say." If other cruelty men invaded pubs to remonstrate with parents it is a safe bet that physical violence sometimes followed. *Register of Inspectors* ("A"), entry for February 1898. See also Appendix B.

30. York Branch Case Recs., Plaint no. 993. Cf. Mylne, p. 90; David Rubinstein, *School Attendance in London, 1870–1904: A Social History* (New York, 1969), p. 51.

31. Fido, pp. 228–29, n. 1.

32. Woodroofe, pp. 44–45; Pringle, p. 209; Morris, *Social Case-Work*, p. 25; Young and Ashton, pp. 123–25.

33. Woodroofe, p. 53; Fido, pp. 217, 228.

34. Young and Ashton, p. 152; B. Harrison, "Animals," p. 809.

35. "Previous Occupations of Inspectors Recruited Between 1890–1894," NSPCC Archives, item no. FXXIV-24.

36. Inspector J. Winter, based in Leeds, supervised this case when Jackson fell ill in March 1903.

37. *The Power of the Parent: A Factor of the State* (NSPCC 15th Annual Report, 1899), p. 46.

38. B. S. Rowntree, pp. 1, 86–87, 117. More precisely, Rowntree found that 9.9 percent of York's population lived in "primary poverty" ("families whose total earnings are insufficient to obtain the minimum necessaries for the maintenance of merely physical efficiency"). A further 17.9 percent of the inhabitants endured "secondary poverty" ("families whose total earnings would be sufficient for the maintenance of merely physical efficiency were it not that some proportion of it is absorbed by other expenditure, either useful or wasteful").

39. *The Discovery* (NSPCC 18th Annual Report, 1902), p. 84.

40. York Branch Case Recs., plaint no. 602.

41. *Ibid.*, plaint no. 656; no. 819.

42. *Ibid.*, plaint no. 568; no. 703; no. 732.

43. *Our Waifs and Strays*, October 1892, p. 11.

44. *C.G.*, September 1898, p. 106.

45. York Branch Case Recs., plaint no. 1415; no. 985.

46. *C.G.*, December 1904, p. 134; [W. Payne,] pp. 134–36. C.O.S. work, by contrast, was more rigidly governed by social Darwinist ideology. Hence, to give material aid to a family that could not or would not provide for itself was a violation of the principle of natural selection. Fido, p. 226.

47. Morrison, *Jago*, p. 69.

48. Loane, *Point of View*, p. 63; *idem, Next Street*, p. 208.

49. S.C. on Children's Life Insurance Bill, P.P., 1890, XI, QQ. 84–85.

50. Reynolds and Woolley, pp. 25–26.

51. York Branch Case Recs., plaint no. 691.

52. R. Roberts, p. 58; Reynolds, pp. 89, 94, 222; Meacham, *A Life Apart*, p. 158.

53. York Branch Case Recs., plaint no. 673; no. 733.

54. *Ibid.*, plaint no. 952.

55. Reynolds, p. 280.

56. *Good Hope for Children*, pp. 46–47; "250", p. 61.

57. R. Roberts, p. 28.

58. *The Champion of the Child* (NSPCC 20th Annual Report, 1904), p. 13.

59. York Branch Case Recs., plaint no. 679.

60. *The Silver Lining*, p. 16.

61. York Branch Case Recs., plaint no. 702; no. 733.

62. Storch, "Policeman," pp. 489–90.

63. Pelling, p. 1.

64. York Branch Case Recs., plaint no. 1566.

65. Loane, *Englishman's Castle*, p. 217.

66. York Branch Case Recs., plaint no. 703. I have altered this letter by inserting periods and capitals in the appropriate places.

67. Townsend, pp. 12–13.

68. Loane, *Neighbours*, p. 84.

69. *Inebriate Mothers and Their Reform* (NSPCC 19th Annual Report, 1903), pp. 4–5.

70. *Day and Night*, May 1885, p. 74.

71. Loane, *Neighbours*, p. 59; P. Thompson, *Edwardians*, p. 59; *The Crown and the Child*, p. 43.

72. *Statements, Illustrations, and Pleas*, p. 12; *Five Years with Cruelty to Children*, pp. 20–21.

73. *Justice to Children*, pp. 42–43; Booth, *Life and Labour*, 3d ser., II, 67.

74. B. S. Rowntree, p. 31. Rowntree's classification system was based on what he designated a "moderate family," that is, a family consisting of a father, mother, and two to four children. More than four children would normally push a family into the next lower income group; fewer than two, into the next higher (pp. 28–29).

75. *Ibid.*, p. viii. As Leroy Pelton notes, the myth of classlessness persists in some modern studies, suggesting, erroneously, that child abuse and neglect are democratically distributed throughout society. Pelton, pp. 608–17. See also Selwyn Smith et al., "Parents of Battered Children: A Controlled Study," in A. W. Franklin, ed., *Concerning Child Abuse* (Edinburgh, 1975), p. 47.

76. See above, p. 71.

77. *The Times*, May 22, 1889, p. 16.

78. Conybeare was attempting to broaden the terms of Parliament's first enactment on the sale of alcohol to young persons: section seven of the Licensing Act of 1872. By this law, no holder of a liquor license could sell "spirits" (thus exempting beer), to be consumed on the premises, to any person "apparently" under sixteen. For a first conviction the 1872 Act set a maximum fine of twenty shillings. See Geoffrey Lushington's memorandum of May 9, 1902; P.R.O., HO45, 10114.

79. *Our Waifs and Strays*, May 1886, p. 6.

80. C.G., March 1887, p. 23; *The Times*, December 27, 1887, p. 11.

81. Rowntree and Sherwell, p. 353; Johnson, pp. 3–5; *Children and the Drink*, p. 108.

82. *Alcohol and Childhood*, pp. 3, 32, 40; Shiman, p. 71. Cf. Urwick, p. 306.

83. R.C. on Liquor Licensing Laws, iii, P.P., 1897, XXXVI, QQ. 29, 124–26, 418–22.

84. *Ibid.*, ii, P.P., 1897, XXXV, QQ. 11,525, 11,998–12,010; *C.G.*, August 1897, p. 89, September, p. 139; Manchester Branch, Ex. Comm. Min. Bk., I, July 27, 1898.

85. NSPCC Council Minutes, March 15, 1900; *C.G.*, April 1900, p. 56, August 1900, p. 104, January 1901, p. 7; *The Miserable Child World* (NSPCC 17th Annual Report, 1902), pp. 11–12.

86. Meacham, *A Life Apart*, p. 124.

87. R.C. on Liquor Licensing Laws, ii, P.P., 1897, XXXV, QQ. 11,364, 11,371–72, 12,180–81, 12,185; iii, P.P., 1897, XXXVI, QQ. 26,321–22; Liverpool SPCC, *Annual Report* for 1905, p. 10.

88. MacLeod, "Edge of Hope," p. 232; Vacher, p. 247. According to the original Act of 1879 (42 & 43 Vic., c. 19), an habitual drunkard was "a person who, not being amenable to any jurisdiction in lunacy, is, not withstanding, by reason of habitual intemperate drinking of intoxicating liquor, at times dangerous to him or herself or to others, or incapable of managing himself or herself, or his or her affairs."

89. *B.M.J.*, September 14, 1895, p. 670; *Civil Rights of Children*, pp. 38, 40.

90. *C.G.*, September 1895, p. 127; *B.M.J.*, February 15, 1896, p. 424; *Children and the Drink*, p. 35; *Inebriate Mothers and Their Reform*, pp. 9, 13–14, 16–17. The 1898 Inebriates' Act was itself weakened by the stipulation that a person could not be committed to a retreat unless he pleaded guilty to drunkenness, or unless he was tried and convicted four times for being intoxicated in public. See Holmes, pp. 744–45.

91. R.C. on Liquor Licensing Laws, viii, P.P., 1899, XXIV, QQ. 73,293–99.

92. B. S. Rowntree, p. 308.

93. *Lancet*, November 26, 1898, pp. 1413–14; *Children and the Drink*, pp. 15, 34; autobiography of Lilian Westall, servant, in Burnett, p. 215; Carter, p. 13; Bayle, p. 4.

94. Loane, *Point of View*, p. 99; P. Thompson, *Edwardians*, p. 60; P. Thompson, "War with Adults," pp. 30–31.

95. R. Roberts, p. 29; Loane, *Point of View*, pp. 3, 154.

96. Booth, *Life and Labour*, 1st ser., IX, 435; Loane, *Neighbours*, p. 134; Cf. John and Elisabeth Newsome, *Infant Care in an Urban Community* (Chicago, 1963), p. 195.

97. Paterson, p. 23; R. Roberts, p. 29; Meacham, *A Life Apart*, p. 160.

98. *The Crown and the Child*, p. 46.

99. MacDonald, pp. 4–5; Supplement to the Seventy-Fifth Report of the Registrar-General, P.P., 1914–16, VIII, pp. xciii–xcv. The only safe generalization to be made about child suicide in the late Victorian and Edwardian period is that adolescent boys most often hanged themselves, whereas young females much preferred drowning.

100. During its first five years, the London SPCC found that approximately one out of every 32 cases ended in the victim's death. By 1905–10 this ratio had fallen to one in 50. "*250*", p. 58.

101. See above, pp. 148–49.

102. Chesser, pp. 13–14.

103. Jackson, p. 756.

104. Light, pp. 560–67. If one accepts Gil's definition of child abuse as "any act of commission or omission by individuals, institutions, or society as a whole . . . which deprive[s] children of equal rights and liberties, and/ or interfere[s] with their development," this social problem assumes epidemic proportions. Gil, "Unraveling," pp. 346–56.

105. J. Turner, p. 134. The abattoir as a source of moral contamination is an idea that dates back at least to Sir Thomas More. See *Utopia* (Crofts Classics edn., 1949), pp. 39, 41.

106. Salt, pp. 18–19; *Humanity: The Journal of the Humanitarian League*, March 1895, end leaf.

107. *The Times*, May 10, 1894, p. 14. American child-savers made the same assumption. See Dailey, p. 377.

108. *New Law and Life for Children*, p. 35; *C.G.*, May 1907, p. 54.

109. Loane, *Neighbours*, pp. 134–35.

110. York Branch Case Recs., no. 602; no. 1732. *A Fourth Year's Work*, pp. 12–13; autobiography of Tom Mullins, laborer, in Burnett, p. 64.

111. L. G. Guthrie, p. 89.

112. See especially Morris and Gould, pp. 31, 47; Steele and Pollock, pp. 97–99; Green et al., pp. 882–83.

113. See above, p. 14.

114. *C.G.*, February 1889, p. 17; "Two Champions of the Children," p. 694. One could argue, of course, that in urging use of the prison treadmill the NSPCC was itself condoning cruelty. See Pearsall, p. 162.

115. *Our Inspectors: A National Duty to Provide More*, p. 57; *The Crown and the Child*, pp. 65–66.

116. Meacham, *A Life Apart*, p. 50.

117. On rebattering, see Skinner and Castle, pp. 9, 12; Oliver and Taylor, p. 473.

118. *The Power of the Parent*, p. 58. Cf. Oscar Craig, "Agencies for the Prevention of Pauperism," in Woods et al., pp. 364–65.

119. *The Power of the Parent*, p. 58. The complete age distribution for all cases from 1884–94 was aged three and under, 21 percent; over three to age six, 21.7 percent; over six to age nine, 23.1 percent; over nine to age twelve, 21.5 percent, over twelve to age seventeen, 12.7 percent.

120. *Proceedings of the Society for Psychical Research*, 1 (1882), p. 12; *Presidential Addresses to the Society for Psychical Research, 1882–1911* (Glasgow, 1912), p. 35.

121. French, pp. 379–83.

122. *The Discovery*, p. 7.

123. B. Waugh, *Some Conditions*, pp. 3–4; Salt, p. 26.

124. Edward Salmon, *Juvenile Literature As It Is* (1888), p. 184, as quoted in M. Lang, p. 28.

125. *The World of Forgotten Children*, p. 60.

126. *C.G.*, December 1891, p. 130.

127. Leeds Branch, Min. Bk., I, December 10, 1896; *Children's League of Pity Paper*, September 1893, p. 9. As F. K. Prochaska has shown, children's charitable work was widespread, particularly in the evangelical missionary movement; see *Women and Philanthropy*, pp. 74–94.

128. Twining, pp. 143–45.

129. *Children's League of Pity Paper*, October 1893, p. 21; March 1894, p. 64. Mary P. Bolton, "The Children's League of Pity," p. 1 [paper read at the Bristol Congress, November 5, 1896], NSPCC Archives, misc. papers.

130. *Inebriate Mothers and Their Reform*, p. 7. *C.G.*, January 1899, p. 6; February 1900, pp. 17–18.

131. *C.G.*, June 1891, p. 52; June 1892, p. 77.

132. *Ibid.*, November 1903, p. 124.

133. *Toynbee Record*, December 1891, p. 32; *The Times*, May 13, 1891, p. 11.

134. Storch, "Problem of Working-Class Leisure," p. 149.

135. London SPCC, *First Annual Report*, p. 9.

136. E. P. Thompson, *Whigs and Hunters*, pp. 262–63.

137. York Branch Case Recs., no. 930; no. 1668.

138. *Ibid.*, no. 1668.

139. *C.G.*, November 1900, p. 139.

140. "Happiness of Children," p. 331. *C.G.*, May 1892, p. 61; January 1903, pp. 1–2; February 1903, p. 17.

141. C. F. G. Masterman, "Realities at Home," in *The Heart of the Empire* (1901), p. 33; *C.G.*, August 1894, p. 106.

Chapter Seven

1. See, for example, Collini, pp. 39–41; Freeden, pp. 15–17.

2. Emy, p. xii.

3. M. J. Moore, p. 85.

4. "One Avoidable Cause," pp. 637–38.

5. Vigne, p. 6; P. Thompson, "War with Adults," p. 29. For many boys and girls, of course, work began before they left school. A parliamentary return of 1899 showed that 150,000 children in full attendance were also employed out of school hours. Adding "half-timers" and allowing for ca-

sual work, perhaps 300,000, or 8.6 percent of all English and Welsh elementary school students, were gainfully employed. P.R.O., HO45, 10215, Report of the Employment of School Children Committee, November 1901, pp. iv-vi; Gorst, "School Children," p. 12.

6. Mosher, p. 67; Gillis, *Youth and History*, p. 103.

7. Helen Dendy, "The Children of Working London," in B. Bosanquet, p. 33; Loane, *Queen's Poor*, p. 68.

8. *Lancet*, July 24, 1869, p. 149.

9. Steelcroft, p. 378. The *B.M.J.* noted that poor women were not alone in parading their offspring: "Demos may be proud of seeing many of its ideas and its forms of enjoyment accepted finally by the upper ten thousand. Thus . . . baby shows have now become the means of manifesting the maternal pride of aristocratic mammas." *B.M.J.*, July 20, 1895, p. 159.

10. *Strand Magazine*, 12 (July-December 1896), 770-76; Jasper, p. 49; Stearns, p. 109.

11. Monroe, p. 2; Cohen, pp. 77-78.

12. Miller, p. 90.

13. H. Bosanquet, *Strength*, p. 227; Greenhough, p. 70; Mosher, pp. 68, 79.

14. Henry, p. 91; Mason, p. 18.

15. N. Smith, p. 148; Mason, pp. 162-63; Henry, pp. 105-6.

16. "The Happiness of Children," p. 331. See also E. H. Cooper, pp. 1060, 1065. Corporal correction of the young is far from rare in mid-twentieth-century England. Of 2,328 parents polled in 1955, 21 percent of the fathers and 14 percent of the mothers favored some type of severe physical punishment for boys. Gorer, *English Character*, pp. 162-63, 193.

17. Bolton, as quoted in Grylls, p. 66; Mangasarian, pp. 495-96.

18. *The Miserable Child World*, pp. 10-11.

19. On the society's early campaign for juvenile courts, see *Five Years with Cruelty to Children*, p. 44; C.G., November 1891, p. 114.

20. C.G., July 1900, p. 89; P.R.O., HO45, 10158, Humanitarian League's *Resolution*, May 26, 1900.

21. P.R.O., HO45, 10158, Howard Association to C. T. Ritchie, December 18, 1900; Hansard, 4th ser., 83 (May 21, 1900), cols. 848-52.

22. Gillis, "Juvenile Delinquency," pp. 108-9.

23. May, "Innocence," p. 18.

24. C.G., March 1890, p. 26.

25. P.R.O., HO45, 9813, *Report of the Head Constable* [of Liverpool], January 16, 1893; Liverpool SPCC, *Annual Report* for 1892, p. 7; Hogg, pp. 235, 243-44.

26. Burke, pp. 720-21; P.R.O., HO45, 10172, printed memorandum on juvenile hawking, 1901.

27. *Lancet*, September 24, 1898, pp. 821-22; Robert Peacock, "Employment of Children, with Special Reference to Street Trading by Chil-

dren," in *Report of the Proceedings of the Third International Congress for the Welfare and Protection of Children*, pp. 192–93; Burke, pp. 724–25; C.G., November 1899, p. 136.

28. Vorspan, p. 59.

29. G. Smith, *Lecture*, p. 79; *idem, Gipsy Life*, p. 98. In 1894 Gertrude Tuckwell estimated that there were closer to 50,000 Gypsy children throughout England and Wales. Tuckwell, pp. 100–101.

30. Vorspan, p. 73.

31. Samuels, pp. 113–14.

32. *Report of the Committee on Vagrant Children* (1899), pp. 5–7, NSPCC Archives, Box 2; P.R.O., HO45, 10182, HO memorandum on vagrant children, 1906.

33. "Memorandum on the Society's Co-operation with Workhouses Respecting Children Accompanying Tramps in Casual Wards" (May 1899), NSPCC Archives; *The Power of the Parent*, p. 64; Report of the Departmental Committee on Vagrancy, P.P., 1906, CIII, Q. 10,965.

34. *C.G.*, December 1898, p. 148; February 1899, p. 14; May 1903, p. 53. [W. Payne,] pp. 75–76.

35. Col. Gerard Clark, "Vagrant Children," in *Report of the Proceedings of the Third International Congress for the Welfare and Protection of Children*, p. 290.

36. W. Anderson, pp. 50–51. The Poor Law Board's order of 1870 applied to orphans, bastards deserted by their mothers, legitimate children deserted by both parents, and legitimate children with one parent dead, mentally incapacitated, or in prison.

37. H. Fawcett, pp. 81–82, 84; Davenport-Hill, pp. 338–39; Tuckwell, pp. 46–48.

38. Davenport-Hill, pp. 20–21.

39. State Children's Aid Association, 1st *Report* (1897), title page; Chance, pp. 328–29, 350.

40. H. O. Barnett, "The Home or the Barrick," pp. 246–48; *Fourth Annual Report of the State Children's Association* (1901), p. 4.

41. H. O. Barnett, *Canon Barnett*, pp. 683–85.

42. Report of the Departmental Committee on the Maintenance and Education of Pauper Children in the Metropolis, P.P., 1896, XLIII, part I, pp. 10–16, 36.

43. H. O. Barnett, *Canon Barnett*, p. 687; *B.M.J.*, July 17, 1897, p. 164; *C.G.*, May 1898, p. 63.

44. *Fourth Annual Report of the State Children's Assoc.*, pp. 7–8.

45. Davenport-Hill, pp. 226, 242; Barrett, pp. 17, 21.

46. State Children's Aid Association, *Leaflet No. 2* (1894); R.C. on the Poor Laws and Relief of Distress, P.P., 1909, XXXVII, "Separate Report," p. 801.

47. Searle, p. 54.

48. G. Smith, *Cry of the Children*, p. 3; Rossiter, p. 616; Pinchbeck and Hewitt, II, 633.

49. Mackintosh, pp. 8–11; Gorst, "Education Bill," p. 576.

50. Gilbert, "Health and Politics," pp. 148–49.

51. Rentoul, pp. xii, 130. Dr. Rentoul later proposed a tax on bachelors, the revenue from which would be distributed among those families with annual incomes under £250 boasting the largest number of healthy children. *B.M.J.*, November 19, 1910, p. 1657.

52. Spargo, pp. xiv–xv.

53. *Hospital*, June 3, 1905, p. 167; M. J. Moore, pp. 91–93.

54. *C.G.*, September 1903, p. 97.

55. *The Society's Majority* (NSPCC 21st Annual Report, 1905), p. 6. *C.G.*, April 1904, p. 38; June 1905, p. 65.

56. Morton, *Early Days*, p. 30; *The Discovery*, pp. 1–2; circular to inspectors marked "private and confidential" (June 7, 1898), NSPCC Archives Box FXXIV-IA; *Sunday School Chronicle*, April 20, 1905, p. 386.

57. *C.G.*, July 1902, p. 73; July 1903, p. 77. R. Waugh, pp. 270–71.

58. Morton, *Directorate*, p. 2; NSPCC Council Minutes, May 23, 1905.

59. *In the Service of the Least* (NSPCC 22d Annual Report, 1906), p. 17.

60. *C.G.*, September 1904, p. 103; June 1905, p. 64. *The Society's Majority*, pp. 5–6.

61. P.R.O., HO45, 10179, NSPCC draft bill to amend the 1894 P.C.C. Act, 1899; HO *Memorandum*, "Bill to amend the Prevention of Cruelty to Children Act, 1894," April 11, 1902.

62. Newsholme, p. 75; *Hospital*, September 22, 1906, pp. 439–41; Bray, p. 95.

63. *Hospital*, June 24, 1905, p. 223; July 29, 1905, p. 303. P.R.O., HO45, 10377, Cree to Samuel, March 4, 1908.

64. *Hospital*, September 22, 1906, p. 439; G. F. McCleary, *Infantile Mortality and Infants Milk Depôts* (1905), pp. 6–7, 10, 13.

65. Hemphill, pp. 2, 15.

66. T. Arthur Helme, "An Address on the Unborn Child: Its Care and Its Rights," reprinted in *B.M.J.*, August 24, 1907, pp. 421–25; Alden, pp. 22, 26.

67. P.R.O., HO45, 10335, Cameron to the HO, March 1906; Newman, pp. 13–15, 60. At no point during the latter half of the nineteenth century did England's infant mortality rate exceed that for 1899, when 163 children under one year died per 1,000 registered births.

68. P.R.O., HO45, 10335, Burns to Gladstone, April 19, 1906; Burns, pp. 7, 11.

69. P.R.O., HO45, 10335, "Infantile Mortality Conference. Resolutions Passed" [June 14, 1906].

70. McCleary, *Infant Welfare Movement*, pp. 112–13. Cf. McCleary's "The State as Over-Parent," p. 53.

71. Rooff, pp. 34–35; McCleary, "Health Visitor," pp. 67, 69.

72. Kanthack, p. 3.

73. Dowling, p. 228. *C.G.*, April 1894, p. 49; December 1896, p. 160; March 1904, pp. 25–26; September 1905, p. 103.

74. R. J. Parr, *Wilful Waste*, pp. 16–17.

75. Morton, *Directorate*, p. 11.

76. *Report of the Proceedings of the Third International Congress for the Welfare and Protection of Children*, pp. 149, 165.

77. *Ibid.*, pp. 166–74.

78. *B.M.J.*, December 20, 1902, p. 1931; January 17, 1903, p. 155. *Hospital*, January 24, 1903, p. 279.

79. *C.G.*, February 1903, p. 20; March 1906, p. 26.

80. *Truth*, August 29, 1906, pp. 502–3; R. J. Parr, *Baby Farmer*, pp. 31–32; P.R.O., HO45, 10361, Zanetti to Samuel, August 26, 1907.

81. H. Bosanquet, *Social Work*, pp. 243–44, 250–51.

82. Gorst, "School Children," pp. 16–17.

83. Gorst, *Children of the Nation*, pp. 86–87.

84. Elliott, pp. 862–63; Countess of Warwick, p. 7; Muirhead, pp. 117–18.

85. Bray, pp. 109–10.

86. Gilbert, *National Insurance*, pp. 116–17, 156–57. See also Donald Read, *Edwardian England, 1901–15* (1972), p. 165; and Freeden, pp. 224–26.

87. Loane, *Next Street*, p. 56; "Underfed Children," *Spectator*, April 1, 1905, p. 467.

88. *C.G.*, August 1902, p. 85; S.C. on the Education (Provision of Meals) Bill, P.P., 1906, VIII, QQ. 1421, 1434, 1441–43, 1447–51.

89. S.C. on the Education (Provision of Meals) Bill, P.P., 1906, VIII, pp. ix–x.

90. L. A. Selby-Bigge's report on the progress of school feeding, published in 1910, acknowledged that outright hunger was not the widespread evil that Gorst and his backers had described five years earlier: "A large proportion of the badly nourished children suffer from unsuitable food rather than from lack of food. It is probably no exaggeration to say that the improvement which would be effected in the physique of elementary school children in the poor parts of our large towns if their parents could be taught or persuaded to spend the same amount of money as they now spend on their children's food in a more enlightened and sensible manner, is greater than any improvement which could be effected by feeding them intermittently at the cost of the rates." Report on the Working of the Education (Provision of Meals) Act, P.P., 1910, XXIII, 5–6.

91. Gray, p. 39.

92. *Hospital*, April 24, 1897, p. 57.

93. E.g., M. K. Inglis, p. 645.

94. MacLeod, "Medico-Legal Issues," pp. 44–47.

95. *Justice to Children*, p. 56.

96. *C.G.*, September 1903, p. 97; October 1906, p. 113.

97. Sidgwick, pp. 50–51.

98. E.g., Richter, pp. 23, 222.

99. Spencer, *Proper Sphere*, p. 5; *C.G.*, June 1891, p. 61; Hallowes, p. 7. Spencer believed that the use of physical force in rearing children was both uncivilized and disruptive of "moral education." See "The Rights of Children," in *Social Statics*, pp. 86–87.

100. Gray, pp. 130–33. Cf. Mess, *Voluntary Social Services*, pp. 205–6.

101. Dailey, p. 381; *Manual of the New York SPCC*, p. 89.

102. *Lancet*, April 28, 1888, p. 842. *The Times*, March 29, 1889, p. 9; April 8, 1889, p. 10.

103. Hansard, 4th ser., 46 (March 2, 1897), col. 1440; *C.G.*, April 1907, p. 38.

104. *C.G.*, October 1888, p. 93; September 1889, p. 165.

105. *Justice to Children*, p. 48.

106. *In the Service of the Least*, p. 15; draft of a letter to Board of Education, January 28, 1909, NSPCC Archives, Box I.

107. Alden, pp. 156–57; "The Cry of the Children," *Quarterly Review*, 205 (July 1906), 53; Hall, *Queen's Reign*, pp. 180–81.

108. Report of the Departmental Committee on Vagrancy, P.P., 1906, CIII, QQ. 11,016, 11,020.

109. R.C. on the Care and Control of the Feeble-Minded, P.P., 1908, XXXVI, QQ. 13,347, 13,354, 13,445–46; *The Care and Control of the Feeble-Minded: The Royal Commission and the NSPCC* (1909), pp. 1–2.

110. Hansard, 4th ser., 172 (April 18, 1907), cols. 1189–90.

111. Samuel, *Grooves of Change*, p. 76.

112. *Ibid.*, pp. 74–75.

113. P.R.O., HO45, 10361, Herbert Samuel, "Children's Bill," printed report marked "Confidential," November 1907, p. 2.

114. See, for example, P.R.O., HO45, 10361, Parr to Samuel printed memorandum, September 30, 1907; State Children's Association, "Memorandum Re Amendment of Infant Life Protection Act, 1897," n.d.; departmental notes on meeting between Samuel and Ollis, May 29, 1907; Mrs. Robert Peel and Mrs. Henniker, "Infant Life Protection Act (Amendment) Bill," n.d.

115. P.R.O., HO45, 10361, Samuel, "Children's Bill," p. 3; S.C. on Infant Life Protection, P.P., 1908, IX, iii, and QQ. 175–93.

116. *Legislation in Regard to Children* (1906), pp. 10–11.

117. *C.G.*, January 1905, p. 7; P.R.O., HO45, 10311, regulations on treatment of children in Metropolitan police courts, June 30, 1905; *Legislation in Regard to Children*, pp. 28–30.

118. Typescript copy of a letter from Clarke Hall to Waugh, 1905, Waugh Papers; Coulter, pp. 517–19; *C.G.*, September 1905, pp. 97–98.

119. *In the Service of the Least*, p. 23; *The Great Awakening* (NSPCC 24th Annual Report, 1908), p. 27. By early 1910, 27 NSPCC inspectors were acting as children's probation officers in 28 petty sessional divisions. *C.G.*, February 1910, p. 14.

120. *C.G.*, May 24, 1908, p. 68.

121. Reynolds and Woolley, pp. 30–32, 38–39. In 1907, NSPCC leaders had cooperated with the British Medical Association and the Coroners' Society of England and Wales to draft a law on overlying and accidental burnings. See "Proposal to Amend the Prevention of Cruelty to Children Act, 1904, Explanatory Memorandum," NSPCC Archives, Box I.

122. *Truth*, March 18, 1908, p. 686; *Daily News*, August 20, 1904, p. 4.

Afterword

1. F. N. S. Silverman, "The Roentgen Manifestations of Unrecognized Skeletal Trauma in Infants," *American Journal of Roentgenology*, 69 (March 1953), pp. 413–27; P. V. Woolley and W. A. Evans, "Significance of Skeletal Lesions in Infants Resembling Those of Traumatic Origin," *Journal of the American Medical Association*, 158 (June 1955), pp. 539–43.

2. C. Henry Kempe et al., "The Battered Child Syndrome," *Journal of the American Medical Association*, 181 (July 1962), pp. 17–24. See also Keith Simpson, "Battered Babies: Conviction for Murder," *B.M.J.*, February 6, 1965, p. 393; and Selwyn M. Smith and Ruth Hanson, "134 Battered Children: A Medical and Psychological Study," *B.M.J.*, September 14, 1974, p. 666.

3. *Journal of the American Medical Association*, 181 (July 1962), p. 42.

4. *B.M.J.*, April 21, 1888, pp. 856–57; Radbill, p. 18.

5. Pfohl, pp. 312–13.

6. Dunn, p. 307; H. Bosanquet, *Family*, p. 261.

7. HO, Children's Branch, *First Report*, pp. 69–70. See also Stewart, p. 26.

8. Bilainkin, pp. 68–69.

Bibliography

Manuscript Sources

British Library, London: Angela Burdett-Coutts Papers.
Deal, Kent (in the possession of Miss Mary Fearnley-Sander): Benjamin
    Waugh Papers.
Huntington Library, San Marino, California: Francis Power Cobbe Papers.
Liverpool University Library, Liverpool: Rathbone Papers.
National Register of Archives, London: Broadlands MSS. (diaries of the
    seventh Earl of Shaftesbury).
NSPCC Archives, London:
    "Council Minutes," 1895–1911.
    "Local Office and Inspectors' Register."
    "Register of Cases," 1884–86, 1888–90.
    "Register of Inspectors," 1888–1904.
    "Record Book of Inspectors," 1889–1910.
    Birmingham Branch, "Executive Committee Minute Book," 2 vols.,
        1888–1910.
    Burton-on-Trent Branch, "Minute Book," 1899–1913.
    Dorchester Branch, "Executive Committee Minute Book," 1892–1924.
    Dover Branch, "Minute Book," 1892–1910.
    Exeter Branch, "Executive Committee Minute Book," 1889–1931.
    Halifax Branch, "Minute Book," 1901–1932.
    Leeds Branch, "Minute Book," 2 vols., 1888–97 and 1903–22.
    Manchester and Salford Branch, "Executive Committee Minute Book,"
        2 vols., 1898–1911; Report from R. Sanders on the founding of the
        Manchester Branch, n.d.
    Morpeth and East Northumberland Branch, misc. minutes, 1895, 1898,
        1901, 1902.
    York Branch, case records, 1898–1903.
Picton Library, Liverpool:
    Liverpool obituary notices, 1883–1929.
    Liverpool SPCC, "Executive Committee Minutes," 1883–1906.

Liverpool SPCC, "General Committee Minutes," 1883–1914.
Liverpool SPCC, misc. correspondence, 1894–1914.
Liverpool SPCC, "Visitors Committee Book," 1906, 1910.
Public Record Office, London:
  Home Office Records, HO45 and HO136.
  Metropolitan Police Papers, Mepo. 2 and Mepo. 3.
  Poor Law Correspondence, M.H. 15.
Royal Scottish SPCC Archives, Edinburgh:
  Glasgow SPCC, misc. minutes, 1884–94.
RSPCA Archives, Horsham, Sussex:
  "Record of Inspectors," 1851–96.
Sheffield University Library, Sheffield:
  Mundella-Leader Correspondence.

Government Documents

SERIES

Annual Reports of the Registrar General of Births, Deaths, and Marriages, 1841–1916.
Census of England and Wales, 1851, 1861, 1871, 1881, 1891, 1901, 1911.
Judicial Statistics for England and Wales, 1856–1910.
Annual Reports of the Poor Law Board, 1860–71.
Annual Reports of the Local Government Board, 1872–1910.
Annual Reports of the Metropolitan Board of Works, 1872–97.
Reports of the Inspector under the Inebriates Acts, 1902–8.
London County Council; Reports of the Medical Officer (Education), 1903–10.
Hansard's Parliamentary Debates, 3d and 4th series.

INDIVIDUAL REPORTS

Report from the Select Committee on . . . the Labour of Children in the Mills and Factories of the United Kingdom; 1831–32, XV.
First Report of . . . His Majesty's Commissioners [on] . . . the Employment of Children in Factories; 1833, XX.
Report from His Majesty's Commissioners [on] . . . the Administration and Practical Operation of the Poor Laws; 1834, XXVII, XXIX.
Report from the Select Committee on the Office of Coroner for Middlesex; 1840, XIV.
A Supplementary Report on the Results of a Special Inquiry into the Practice of Interment in Towns; 1843, XII.
Report of the Poor Law Commissioners . . . on the Law Concerning the Maintenance of Bastards; 1844, XIX.
Second Report of the Commissioners for Inquiring into the State of Large Towns and Populous Districts, Appendix, Part II; 1845, XVIII.

First Report from the [Lords] Select Committee . . . [on] the Execution of the Criminal Law, especially respecting Juvenile Offenders and Transportation; 1847, VII.

Board of Health. Report on a General Scheme for Extramural Sepulture; 1850, XXI.

Report from the Select Committee on Criminal and Destitute Juveniles; 1852, VII.

Report from the Select Committee on Criminal and Destitute Children; 1852–53, XXIII.

Report from the Select Committee on Friendly Societies Bill; 1854, VII.

Return of the Number of Persons Tried in England and Wales in Each of the Last Ten Years, 1844 to 1853 Inclusive, for the Murders of Children Under Ten Years of Age, Who Are Members of Burial Societies; 1854, LIII.

Return Relating to Charges Preferred Against Male Persons for Assaults on Women and Children, at Each Court within the Metropolitan Police District, from 1 June 1850 to 1 June 1853; 1854, LIII.

Report from the Select Committee on the Office of Coroner; 1860, XXII.

Return of the Number of Coroners' Inquests Held in Each Year Upon the Bodies of Infants from 31st December 1855 to 31st December 1860, within the Metropolitan District; 1861, LI.

Return of the Verdicts of Coroners' Inquests, in the Metropolis, on Infants Under Two Years of Age, During the Year 1861; 1862, XLIV.

Return of the Verdicts of Coroners' Inquests in England and Wales on Children under Two Years of Age, During the Year 1861, and the First Six Months of 1862; 1863, XLVIII.

Special Report from the Select Committee on the Chemists and Druggists Bill; 1865, XII.

Report of the Capital Punishment Commission; 1866, XXI.

Children's Employment Commission. Sixth Report of the Commissioners; 1867, XVI.

Report from the Select Committee on Protection of Infant Life; 1871, VII.

Second Report of the Royal Sanitary Commission; 1871, XXXV.

Report of the Select Committee on Habitual Drunkards; 1872, IX.

Special Report from the Select Committee on Homicide Law Amendment; 1874, IX.

Fourth Report of the Commissioners [on] . . . Friendly and Benefit Building Societies; 1874, XXIII.

Reports . . . on the State of the Law Relating to Brutal Assaults; 1875, LXI.

Reports of the Chief Registrar of Friendly Societies for the Year Ending 31st December 1875; 1876, LXIX.

First, Second, and Third Reports from the [Lords] Select Committee . . . on Intemperance; 1877, VIII.

Reports on the Laws of Foreign Countries Respecting Homicidal Crime; 1881, LXXVI.

Report from the Select Committee on Artizans' and Labourers' Dwellings; 1882, VII.

Report from the Select Committee on Police and Sanitary Regulations; 1882, XII.

Report of the Select Committee on Post Office (Annuities and Life Assurance Policies); 1882, XII.

Report from the [Lords] Select Committee on the Law Relating to the Protection of Young Girls; 1882, XIII.

Reformatories and Industrial Schools Commission. Report of the Commissioners; 1884, XLV.

First Report of Her Majesty's Commissioners [on] . . . the Housing of the Working Classes; 1884–85, XXX.

Return of the Number of Women in Convict Prisons on Commuted Capital Sentences for Infanticide on 7th August 1886; 1886, LIII.

Report from the Select Committee on Friendly Societies; 1888, XII.

Report from the [Lords] Select Committee . . . on Poor Law Relief; 1888, XV.

Final Report of the Commissioners [on] . . . the Elementary Education Acts; 1888, XXXV.

Report from the Select Committee on the Friendly Societies Act, 1875; 1889, X.

Report from the [Lords] Select Committee on the Children's Life Insurance Bill; 1890, XI.

Report from the Select Committee on the Infant Life Protection Bill; 1890, XIII.

Report from the [Lords] Select Committee . . . on the Children's Life Insurance Bill; 1891, XI.

Report from the [Lords] Select Committee . . . on the Infant Life Protection Bill and Safety of Nurse Children Bill; 1896, X.

Report of the Departmental Committee on the Maintenance and Education of Pauper Children; 1896, XLIII.

Report from the Standing Committee on Law . . . on the Infant Life Protection Bill; 1897, X.

Minutes of Evidence Taken Before the Royal Commission on Liquor Licensing Laws; 1897, XXXIV, XXXV, XXXVI; 1899, XXXIV.

Final Report [on] . . . the Laws Relating to the Sale of Intoxicating Liquors; 1899, XXXV.

Special Report . . . from the Select Committee on the Education (Provision of Meals) Bill; 1906, VIII.

Report of the Departmental Committee on Vagrancy; 1906, CIII.

Report of the Select Committee on Infant Life Protection; 1908, IX.

Report of the Royal Commission on the Care and Control of the Feeble-Minded; 1908, XXXV, XXXVI, XXXVII.
Children Under the Poor Law, A Report . . . by T. J. Macnamara; 1908, XCII.
Report of the Departmental Committee on the Probation of Offenders Act, 1907; [H.M.S.O.] 1909.
Report of the Royal Commission on the Poor Laws and Relief of Distress; 1909, XXXVII; 1910, LII.
Report on the Working of the Education (Provision of Meals) Act; 1910, XXIII.
Memorandum of the Local Government Board as to Numbers of Children Under the Poor Law . . . ; [H.M.S.O.] 1912.
Report of the Royal Commission on Divorce and Matrimonial Causes; 1912–13, XVIII, XIX, XX.
Home Office, Children's Branch, First Report, 1923.
Report of the Departmental Committee on Industrial Assurance; 1932–33, XIII.
Report of the Select Committee on Violence in the Family; 1977, LXXXII.

Other Works

(Unless otherwise noted, all books listed below were published in London.)
Abbott, Grace. *The Child and the State.* 2 vols. Chicago, 1938.
Acland, Emily. "The Training of Midwives," *Nineteenth Century and After*, 62 (November 1907), 787–92.
Adams, W. H. *Woman's Work and Worth in Girlhood, Maidenhood, and Wifehood.* 1880.
Adler, Nettie. "Children as Wage-Earners," *Fortnightly Review*, n.s. 73 (May 1903), 918–27.
Agnew, T. F. A. *Work in Early Days for the Prevention of Cruelty to Children.* n.d.
Alcohol and Childhood: A Report of Two Conferences Promoted by the Church of England Temperance Society. 1891.
Alden, Margaret. *Child Life and Labour.* 1908.
Alford, Violet. "Rough Music or Charivari," *Folk-Lore*, 70 (December 1959), 505–18.
Allen, Anne, and Arthur Morton. *This Is Your Child.* 1961.
Alverstone, Viscount. *Recollections of Bar and Bench.* 1914.
Analysis and Review of the Blue Book of the Royal Commission on Capital Punishment. [1866.]
An Appeal to Humanity, in an Account of the Life and Cruel Actions of Elizabeth Brownrigg. 1767.
Anderson, Michael. *Family Structure in Nineteenth Century Lancashire.* Cambridge, 1971.

Anderson, Olive. "Did Suicide Increase with Industrialization in Victorian England?," *Past and Present*, 86 (February 1980), 149–73.
Anderson, R. "Morality by Act of Parliament," *Contemporary Review*, 59 (January 1891), 77–88.
Anderson, William. *Children Rescued from Pauperism: or the Boarding-Out System in Scotland*. Edinburgh, 1871.
Annual Register, Or a View of the History and Politics of the Year 1860. 1861.
Ariès, Philippe. *Centuries of Childhood*. Trans. Robert Baldick. New York, 1962.
———— *Western Attitudes Toward Death*. Trans. Patricia Ranum. Baltimore, 1975.
Armstrong, R. A. *The Overstrain in Education*. [1883.]
Armytage, W. H. G. *A. J. Mundella 1825–1897*. 1951.
Arnott, John. *The Investigation into the Condition of the Children in the Cork Workhouse, with an Analysis of the Evidence*. Cork, 1859.
Aschaffenburg, Gustav. *Crime and Its Repression*. Boston, 1913.
Atkinson, Stanley B. "Life, Birth, and Live-Birth," *Law Quarterly Review*, 20 (April 1904), 134–59.
At Risk: An Account of the Work of the Battered Child Research Department, NSPCC. 1976.
Attlee, M. A. *The Social Worker*. 1920.
Avery, Gillian. *Nineteenth Century Children*. 1965.
Baernreither, J. M. *English Associations of Working Men*. 1889.
Baines, M. A. *On the Prevention of Excessive Infant-Mortality*. 1868.
Baines, Thomas. *History of the Commerce and Town of Liverpool*. 1852.
Baker, Charles E. *The Law of Husband and Wife*. 1880.
Banks, J. A. *Prosperity and Parenthood. A Study of Family Planning Among the Victorian Middle Class*. 1954.
Banks, J. A., and Olive Banks. *Feminism and Family Planning in Victorian England*. 1964.
Barbero, Giulio, Marian G. Morris, and Margaret T. Reford. "Malidentification of Mother-Baby-Father Relationships Expressed in Infant Failure to Thrive," in *The Neglected Battered-Baby Syndrome*. New York, 1963.
Barker, Joseph. *The History and Confessions of a Man, As Put Forth by Himself*. 1846.
Barlee, Ellen. *Pantomime Waifs, or, A Plea for Our City Children*. 1884.
Barnardo, Mrs. T. J., and James Marchant. *Memoirs of the Late Dr. Barnardo*. 1907.
Barnardo, T. J. *A Year's Work in Dr. Barnardo's Homes*. 1884.
Barnett, Henrietta O. *Canon Barnett: His Life, Work, and Friends*. 1921.
———— "The Home or the Barrack for the Children of the State," *Contemporary Review*, 66 (August 1894), 243–58.

Barnett, Samuel A. "Sensationalism in Social Reform," *Nineteenth Century*, 19 (February 1886), 280–90.

Baron and Feme. A Treatise on the Common Law Concerning Husbands and Wives. 1719.

Baroness Burdett-Coutts. A Sketch of Her Public Life and Work Prepared for the Lady Managers of the World's Columbian Exposition by Command of Her Royal Highness, Princess Mary Adelaide, Duchess of Teck. Chicago, 1893.

Barrett, Rosa M. *Foreign Legislation on Behalf of Destitute and Neglected Children.* Dublin, 1896.

"The Bar Sinister," *British and Foreign Medico-Chirugical Review*, 31 (January 1863), 1–27.

Bayle, Elisabeth Boyd. *England's Answer to the Children's Cry.* 1908.

Bayne-Powell, Rosamond. *The English Child in the Eighteenth Century.* New York, 1939.

Beattie, J. M. "The Pattern of Crime in England 1660–1800," *Past and Present*, 62 (February 1974), 47–95.

Beaver, M. W. "Population, Infant Mortality, and Milk," *Population Studies*, 27 (July 1973), 243–54.

Behlmer, George K. "Deadly Motherhood: Infanticide and Medical Opinion in Mid-Victorian England," *Journal of the History of Medicine and Allied Sciences*, 34 (October 1979), 403–27.

Bensusan, S. L. "The Training of Child Acrobats," *English Illustrated Magazine*, 16 (October 1896), 41–45.

Berdoe, Edward. "Slum-Mothers and Death Clubs: A Vindication," *Nineteenth Century*, 29 (April 1891), 560–63.

Berger, Nan. "The Child, the Law, and the State," in Julian Hall, ed., *Children's Rights.* 1971.

Beveridge, William Henry. *Voluntary Action.* 1948.

Beyond the Law: Some Facts on Illegitimacy in Ireland [NSPCC]. n.d.

Bilainkin, George. "Children in Peril," *Contemporary Review*, 201 (February 1962), 67–71.

Blackburn, Helen. *Women's Suffrage.* 1902 [reprinted, 1970].

Blackley, William Lewery. *Thrift and Independence.* 1885.

Blackstone, William. *Commentaries on the Laws of England.* 4 vols. 1765–69 [reprinted, 1966].

Bonger, William Adrian. *Criminality and Economic Conditions.* Boston, 1916.

Booth, Bramwell. *Echoes and Memories.* 1925.

Booth, Charles. *Life and Labour of the People in London.* 17 vols. 1892–1903.

———— "Occupations of the People of the United Kingdom, 1801–81," *Journal of the Statistical Society*, 49 (June 1886), 314–435.

Bosanquet, Bernard, ed. *Aspects of the Social Problem*. 1895 [reprinted, 1968].

Bosanquet, Helen. *The Family*. New York, 1923.

—— *Rich and Poor*. 1898.

—— *Social Work in London, 1869 to 1912*. 1914.

—— *The Strength of the People*. 1902.

Boudouris, James. "Homicide and the Family," *Journal of Marriage and the Family*, 33 (November 1971), 667–76.

Bowerman, E. E. *The Law of Child Protection*. 1933.

Bowley, Arthur L. *Wages in the United Kingdom in the Nineteenth Century*. Cambridge, 1900.

Brabrook, W. E. *Provident Societies and Industrial Welfare*. 1898.

Brand, Jeanne L. *Doctors and the State: The British Medical Profession and Government Action in Public Health, 1870–1912*. Baltimore, 1965.

Bray, Reginald A. *The Town Child*. 1907.

Bready, J. Wesley. *Doctor Barnardo*. 1930.

—— *Lord Shaftesbury and Social-Industrial Progress*. 1926.

Brice, A. W. C., and K. J. Fielding. "Dickens and the Tooting Disaster," *Victorian Studies*, 12 (December 1968), 227–44.

Briggs, Asa. *Victorian Cities*. 1970.

Bristow, Edward Jay. "The Defence of Liberty and Property in Britain, 1880–1914." Ph.D. diss., Yale University, 1970.

Brockington, C. Fraser. *A Short History of Public Health*. 1956.

Brown, James Baldwin. *The Home: In Its Relation to Man and to Society*. 1883.

Brown, John. *A Memoir of Robert Blincoe*. Manchester, 1832 [reprinted, 1966].

Browning, Elizabeth Barrett. *The Poetical Works of Elizabeth Barrett Browning*. 1900.

Brownlow, John. *Memoranda; or, Chronicles of the Foundling Hospital, Including Memoirs of Captain Coram, &c. &c.* 1847.

Bruce, Henry Austin. *Letters of the Rt. Hon. Henry Austin Bruce*. 2 vols. Oxford, 1902.

Burdett-Coutts, Angela, ed. *Woman's Mission: A Series of Congress Papers on the Philanthropic Work of Women*. 1893.

Burke, Thomas. "Street-Trading Children of Liverpool," *Contemporary Review*, 78 (November 1900), 720–26.

Burn, W. L. *The Age of Equipoise*. New York, 1965.

Burnett, John, ed. *Useful Toil*. 1976.

Burns, John. *Address . . . Delivered at the Conference on Infantile Mortality*. 1906.

Butler, Josephine. *Personal Reminiscences of a Great Crusade*. 1896.

Carpenter, Mary. *Reformatory Schools for the Children of the Perishing and Dangerous Classes, and for Juvenile Offenders.* 1851.

Carter, Henry. *Liquor Versus Life.* 1908.

Caulfield, Ernest. *The Infant Welfare Movement in the Eighteenth Century.* New York, 1931.

"Cemeteries and Churchyards—Funerals and Funeral Expenses," *Quarterly Review*, 73 (March 1844), 438–77.

Chance, W. *Children Under the Poor Law.* 1897.

Channing, Francis Allston. *Memories of Midland Politics 1885–1910.* 1918.

Chesser, Eustace. *Cruelty to Children.* 1951.

Chevalier, Louis. *Laboring Classes and Dangerous Classes in Paris During the First Half of the Nineteenth Century.* New York, 1973.

"Child Murder—Obstetric Morality," *Dublin Review*, 45 (September 1858), 54–106.

The Children and the Drink. 1901.

"Children in Theatres," *Saturday Review*, July 23, 1887, pp. 108–9.

Clarke, Peter. *Liberals and Social Democrats.* Cambridge, 1978.

Clay, Walter Lowe. *The Prison Chaplain: A Memoir of the Rev. John Clay, B.D.* Cambridge, 1861.

Clotten, Francis Egon. *The Necessity of Sanitary Reform in Infant Rearing: Why and How It Should Be Effected.* Liverpool, 1888.

C.M.C. *The Legislation of 1889; or, One Year of Conservative and Unionist Government.* 1890.

Cobbe, Frances Power. *The Higher Expediency.* 1882.

——— *Life of Frances Power Cobbe.* 1904.

——— "Wife-Torture in England," *Contemporary Review*, 32 (April 1878), 55–87.

Cohen, Emmeline W. *English Social Services.* 1949.

Colam, Robert Frederick. *Prevention of Cruelty to Children: A Manual* [London SPCC]. 1885.

Coleman, Sydney. *Humane Society Leaders in America.* Albany, N.Y., 1924.

Collier, J. F. "The Prevention of Cruelty to Children," *Good Words*, 1884, pp. 537–40.

Collini, Stefan. *Liberalism and Sociology: L. T. Hobhouse and Political Argument in England 1880–1914.* Cambridge, 1979.

Collins, P. A. W. "Dickens and the Ragged Schools," *Dickensian*, 55 (May 1959), 94–109.

Collis, Arthur T., and Vera E. Poole. *These Our Children.* 1950.

[Cooper, Anthony Ashley.] "Infant Labour," *Quarterly Review*, 67 (December 1840), 171–81.

Cooper, Edward H. "The Punishment of Children," *Fortnightly Review*, n.s. 73 (June 1903), 1060–67.

Coote, William Alexander. *A Romance of Philanthropy.* 1916.
Coulter, Ernest K. "The New York Children's Court," *Contemporary Review*, 87 (April 1905), 516–23.
Coveney, Peter. *The Image of Childhood.* Harmondsworth, Middlesex, 1967.
[Crawford, Virginia M.] *Fairness to Catholics* [NSPCC pamphlet]. 1891.
"A Crime and Its Causes," *Westminster Review*, 151 (February 1899), 131–39.
"Cruelty to Children," *The Shaftesbury Magazine*, January 1908, pp. 5–6.
"The Cry of the Children," *Quarterly Review*, 408 (July 1906), 29–53.
Curgenven, J. Brendon. *A Bill for the Better Protection of Infant Life.* 1871.
——— "Infanticide, Baby-Farming, and the Infant Life Protection Act, 1872," *Sanitary Record*, n.s. 10 (1888–89), 409–10, 461–63.
——— *Infant Life Protection Society Prospectus.* [1870.]
——— *On Baby-Farming and the Registration of Nurses.* 1869.
——— "On the Laws of Belgium Relative to Illegitimate Children and Foundlings," *Transactions of the N.A.P.S.S.* (1868), 531–39.
——— *On the Laws of France Relating to Illegitimate Children, Foundlings, and Orphans; and also Those Relating to the Registration of Births and Deaths.* 1871.
——— *Reply of the Infant Life Protection Society to a Memorial of Members of the National Society for Women's Suffrage Objecting to the Proposed Measure.* 1870.
——— *The Waste of Infant Life.* 1867.
Curl, James Stevens. *The Victorian Celebration of Death.* Detroit, 1972.
Dailey, Abram. "The Conflict Between Parental Authority and the Society for the Prevention of Cruelty to Children," *Medico-Legal Journal*, 10 (1892), 376–85.
Davenport-Hill, Florence. *Children of the State.* 2d ed., 1889.
Davey, Richard. *A History of Mourning.* [1890.]
Davies, D. Seaborne. "Child-Killing in English Law," *Modern Law Review*, 1 (December 1937 and March 1938), 203–23, 269–87.
Degler, Carl. *At Odds: Women and the Family in America from the Revolution to the Present.* New York, 1980.
de Mause, Lloyd. "The Evolution of Childhood," in *idem*, ed., *The History of Childhood.* 1975.
Demos, John. "Demography and Psychology in the Historical Study of Family-Life: A Personal Report," in Peter Laslett, ed., *Household and Family in Past Time.* Cambridge, 1972.
——— *A Little Commonwealth.* New York, 1970.
The Dens of London. Forty Years' Mission Work Among the Outcast Poor of London. 1884.

Dewi. "Save the Children: A Plea," *Westminster Review,* 160 (November. 1903), 559–62.
Dickson, Thompson. "On Baby Farming," *Medical Press and Circular,* n.s. 10 (October 1870), 323–27.
Dingle, A. E., and B. H. Harrison. "Cardinal Manning as a Temperance Reformer," *Historical Journal,* 12 (1969), 485–510.
Donzelot, Jacques. *The Policing of Families.* New York, 1979.
Dowling, William Charles. "The Ladies' Sanitary Association and the Origins of the Health Visiting Service." M.A. thesis, University of London, 1963.
Driver, Cevil. *Tory Radical. The Life of Richard Oastler.* New York, 1946.
Duffy, John. "Mental Strain and 'Overpressure' in the Schools: A Nineteenth-Century Viewpoint," *Journal of the History of Medicine and Allied Sciences,* 23 (January 1968), 63–79.
Dunckley, Henry. "Child Labour: II. The Half-Timers," *Contemporary Review,* 59 (June 1891), 798–802.
Dunelm, J. B. "The White Cross," *Contemporary Review,* 48 (August 1885), 262–68.
Dunn, Courtenay. *The Natural History of the Child.* New York, 1920.
Dyos, H. J. "The Slums of Victorian London," *Victorian Studies,* 11 (September 1967), 5–40.
E. C. *Statute Mongery.* 1901.
Edinburgh SPCC. *Preliminary Report.* Edinburgh, 1884.
Elliott, C. A. "State Feeding of School Children in London," *Nineteenth Century and After,* 65 (May 1909), 862–74.
Ellis, Sarah Stickney. *The Mothers of England: Their Influence and Responsibility.* 1843.
Elmy, Elizabeth Wolstenholme. *The Custody and Guardianship of Children.* 1884.
Elyot, Thomas. *The Boke Named the Governour.* 2 vols. 1883 [first published in 1531].
Emy, H. V. *Liberals, Radicals, and Social Politics 1892–1914.* Cambridge, 1973.
Engels, Friedrich. *The Condition of the Working Class in England.* Stanford, Calif., 1958.
Ensor, R. C. K. *England 1870–1914.* Oxford, 1936.
Erlanger, Howard S. "Social Class and Corporal Punishment in Childrearing: A Reassessment," *American Sociological Review,* 39 (February 1974), 68–85.
Evans, George Ewart. *The Pattern Under the Plow: Aspects of the Folk-Life in East Anglia.* 1966.
Eversley, William Pinder. *The Law of the Domestic Relations.* 1885.
Eyler, John M. "Mortality Statistics and Victorian Health Policy: Program

and Criticism," *Bulletin of the History of Medicine*, 50 (Fall 1976), 335–55.

Fairholme, Edward, and Wellesley Pain. *A Century of Work for Animals*. 1924.

Fawcett, Henry. *Pauperism: Its Causes and Remedies*. 1871.

Fawcett, Millicent Garrett. "The Employment of Children in Theatres," *Contemporary Review*, 56 (November 1889), 822–29.

Fido, Judith. "The Charity Organisation Society and Social Casework in London 1869–1900," in A. P. Donajgrodzki, ed., *Social Control in Nineteenth Century Britain*. 1977.

Fielden, John. *The Curse of the Factory System*. 2d ed. 1836 [reprinted, 1969].

Fifty Years' Record of Child-Saving and Reformatory Work (1856–1906), Being the Jubilee Report of the Reformatory and Refuge Union. 1906.

The First Forty Years: A Chronicle of the Church of England Waifs and Strays Society, 1881–1920. 1922.

Fitzgerald, William G. "Dandy Dogs," *Strand Magazine*, 11 (January-June 1896), 538–50.

Folks, Homer. *The Care of Destitute, Neglected, and Delinquent Children*. New York, 1902.

Forbes, Thomas R. "The Regulation of English Midwives in the Eighteenth and Nineteenth Centuries," *Medical History*, 15 (October 1971), 352–60.

Forwood, Arthur B. *The Dwellings of the Industrial Classes in the Diocese of Liverpool, and How to Improve Them*. Liverpool, 1883.

Fraser, Derek. *The Evolution of the British Welfare State*. New York, 1973.

Freeden, Michael. *The New Liberalism: An Ideology of Social Reform*. Oxford, 1978.

French, Richard. *Antivivisection and Medical Science in Victorian Society*. Princeton, N.J., 1975.

"Friendly Societies," *Quarterly Review*, 166 (April 1888), 377–406.

Fryer, Peter. *The Birth Controllers*. New York, 1966.

Fyffe, C. A., "The Punishment of Infanticide," *Nineteenth Century*, 1 (June 1877), 583–95.

Garnett, W. H. Stuart. *Children and the Law*. 1911.

Gaskell, P. *The Manufacturing Population of England*. 1833 [reprinted, 1972].

Gatrell, V. A. C., and T. B. Hadden. "Criminal Statistics and Their Interpretation," in E. A. Wrigley, ed., *Nineteenth Century Society*. Cambridge, 1972.

Gelles, Richard J. "The Social Construction of Child Abuse," *American Journal of Orthopsychiatry*, 45 (April 1975), 363–71.

George, M. Dorothy. *London Life in the Eighteenth Century*. 1925.

George Smith of Coalville: A Chapter in Philanthropy. 1880.

Gerry, Elbridge T. "Cruelty to Children," *North American Review*, 137 (1883), 68–75.

Gibson, Ian. *The English Vice: Beating, Sex, and Shame in Victorian England and After.* 1978.

Gil, David G. "Unraveling Child Abuse," *American Journal of Orthopsychiatry*, 45 (April 1975), 346–56.

——— *Violence Against Children: Physical Child Abuse in the United States.* Cambridge, Mass., 1970.

Gilbert, Bentley. *The Evolution of National Insurance in Great Britain.* 1966.

——— "Health and Politics: The British Physical Deterioration Report of 1904," *Bulletin of the History of Medicine*, 39 (March-April 1965), 143–53.

Gillis, John R. "The Evolution of Juvenile Delinquency in England 1890–1914," *Past and Present*, 67 (May 1975), 96–126.

——— *Youth and History.* New York, 1974.

Giovannoni, Jeanne M. "Parental Mistreatment: Perpetrators and Victims," *Journal of Marriage and the Family*, 33 (November 1971), 649–57.

Glasgow SPCC. Annual Reports for 1884–87.

Gorer, Geoffrey. *Death, Grief, and Mourning.* New York, 1967.

——— *Exploring English Character.* 1955.

Gorham, Deborah. "The 'Maiden Tribute of Modern Babylon' Re-Examined: Child Prostitution and the Idea of Childhood in Late-Victorian England," *Victorian Studies*, 21 (Spring 1978), 353–79.

Gorst, Sir John. *The Children of the Nation: How Their Health and Vigour Should be Promoted by the State.* 1906.

——— "The Education Bill," *Nineteenth Century and After*, 52 (October 1902), 576–90.

——— "School Children as Wage-Earners," *Nineteenth Century*, 46 (July 1899), 8–17.

Gosden, P. H. J. H. *The Friendly Societies in England, 1815–1875.* Manchester, 1961.

——— *Self-Help.* 1973.

Gray, B. Kirkman. *Philanthropy and the State, or Social Politics.* 1908.

Greaves, George. "Observations on Some of the Causes of Infanticide," *Transactions of the Manchester Statistical Society*, 1863, pp. 1–24.

——— "On the Laws Referring to Child-Murder and Criminal Abortion, with Suggestions for Their Amendment," *Transactions of the Manchester Statistical Society*, 1864, pp. 19–41.

Green, Arthur H., Richard W. Gaines, and Alice Sandgrund. "Child Abuse: Pathological Syndrome of Family Interaction," *American Journal of Psychiatry*, 131 (August 1974), 882–86.

Greenhough, J. G. *Our Dear Home Life.* 1896.

Greenwood, James. *Low-Life Deeps: An Account of the Strange Fish to be Found There.* 1876.

────── *The Seven Curses of London.* Boston, 1869.

Greg, William R. *An Enquiry Into the State of the Manufacturing Population, and the Causes and Cures of the Evils Therein Existing.* 1831.

Gregory, Alice S. "Midwifery as a Profession for Educated Women," *Nineteenth Century and After*, 63 (January 1908), 90–97.

Grylls, David. *Guardians and Angels.* 1978.

Guthrie, Leonard G. *Functional Nervous Disorders in Childhood.* 1909.

Guthrie, Thomas. "A Plea for Ragged Schools; or, Prevention Better than Cure," *Edinburgh Review*, 85 (April 1847), 520–35.

Hair, P. E. H. "Deaths from Violence in Britain: A Tentative Secular Survey," *Population Studies*, 25 (March 1971), 5–24.

Hall, W. Clarke. *Children's Courts.* 1926.

────── *The Law Relating to Children.* 1894.

────── *The Queen's Reign for Children.* 1897.

────── *The State and the Child.* 1917.

Hallowes, Frances S. *The Rights of Children in Spirit, Mind, and Body.* 1896.

Hammond, J. L., and Barbara Hammond. *James Stansfeld: A Victorian Champion of Sex Equality.* 1932.

Handbook for Workers [C.E.W.S.S.]. 1895.

Hanson, Harry. *The Canal Boatmen 1769–1914.* Manchester, 1975.

Hanson, John. *Infant Salvation; or, Words of Instruction and Comfort Concerning Little Children.* Leeds, 1864.

"The Happiness of Children," *The Spectator*, 68 (March 5, 1892), 331–32.

Hardwick, Charles. *The History, Present Position, and Social Importance of Friendly Societies.* 2d ed. Manchester, 1869.

Harris, John. *Patriarchy; or, The Family: Its Constitution and Probation.* 1855.

Harrison, Brian. "Animals and the State in Nineteenth-Century England," *English Historical Review*, 88 (October 1973), 786–820.

────── *Drink and the Victorians.* Pittsburgh, Penn., 1971.

────── "For Church, Queen, and Family: The Girls' Friendly Society 1874–1920," *Past and Present*, 61 (November 1973), 107–38.

────── "Philanthropy and the Victorians," *Victorian Studies*, 9 (June 1966), 353–74.

────── *Separate Spheres: The Opposition to Women's Suffrage in Britain.* 1978.

────── "State Intervention and Moral Reform in Nineteenth-Century England," in Patricia Hollis, ed., *Pressure from Without in Early Victorian England.* 1974.

————— "Underneath the Victorians," *Victorian Studies*, 10 (March 1967), 239–62.

Hartwell, R. M. *The Industrial Revolution and Economic Growth.* 1971.

Harwood, Dix. *Love for Animals and How It Developed in Great Britain.* New York, 1928.

Havard, J. D. J. *The Detection of Secret Homicide: A Study of the Medicolegal System of Investigation of Sudden and Unexplained Deaths.* 1960.

Head, Sir George. *A Home Tour Through the Manufacturing Districts of England in the Summer of 1835.* 1836 [reprinted, 1968].

The Heart of the Empire. 1901.

Heasman, Kathleen. *Evangelicals in Action.* 1962.

Heath, H. Llewellyn. *The Infant, the Parent, and the State.* 1907.

Heath-Stubbs, Mary. *Friendship's Highway, Being the History of the Girls' Friendly Society, 1875–1925.* 1926.

Hemphill, Samuel. *The Murderess of the Unseen: A Tract on Race-Suicide.* 2d ed. Dublin, 1908.

Hennock, E. P. "Poverty and Social Theory in England: The Experience of the Eighteen-Eighties," *Social History*, 1 (January 1976), 67–91.

Henriques, U. R. Q. "Bastardy and the New Poor Law," *Past and Present*, 37 (July 1967), 103–29.

Henry, Mrs. S. M. I. *Confidential Talks on Home and Child Life.* Edinburgh, 1898.

Hewitt, Margaret. *Wives and Mothers in Victorian Industry.* 1958.

Heywood, Jean. *Children in Care: The Development of the Service for the Deprived Child.* 1959.

Hicks, A. Braxton. *Hints to Medical Men Concerning the Granting of Certificates of Death.* 1889.

Hill, Florence. "The Family System for Workhouse Children," *Contemporary Review*, 15 (September 1870), 240–73.

Hillocks, James I. *Hard Battles for Life and Usefulness.* 1884.

Hird, Frank. *The Cry of the Children.* 2d ed. 1898.

Hobbes, Thomas. *Leviathan.* Harmondsworth, Middlesex, 1968.

Hobhouse, Rosa. *Benjamin Waugh, Founder of the National Society for the Prevention of Cruelty to Children and Framer of the 'Children's Charter.'* 1939.

————— *An Interplay of Life and Art.* Broxbourne, Herts., 1958.

Hocking, Silas K. *Her Benny.* 2d ed. Chicago, 1890.

Hodder, Edwin. *George Smith (of Coalville).* 1896.

————— *John MacGregor ('Rob Roy').* 1894.

————— *The Life and Work of the Seventh Earl of Shaftesbury, K.G.* 3 vols. 1886.

Hodgkinson, Ruth G. "Poor Law Medical Officers in England 1834–1871," *Journal of the History of Medicine and Allied Sciences*, 11 (July 1956), 299–338.

Hoffman, Frederick L. *The Life Insurance of Children*. Newark, N.J., 1903.

Hogg, Edith F. "School Children as Wage Earners," *Nineteenth Century*, 42 (August 1897), 235–44.

Hole, James. *The Homes of the Working Classes with Suggestions for Their Improvement*. 1866.

Holmes, Thomas. "Habitual Inebriates," *Contemporary Review*, 75 (May 1899), 740–46.

Hood, Thomas. *The Choice Works of Thomas Hood*. Boston, n.d.

Hopkins, Ellice. "The Apocalypse of Evil," *Contemporary Review*, 48 (September 1885), 332–42.

——— "The Industrial Training of Pauper and Neglected Girls," *Contemporary Review*, 42 (July 1882), 140–54.

Hopley, Thomas. *Facts Bearing on the Death of Reginald Channell Cancellor: With a Supplement and a Sequel*. 1860.

Horn, Pamela. *The Victorian Country Child*. Kineton, Warwick, 1974.

Horsley, J. W. *How Criminals Are Made and Prevented*. 1913.

Housden, Leslie George. *The Prevention of Cruelty to Children*, 1955.

Howell, George. "The Dwellings of the Poor," *Nineteenth Century*, 13 (June 1883), 992–1007.

Hull, Charles H., ed. *The Economic Writings of Sir William Petty*. 2 vols. Cambridge, 1899.

Hull SPCC. Annual reports for 1888–90, 1892, 1894, and 1898–99.

Hume, A. *Conditions of Liverpool, Religious and Social; Including Notices of the State of Education, Morals, Pauperism, and Crime*. Liverpool, 1858.

Hume-Rothery, Mary C. *Women and Doctors: or Medical Despotism in England*. Manchester, 1871.

Hunt, David. *Parents and Children in History*. New York, 1972.

Hutchins, B. L., and A. Harrison. *A History of Factory Legislation*. 1911.

Hutchins, John H. *Jonas Hanway 1712–1786*. 1940.

Huxley, Leonard, ed. *Life and Letters of Thomas Henry Huxley*. 2 vols. 1900 [reprinted, 1969].

Huxley, T. H. *Social Diseases and Worse Remedies*. 1891.

Ignatieff, Michael. *A Just Measure of Pain: The Penitentiary in the Industrial Revolution, 1750–1850*. New York, 1978.

Infant Mortality: Its Causes and Remedies. Manchester, 1871.

Inglis, K. S. *Churches and the Working Classes in Victorian England*. 1963.

Inglis, M. K. "The State Versus the Home," *Fortnightly Review*, n.s. 84 (October 1908), 643–58.

Jackson, Graham. "Child Abuse Syndrome: The Cases We Miss," *British Medical Journal*, June 24, 1972, pp. 756–57.

James, T. E. *Child Law*. 1962.

Jasper, A. S. *A Hoxton Childhood*. 1969.

Jeune, Mary. "Children in Theatres," *English Illustrated Magazine*, 6 (1889–90), 6–14.

—— "Saving the Innocents," *Fortnightly Review*, 44 (September 1885), 345–56.

Johnson, Harriet M. *Children and Public-Houses*. 3d ed. Seacombe, Cheshire, 1897.

Jones, Gareth Stedman. *Outcast London*. 1971.

—— "Working-Class Culture and Working-Class Politics in London, 1870–1900; Notes on the Remaking of a Working Class," *Journal of Social History*, 7 (Summer 1974), 460–508.

Jones, Hugh R., "The Perils and Protection of Infant Life," *Journal of the Royal Statistical Society*, 57 (March 1894), 1–98.

"Juvenile Criminals," *North British Review*, 10 (1848), 2–38.

Kanipe, Esther Sue. "The Family, Private Property, and the State in France, 1870–1914." Ph.D. diss., University of Wisconsin at Madison, 1976.

Kanthack, Emilia. *The Preservation of Infant Life: A Guide for Health Visitors*. 1907.

Kay, Joseph. *The Social Condition and Education of the People in England and Europe*. 2 vols. 1850.

Kempe, C. Henry, et al. "The Battered Child Syndrome," *Journal of the American Medical Association*, 181 (July 7, 1962), 17–24.

Kenny, Courtney Stanhope. *The History of the Law of England as to the Effects of Marriage on Property and on the Wife's Legal Capacity*. 1879.

Kern, Stephen. "Explosive Intimacy: Psychodynamics of the Victorian Family," *History of Childhood Quarterly: The Journal of Psychohistory*, 1 (Winter 1974), 437–61.

Kerr, Madeline. *The People of Ship Street*. 1958.

Key, Ellen. *The Century of the Child*. New York, 1909.

Lamb, G. F. *The Happiest Days*. 1959.

Lane-Claypon, Janet E. "The Waste of Infant Life," *Nineteenth Century and After*, 65 (January 1909), 48–64.

Lang, Andrew. *Life, Letters, and Diaries of Sir Stafford Northcote*. 2 vols. 1890.

Lang, Marjory. "Childhood's Champions: Mid-Victorian Children's Periodicals and the Critics," *Victorian Periodicals Review*, 13 (Spring & Summer 1980), 17–31.

Lankester, Edwin. "Can Infanticide be Diminished by Legislative Enactment," *Transactions of the N.A.P.S.S.*, 1870, pp. 205–08.

—— "Infanticide, with Reference to the Best Means of its Prevention," *Transactions of the N.A.P.S.S.*, 1867, pp. 216–24.

Laslett, Peter. *The World We Have Lost*. 2d ed. 1971.

Laslett, Peter, and Karla Oosterveen. "Long-term Trends in Bastardy in England," *Population Studies*, 27 (July 1973), 255–86.

Lawson, Joseph. *Letters to the Young on Progress in Pudsey During the Last Sixty Years.* 1887.

The Laws Respecting Women, As They Regard Their Natural Rights, or Their Connections and Conduct. 1777 [reprinted, 1974].

Ledbeater, C. W. *Our Relations to Children.* 1898.

Ledbetter, Rosanna. *A History of the Malthusian League 1877–1927.* Columbus, Ohio, 1976.

Lees, Lynn. *Exiles of Erin: Irish Migrants in Victorian London.* Ithaca, N.Y., 1979.

Legislation in Regard to Children. 1906.

Leis, Gordon L. "A Sociological Study of Voluntary Organization with Special Reference to the National Society for the Prevention of Cruelty to Children." M.Sc. thesis, London School of Economics, 1959.

Lewis, Jane. *The Politics of Motherhood.* 1980.

The Life and Trial of the Child Murderess, Charlotte Winsor, n.d.

The Life of W. T. Stead. 1886.

Light, Richard J. "Abused and Neglected Children in America: A Study of Alternative Policies," *Harvard Educational Review,* 43 (November 1973), 556–98.

Little, Ernest M. *History of the British Medical Association 1832–1932.* 1932.

Liverpool SPCC. Annual Reports for 1883–1910.

⸻ *Jubilee Report.* 1933.

Loane, M. *An Englishman's Castle.* 1909.

⸻ *From Their Point of View.* 1908.

⸻ *Neighbours and Friends.* 1910.

⸻ *The Next Street But One.* 1907.

⸻ *The Queen's Poor.* 1905.

Loch, C. S. *Charity and Social Life.* 1910.

⸻ *Charity Organisation.* 1890.

⸻ *A Great Ideal and Its Champion: Papers and Addresses by the Late Sir Charles Stewart Loch.* 1923.

Lomax, Elizabeth. "The Uses and Abuses of Opiates in Nineteenth-Century England," *Bulletin of the History of Medicine,* 47 (March-April 1973), 167–76.

London SPCC. Annual Reports for 1884–89.

Low, Frances H. "A Remedy for Baby-Farming," *Fortnightly Review,* 69 (February 1898), 280–86.

Lowndes, Frederick. "The Destruction of Infants Shortly after Birth," *Transactions of the N.A.P.S.S.,* 1877, pp. 586–93.

Ludlow, J. M., and Lloyd Jones. *Progress of the Working Classes, 1832–1867.* 1867.

Macadam, Elizabeth. *The New Philanthropy,* 1934.

Macaulay, T. B. *Critical and Historical Essays.* 3 vols. New York, 1903.

MacDonald, Arthur. *Statistics of Child Suicide.* [1908.]

MacDonnell, John Cotter. *The Life and Correspondence of William Connor Magee, Archbishop of York.* 2 vols. 1896.

Macgill, Patrick. *Children of the Dead End: The Autobiography of a Navvy.* 6th ed. 1914.

Mackintosh, J. M. *Trends of Opinion about the Public Health, 1901–51.* 1953.

MacLeod, Roy M. "The Edge of Hope: Social Policy and Chronic Alcoholism 1870–1900," *Journal of the History of Medicine and Allied Sciences,* 22 (July 1967), 215–45.

——— "Medico-Legal Issues in Victorian Medical Care," *Medical History,* 10 (January 1966), 44–49.

——— "Social Policy and the 'Floating Population': The Administration of the Canal Boats Acts 1877–1899," *Past and Present,* 35 (December 1966), 101–32.

MacQueen, John Fraser. *The Rights and Liabilities of Husband and Wife.* 2d ed. 1872.

Maddison, Arthur J. S. *Hints on Rescue Work.* 1898.

Magee, W. C. *Speeches and Addresses.* 1892.

Mager, Alfred W. *Children's Rights: A Social and Philanthropic Question.* Bolton, 1886.

Mangasarian, M. M. "The Punishment of Children," *International Journal of Ethics,* 4 (July 1894), 493–98.

Manning, Henry Edward. "Child Labour: I. The Minimum Age for Labour of Children," *Contemporary Review,* 59 (June 1891), 794–97.

——— *The Temperance Speeches of Cardinal Manning.* Ed. C. Kegan Paul. 1894.

Manning, Henry Edward, and Benjamin Waugh. "The Child of the English Savage," *Contemporary Review,* 49 (May 1886), 687–700.

Marsh, Benjamin C. "The National Conference, and Societies to Protect Children from Cruelty," *Charities,* 15 (March 1906), 867.

Marshall, Captain Pembroke. "Child-Life Insurance: A Reply to the Rev. Benjamin Waugh," *Fortnightly Review,* n.s. 48 (December 1890), 830–51, n.s. 49 (June 1891), 939–46.

Martin, J. P. "Family Violence and Social Policy," in J. P. Martin, ed., *Violence and the Family.* Chichester, 1978.

Mason, Charlotte M. *Parents and Children.* 1897.

Masterman, N. C. *John Malcolm Ludlow.* Cambridge, 1963.

Matthews, Joseph Bridges. *The Law Relating to Children and Young Persons.* 1895.

May, Margaret. "Innocence and Experience: The Evolution of the Concept of Juvenile Delinquency in the Mid-Nineteenth Century," *Victorian Studies,* 17 (September 1973), 7–29.

——— "Violence in the Family: An Historical Perspective," in J. P. Martin, ed., *Violence and the Family*. Chichester, 1978.

Mayhew, Henry. *London Labour and the London Poor*. 4 vols. 1861–62 [reprinted, 1968].

McCabe, Anthony Thomas. "The Standard of Living in Liverpool and Merseyside, 1850–1875." M.Litt. thesis, University of Lancaster, 1974.

McCleary, G. F. *The Early History of the Infant Welfare Movement*. 1933.

——— "The State as Over-Parent," *Albany Review*, October 1907, pp. 46–59.

——— "The Work of the Health Visitor," *Albany Review*, April 1907, pp. 64–74.

McClelland, Vincent Alan. *Cardinal Manning: His Public Life and Influence 1865–1892*. 1962.

McGregor, O. R. "Social Research and Social Policy in the Nineteenth Century," *British Journal of Sociology*, 8 (1957), 146–57.

McHugh, Paul. *Prostitution and Victorian Social Reform*. New York, 1980.

McKendrick, Neil. "Home Demand and Economic Growth: A New View of the Role of Women and Children in the Industrial Revolution," in Neil McKendrick, ed., *Historical Perspectives: Studies in English Thought and Society in Honour of J. H. Plumb*. 1974.

McLaren, Angus. *Birth Control in Nineteenth-Century England*. New York, 1978.

McLoughlin, William G. "Evangelical Childrearing in the Age of Jackson: Francis Wayland's Views on When and How to Subdue the Willfulness of Children," *Journal of Social History*, 9 (Fall, 1975), 20–39.

Meacham, Standish. "The Evangelical Inheritance," *Journal of British Studies*, 3 (November 1963), 88–104.

——— *A Life Apart: The English Working Class 1890–1914*. Cambridge, Mass., 1977.

Mearns, Andrew. *The Bitter Cry of Outcast London*. Ed. Anthony W. Wohl. New York, 1970.

Mence, R. *The Mutual Rights of Husband and Wife*. 1838.

Mess, Henry A. *Voluntary Social Services since 1918*. Ed. Gertrude Williams. 1948.

Midwinter, E. C. *Social Administration in Lancashire 1830–1860*. Manchester, 1969.

Mill, John Stuart. *On Liberty*. Arlington Heights, Ill., 1947 edn.

Miller, J. R. *Home-Making, or the Ideal Family Life*. [1895.]

Mitchell, William. *House and Home: or, The Value and Virtue of Domestic Life*. [1896.]

——— "Neglected Children in our Towns and Cities," *Transactions of the*

Seventh International Congress of Hygiene and Demography, 4 (1892), 131–37.
———— *Rescue the Children*. 1886.
Monroe, Will S. *Status of Child Study in Europe*. Worcester, Mass., 1899.
Montague, C. J. *Sixty Years of Waifdom: Or, The Ragged School Movement in English History*. 1904.
Moore, Michael J. "Social Work and Social Welfare: The Organization of Philanthropic Resources in Britain, 1900–1914," *Journal of British Studies*, 16 (Spring 1977), 85–104.
Moore, S. G. *Report of the Medical Officer of Health on Infant Mortality*. Huddersfield, 1904.
Morley, John. *Death, Heaven, and the Victorians*. Pittsburgh, 1971.
Morley, John. "Liberalism and Social Reforms" [speech delivered at the dinner of the "Eighty" Club]. 1890.
———— *Recollections*. 2 vols. 1917.
Morris, Cherry, ed. *Social Case-Work in Great Britain*. 1950.
Morris, Marian G., and Robert W. Gould. "Role Reversal: A Concept in Dealing with the Neglected/Battered-Child Syndrome," in *The Neglected Battered-Child Syndrome*. New York, 1963.
Morrison, Arthur. *A Child of the Jago*. 1896 [reprinted, 1969].
———— *Tales of Mean Streets*. Boston, 1895.
Morton, Arthur. *The Directorate of Sir Robert Parr*. n.d.
———— *Early Days*. n.d.
Mosher, Martha B. *Child Culture in the Home*. 1898.
Moss, Arthur W. *Valiant Crusade: The History of the R.S.P.C.A.* 1961.
Muir, Ramsay. *A History of Liverpool*. 1907.
Muirhead, J. H. "The Family," in Stanton Coit, ed., *Ethical Democracy: Essays in Social Dynamics*. 1900.
Muraskin, William A. "The Social-Control Theory in American History: A Critique," *Journal of Social History*, 9 (June 1976), 559–69.
Musgrove, F. "Population Changes and the Status of the Young in England Since the Eighteenth Century," *Sociological Review*, n.s. 11 (March 1963), 69–93.
Mylne, Jessy Louisa. *Holding Up the Standard on Behalf of the Weak Against the Strong: A Life of Thomas Oliver*. 1913.
Newman, George. *Infant Mortality: A Social Problem*. 1906.
Newsholme, Sir Arthur. *The Elements of Vital Statistics*. 3d ed. 1899.
New York SPCC. Annual Reports for 1875, 1887–95.
———— *Manual of the New York SPCC*. New York, 1888.
NSPCC. Annual Reports for 1884–1910.
———— *Inspector's Directory*. 1901.
Oastler, Richard. *Richard Oastler: King of the Factory Children*. New York, 1972.

Oates, Austin. "The Lost, Strayed, and Stolen of Our Catholic Poor Children," *Dublin Review*, 100 (January 1887), 157–76.
Oliver, J. E., and Audrey Taylor. "Five Generations of Ill-Treated Children in One Family Pedigree," *British Journal of Psychiatry*, 119 (1971), 473–80.
"One Avoidable Cause of Cruelty," *The Spectator*, May 13, 1893, pp. 637–38.
O'Neill, James E. "Finding a Policy for the Sick Poor," *Victorian Studies*, 7 (March 1964), 265–84.
Owen, David. *English Philanthropy 1660–1960.* 1965.
Paget, Charles E. "An Objectionable Feature of Some Burial Societies in Their Relation to Infant Life Insurance," *Transactions of the Seventh International Congress of Hygiene and Demography*, 4 (1892), 67–71.
Parr, Joy. *Labouring Children: British Immigrant Apprentices to Canada, 1869–1924.* 1980.
Parr, Robert J. *The Baby Farmer: An Exposition and an Appeal.* 1909.
——— *Benjamin Waugh: An Appreciation.* 1908.
——— *Canal Boat Children.* 1910.
——— *The Seed of Hope: How the N.S.P.C.C. Helps the State.* 1910.
——— *Wilful Waste: The Nation's Responsibility for its Children.* 1910.
Paterson, Alexander. *Across the River, or Life by the South London Riverside.* 1911.
Pattison, Robert. *The Child Figure in English Literature.* Athens, Ga., 1978.
Payne, George Henry. *The Child in Human Progress.* New York, 1916.
[Payne, W.] *The Cruelty Man: Actual Experiences of an Inspector of the N.S.P.C.C. Graphically Told by Himself.* 1912.
Pearsall, Ronald. *Night's Black Angels.* New York, 1975.
Pelling, Henry. *Popular Politics and Society in Late Victorian Britain.* 1968.
Pelton, Leroy. "Child Abuse and Neglect: The Myth of Classlessness," *American Journal of Orthopsychiatry*, 48 (October 1978), 608–17.
Perkin, Harold. "Individualism Versus Collectivism in Nineteenth-Century Britain: A False Antithesis," *Journal of British Studies*, 17 (Fall 1977), 105–18.
——— *The Origins of Modern English Society 1780–1880.* 1976.
Peterson, M. Jeanne. *The Medical Profession in Mid-Victorian London.* Berkeley, Calif., 1978.
Pfohl, Stephen J. "The 'Discovery' of Child Abuse," *Social Problems*, 24 (February 1977), 310–23.
Pinchbeck, Ivy, and Margaret Hewitt. *Children in English Society.* 2 vols. 1969, 1973.

Place, Francis. *The Autobiography of Francis Place*. Ed. Mary Thale. Cambridge, 1972.

Plumb, J. H. "The New World of Children in Eighteenth-Century England," *Past and Present*, 67 (May 1975), 64–95.

Pope, Norris. *Dickens and Charity*. New York, 1978.

Porter, Enid. *Cambridgeshire Customs and Folklore*. New York, 1969.

Powers, Edwin. *Crime and Punishment in Early Massachusetts, 1620–1692*. Boston, 1966.

Pringle, J. C. *Social Work of the London Churches*. 1937.

Prochaska, F. K. "Charity Bazaars in Nineteenth-Century England," *Journal of British Studies*, 16 (Spring 1977), 62–84.

————— *Women and Philanthropy in Nineteenth-Century England*. Oxford, 1980.

"The Protection of Children," *The Spectator*, July 12, 1884, p. 910.

Public Nurseries. 1850.

Radbill, Samuel X. "A History of Child Abuse and Infanticide," in Ray Helfer and Henry Kempe, eds., *The Battered Child*. Chicago, 1968.

Radzinowicz, Leon. *A History of English Criminal Law and Its Administration from 1750*. 4 vols. New York, 1948–68.

Reeves, Mrs. Pember. *Round About a Pound a Week*. 1913.

Rentoul, Robert R. *Race Culture; or Race Suicide?* 1906.

Report of the Committee on Vagrant Children. 1899.

Report of the Proceedings of the Third International Congress for the Welfare and Protection of Children. Ed. Sir William Chance. 1902.

"Reports of the Royal Commission on Friendly and Benefit Building Societies, 1872–4," *Quarterly Review*, 138 (January 1875), 206–29.

A Report Upon the Finances and General Management of the National Society for the Prevention of Cruelty to Children [C.O.S.]. 1897.

Reynolds, Stephen. *A Poor Man's House*. 1909.

Reynolds, Stephen, Bob Woolley, and Tom Woolley. *Seems So! A Working-Class View of Politics*. 1911.

Ribton-Turner, C. J. *A History of Vagrants and Beggars and Begging*. 1887.

Richmond, Mary E. *Friendly Visiting Among the Poor*. New York, 1914.

Richter, Melvin. *The Politics of Conscience: T. H. Green and His Age*. Cambridge, Mass., 1964.

"The Rights of Children," *The Nation*, 9 (December 1869), 503–4.

Riis, Jacob A. *The Children of the Poor*. 1892.

Ritt, Lawrence. "The Victorian Conscience in Action: The National Association for the Promotion of Social Science, 1857–1886." Ph.D. diss., Columbia University, 1959.

R. J. *'I Was in Prison': A Plea for the Amelioration of the Criminal Law*. 1893.

Roberts, David. "How Cruel Was the Victorian Poor Law," *Historical Journal*, 6 (1963), 97–107.

——— "The Paterfamilias of the Victorian Governing Classes," in Anthony Wohl, ed., *The Victorian Family*. New York, 1978.

Roberts, Robert. *The Classic Slum*. Manchester, 1971.

Robertson, A. B. "Children, Teachers, and Society: The Over-Pressure Controversy, 1880–1886," *British Journal of Educational Studies*, 20 (October 1972), 315–23.

Rooff, Madeline, *Voluntary Societies and Social Policy*. 1957.

Ross, Catherine J. "Society's Children: The Care of Indigent Youngsters in New York City, 1875–1903." Ph.D. diss., Yale University, 1977.

Rossiter, Elizabeth. "Child Life for Children," *Nineteenth Century*, 10 (October 1881), 567–72.

——— "Unnatural Children," *Fortnightly Review*, 37 (May 1882), 612–19.

Routh, C. H. F. *Infant Feeding and Its Influence on Life: or, the Causes and Prevention of Infant Mortality*. 1860.

Rowntree, B. Seebohm. *Poverty: A Study of Town Life*. 1901.

Rowntree, Joseph, and Arthur Sherwell. *The Temperance Problem and Social Reform*. 5th ed. 1899.

RSPCA. Annual Reports for 1880–1910.

——— *Rules and Instructions* [for inspectors]. 1906.

Rumsey, H. W. "On Certain Departments of Medico-Sanitary Police and Medico-Legal Inquiry, in Connexion with the Scientific Superintendence of Mortuary Registration," *Transactions of the N.A.P.S.S.*, 1860, pp. 585–95.

Salt, H. S. *Humanitarianism: Its General Principles and Progress*. 1893.

Samuel, Herbert. *Grooves of Change*. Indianapolis, 1946.

——— *Liberalism: An Attempt to State the Principles and Proposals of Contemporary Liberalism in England*. 1902.

Samuels, Emma. "The Adoption of Street Arabs by the State," *Fortnightly Review*, 69 (January 1898), 111–18.

Samuelson, James. *The Children of Our Slums*. Liverpool, 1911.

Sangster, Paul. *Pity My Simplicity*. 1963.

Saunders, L. D. *Before the Doctor Comes*. 1909.

Schupf, Harriet Warm. "The Perishing and Dangerous Classes: Efforts to Deal With the Neglected, Vagrant, and Delinquent Juvenile in England, 1840–1875." Ph.D. diss., Columbia University, 1971.

Scott, Joan, and Louise Tilly. "Women's Work and the Family in Nineteenth Century Europe," in Charles Rosenberg, ed., *The Family in History*. Philadelphia, 1975.

Searle, G. R. *The Quest for National Efficiency*. Berkeley, Calif., 1971.

"The Second Annual Report of the Ragged School Union," *Quarterly Review*, 79 (1846), 127–41.

Selby, D. E. "Cardinal Manning, Campaigner for Children's Rights," *Journal of Ecclesiastical History*, 27 (October 1976), 403–12.
Sherard, Robert Harborough. *The Child-Slaves of Britain*. 1905.
Shiman, Lilian Lewis. "The Band of Hope Movement: Respectable Recreation for Working-Class Children," *Victorian Studies*, 17 (September 1973), 49–74.
Shimmin, Hugh. *Liverpool Sketches*. 1862.
[———] *Town Life*. 1858.
Shorter, Edward. *The Making of the Modern Family*. New York, 1975.
Shultz, William J. *The Humane Movement in the United States, 1910–1922*. New York, 1924.
Sidgwick, Henry. *The Elements of Politics*. 1891.
Simey, Margaret. *Charitable Effort in Liverpool in the Nineteenth Century*. Liverpool, 1951.
Sims, George R. *The Black Stain*. 1907.
——— *How the Poor Live*. 1898.
——— *My Life*. 1917.
——— *The Social Kaleidoscope*. 1881.
Skinner, Angela, and Raymond Castle. *Seventy-Eight Battered Children: A Retrospective Study*. 1969.
Smelser, Neil. *Social Change in the Industrial Revolution*. 1959.
Smiles, Samuel. *Thrift*. 1876.
Smith, George. *The Cry of the Children from the Brickyards of England: A Statement and Appeal, with Remedy*. 3d ed. 1871.
——— *Gipsy Life: Being an Account of Our Gipsies and Their Children, with Suggestions for Their Improvement*. 1880.
——— *A Lecture by George Smith of Coalville Delivered before the Association of Public Sanitary Inspectors*. 1888.
Smith, Nora. "How Shall We Govern Our Children," in Kate Douglas Wiggin, ed., *Children's Rights*. Cambridge, Mass., 1892.
Smith, Samuel. *My Life-Work*. 1902.
——— "Social Reform," *Nineteenth Century*, 13 (May 1883), 896–912.
Smith, Steven R. "The London Apprentices as Seventeenth-Century Adolescents," *Past and Present*, 61 (November 1973), 149–61.
Smyth, A. Watt. *Physical Deterioration, Its Causes and the Cure*. 1904.
Snead-Cox, J. G. *The Life of Cardinal Vaughan*. 2 vols. 1910.
"The Society for the Prevention of Cruelty to Children," *Saturday Review*, May 12, 1883, pp. 596–97.
Sommerville, C. John. "Toward a History of Childhood and Youth," *Journal of Interdisciplinary History*, 3 (Autumn 1972), 439–47.
Spargo, John. *The Bitter Cry of the Children*. New York, 1906.
Spencer, Herbert. *The Proper Sphere of Government*. 1843.
——— *Social Statics, Abridged and Revised*. New York, 1896.

Stack, John Andrew. "Social Policy and Juvenile Delinquency in England and Wales: 1815–1875." Ph.D. diss., University of Iowa, 1974.

Stead, Estelle W. *My Father.* 1913.

Stead, W. T. *My First Imprisonment.* 1886.

Stearns, Peter N. "Working-Class Women in Britain, 1890–1914," in Martha Vicinus, ed., *Suffer and Be Still.* Bloomington, Ind., 1974.

Steelcroft, Framley. "At a Baby Show," *Strand Magazine,* 14 (October 1897), 378–84.

Steele, Brandt, and Carl Pollock. "A Psychiatric Study of Parents Who Abuse Infants and Small Children," in Ray Helfer and Henry Kempe, eds., *The Battered Child.* Chicago, 1968.

Steele, F. A. "Consider the Children," *Saturday Review*, July 16, 1904, pp. 72–73.

Stewart, J. D. *British Pressure Groups.* Oxford, 1958.

Stone, Lawrence. *The Family, Sex, and Marriage in England, 1500–1800.* New York, 1977.

Storch, Robert. "The Policeman as Domestic Missionary: Urban Discipline and Popular Culture in Northern England, 1850–1880," *Journal of Social History*, 9 (June 1976), 481–509.

——— "The Problem of Working-Class Leisure: Some Roots of Middle-Class Moral Reform in the Industrial North, 1825–1850," in A. P. Donajgrodzki, ed., *Social Control in Nineteenth Century Britain.* 1977.

Sutherland, Neil. *Children in English-Canadian Society: Framing the Twentieth-Century Consensus.* Toronto, 1976.

Symons, Jelinger C. *Tactics for the Times: As Regards the Conditions and Treatment of the Dangerous Classes.* 1849.

Tabor, Mary C. "The Rights of Children," *Contemporary Review*, 54 (September 1888), 408–17.

Taine, Hippolyte. *Notes on England.* 1957 edn.

Tarn, John Nelson. *Five Per Cent Philanthropy.* 1973.

Teale, T. Pridgin. *Hurry, Worry, and Money: The Bane of Modern Education.* Leeds, 1883.

Terrot, Charles. *The Maiden Tribute.* 1959.

Thomas, Keith. "The Beast in Man," *New York Review of Books*, April 30, 1981, pp. 47–48.

Thomas, Mason P. "Child Abuse and Neglect. Part I: Historical Overview, Legal Matrix, and Social Perspectives," *North Carolina Law Review*, 50 (1972), 293–349.

Thompson, E. P. *The Making of the English Working Class.* New York, 1963.

——— "'Rough Music': Le Charivari Anglais," *Annales: Économies, Sociétés, Civilisations*, 27 (March-April 1972), 285–312.

———— *Whigs and Hunters*. New York, 1975.

Thompson, Paul. *The Edwardians*. Bloomington, Ind., 1975.

———— "The War with Adults," *Oral History*, 3 (Autumn 1975), 29–38.

Thompson, Thea. "A Lost World of Childhood," *New Society*, October 5, 1972, 20–23.

Tomes, Nancy. "A 'Torrent of Abuse': Crimes of Violence Between Working-Class Men and Women in London, 1840–1875," *Journal of Social History*, 11 (Spring 1978), 328–45.

Townsend, Edward W. *A Daughter of the Tenements*. New York, 1895.

Trench, Maria. "Girl-Children of the State," *Nineteenth Century*, 13 (January 1883), 76–87.

Trudgill, Eric. *Madonnas and Magdalens*. New York, 1976.

Trumbach, Randolph. *The Rise of the Egalitarian Family*. New York, 1978.

Tuckwell, Gertrude. *The State and Its Children*. 1894.

Turner, James. *Reckoning with the Beast: Animals, Pain, and Humanity in the Victorian Mind*. Baltimore, 1980.

Turner, Sydney. "Juvenile Delinquency," *Edinburgh Review*, 94 (October 1851), 403–29.

Twining, Louisa. *Recollections of Life and Work*. 1893.

"Two Champions of the Children," *Review of Reviews* [American ed.], 4 (January 1892), 689–701.

"Underfed Children," *The Spectator*, April 1, 1905, pp. 467–68.

Ure, Andrew. *The Philosophy of Manufactures*. 1835 [reprinted, 1967].

Urwick, E. J., ed. *Studies of Boy Life in Our Cities*. 1904.

Vacher, Francis. "Infanticide: An Inquiry into Its Causes, and Their Remedy," *Provincial Medical Journal*, 7 (May 1, 1888, and June 1, 1888), 212–14, 246–48.

"Vagrants, Beggars, and Tramps," *Quarterly Review*, 209 (October 1908), 388–408.

Vigne, Thea. "Parents and Children 1890–1918; Distance and Dependence," *Oral History*, 3 (Autumn 1975), 6–11.

Voluntary Social Services. Ed. A. F. C. Bourdillon. 1945.

Vorspan, Rachel. "Vagrancy and the New Poor Law in Late-Victorian and Edwardian England," *English Historical Review*, 92 (January 1977), 59–81.

[Wade, John.] *History of the Middle and Working Classes*. 1833 [reprinted, 1966].

Walford, Cornelius, "On the Number of Deaths from Accidents, Negligence, Violence, and Misadventure in the United Kingdom and Some Other Countries," *Journal of the Statistical Society*, 44 (September 1881), 429–521.

Walker, Arthur De Noé. *The Right Reverend Father in God the Bishop of Peterborough, on Vivisection*. 2d ed. Norwich, 1882.

Walker, R. B. "Religious Changes in Liverpool in the Nineteenth Century," *Journal of Ecclesiastical History*, 19 (October 1968), 195–211.

Walkowitz, Judith R. *Prostitution and Victorian Society*. Cambridge, 1980.

Ward, J. T. *The Factory Movement 1830–1855*. 1962.

Warwick, Countess of [Frances Greville]. *A Nation's Youth: Physical Deterioration; Its Causes and Some Remedies*. 1906.

Waugh, Benjamin. "Baby Farming," *Contemporary Review*, 57 (May 1890), 700–714.

―――― "Child-Life Insurance," *Contemporary Review*, 58 (July 1890), 40–63.

―――― *The Child of Nazareth*. 1906.

―――― *Come Ye Children: Heart Stories for the Young*. 1889.

[――――] *The Gaol Cradle, Who Rocks It?* 3d ed. 1876.

―――― *A New Public Policy for Children*. 1894.

―――― *The Next-Door Neighbour: A Justification*. n.d.

―――― "Prevention of Cruelty to Children," *Dublin Review*, 110 (January 1892), 140–51.

―――― "Reminiscences of Cardinal Manning," *Contemporary Review*, 61 (February 1892), 188–194.

―――― *The Results of Child-Life Insurance*. 1891.

―――― *Some Conditions of Child Life in England*. 1889.

―――― "Street Children," *Contemporary Review*, 53 (June 1888), 825–35.

―――― *William T. Stead: A Life for the People*. 1885.

Waugh, Rosa. *The Life of Benjamin Waugh*. 1913.

Webb, Sidney, and Beatrice Webb. *English Poor Law Policy*. 1910.

―――― *The Prevention of Destitution*. 1911.

Weber, Adna Ferrin. *The Growth of Cities in the Nineteenth Century*. New York, 1899.

Wilkinson, John Frome. *The Friendly Society Movement*. 1886.

―――― *Mutual Thrift*. 1891.

Wing, Charles. *Evils of the Factory System*. 1837 [reprinted, 1967].

Wohl, Anthony. *The Eternal Slum*. Montreal, 1977.

―――― "Sex and the Single Room: Incest Among the Victorian Working Classes," in *idem*, ed., *The Victorian Family*. New York, 1978.

Wood, Emma Caroline. *Sorrow on the Sea*. 3 vols. 1868.

Woodroofe, Kathleen. *From Charity to Social Work in England and the United States*. 1962.

Woods, Robert A., et al. *The Poor in Great Cities: Their Problems and What Is Being Done to Solve Them*. 1896.

Worsley, Henry. *Juvenile Depravity*. 1849.

Wrigley, E. A. *Population and History*. New York, 1969.

Wrongs Righted: Being a Brief Record of the Work of the Manchester &
Salford Society for the Prevention of Cruelty to Children. 1892.

Young, A. F., and E. T. Ashton. *British Social Work in the Nineteenth Century.* 1956.

Young, Michael, and Peter Willmott. *Family and Kinship in East London.* Harmondsworth, Middlesex, 1976.

Index